COSTUME AND FASHION

VOLUME THREE

THE TUDORS

Book II: 1547–1603

UNIFORM WITH THIS VOLUME

COSTUME AND FASHION

VOLUME ONE

The Evolution of European Dress through
the Earlier Ages

VOLUME TWO

Senlac to Bosworth.   1066–1485

BY

HERBERT NORRIS

VOLUME SIX

The Nineteenth Century

BY

HERBERT NORRIS & OSWALD CURTIS

PLATE XIX.   KING EDWARD VI, 1548
Founded on the portrait in Christ's Hospital, Horsham
By kind permission of the Governors

COSTUME & FASHION

VOLUME THREE

THE TUDORS
Book II: 1547-1603

BY

HERBERT NORRIS

ILLUSTRATED
IN COLOUR & BLACK AND WHITE
BY THE AUTHOR

LONDON
J. M. DENT AND SONS LTD

391

C 6121 104 4

20 452

26.2.39

ERRATA

CONTENTS

Book II

v

vi   CONTENTS

ILLUSTRATIONS

IN COLOUR AND HALF-TONE

Book II

ILLUSTRATIONS

IN BLACK AND WHITE

Book II

CHAPTER III

THE REIGN OF KING EDWARD VI
1547–53

THE REIGN OF QUEEN MARY
1553–8

CONTEMPORARY SOVEREIGNS

	ENGLAND	SCOTLAND	FRANCE	GERMANY	SPAIN	SWEDEN	DENMARK
						Gustavus Vasa	Christian III
1547	Edward VI	Mary Stuart Francis II of France	Henry II 1547–59 Catherine de' Medici	Charles V	Charles I		
1553	Mary						
1556					Philip II 1556–98 1. Maria of Portugal 2. Mary Tudor 3. Elizabeth de Valois 4. Anne of Austria		
1558				Ferdinand I 1558–64 Anne of Hungary and Bohemia			

383

HISTORICAL DATA, 1547-1558

1547. Accession of Edward VI and the establishment of Protestantism.

Protectorate of the Duke of Somerset, until 1549.

1548. First Act of Uniformity.

French alliance with Scotland.

1549. The first Prayer Book published.

The new Pilgrimage of Grace in the south-west.

Robert Ket's rebellion in Norfolk and Suffolk, August.

1550. Treaty of Peace between England, Scotland, and France.

1551. William Camden born in the Old Bailey, son of a painter - stainer of Lichfield. Wrote *Britannia*, published in 1586, the first systematic survey of antiquities of England, partly based on John Leland. First English version 1610. Head master of Westminster 1593. Clarenceux King of Arms. Died at Chislehurst 1623.

War between France and Germany, until 1554.

1552. The second Prayer Book published; second Act of Uniformity.

1553. Richard Chancellor reaches Moscow and opens up trade with Russia.

John Lyly born. Wrote many plays, chiefly upon classic subjects, founder of the popular style called 'euphuism,' the type in literature and polite conversation much used in the sixteenth century. Died 1606.

Death of Edward VI, 6th July.

Lady Jane Grey. Queen from 8th July to the 19th.

Accession of Mary and the beginning of the Romanist reaction.

1554. 'England returns to the bosom of the Roman Church,' November.

Insurrection of Kent, headed by Sir Thomas Wyatt, to dethrone Queen Mary and replace Lady Jane Grey on the throne.

1555. The old laws against heresy revived and enforced with great severity.

Diet of Augsburg, in which 'a complete liberty of conscience was granted to those States and Princes in the Empire who had embraced Protestant opinions.'

1555-6. Charles V resigned the Netherlands, the Spanish possessions in 1556 and, formally, the Empire in 1558.

The era of the Protestant martyrs. Bishop Hooper, 9th February. Bishops Ridley and Latimer, 16th October. Archbishop Cranmer, 21st March.

1557. War with France, until 1559.

1558. Surrender of Calais to the French. Mary of Scotland marries the Dauphin.

George Peele born. Wrote comedies and tragedies, and devised the Lord Mayor's pageant in 1585 and in 1591. Died 1597/8.

Death of Queen Mary and accession of Queen Elizabeth.

THE ARTS, 1547-58

SCULPTURE: MONUMENTAL EFFIGIES (*continued from p. 145*)

THE years covered by the reigns of Edward VI and Mary were not propitious for the craft of the monumental masons. A period of transition had arrived: the reckless destruction of many monumental effigies dating from the earlier centuries has deprived us of much detail of value and interest. Craftsmen of the Gothic tradition were dying out, and, when new monuments were required, the younger generation sought inspiration from Italy and from the Classic style which was just beginning to reach England.

At the same time, the conservative Englishman was not too eager to have the memory of his children, parents, and grandparents surrounded with the trappings of a foreigner. However, by degrees a compromise was achieved between the old and the new, and one notices the introduction of some Classic feature here and there into what at first appears to be the work of an earlier generation.

(*Continued on p. 472*)

MEMORIAL BRASSES (*continued from p. 145*)

During this period, the reigns of Edward VI and Mary, very few (if any) brasses were laid down: and this was a direct consequence of the religious controversies and political dissensions of the times.

(*Continued on p. 472*)

TAPESTRY (*continued from p. 145*)

Temp. Edward VI and Queen Mary

As a matter of course Edward VI and Queen Mary inherited most, if not all, the sets of tapestry previously possessed by their father. The subject of at least one set in use at this time is known, 'The Siege of Antioch.' It was hung in the Audience Chamber at Hatfield, while the Princess Elizabeth was in residence there in 1557.

During the period between 1547 and 1558, little of importance occurred in the history of tapestry, but some interesting details are at hand regarding the production of a masterpiece of the time. Detailed instructions issued to the famous Flemish tapestry weaver, William Pannemaker, are still extant in the 'Imperial Command' received by him in 1548 from the Emperor Charles V. These instructions had been revised and elaborated by the Emperor's business-like sister Mary, Queen of Hungary, widow of Louis II, who edited a stringent contract by which Pannemaker was bound to supply the very best materials, etc. The silk used was to come from Granada, the gold from Milan. Eighty-three different tints of colour, each subdivided into twenty-two series, each of which again comprised from two to five tones, making altogether something like eight thousand shades of colour, are specified. The subject was to commemorate 'The Conquest of Tunis.' [1] In the year 1535, the Emperor had taken the artist, Jan Vermeyen, with him on this expedition as a member of his retinue, to enable him to design with strict truthfulness the cartoons representing various events in the campaign.

The execution of Vermeyen's cartoons occupied Pannemaker and eighty-four picked weavers for five years. The set was completed early in 1554.

The tapestries were justly prized by their owner, for they are reckoned among the most beautiful in existence. They consist of twelve panels, and are extremely useful for the study of military equipment, ships, and the costume of the Turks in the sixteenth century.

These twelve panels were sent on their completion to England for the marriage festivities of Queen Mary and Philip II. They were hung from pillar to pillar in the nave of Winchester Cathedral; the iron hooks which held the supporting rods are still in position. After the wedding the tapestries were returned to Spain with the utmost care, and thereafter were constantly used at Spanish Court functions. They used to ornament the palace of King Alphonso XIII in Madrid.

A reference to these tapestries in John Elder's letter is of sufficient interest to be inserted here:

'Where [Whitehall] in the mean season two princely presents came to Their Majesties. The one from the Emperor, which is XII pieces of Arras work, so richly wrought with gold, silver, and silk, as none in the world may excel them. In which pieces be so excellently wrought and set out all the Emperor's Majesties procedings and Victories against the Turks as Apelles were not able (if he were alive) to mend any parcel thereof with his pencil.'

(Continued on p. 473)

---

[1] The campaign in Tunis took place in 1535, and was undertaken to quell the invasion of northern Africa by the Turks. Charles V dispatched a fleet under the command of Doria, who achieved the conquest of Tunis.

Andrea Doria was born at Oneglia, near Genoa, in 1468. After having been in the service of the Genoese as Captain-General, he had sided with Francis I against the Emperor; but upon his native place being attacked by the French, he joined the Emperor Charles, and drove the French out of Genoa in 1528. This hero of the conquest of Tunis lived in great state in Genoa, and even at the age of ninety continued to command his galleys. He died in his bed in 1560.

PORTRAITS AND PAINTERS (*continued from p. 153*)

Temp. Edward VI and Mary, 1547 to 1558

In addition to Hans Eworth and Corneille de Lyon, both of whom lived until 1574, the most important Flemish painters whose works are useful for the study of costume in fashion during the reigns of Edward VI and Queen Mary are the following:

The family POURBUS, father, son, and grandson, were artists to whom we owe much information on costume. PIETER POURBUS, the father, born at Gouda in 1510, was specially a painter of portraits. He died at Bruges in 1584.

ANTONIO MORO, born at Utrecht in 1517. The dates of his itinerary are useful:

In Italy	1550–1	In Madrid	1559
In Madrid	1552	In Utrecht	1564
In England	1553	In Antwerp	1568
In Utrecht	1555		

He was sent to England by Marie, Queen of Hungary, to paint for her nephew, Prince Philip of Spain, a portrait of Queen Mary. The exact date of his receiving the honour of knighthood is not known, but since it was for services rendered to Queen Mary, the year must have been 1553. Sir Antonio died about 1576.

GWILLIM STRETES, STREETES, or STREATE, born in Holland. He flourished 1546–56, and was one of the successors to Holbein. His first portrait of any importance is that of the Earl of Surrey, at Hampton Court (considered by some to represent the Duke of Richmond, natural son of Henry VIII). He became painter to the King.

LUCAS DE HEERE, born at Ghent in 1534, did not come to England until 1568. He died in Paris in 1584.

HANS EWORTH came into prominence about 1550 and remained a fashionable portrait painter until 1575. During this period he signed himself HE. Up to quite recently (1912) some of his works were attributed to Antonio Moro and Lucas de Heere. His paintings are characterized by the truthful, yet perhaps unflattering, portraiture of his sitters, the detail of accessories, and the introduction of armorial bearings into the general design of his composition. He died about 1575–6.

ALONZO SANCHEZ COELLO, born at Bonifacio near Valencia in 1515, though of Portuguese nationality, is known as a Spanish painter. He studied in Italy for many years and returned to Spain in 1541, settling in Madrid where he was appointed Court painter to Philip II. Although religious themes were his chief interest, there are portraits by him of the Infante Don Carlos and the Infanta Isabella in the Prado.

The paynter-stayners who flourished during these two reigns were:

NICHOLAS DE MODENA, an Italian who supervised the ornaments for Henry VIII's funeral obsequies, and became later 'art decorator' of the various 'dysguisings,' masques, and revels which took place at Court. He died 1571.

BARTOLOMMEO PENNI was another Italian, born at Florence, who became paynter-decorator to Edward VI.

JOHN BOSSAM flourished from 1550: 'that most rare English drawer of story works in black and white.'

NICHOLAS LYZARD continued in the office of paynter-stayner during Edward VI's reign, and was appointed serjeant-paynter by Queen Mary.

(*Continued on p. 476*)

SECTION I: 1547-58

ROYALTY AND NOBILITY—MEN: 1547-58

KING EDWARD VI, 1537-53

Edward VI, fifth child of Henry VIII, was born at Hampton Court, 12th October 1537. His mother was Queen Jane Seymour who died twelve days later, a victim to bad judgment on the part of her physicians. The third of our bachelor kings, he was crowned 25th February 1547 at Westminster by Thomas Cranmer, Archbishop of Canterbury. In appearance Edward was fragile, moderately good looking with grey eyes, delicate complexion, and fair hair worn cut close to the head. His health was always precarious; at fourteen he writes in his *Journal* (2nd April 1551): 'I fell sick of the Measels and Small Pox.' His early portraits show him with a round pleasant face, but in those painted towards the end of his reign the face is long and rather narrow with a pointed chin. A celebrated Milanese physician who visited him in 1552 said: 'His stature was below the medium . . . his general appearance dignified and formal.'

Fig. 482. A Badge of King Edward VI

The early education forced upon him at the age of six, and a slight deafness, somewhat tempered the exuberance of youth. He was eager to acquire knowledge, but at the same time, despite his serious outlook on life, he was as fond of fun and games as any other boy. His tutors were selected with great discernment: Dr. John Cheke, born at Cambridge 1514, and Professor of Greek at St. John's College, taught him classics; Dr. Christopher Tye instructed the Prince in the art of music, Philip van Wilder being specially engaged to teach him to play the lute.

Very religious by nature, he was an ardent student of the Scriptures, and took exceptional pleasure in listening to sermons; so it is not to be wondered at that from his early years he was an enthusiastic religious reformer. Somewhat later he showed signs of developing many of the better traits of his father's character.

Edward was never created Prince of Wales, although preparations for the ceremony of his crowning were in progress when his father died. Nor was he created a Knight of the Garter, though on his accession to the throne he automatically became sovereign of that Most Noble Order.

390 THE REIGNS OF EDWARD VI AND MARY

Henry VIII had planned a carefully balanced Council of Regency in the event of his death during Edward's minority, but on Henry's demise this council was set aside, and the Earl of Hertford, a moving spirit of the Reforming Party, became Lord Protector, assuming the title of Duke of Somerset. He remained in office until October 1549, and was followed by the self-seeking John Dudley, Earl of Warwick, created Duke of Northumberland by Edward VI in 1551. Dudley was a son of Henry VII's infamous lawyer (*see* Chapter I, p. 14) and eventually died on the scaffold 22nd August 1553, after a shameful apostasy from the faith for which he had plunged England into bloodshed.

As early as 1542, Henry VIII endeavoured to arrange a marriage between his son, aged five years, and Mary Queen of Scotland—then only a few weeks old. During the following year the betrothal became an actuality by treaty concluded at Greenwich on 1st July 1543. But the Scottish Catholics favoured an alliance with France, and at the end of the same year Scotland repudiated the Greenwich agreement, with dire results to herself. In 1548 the infant Queen was sent to France to be educated as the destined bride of a future King—Francis II. At this juncture certain persons of high standing in the English Government were occupied in arranging a suitable marriage among the nobility of England for Edward, who had become King the year before. On 21st May 1550 Edward refers to the subject himself in his *Journal*. He writes: 'My Lord Marquess of Northampton had Commission . . . to treat of all things, and chiefly of Marriage for Me to the Lady Elizabeth his Daughter.' On the 26th of October the same year this entry occurs: 'The Lord Strange confessed how the Duke [of Suffolk] willed him to stir me to marry his third Daughter, the Lady Jane.' This was the Lady Jane Grey to whom he left in his will the crown of England, although he had no legal power to do so.

On 19th February 1547 the coronation festivities began. Mounted on a white horse *before* a canopy of gold, the boy King must have made an imposing figure as he rode from the Tower through London to the Palace of Westminster. He inherited much of his father's splendid dignity of bearing, and his costume, described by a contemporary, proves that on occasion he was thoroughly well dressed:

'The kynges Royall Maj^{tie} walking a lytell before his canopy, because the people might the better see his grace, his highness being richly apparelled with a riche gowne of cloth of silver all over embrodered with damaske golde, with a girkyn of white velvett, wrought with Venyce silver, garnished with precious stones, as rubies and diamonds, with true-loves of pearles, a doblet of white velvet according to the same, with like precious stones and pearls, a white velvet cappe garneshed with lyke stones, and perles, and a pere of buskenes of white velvet. His horse caparison of crymoysyn sattyn, imbrodered with perles and damaske gold.'

A painting of the procession existed at Cowdray House (*see* p. 420).

Another interesting feature in this cavalcade was the presence of the Lady Elizabeth and the Lady Anne of Cleves, both dressed in the latest French fashion all in silver. They were seated side by side in a chariot covered with cloth of silver. Unfortunately this is not shown in the painting above mentioned.

According to custom special robes were prepared for King Edward's coronation ceremonies. The first set was of the usual crimson velvet, the mantle 'with a longe trayne,' the surcote and hood all furred with powdered ermine throughout. These 'were called his parliament robes, wering on his hede a cappe of black velvett.' After the crowning and the hearing of Mass he changed into robes of purple, velvet, and ermine. Altogether the King's appearance was like the drawing, Fig. 211, which shows his father as a young man wearing similar robes.

It is interesting to know what garments King Edward wore under these regal trappings. Fortunately a list of them is extant:

'ij shertes, oone of Lawne, the other crymesyn sarsenet wyde in the collers.

'A breche of camerycke to the myd thighe, gathered together before and behynde, and a breche belt of crymesyn velvet sette the same.

'A payr of hosen of crymesyn sarsenet, Vaumpes and all.

'A payre of Sabetynes [shoes] of clothe of bawkekyn.'

A painting by Stretes showing Edward VI in state robes is in the possession of the Bridewell Royal Free Hospital. In this he wears over his doublet only the Royal mantle lined with ermine and a cape with hood of the same. The crown appears to be set on the bonet. The Garter Collar and the sceptre are the only other emblems of sovereignty.

On 12th June 1550 King Edward writes in his *Journal*: 'I was elected of the Company of St. Michael in France by the French King and his Order.' And on 20th of the same month the following information is given: 'The French King was invested with the Order of the Garter in his Bed-Chamber, where he gave a Chain to the Garter worth 200*l* and his Gown dressed with Auglets worth 25*l*, the Bishop of Ely making an Oration, and the Cardinal of Lorrain making him Answer.' Edward did not receive the French Order until 17th July. On that day 'Monsieur le Mareschal . . . came to present the Order of Monseigneur Michael; whereafter with Ceremonies accustomed, he had put on the Garments, he, and Monsieur Gye likewise of the Order, came one at my right Hand, the other at my left to the Chappel, whereafter the Communion celebrated, each of them kissed my cheek. After that they dined with Me, and talked after Dinner, and saw some Pastime and so went home again.' Monsieur le Mareschal Saint-André seems to have been popular with the King, for we read: 'The next Morning he came to Me to mine Arraying, and saw my Bed-Chamber, and went a hunting with Hounds; and saw Me shoot, and saw all my Guards shoot together. He dined with Me, heard Me play on the Lute, Ride; came to Me to my study, supped with Me, and so departed to Richmond.' The King was then in residence at Hampton Court.

Edward VI has received much undeserved credit as an extensive founder of grammar schools.[1] He did, however, use part of the vast sums accumulated by his father from the suppressed ecclesiastical institutions to endow some such schools, including the famous Christ's Hospital (1553) (*see* p. 424), together with three other foundations for three classes of indigent poor.

St. Bartholomew's and St. Thomas's Hospitals, founded in 1102 and 1228 respectively, were endowed, and the Royal Palace of Bridewell was given up as a home for the reform of vagrants and disorderly persons. Besides the grammar schools which owed their origin to Edward's initiative, the Royal example inspired similar foundations in various parts of the country, and other schools were started in certain towns, by petition and help of the burgesses.

The Puritans made their first appearance in this reign. This fact may have influenced some writers [2] to suggest that the Court of Edward VI was sombre and funereal. This view seems to be far from the truth, for Edward's own journal makes frequent references to the gaieties and splendid entertainments which took place. As for dress, examination of the portraits of the time shows apparel fully as gorgeous as ever was worn in the last reign.

Plate XIX is taken from a portrait of King Edward VI at Christ's Hospital painted about 1548. There is another almost identical at Windsor Castle. It will be seen that the costume worn by Edward is similar in most details to that of his father. The surcote is of vermilion velvet, garded with gold passamayne and lined with ermine. A feature to be noticed is that the collar, or turned-back lining of ermine, surrounds the neck, and does not, as previously, fall back wide on the shoulders. This gives a view of the way the full sleeve is pleated, or gathered, into the armhole. The King's slender figure appears somewhat overwhelmed in this ample garment. The doublet, with sleeves of white cloth of silver of damask bordered with a wide design in squares of silver embroidery, is slightly different from the earlier vogue. It is closed higher at the throat, with a stand-up collar; a narrow collar of white lawn is inside, and turns down over it. The skirt part (originally the bases, and later a pleated skirt) is shorter, and forms a deep basque. In consequence the slops are more conspicuous. They are of silver embroidery worn over white silk hosen. Edward VI was the first English monarch to wear knitted hose of silk. A pair of long silk STOCKINGS was presented to him by Sir Thomas Gresham. Sir Thomas had procured them from some Spanish merchants and this unusual gift greatly pleased his youthful majesty. About this same time Diane de Poitiers made a present of some knitted silk stockings manufactured in Italy to Henry II of France and Catherine de' Medici. Shoes had now become more normal in the toe, though somewhat rounded, and followed the shape of the foot.

A noticeable feature of this costume is the bonet. At this time it was

---

[1] The name 'grammar school' was given to schools before the grammar of the English language was written or taught, and when all grammatical knowledge was obtained by the study of ancient languages. Latin was the chief subject of instruction in the early grammar schools, and the language in which teaching was given.

[2] For example, the ambassador, Antoine de Noailles, and Henri Griffet (1698–1771), who wrote *A New Light on the History of Mary, Queen of England*, which influenced David Hume (1711–76) and Dr. Lingard (1771–1851).

PLATE XX. KING EDWARD VI: Portrait by Gwillim Stretes
Hampton Court Palace.   *By gracious permission of H.M. the King.*
Photo by Mansell

not so flat as hitherto and the band of jewels was placed round the crown on top of the brim; the white feather drooping over the left side, with a fancy gold tassel hanging from it; a gold dagger in a black sheath, slung from a narrow white and silver waistbelt, and ornamented with a large black silk tassel. The background shows a repetition of the Vol, the armorial bearings of the Seymours. Birds on the wing see more than beings and beasts.

Another portrait of King Edward shows a handkerchief attached by one corner to the waistbelt. It is of fine white lawn, with the hem embroidered in red silk. It measures about fifteen inches square. '6 handkerchers edged with passamayne of gold and silk' is an item which appears in one of the lists of New Year's gifts to the King.

Fig. 483

A pleasing design, embroidered in black silk on a linen neck-frill, is seen in a portrait of Edward VI at Packwood House (Figs. 483 and 484). The edge of the frill is worked in double blanket-stitch, and on top of each fold is a quatre-foil with fleur-de-lys motifs at the corners. This frill is particularly interesting because it shows for the first time a method, much used at a later period, of catching the edges together to form what was known in heraldry as nebulée and dovetail.

Plate XX reproduces a later portrait of Edward VI by Gwillim Stretes at Hampton Court. The costume is carried out entirely in black satin, elaborately braided in gold, with emeralds in gold settings placed thereon at intervals (see Fig. 268). The surcote is not so ample as that shown in Plate XIX, and the turn-back sets wide on the shoulders, a return to the mode characteristic of the latter part of Henry VIII's reign. The slops are even more conspicuous below the basque and have vertical bands of the same braiding as on the doublet and the surcote.

Fig. 484

For centuries it had been, and was still, the privilege of all gentlemen when wearing civil full dress to carry swords unless fashion during certain periods dictated otherwise. Attention is called to the sword. A drawing of one of this period is shown in Fig. 485; the hilt is of the cross type. The tapering *grip* is bound with wire, and finished with an ornamental pointed *pommel*;

Fig. 485

the *quillons* are straight with circular ornaments at the ends, and the *pas-d'âne* are seen below them. The scabbard of plain velvet, ending in a metal *chape*, encloses the steel blade which is probably richly damascened. This sword is slung from the waistbelt by two straps fixed to the scabbard by circular ornaments. One strap is hooked to the waistbelt in front, the other on the left side towards the back. The waistbelt (Fig. 486) fastens low down in front, the ends of the belt having metal ornaments, one with a ring, the other with a hook at A.

A more elaborate sword handle with part of the scabbard of the same date is shown in Fig. 563.

Edward VI's Lord Chamberlain of the Household was Thomas, first Baron Wentworth (born 1501, died 1551). 'The Lord Wentworth Lord Chamberlain, died about ten of the Clock at Night, leaving behind him sixteen Children,' writes Edward in his *Journal* under date 3rd March 1550-1. Fig. 487 is made from his portrait by Hans Eworth dating 1547, and in it is seen the latest development of the style of dress worn in Henry VIII's time. The doublet is of black silk, braided at the edge with black and buttoned down the front. From the high collar falls a white turn-back collar. Over the doublet is worn the surcote of black velvet, lined and turned back with ermine. The sleeves are made loose enough on the lower arm to allow for the sleeve of the doublet underneath, and there are large puffs on the shoulders. When the sleeve was raised high above the shoulder it was said to be MAHOITERED, viz. stuffed with wadding (French *maheutre* or *mahoitre*, a wadded sleeve). It appears for the first time in this drawing (for the cut, reference should be made to Fig. 522 C). The sleeves in Fig. 487 are decorated with three narrow bands of ermine, the centre one descending the full length of the arm. These bands are fixed at intervals with pairs of gold aiglettes. A pocket like that shown in Fig. 495 would be attached to the narrow waistbelt. The slops

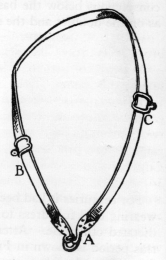

Fig. 486. Waistbelt

are of black velvet gathered or pleated into a narrow band which surrounds the thigh. The black velvet bonet has a turned-down brim, with a flat crown, and is without ornament or feather.

An excerpt from Edward VI's *Journal*, under date 4th November 1550, when the King received Mary of Guise, Queen-Dowager of Scotland, is given below as an example of Court ceremonial:

The '*Duke of Suffolk*, the Lord Fitzwater, the Lord Bray, and divers other Lords and Gentlemen, accompanied with his wife the *Lady Francis*, the *Lady Margaret*, the Dutchesses of Richmond and of Northumberland, the Lady Jane daughter to the Duke of Suffolk; the Marquess of Northampton and Winchester; the Countesses of Arundel, Bedford, and Huntingdon, and Rutland; with 100 other Ladies and Gentlewomen went to her, and brought her through London to Westminster. At the Gate there received her the Duke of Northumberland, Great Master, and the Treasurer, and Comptroller, and the Earl of Pembrook, with all the Sewers, and Carvers, and Cup-bearers, to the number of thirty. In the Hall I met her, with all the rest of the Lords of my Council, as the Lord Treasurer, the Marquis of Northampton, etc., and from the outer-Gate up to the Presence-Chamber, on both sides, stood the *Guard*. The Court, the Hall, and the Stairs, were full of Servingmen; the Presence-Chamber, Great-Chamber, and her Presence-Chamber, of Gentlemen. And so having brought her to her Chamber, I retired to Mine.

Fig. 487. The first Baron Wentworth, 1547. After Hans Eworth
(*National Portrait Gallery*)

'I went to her to Dinner; she dined under the same Cloth of State, at my Left Hand; at her *rereward* dined my Cousin Francis, and my Cousin Margaret; at Mine sat the French Ambassadour. We were served by two Services, two Sewers, Cupbearers, Carvers, and Gentlemen. Her *Master-Hostel* came before her Service, and my Officers before Mine. There were two Cupboards, one of Gold four Stages high, another of massy Silver six Stages: In her great Chamber dined at three Boards the Ladies only. After Dinner, when she had heard some Musick, I brought her to the Hall, and so she went away.'

One or two notes on the above may be helpful. The 'Duke of Suffolk' was Henry Grey, who married the Lady Frances Brandon, second daughter of Charles Brandon, Duke of Suffolk, see pp. 176 and 213.

'My cousin Margaret' was the Lady Margaret Douglas, the mother of Lord Darnley. The 'Guard,' of course, means the Yeomen of the Guard. The King does not mention the Gentlemen Pensioners, but doubtless they also were present.

'At her rereward' must mean, according to the usual precedence at banquets, that the 'cousins' sat on the Queen's left, and the 'French Ambassadour' —invited doubtless out of compliment to the Queen—on the King's right.

The 'Master-Hostel' was the Queen's Chamberlain, or Comptroller of her household.

At the premature age of sixteen, the young King, who had been ailing for most of his short life, died of lung trouble at Greenwich, 6th July 1553. The nostrums of the female quack, to whose tender care he was committed after the physicians had pronounced his case hopeless, probably hastened his end.

FRENCH FASHIONS

HENRY II

King of France, 1518–59

In the portrait of Henry II of France, painted by François Clouet and now in the Musée Condé at Chantilly, is seen the characteristic French fashion of this period. Fig. 488 is a drawing made from this portrait.

Henry, the second son of Francis I and Queen Claude, was born in 1518. He married Catherine de' Medici in 1533, and was father of three successive kings of France. On the death of his elder brother Francis in 1536, he became Dauphin and ascended the throne of France in 1547 as Henry II. In appearance he was tall with broad shoulders and short neck; of dark complexion with sharp black eyes, large nose, black hair, and at the age of thirty-two a 'beard coming to a point, two fingers long.' He was extremely active, possessing abnormal muscular strength combined with great dignity, which served him in good stead as a great sportsman, keen tennis player, and expert tilter. At the age of thirty-six, however, he became rather corpulent, and his hair turned grey.

When the time came to make the arrangements for his crowning, the King surveyed the robes and consecration ornaments which had been used by his predecessors. Finding them unsatisfactory and somewhat impaired by time, he had very gorgeous new ones made for his own coronation.

The costume worn by Henry II in the portrait referred to above is carried out entirely in black and white. The doublet is close-fitting (JUSTAU-CORPS) and has a high collar, short puffed sleeves, and basque. It is constructed of *bands* of white silk, ornamented with cuttes and attached at the

PLATE XXI. HENRY II, KING OF FRANCE, 1558: Portrait by Francis Clouet
Private collection. *Photo by Fleming*

edges by heavy black silk stitchery. The separate sleeves are white decorated with very small cuttes between transversal groups of three rows of black silk stitches. The treatment of garments with these minute cuttes was called 'pinking.' The slops are composed of bands called PANES of white silk worked with black, between which the white silk puffed foundation is seen. The bonet is black velvet with a white ostrich tip. It is said that Henry II usually wore a suit of black and white out of compliment to Diane de Poitiers, who favoured this combination. Some of his doublets were embroidered with 'three crescents intertwined and carrying the cipher of the double D linked and joined with an H.' A portrait of this King at the age of thirty-seven (1556) in the Musée du Puy (Fig. 489) shows him in a doublet of white soft leather treated in the same manner as the JERKIN described under Fig. 495. Over it he has a black velvet surcote lined and turned back with white fur through the short sleeve of which his left arm passes, his forearm resting on the chair, with his hand on the hilt of his sword; the right arm is outside the surcote sleeve and gloves are held in the hand. The usual black velvet flat cap with white feather is worn.

Fig. 488. Henry II, King of France (*after Clouet*)

Plate XXI is a reproduction from a private collection of a very fine equestrian portrait of Henry II painted by François Clouet about 1558. The black velvet doublet is ornamented with very beautiful gold embroidery at the front, sides, and edges, while lines of gold cord converge to the waist and spread out over the rather deep basque. The sleeves, which are treated in the same way, are not worn, but hang from the back of the shoulder. The close sleeves and slops are of white satin having bands of gold with pinking between. The most interesting details are the elaborately embroidered white tops of the BOOT HOSE and the JACK BOOTS. The horse furniture, too, is of exceptional interest. The saddle, saddle-cloth, and well-padded front bate are white embroidered with gold. The rest of the trappings are of gold with coloured silk tassels in a beautiful design, incorporating the cipher D and D reversed with H. The first, of course, refers to Diane de Poitiers, but in the opinion of the author there is some doubt if both initials are D's; the right one *could* pass for a C, in which case the Queen has not been overlooked. The King carries a long riding-rod in his right hand, and wears the fashionable gloves cutte at the wrist and folded over to form loops (*see* Fig. 645).

III²—C

Fig. 489. HENRY II, KING OF FRANCE, 1555

A Venetian gentleman, who saw him at the age of thirty-six playing tennis with a racquet (Fig. 490), describes this costume thus:

'He is clad all in white, with white shoes, too, and a straw hat of the finest on his head. He played in his doublet.' Unfortunately the shape of the straw hat is not mentioned. In all probability it had a basin crown fitting close to the head, and a wide brim. His death, which created a sensation in sporting circles throughout Europe, was caused by a fatal wound in the eye inflicted by his opponent, the Comte de Montgoméry,[1] at a Royal wedding tournament in 1559.

Fig. 367 shows another decorative treatment of a black velvet jerkin worn by a Frenchman in 1543. Lines of fine gold cord are sewn horizontally across it, and the manner in which they join the arm openings demonstrates that the latter are cut at right angles to the jerkin with shoulder seams.

Fig. 490. Racquet

Fig. 491. William West, Esq., 1551.
National Gallery

There is a three-quarter portrait, No. 4252, in the National Gallery, London, of 'William West, Esq.,' born 1519 and created Baron de la Warr in 1570. It was painted about 1551, and depicts the ordinary attire of a young gentleman of Edward VI's reign (Fig. 491). The doublet of fine black cloth has vertical cuttes below the chest and a long basque edged with strands of bullion like the cloak. It is worn over crimson silk, and the sleeves, moderately full at the shoulders and close at the wrists, are of the same colour and material. At the neck and wrists are frills embroidered with Spanish work. The slops are of more ample proportions, and are composed of panes of black velvet with the black satin lining very much pulled through. A full and rather deep cloak of cloth without lining, bound with flat gold bullion with loops of

[1] Gabriel de Montgoméry (1533–74) was a captain in the French King's Scottish Bodyguard and son of James de Lorge, a Scottish gentleman who purchased, in Normandy, the Seignory of Montgoméry, which conferred upon him the title of Count.

the same at the edge (*see* inset), hangs from the shoulders; and the cap of black velvet with a narrow brim is decorated with groups of three gold buttons and a long white drooping plume.

Fig. 492 is taken from a portrait dating about 1550, and shows the black velvet jerkin, now decorated with narrow vertical lines of gold closely worked with bullion strands. Notice the way the lines are arranged, particularly those from shoulder to waist and continuing on the basque. The shape of the collar is very characteristic; it is very straight, close under the chin in front and high at the back. Observe also the shoulder pieces in the form of epaulets obviously derived from the wide shoulders of Fig. 504. The epaulet or narrow piece of material formed on the shoulder of the armhole was known as a 'welt' or 'pinion.' The basque is cut in one piece with the body part, and is edged with a row of indentations.

Fig. 492. Jerkin, 1549   Fig. 493. Jerkin, 1555

THE EMPEROR CHARLES V, 1548–58 (*continued from p. 250*)

In later life the Emperor was painted by Titian in 1548 as he appeared at the Battle of Mühlberg, in full steel armour inlaid with gold,[1] mounted upon a chestnut Andalusian charger. The scarf and feathers in the helmet are scarlet. The horse furniture is scarlet and gold. When Charles reached middle life he appears to have lost interest in his personal appearance. Bernardo Navagero, the Venetian envoy, writes in 1548: 'His personal tastes were simple, his clothes, his table, his kennel and his stables were those of a modest prince rather than a mighty Emperor.'

It has been suggested that His Imperial Majesty adopted this course on purpose to counteract the insensate passion for dress among the gentry. In Germany he would wear a fustian cap and a woollen costume not worth a crown, all of one colour, and so the great nobles did likewise.

[1] Several of Charles V's suits of armour, including this one, are preserved in the Royal Armoury of Madrid.

Another portrait by Titian (1548) in the Pinakothek, Munich, displays simple richness combined with great dignity. Charles is seated in a purple velvet chair in front of a dorsal of orange damask. He is dressed entirely in black velvet without any decoration, a short sable-lined cloak is drawn closely around him, and he wears a plain flat black velvet bonet. The severity of this costume is relieved only by the turned-down white collar, the Golden Fleece, and dark brown leather gloves. Another Venetian, Alvise Mocenigo, states that the Emperor 'was most economical in his person, thinking it folly to give more than two hundred crowns for a fur; he often had his clothes mended, knew every detail, and missed a straying shirt or handkerchief.' During his last ten years he was possessed by a mania for frugality, and it was not beneath his dignity to wear threadbare clothes, old hats, and patched boots. On one occasion when about to make his entry into Nuremberg, for fear of his new cap being spoilt by the rain he sent forward into the town for an old one, and carried the new one under his arm.

We have a pathetic description of this great man in 1551 given by the English ambassador. He writes: 'I . . . found the Emperor at a bare table, without a carpet [1] or anything else upon it, saving his cloak, his brush, his spectacles, and his picktooth. Here His Majesty received the King's Highness's [Edward VI] letters very gently putting his hand to his bonet and uncovering the upper part of his head . . . he was newly rid of his gout and fever, and therefore his nether lip was in two places broken out, and he forced to keep a green leaf within his mouth at his tongue's end—a remedy, as I took it, against such his dryness as in his talk did increase upon him.'

The Emperor resigned the Empire to his brother Ferdinand,[2] 25th October 1558, and the crown of Spain to his son Philip, 15th January 1556; and, as a consequence, the Grand Mastership of the Order of the Golden Fleece became divided between Austria and Spain (see vol. ii, p. 402).

Charles retired to the monastery of S. Yuste, near Placentia, Estremadura, and died 21st September 1558. 'Not quite a great man nor quite a good man, but an honourable Christian gentleman,' says a biographer.

To him his son Philip erected an elaborate monument in his newly finished Escorial shortly after 1584. It stands on the north side of the high altar, and contains the kneeling effigies of Charles V and his wife Isabella, their daughter the Empress Maria, and his sisters, Queens Eleanor of France and Marie of Hungary. The figures are full size, in bronze, and with armorial mantles in colour. The artist, Pompeo Leoni, also executed Philip's own monument.

[1] Very rich carpets were frequently used as table covers.
[2] The Emperor Ferdinand I was educated by Spanish Dominicans, and spoke Spanish only, even when he had already long been ruling in German lands.

SPANISH STYLES: 1547–58

For the contemporary Spanish fashion, Fig. 494, reproducing a three-quarter portrait of a Spanish gentleman by the Italian artist, Moroni (by courtesy of the Earl of Warwick), is chosen as an example. Although it is dated 1560 the style was in vogue quite ten years earlier. The drawing shows a Spanish jerkin. This garment was worn over the doublet, and had no sleeves to be worn on the arm; but at this time it often had short sleeves, and sometimes short puffed sleeves reaching half-way down the upper arms. 'The jerkin was merely an outside coat worn generally over the doublet which it greatly resembled.' The jerkin in Fig. 494 has a short basque and cutte shoulder sleeves of black velvet, without any other decoration. It has a high collar, and from the top of it falls a square-shaped collar of cut-work, mounted on rose-coloured satin, having tiny tassels at the corners (a similar collar is shown in Fig. 688). The cuffs match the collar. The sleeves of the doublet are of deep rose satin, decorated with pinking in the manner described under Fig. 488. The slops have wide panes of crimson velvet edged and braided diagonally with rose silk cord, with deep rose satin linings pulled through. The pattern of the braid is shown below the picture.

Fig. 494. A Spanish Gentleman
(*after Moroni*)

The bonet is black velvet without jewel or feather. The hosen, the tops of which are just visible in the original painting, are of rose-coloured silk.

Jerkins similar in shape to the one described above are depicted in several portraits of Spanish and Italian gentlemen painted by Italian artists about the same date.

MAXIMILIAN

Archduke of Austria, 1522 until 1558

The Archduke Maximilian of Austria, later Maximilian II, Holy Roman Emperor (1564–75), is shown in Fig. 495, taken from a portrait in the Prado, Madrid, painted in 1551 by Antonio Moro. Maximilian was the son of the Emperor Ferdinand I, and a nephew of Charles V. He was born about 1522 and married his cousin the Archduchess Maria.

Although a German his costume is regulated by French fashion as regards all details except the jerkin, which is of Spanish type. The jerkin and shoulder sleeves in Fig. 495 are of soft white leather. After the garment was made up, the body part from high breast level to waist - line was cut vertically in narrow strips half an inch in width, finishing in a row of scallops 'lired' or bound with gold thread. A second similar row of scallops was fixed at the waist under the first. The doublet and sleeves are of white silk, also cut vertically in strips and banded transversely with gold braid, the body part being occasionally visible between the strips of the jerkin. The white panes

Fig. 495. The Archduke Maximilian, 1551
(after Moro)

of the slops are heavily braided with gold, with the lining of white taffety 'pulled out' between them. Panes were fixed to a hip-yoke which descended from waist-line to hip-bone level, and fitted close to the figure (*refer to* Fig. 496), the lower part of the slops gradually bulging out. A black velvet bonet is worn and the Toison d'or encircles the neck. The pocket or pouch is a fine example of those in use among fashionable people of this period. Variants of the jerkin described above are chiefly foreign, dating about this time to be seen in several portraits, (*see* Fig. 489).

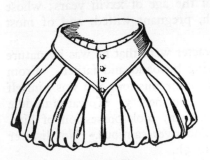

Fig. 496. Slops

PHILIP OF SPAIN

King of Naples and Jerusalem, 1527 until 1558

Philip of Spain, only son of the Emperor Charles V and Isabella of Portugal, was born at Valladolid, 21st May 1527. In his early years he was surrounded by strict and narrow-minded devotees, and not until the termination of hostilities with Italy, and the subsequent return of the Emperor in 1533, did he see his father for the first time. Heir to the largest empire in the world, he was educated with great care by a Professor of Salamanca called Siliceo, whom Philip afterwards made Archbishop of Toledo and Primate of Spain, and Don Juan Zuniga, who taught the young Prince the various accomplishments necessary for one in so exalted a position. At the age of fourteen the Emperor took charge of his son's education in politics.

The various portraits of Philip show him as a good-looking young man of fair complexion with yellow hair, grey eyes, and a pleasant expression. Another description refers to 'a fine broad brow, large blue eyes, dense fair eyebrows very close together, a nose well formed, a large mouth with a thick and pendent under-lip which rather spoiled his appearance. His skin was white and his hair flaxen.' He was a little below the average height, graceful, erect, and dapper of person. Grave and reserved, he relaxed when occasion required, and could become most courteous and affable. Dancing was, in fact, the one frivolity that this solemn Prince allowed himself.

An eyewitness of Philip's entry into London on the occasion of his visit in 1554, describes him in these words:

'Of visage he is well favoured, with a broad forehead, and grey eyes, straight nosed, and manly countenance. From the forehead to the point of his chin, his face groweth small. His pace is princely, and gate so straight and upright, as he loseth no inch of his height; with a yellow head and a yellow beard. And thus to conclude, he is so well proportioned of body, arm, leg, and every other limb to the same, as nature cannot work a more perfect pattern; and, as I have learned, of the age of xxviij years; whose Majesty I judge to be of a stout stomach, pregnant witted, and of most gentle nature.'

The chief points of Philip of Spain's character were that he was by nature a kind man, a loyal and dutiful son, a loving husband and father. From birth he firmly believed that he had a semi-divine mission, and was himself God's instrument to fight His battles and wipe out heresy. Towards middle age a hereditary gloom, deepened by fanaticism, took possession of him, and he became distrustful, secret, crafty, and over-cautious. No disaster thwarted him; it was God's will, that was enough.

Biased historians have hitherto held Philip responsible for the drastic extirpation of heresy in this country. As a matter of fact, his energies were directed against the rash zeal of the Catholic party, and the era of martyrs did not begin until six months after he left England for the first time. During

Fig. 497. PRINCE PHILIP OF SPAIN, 1548. After Titian

his second visit in 1557 he was the means of saving many victims from the flames by his active intercessions.

Philip's titles were many. Those proclaimed in conjunction with Queen Mary's at their marriage were: 'Philip and Mary, by the Grace of God King and Queen of England, France, Naples, Jerusalem, and Ireland, Defenders of the Faith, Princes of Spain and Sicily, Archdukes of Austria, Dukes of Milan, Burgundy, and Brabant, Counts of Hapsburg, Flanders, and Tyrol.'

On the day of Prince Philip's marriage in 1554 with Mary Tudor, the Emperor equalized his son's rank with that of Queen Mary by making him King of Naples and of Jerusalem. The crowns of Spain were also transferred to Philip on the abdication of his father, together with the sovereignty of the New World, 16th January 1556. Henceforth he was known as King Philip II.[1]

Prince Philip had previously married (15th November 1542) the Princess Maria, daughter of Joam III, King of Portugal, and Catalina, youngest daughter of Philippe le Beau. Don Carlos (died 1568) was their only son. The Princess died November 1543.

One of the Emperor Charles V's schemes, evolved in 1548, for centralizing the government of Spain, was to form an entourage around his son Philip, consisting of members of the most powerful Spanish noble families; and he also introduced into the Royal household the punctilious formulae of the Court [2] of his ancestor, the magnificent Philippe le Bon, Duke of Burgundy (see vol. ii, p. 400).

This change in the regime was not altogether congenial to Prince Philip, whose personal tastes were of the simplest. He disliked the pomp, glamour, and flattery inevitable to the life of Royal personages under such a system, and from early manhood preferred the domestic circle of his own family. In dress he was moderate and his usual attire was plain though rich. Nevertheless on all necessary occasions he would appear garbed in the superb raiment befitting his exalted position. Of this type Fig. 497 is a good example.

It is made from the portrait of Prince Philip in the Royal Pitti Gallery, Florence. The original was painted by Titian from a sketch made either in 1548 at Milan, or in 1550 at Augsburg, and was presented to Duke Cosimo I. It has been suggested that this is a copy of another portrait of Philip, in the Gallery at Naples. The Naples portrait is exactly the same, but the background is slightly different.

In Fig. 497 the doublet, sleeves, and slops (now still more pronounced) are composed of bands of pale yellow satin edged with passamayne, having pairs of aiglettes, called in Spanish 'puntas,' set at intervals. One such aiglette is shown in Fig. 455. The bands are embroidered with a design

[1] Philip's grandfather, Philippe le Beau, is known as Philip I, King of Spain.
[2] The elaborate ceremonial and etiquette of the Burgundian Court, adopted by that of Spain in the middle of the sixteenth century, retained its hold until the end of the Spanish monarchy in April 1931.

shown again in Fig. 498. The floral motifs are worked in silver thread, and the stems are silver chainlets. The collar and wrists are edged with a series of loops like Fig. 499. A plain white lawn collar surrounds the neck, and the Toison d'or is worn.

The doublet is now slightly padded from below chest level to the sloping waist. The surcote is of rich brown satin, the fronts turned back with sable; it has large sleeves with bands in the same design as those on the doublet; the sleeves are sufficiently short to show those of the doublet worn beneath it at the wrists. The hosen are of pale yellow silk, and the cutte shoes, of the same shade in velvet, have a series of very small loops at the edge. The Prince holds his dagger in the right hand with the hilt pointing downwards.

The portrait of Philip, painted by Titian at Augsburg in 1550–1 and now in the Prado, Madrid, shows him wearing a beautiful suit of damascened armour, over slops, hosen, and shoes of white silk. This portrait, one of the finest in the world, was sent to Queen Mary at the time the Spanish marriage was arranged.

Fig. 498.
Embroidery

An inventory of his costumes, besides other items for his personal use, to be worn during his sojourn in England, was compiled by a certain Andres Muñoz, valet to his young son, Don Carlos. It is of exceptional interest, as it gives numerous details of the costumes worn not only by Philip himself, but by many of his courtiers, attendants, servants, and military escort. It appears that this wonderful masculine trousseau, chiefly prepared in the city of Valladolid, caused a great sensation throughout Spain. Previous to this date, 1554, lavish display and ostentation in the dress of the middle classes, as has been already noted, was strictly prohibited. Gradually these laws had been applied with less and less stringency, but now the opportunity for release seemed to have been reached. The Cortes of Castile boldly presented a petition to the Emperor, asking that these sumptuary laws should be repealed. The petition, however, was not granted, because both the Emperor and his son realized that instead of the wealth of the country flowing into their own coffers, it would probably be 'used in decking the undistinguished persons of private citizens.'

Fig. 499

Fig. 500. Button

Philip's portrait, painted by Antonio Moro in 1554 (Plate XXII), shows him in a jerkin composed of wide bands of velvet each edged with passamayne, the centre portion of the velvet being cutte to show the doublet underneath. These bands are held together at intervals by fancy buttons (Fig. 500), often very elaborate and set with jewels. The jerkin is long enough to form a

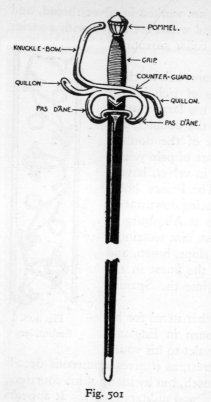

POMMEL.

KNUCKLE-BOW.

GRIP.

COUNTER-GUARD.

QUILLON

QUILLON.

PAS D'ÂNE.

PAS D'ÂNE.

Fig. 501

basque shorter than that previously worn, and has a moderately high collar. Underneath the jerkin is worn the doublet of white satin, and banded with silver and pearls, having close sleeves to the wrist. The slops, now appearing much larger owing to the reduction of the basque, match the doublet in treatment of decoration and material. These three garments, the jerkin, the doublet, and the slops, together with hose and shoes of white silk, comprise a 'suit.'

Fig. 501 shows the type of sword-hilt with spherical pommel, used during the second half of the sixteenth century. It is the type carried by Englishmen, Frenchmen, and Spaniards. A curved guard for the hand, or knuckle-bow, appears at this time fixed to the top of the 'grip' and in a line with one of the *quillons*. The *pas-d'âne*, formed of two rings curving below the quillons on each side of the base of the hilt, was a further addition. The whole of the hilt was often decorated with chasing, and was sometimes much jewelled. Fig. 502 shows the sword carriage, or HANGER, of the second half of the sixteenth century. It is made of two pieces of leather fixed at the top with a hook, E, which is hooked to the waist-belt on the left side at C (*refer to* Fig. 486). The ends of each are cut into three straps—F is one of them—and these are buckled back to form loops through which the scabbard of the sword is passed. A belt, having a hook, or toggle, D, is attached to the carriage, and hooks across the front into the ring, B (*see* Fig. 486), on the right side of the waistbelt, *not* to the centre fastening, A, as hitherto. The Archduke Maximilian, Fig. 495, carries a sword, the hilt of which is shown in Fig. 503.

For a jewelled sword-handle, see Fig. 563.

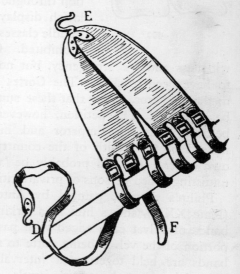

E

D

F

Fig. 502. Hanger

PLATE XXII. PRINCE PHILIP OF SPAIN, 1554: Portrait by Antonio Moro
Prado, Madrid.   *Photo by Mansell*

When Philip disembarked from his galleon at Southampton, 19th July 1554, and proceeded along the High Street, he presented a very gracious and attractive appearance, his slight dapper figure sitting erect upon the beautiful white charger, caparisoned in crimson velvet embroidered in gold, which Sir Anthony Browne, Master of the Horse, presented to him in the Queen's name.[1]   He then made his way to the Church of the Holy Rood, and there returned thanks for his safe voyage.   Afterwards the Prince was conducted to a house prepared for his reception near the Watergate, and not far from the church. The rooms occupied by Philip had been specially garnished, by order of the Queen, the walls being covered with gold embroidered damask hangings from the Royal collection.   The furniture, as was usual at this period, consisted of exceptional pieces of a most sumptuous nature.   The English household servitors were dressed in the red and yellow liveries of Aragon by special direction of the Queen.

He was dressed on this occasion more or less as shown in Plate XXII, in black velvet and silver, with massive gold chains and jewels around his neck.   His black velvet bonet, worn at the correct rakish angle, was decorated with jewels, and a white plume fell in graceful lines over the left ear—a costume well suited to set off his pink and white complexion, close-cropped yellow hair and close-cut beard.   The Earl of Arundel had been sent by the Queen to invest him with the Order of the Garter on his landing. The Order of the Golden Fleece, hung from a gold chain, was doubtless also worn.

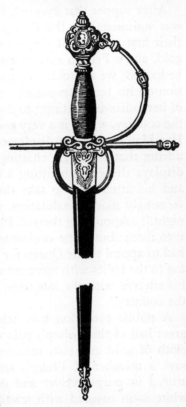

Fig. 503

Having stayed four days in Southampton [2] His Highness proceeded to Winchester.   The journey of twelve miles was made in torrents of rain; and despite the scarlet felt cloak and black sombrero—substitutes for a modern mackintosh and umbrella — Philip's magnificent black velvet surcote, smothered with silver and diamond embroidery, and worn over doublet and slops of white satin embroidered in gold, was soaked through and

[1] Horses for Philip's use had been shipped to England, and in addition to these he brought six hundred Andalusian jennets to improve the English breed of horses.

[2] In Speed's *History of Southampton*, 1909, occurs the statement that Philip 'remained three days in the town, during which time he appears to have done little but hear mass at Holy Rood and drink beer.   He made a very unfavourable impression on the townspeople by his ungracious manners.'   This criticism ignores contemporary evidence which emphatically contradicts these accusations.

through. He was quite unperturbed by these somewhat trying conditions, which necessitated a call at the Hospital of St. Cross to change into an equally gorgeous costume. This consisted of a black velvet surcote covered with gold BUGLES, and a suit of white silk-velvet trimmed in similar fashion. Thus fortified Philip continued on his way to Winchester, where, on arrival, he and his numerous train of nobles entered the cathedral to hear Mass, and then on to the deanery where he was housed.

After supper that evening, the clock chiming the hour of ten, Prince Philip was summoned to the Bishop's palace where the Queen awaited him. For their first meeting he chose a suit of white silk and white kid embroidered in gold, and a French surcote embroidered in gold and silver, 'and very gallant he looked' we are told. At any rate, it is known that he made a great impression on his ten-years-senior bride. In due course the Queen presented each of her ladies-in-waiting [1] to the Prince, who, 'so as not to break the custom of the country, which is a very good one,' kissed them all 'in his way.' Evidently Her Majesty was not displeased, for it is on record that she was in high spirits during that evening, 'chatting gaily, and although she is a little elderly she displays the grace befitting a Queen.' When the time came for the Prince and his attendants to take their leave, the Queen instructed Philip in that seemingly modern salutation, which may mean so much or so little—'Good night.'[2] Approving thereof, Philip approached the ladies-in-waiting to repeat it to them; but as he confronted them the words slipped his memory and he had to appeal to the Queen for help, 'whereat she was well pleased.' Returning to the ladies with more assurance, he made another attempt, and, whatever his success with the language, he did not neglect the very good 'custom of the country.'

A public reception was held by the Queen on the following day in the great hall of the Bishop's palace. 'The Hall, which is beautifully hung with cloth of gold and silk, measures forty of my paces long and twenty wide,' says a member of Philip's entourage. For the ceremony the Prince was attired in purple velvet and gold. His wedding suit on 25th July was of white satin covered with jewelled embroidery, and over it a long mantle of cloth of gold and ermine ornamented with pearls and precious stones surmounted by the Collar of the Garter. The mantle was a present from the Queen, who wore one like it. Simon Renard, the Emperor's representative, reports to his master that 'the Queen has had a collar [of the Garter] made, which cost seven or eight thousand crowns, besides several rich dresses for His Highness.' It is not stated in which style these rich dresses were fashioned, neither do we learn where they were made—whether in London or ordered from Valladolid.

These descriptions of other costumes in Philip's wardrobe are taken from the inventory by Andres Muñoz, to which reference has already been made. They are more or less literal translations from the original Spanish, and are

---

[1] One was the Lady Jane Dormer, who afterwards became the wife of the Duke of Feria.

[2] This phrase has been in use since mediæval times.

valuable here for the reason that Philip and his attendant nobles influenced the English fashions, and introduced many details into the costume of the people during the reign of Queen Mary.

Here are eight suits worn by His Imperial and Royal Highness:

(1) A costume of crimson velvet completely covered with embroidery of an heraldic pattern of large flowers in seed pearls, the leaves formed of *half-braids* of silver, the interstices being filled with silver bullion. The lining of the short cloak or MUCETA was of flat [dull] cloth of silver embroidered in the same manner. The hosen were of silk.

(2) Another very pretty costume was a brown satin cloak with trimmings of *chainlets* formed of silk twist in gold and pipings of silver. The linings were of a lighter shade encrusted with silver. The doublet and slops were of white silk-velvet embroidered in the same manner.

(3) A very handsome costume made in the French fashion had a cloak of black velvet with two different designs of embroideries of pipings in gold and silver twist. The jerkin and hosen were of crimson velvet, and the doublet was of satin with the same embroidery of very beautiful workmanship.

(4) A second very rich French costume had very gorgeous and costly embroidery of narrow trimmings of gold and silver, lined with a light material of *frizzed silver*. The jerkin, doublet, slops, and hosen were of white silk-velvet.

(5) A very pretty surcote was of black velvet embroidered with *quills* of gold and twists of silver in a manner that showed some silver slashings and unfinished weaving (cuttes) with a ground of embroidery of leaves formed of twists of gold thread enclosing narrow strands of silver bullion. The suit worn underneath was of white silk-velvet embroidered with gold and silver.

(6) A beautiful costume had a surcote of grey satin covered with alternate stripes of applied gold chains and silver bugles, and lined with embossed cloth of silver. The suit was of white satin ornamented in the same way.

(7) Another suit consisted entirely of white silk-velvet covered with costly gold embroidery and gold *filigree*.

(8) One of the most elaborate costumes in Philip's wardrobe included a surcote of black velvet, with a border of gold bugles and heavy twisted silver cord worked into a design similar to that in fashion during Henry VIII's reign (*see* Fig. 267). The garment itself was almost hidden under closely embroidered sprigs in gold, the leaves being filled in with silver filigree. The spaces between the sprigs were cutte showing the white satin lining. With this surcote was worn a suit of white silk-velvet and gold embroideries.

Costumes (1), (2), (3), (4), (7) are well represented in Plate XXII and (5), (6), (8) in Fig. 497.

It is interesting to notice that many of Philip's costumes were carried out in schemes of black and white, gold and silver.

Space will permit only of a few of the costumes made for the members of Philip's suite as described by Andres Muñoz.

The Admiral of Castile, Don Antonio de Toledo, amongst other costumes had one suit of white silk-velvet and satin trimmed with gold passamayne, very fine, that was made with consummate workmanship. His muceta was of black velvet embroidered with a marvellous plated ornamentation of gold, half a yard in breadth, with a stitching of silver spirals and a border of embroidery of thick tendrils of gold. This cape was lined with cloth of silver. The admiral's pages wore liveries of purple velvet lined with yellow satin. Over their jackets they had mantles of the same garnished with loops of cloth of gold. The other attendants were several lackeys, six servants, four trumpeters, and three kettle-drummers all dressed in the same livery.

The Marqués de los Valles appeared in a suit of purple velvet and satin. The gold embroidery embodied a scale design with pearl-drop pendants. The muceta worn with it was also of purple velvet, decorated with the same embroidery and lined with cloth of silver. His lackeys wore jackets and hosen of black velvet and doublets of satin, garnished with *welts* of the same velvet, and on top of them two backstitches of brown silk; over this dress they had capes of black cloth with the same garniture. The pages wore GALDRESES of the same cloth and braiding, and capes of velvet.

A black velvet muceta embroidered with quills of silver about eight inches in width showed many a graceful difference of working, and was very lucent and costly. This was worn by the Duke of Alba over a suit of white satin of the same workmanship. The Duke of Medina Celi had a French costume in purple and white velvet, with two trimmings of gold and silver quills embroidered with YY and with interlaced letters which spelt 'Juana Manuel.' This [says Muñoz] was a satisfactory garment to see.

The costume made for the Marquis de Pescara was also in the French style, carried out in black velvet and crimson satin. The cape of black velvet was trellissed with silver and loops of gold, showing a gold rose in each square of trellissing. The lackeys attending this nobleman wore capes of black cloth with two gards of black velvet, slashed in the centre, on both sides of which there was a design embroidered in brown silk flanked by two rows of gold passamayne. The jackets were of the same velvet garnished in like manner; the pages were similarly attired but wore gold chains. Five gentlemen of the household were garbed in the same style.

The Marqués de Aguillara had a costume of brown velvet, the muceta embroidered with large raised roses and crossings, in a manner that formed several squares of graceful outline. The embroidery required twenty-seven marks' weight of gold. The lackeys wore jackets, doublets, and hosen of scarlet velvet garnished with black and white embroidery; sufficiently costly and handsome to see. The pages wore under-dresses and galdreses of scarlet velvet with ornamentations called *entranzado*.

The costume made for the Duke of Saldanha had a cape and suit all of worked gold on black velvet, with an embroidery of quills of gold using twenty-two marks' weight of bullion. The Duke had another costume of brown velvet and a muceta of crimson velvet, also a jerkin of Cordoban leather dressed with amber, with an embroidery of quills of gold; very costly. Further he had a collar of gold with thick stems enchased with emeralds, rubies, and diamonds of great value, the intermediate pieces being studded with large pearls. More than this, he possessed a great number of jewels, medals, and buttons of great worth.

The costume of the guards who accompanied Philip to England, as noted by Muñoz, was exceptionally rich. This display turned out to be a prodigious waste of good material, as the guards were allowed no part in the show. Neither bodyguard nor men-at-arms were allowed to land, on pain of death; and they remained, perforce, cooped up on board the Spanish galleons. The reason for this was that it was believed that Spanish troops, if brought ashore, might create a feeling of distrust among the English people. Eventually the fleet was sent to Portsmouth to revictual, before sailing to Flanders to join the Emperor's forces.

The hundred halberdiers of the Spanish guard were very well clad and a very good set of men. Among them were their sergeants and lieutenants, chiefs of squadrons. These wore doublets of red and yellow (the livery colours of Aragon) garnished with sashes of crimson velvet, one-sixth of a yard in width, with others of the same width of white velvet; the crimson sash had slashes formed in a kind of square with thick cordons of silk for edging of the braid; these were of white, scarlet, and yellow, the colours of His Highness's livery. The caps, shoon, hosen, scabbards, and sword-belts were of yellow velvet with the same braid. The Count de Feria was their captain and Hernando de Sayavedre their lieutenant.

A hundred German halberdiers, all well-disciplined men, and garbed similarly to the Landsknechten (Fig. 224), were in the same device and costume, except that all the silk of their dress was doubled, because it was their custom and habit to carry themselves with bravura, in the German fashion. Their captain was Christopher, a German. A hundred German mounted archers were dressed in the same device and uniform, except that they wore cloaks of yellow velvet, with frocks of velvet of the same colour and braiding. Their captain was the Count de Hornes, and their ensign Monsieur Turlon.

The following explanations of the various terms used in describing the decoration of these costumes may be of interest:

Bugle, a glass bead. The Venetians were the first to manufacture bugles, and from them most countries of Europe derived their supplies. In the sixteenth century bugles were of gold or silver. *Jet* bugles were also very fashionable, the mineral being found at this period chiefly at Whitby, in Aude (France), and Asturia (Spain).

Half-braids were very narrow braids.

Muceta, or museta, a short cloak. For details see under diagram, Fig. 507.

Chains or *chainlets* were either small chains of metal in gold or silver sewn on to the garment, or embroidery in a chain pattern.

Material of *frizzed silver* was a fabric woven with very fine silver or gold thread upon a coloured silk, satin, velvet, or cloth of silver or gold ground, so giving the appearance of silver or gold hair.

III²—D

Quills or *quilling* were plaits or pipings of folded or quilled material, somewhat resembling cords. These quills were sewn on in straight lines and curves, and wrought into patterns, in the same manner as cord or braid: designs were frequently of the interlaced type (*see* p. 227).

Filigree, small motifs of metal in gold or silver, sewn on and embodied in the design of the embroidery.

Welt, a narrow strip of material put on the edge of a garment as a border, binding, or hem; also a narrow ridge or raised stripe.

Galdres, a gown worn by men and women. Gowns or robes such as were worn by gentlemen in Henry VII's reign. Galdreses, when applied to women, meant any fashionable gowns or dresses.

Entranzado, garniture, decoration, usually plaited gold, silver, or silk braid.

NOBILITY: MEN, 1553–8

'The nobility are by nature very courteous, especially to foreigners . . . they, save such as are employed at Court, do not habitually reside in the cities but in their own country mansions, where they keep up very grand establishments.'—VENETIAN CALENDAR.

EDWARD COURTENAY

Earl of Devonshire, Baron Courtenay of Okehampton and Plympton, 1526–56

It is obvious that the black velvet jerkin worn by the English gentleman in Fig. 504 is influenced by the Spanish mode. The drawing is made from a portrait by Hans Eworth of Edward Courtenay, who was born about 1526, and at the age of thirteen was confined by Henry VIII to the Tower, chiefly because he was unfortunate enough to be a great-grandson of King Edward IV. He was released by Queen Mary and created Earl of Devonshire in 1553. He bore the Sword of State at her coronation, and for this office he had intended to appear in a very splendid suit of blue velvet embroidered with gold, but the Queen, being desirous of wearing the same shade, instantly commanded this young man of twenty-seven to set aside such fine array for more sober attire. By common consent the earl was chosen as a husband for the Princess Elizabeth, but becoming implicated in Wyatt's rebellion he was again sent to the Tower for a year in 1554. In 1555 he was sent abroad out of the way and died of fever at Padua, 1556.

. Courtenay is described by his contemporaries as one of the handsomest and most agreeable young noblemen of his age.

The jerkin in Fig. 504 has a high upstanding collar supporting a pleated linen frill, and the shoulders are cut wide. It is tied by laces and aiglettes down the front. The sleeves of the doublet and the paned slops are of white silk. The increased size of the latter should be noticed.

Fig. 504.
Edward Courtenay, Earl
of Devonshire, 1553

Lord Guyldeford Dudley is described as a very tall strong youth with light hair. On one occasion it is stated that he wore a suit of white silk embroidered with gold. On the scaffold his costume was of black velvet cutte over satin white and would have been made like that shown in Fig. 504.

In the group (Fig. 531) of Philip and Mary, the original of which was painted by Hans Eworth in 1558, Philip is in a black velvet jerkin ornamented with silk braid and bugles. It is cut sloping to a point at the waist with deep basques. The sleeves of the doublet, and the slops, are of cutte pale yellow satin. A short Spanish cloak—the muceta—made of black velvet and lined with black silk, hangs from his shoulders. The bonet is of black velvet with a small white plume, and the blue and gold garter is buckled on his yellow behosed left leg.

Fig. 493 shows a characteristic jerkin worn during the later part of Queen Mary's reign and the early part of Elizabeth's. It is taken from a portrait by Antonio Moro, dating about 1555, and is made of black velvet braided with narrow gold, either cord or braid. The epaulets are composed of a series of braided loops; and the basque is divided into tabs, the front ones cut in one with the front widths of the body part, and the tabs next to these joined on to the body part at the waist-line and overlapping each other to the centre of the back. The bulging over the waist is due to padding. One of the gold buttons is inset.

Fig. 505 shows the type of costume worn by a fashionable young English nobleman towards the close of Queen Mary's reign. The illustration is adapted from a three-quarter-length portrait of Henry FitzAlan, Lord Maltravers, a youth of nineteen, who died in Brussels in 1556. The portrait was almost certainly painted by Hans Eworth. The jerkin is of a material, probably thick white silk, woven or embroidered with a design (Fig. 506) in gold; the converging cuttes down the centre and sides are edged

Fig. 505. LORD MALTRAVERS, 1556.   After Hans Eworth

with gold passamayne which also decorates the collar and basque. The edge of the basque is finished with escallopes or indentations (heraldic term: engrailed). The high collar is surmounted by a small close frill, or RUFF. The doublet closely fits the figure and the jerkin is cut to fit over it. The sleeves and paned slops are of white damask.

Over the shoulders his lordship wears the newest thing—the muceta — just introduced from Spain. The diagram (Fig. 507) gives the shape — three-fourths of a circle—which produces many voluminous folds in wear. It often had ornaments down the front for fastening with buttons, cords, loops and buttons, or, in place of buttons, small tassels, sometimes both. This Spanish cloak is distinguished by a long hood rounded or pointed at the top

Fig. 506

and usually fastened down the front in the manner described above. Fig. 508 shows the shape of the hood, the portion AA being sewn to the neck opening of the cloak. The projecting ends, BB, form lapels on both sides of the

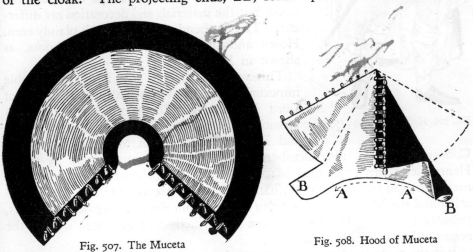

Fig. 507. The Muceta

Fig. 508. Hood of Muceta

neck. The muceta worn by Lord Maltravers is of black silk or satin, having a hood of black velvet studded with gold buttons. In fact, the enormous number of buttons worn by English gentlemen at this time was commented upon by the Spaniards in Philip's retinue.

The cloak is lined and turned back with ermine, forming revers and a deep collar. With a practical hood this collar would be superfluous; hence the hood, in this case, is flat,[1] and merely ornamental—quite a usual fancy.

The black velvet bonet is decorated with gold buttons round the crown, and a small white ostrich tip droops on the left side.

Legs have been added to the drawing (Fig. 505) and these are clothed in white silk hosen and long black leather boots.

In the Prado, Madrid, there is a portrait of Don Carlos, son of Philip II, painted by Sanchez Coello. The boy's age cannot be less than eleven years, which dates the portrait at 1556, and makes it contemporary with the portrait of Lord Maltravers. On comparing the two portraits it is seen that the Prince's doublet and slops are of different material and decoration, but the same shape. The bonet is identical, and the muceta, which stands out from the shoulders in large radiating folds, is of black satin with a six-inch border of black velvet, and is lined and turned back with ermine. The portrait of Don Carlos is a front view; but it is probable that there is a similar hood arrangement at the back.

Fig. 509. Henry Lee, Esq., 1555

There is another portrait of Don Carlos by Coello in the Kunsthistorisches Museum, Vienna. In it the details of the Infante's dress are the same, but the materials and decoration are different. The flat hood of the muceta is plainly seen. Hosen and shoes take the place of boots, as shown in Fig. 505.

This young man (Fig 509) is of considerable importance, for he is seen sitting on the left of Lord Williams of Thame amongst the commissioners at the burning of Bishops Latimer and Ridley 'in the ditch over against Balliol College,'[2] Oxford, 16th October 1555. It seems probable that he is Sir Henry Lee (born 1530, died 1610), to whom Ridley gave a new groat as a memento; the two on Lord Williams's right are presumably the Vice-Chancellor and the Mayor. The drawing is taken from Foxe's *Acts and Monuments*, published in 1563, but the costume is distinctly that in vogue during the reigns of Edward VI and Mary.

It is the everyday dress of the upper classes, and consists of a doublet with a deep basque and close-fitting sleeves raised on the shoulders. On top of

[1] Flat unpractical hoods of this kind can be seen to-day on the backs of ecclesiastical copes.
[2] The cross, commemorating the burning of Latimer and Ridley, is to be seen in the centre of the road in Broad Street immediately opposite Messrs Lindsey & Sons, opticians. It is a Greek cross in plain stone. Originally it was placed nearer St Michael's Church.

this is draped a cloak with a high collar braided deeply round the shoulders. Over his hosen he has drawn boot hose to protect them from the slush—practical though unusual, as they were generally worn inside boots; these he has probably used when on the road but left behind at his lodging. A flat cap with feather, a gold chain wound twice round his neck, sword, stout leather shoes, and gloves complete this young aristocrat's outfit.

We are informed that on this occasion the Mayor of Oxford, Richard Whittington, entertained the commissioners very lavishly.   In the City accounts appear the following:

'Item. For wine to my Lord Williams and his retinue at the burning of the Bishops, 3s. 4d.   Item. For 2 pair of gloves double garnished for my Lord and Lady Williams 4s.

'Item [the next morning] a bottle of Malmsey 14d.'

EMBROIDERY (*continued from p. 230*)

After the abbeys and monasteries had been ruthlessly looted of their sacred belongings, it became the fashion, about 1550, to use embroidered vestments and Church hangings as decorations in the rooms of private houses.

Fig. 510. Gold Braiding

During the reigns of Edward VI and Queen Mary, Spanish work was very much in favour. Queen Mary had inherited her Spanish mother's taste in needlework.

(*Continued on p. 583*)

Fig. 511. Gold Embroidery

LACE (*continued from p. 231*)

Lace now seems to be called indifferently purle, passamayne, or bone lace (1556).

Frequent mention of lace is made in wardrobe accounts during this time, and bone lace constantly appears in the same records.

Bobbin lace is of less frequent occurrence. It is made of coarser thread than bone lace.

Ruffles made or wrought out of England, commonly called cutwork, were forbidden to any one under the degree of a baron.

(*Continued on p. 589*)

THE YEOMEN OF THE GUARD (*continued from p. 292*)

Temp. EDWARD VI

In the reign of Edward VI the full corps of the Yeomen of the Guard numbered sixty-six 'Yeoman in Ordinary,' who were on duty on ordinary occasions, 141 'Yeomen Extraordinary,' in reserve for ceremonial and state

functions, and 15 'Tower Warders' permanently stationed at the Tower in readiness to guard the King when he was lodged there.

The livery worn by the Yeomen of the Guard during this reign was practically the same as that of Henry VIII's time. The only remaining representation of the guard of this period was in a picture of the coronation procession of Edward VI at Cowdray House, but unfortunately this was destroyed in the disastrous fire which occurred there in 1793. The existing reproduction [1] of this picture is not too satisfactory, but in it the hat worn appears to be rather larger than before, and the bases of the tunics are sufficiently long to obscure the small slops fashionable in Edward VI's reign. At one time during this reign hats were scarlet, but more usually they were of black velvet or cloth.

Temp. QUEEN MARY

At the accession of Mary the corps numbered 207 picked men. This number was immediately increased by another 200, an augmentation deemed necessary in view of the disturbances which had arisen from the ferment of controversy as to whether the Princess Mary or the Lady Jane Grey was the rightful successor to the crown.

[1] *Archaeologia*, vol. viii, 1787, p. 406.

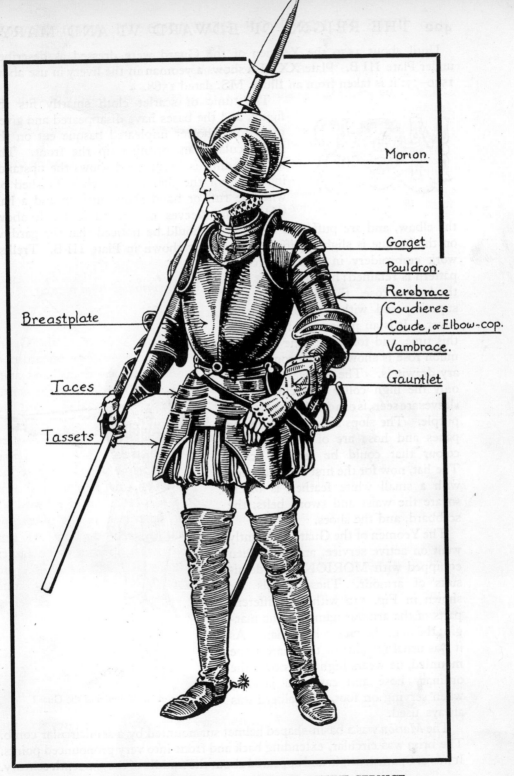

Morion.

Gorget

Pauldron.

Rerebrace
Coudieres
Coude, or Elbow-cop.

Vambrace.

Gauntlet

Breastplate

Taces

Tassets

Fig. 512. YEOMAN OF THE GUARD ON ACTIVE SERVICE

Until about 1550 the Yeomen of the Guard were dressed as described under Plate III B. Plate XXIII A shows a yeoman in the livery in use about 1550–75: it is taken from an Illum. MS. dated 1568.

The tunic of scarlet cloth smartly fits the figure, and the bases have disappeared and given place to a shorter unpleated basque cut on the semicircular plan, opening up the front. The neck opening is higher and shows the upstanding collar of the doublet, which is finished off with the ruff or band about an inch and a half wide. The sleeves of the tunic finish above the elbow, and are puffed as of old. It should be noticed that the garding on the basque is slightly different from that shown in Plate III B. Trellis-work embroidery in gold in a closer pattern is retained; but the rose is now the 'union rose,' that is, one of gold superimposed with a second rose of silver. It is an interesting fact that at this time, and for some time later, the union rose is shown on all contemporary drawings. The doublet, of which only the high collar and close-fitting sleeves are seen, is of a dull liver-coloured purple. The slops are purple, and the panes and hose are of a dull yellow colour that could be termed ochre. The hat, now for the first time adorned with a small white feather, is black, so are the waist and sword belts, the scabbard, and the shoes.

The Yeomen of the Guard frequently went on active service, and were then equipped with MORIONS and demi-suits of armour. These details are shown in Fig. 512 with the different parts of the armour named in the margin; the man shown is a horseman. As it was usual for part of the guard to be mounted, he wears high boots over the ordinary hose and carries a javelin; when serving on foot, the halberd was always used.

Fig. 513.
Archer of the Yeomen of the Guard

The *Morion* was a basin-shaped helmet surmounted by a semicircular comb. The brim was circular, extending back and front into very pronounced points. It was of Spanish origin and appeared about the middle of the sixteenth century.

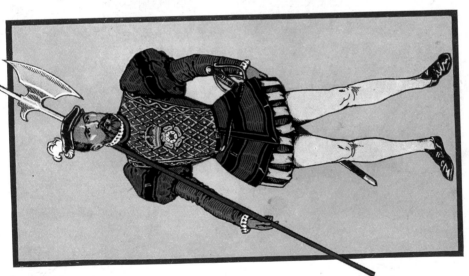

The CABASSET is very like the morion, but is distinguished from it by the pointed apex in place of the comb.

Archers of the Yeomen of the Guard wore leather tunics, the sleeves of which were sometimes of chain-mail over slops and hose. Above the tunic was placed the BRIGANDINE, and upon the head the morion or SALADE. The arms carried were large bows and long arrows (*see* Fig. 513).

The *brigandine* was a jacket composed of some strong material—canvas or linen—on the inside, with an outer covering of velvet or silk when worn by important people, and of linen or leather in the case of the rank and file of the army. Between these layers of material were small strips of thin iron, disposed like taces, or the slats of a Venetian blind, kept in place by rivets set close together, the metal heads being visible externally. Brigandines sometimes had sleeves, and usually descended to the hips; they were fastened down the front or sides by hooks, laces, or buttons. They formed a useful item of war equipment, being less expensive than plate armour, serviceable, pliable to the movement of the body, and at the same time resisting sword, dagger, and spear thrusts.

The *salade* was a shallow loose-fitting helmet, the rear peak prolonged over the back of the neck. It had usually a vision-slit in front, but sometimes this was cut in a pivoted visor, which could be thrown back.

GENTLEMEN PENSIONERS

The corps, 'all in red damask with pole-axes in hand,' attended Edward VI at his coronation. They 'went on either side the way on foot.' By this arrangement they were placed longitudinally, at proper distances, so that the King was as nearly as possible in the centre of the band. In the procession to the Abbey they followed the peers in the rear, immediately before the Yeomen of the Guard. Shortly afterwards they are described as riding five in a row and clad in white and black and 'in harness [1] from top to toe, and goodly bases of cotes, and their men in like colours of cloth.'

The first great opportunity of proving their worth occurred during the attack on Whitehall Palace by the rebels under Sir Thomas Wyatt. On this occasion the corps were equipped in full armour.

Queen Mary behaved with great courage, and refused to leave the palace by the Watergate as Her Majesty's dependence on her loyal bodyguard in the time of danger was absolute, and her gratitude was most gracious and sincere. The full corps was in attendance on the Queen during her marriage celebrations at Winchester; they were her own special guard, her bridegroom having his own corps of 'Allemains and Spaniards,' and Swiss and some English gentlemen.

In 1556 we have the earliest description of the banner of the corps: this was

[1] 'Harness' means armour.

red and yellow, and bore, on one side, a white hart, and on the other a black eagle with gilded legs, the former being one of the cognizances of Queen Mary and the black eagle part of the armorial bearings of King Philip.

The colour of the costume was now changed to the Tudor livery colours of white and green, and the attendants were dressed in the same but of less rich material.

(Continued on p. 686)

MIDDLE CLASSES

The period covered by these two reigns was too short for any notable changes to take place in the dress worn by the middle and lower classes of both sexes. Men and women of the upper class followed the prevailing fashions with moderation as their means and social position allowed, the general style of their clothes being as a rule some years behind that of their betters. Much the same applies to the burgesses and lower classes, who continued to dress in the same manner as described under Chapter II.

There is an exception, however, and this definitely falls within the scope of this chapter—the costume worn by

Fig. 514.
Christ's Hospital Boy, 1553

The Boys of Christ's Hospital

At their first appearance after the foundation of Christ's Hospital, when they lined the streets for the procession of the Lord Mayor and aldermen to St. Paul's on Christmas Day, 1552, the children, numbering three hundred and forty, were clothed in a livery of russet cotton. When they attended the Spittal Sermon at the Easter following they were dressed in blue, 'and so have continued ever since,' says Stow.

Edward VI received the Hospital Corporation and presented them with their Charter, June 1553. This event is commemorated in the picture at Christ's Hospital, Horsham, and on this occasion the boys were dressed in their new livery as shown in Fig. 514.

It consisted of a long dark blue cloth gown reaching to the ankles and fastened up the front with pewter buttons having thereon a bust of Edward VI and the inscription 'EDWARDUS VI D G REX F.' It was girt about the waist by a red leather belt, and had an upstanding collar about one and a half or two inches wide, finishing with a white gathered neckband.[1] Under the gown was

[1] This neckband gave place to the Geneva band in the reign of Charles II, and buckles were added to the shoes early in the eighteenth century.

worn a long russet kersey cassock, with russet worsted hosen and black leather shoes.   A flat black felt cap and brown leather or white cotton gloves completed the livery.   It should be pointed out that a blue coat was not entirely the distinctive or monopolized livery of Christ's Hospital (*see* Apprentices, p. 302).

ROYALTY AND NOBILITY—WOMEN: 1547-58

THE LADY JANE GREY, 1537-54

Of the women, other than the Royal Princesses, the Lady Mary, the Lady Elizabeth, and the vacuous Anne of Cleves, who occupied important positions during Edward VI's reign, the most prominent was the Lady Jane.   She was the eldest daughter of the Lady Frances Brandon who married Henry Grey, Marquess of Dorset, later (1551) Duke of Suffolk, and great-great-grand-daughter of Queen Elizabeth Wydeville.   The Lady Jane was born at Bradgate in 1537.

In appearance she was petite : her face was what we should call to-day pretty, with small features, well-shaped nose, light hazel eyes, and auburn hair.   She possessed firmness, capacity, and knowledge of affairs.   Her learning in divinity and religious controversial subjects acquired under her tutors, Roger Ascham and John Aylmer, Bishop of London, was profound.   Gentle, affectionate, firm as a rock where any principle was concerned, she would have made an ideal queen-consort and a perfect queen-regnant.

Fig. 515. The Lady Jane Grey
(*from a contemporary portrait*)

In adversity she displayed great nobility and beauty of character.   Lady Jane's first appearance in public was made at the age of fourteen when she

Fig. 516. The Lady Jane Grey

accompanied her mother, the Duchess of Suffolk, on the occasion of the visit of Mary of Guise, the Dowager-Queen of Scotland, to Greenwich Palace. She afterwards became the guest of the Princess Mary. On 21st May 1553 the Lady Jane married Guyldeford, fourth son of John Dudley, created Earl of Warwick in 1547, and Duke of Northumberland in 1551. She was proclaimed Queen in London, 10th July 1553, but nine days later her reign was at an end; after imprisonment in the Tower, both she and her husband were executed 12th February 1554.

In dress the Lady Jane displayed great taste, so Ascham considered, as he suggested that her 'seemly apparelling' should form the model for the Princess Elizabeth.

The drawing (Fig. 515) is made from an original portrait of this lady. Her dress is of nasturtium-red velvet with sleeves turned back showing a deep peacock-blue lining. The yoke and false sleeves are of the same blue in satin with a cornflower design worked in gold. Spanish work decorates the inside of the open collar to match the wrist-frills, and above it is a second collar of white gauze embroidered with red silk. (*Refer to* Fig. 541 for details of the French hood.)

A costume worn by the Lady Jane in July 1553 has been described by a Genoese, Baptist Spinola, and Plate XXIV is a drawing made from these details. The dress is of cloth of gold woven with a raised Renaissance pattern in green velvet: the shoulder yoke, underskirt, and turned-back part of the sleeves are of plain green velvet, and the false sleeves of cloth of gold. The collar is turned back as in Fig. 515, lined with gold, and a second collar inside is of fine lawn decorated with Spanish work to match the wrist-frills. The French hood is described under Fig. 541. It is said that the lady wore many

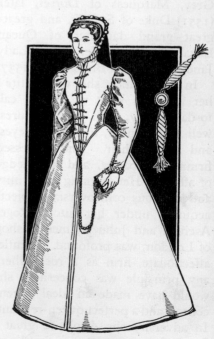

Fig. 517

PLATE XXIV. THE LADY JANE GREY, 1553
Watercolour by the Author
By kind permission of Madame Tussauds, Ltd.

jewels about her person. Sometimes, especially on state occasions, she was mounted on CHOPINS to make her look taller (*see* Fig. 560).

There is a portrait of Lady Jane at Melton Constable showing her in a costume similar to Plate XXIV, and carried out in white damask, with false sleeves and underskirt in cream and gold brocade. The painting has suffered a great deal from restoration, but from a costume point of view it is interesting. (See *Country Life*, 22nd September 1928.)

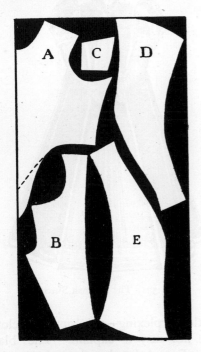

Fig. 518. Bodice

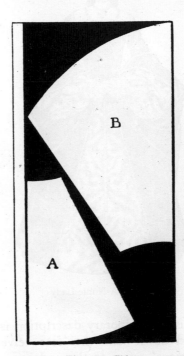

Fig. 519. Skirt

The head-and-shoulders portrait of Lady Jane, by Eworth, in the National Portrait Gallery, London (No. 764), is the latest, if one may judge by the headdress. The only visible part of her dress suggests a black velvet surcote, with a double row of narrow miniver edging on the moderately mahoitered sleeves, collar, and down the front. This surcote is influenced by Spanish fashions, and its style was known as 'à l'Espagnolle.' (See Fig. 521 which shows it in detail.)

The headdress is the flat-fronted, rather wide French hood of black velvet, without the slightest ornamentation.

The costume is a simple dress as Fig. 516 shows, and one that would be worn on ordinary occasions by great ladies, at home or out of doors. A similar costume is depicted in a portrait dated as early as 1551.

On the day of her execution, 13th November 1553, amongst those led out of the Tower on foot was 'The Lady Jane in a blacke gown of cloth, turned down; the Cape lined with fese velvet, and edged about with the same, in a French hood, all black, with a black byllyment, a black velvet book hanging before her, and another book in her hand open.'

Fig. 520. A Noble Lady

Fig. 521. The Spanish Surcote

This contemporary description is a little perplexing—the 'gown of cloth, turned down' and the 'fese velvet' are not easy to explain. The 'black byllyment' refers to the under-cap of the French hood and to the partlet: the 'black velvet book hanging before her' was suspended from her girdle.

In Fig. 517 is seen a lady's simple dress. The close-fitting bodice, high collar, sleeves pleated into the armhole, and skirt without a train worn over the Spanish farthingale, are the foundations on which much ornamentation was lavished during the following fifty years.

Fig. 518 gives the pattern of this bodice and sleeve, shown white, laid upon a piece of silk or cloth, shown black. The material is folded double.

A is half the front, the dotted line showing where the point of the waist finished in this its earliest version; B the half back; C the half-collar; and D and E the over and under part of the sleeve.[1]   Fig. 519 gives on a smaller scale the cut of the skirt.   A is half the front, and B half the back without a train.   Under the all-round surcote a train would have been incongruous. These diagrams are taken from a sixteenth-century pattern book.

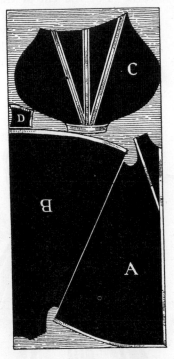

Fig. 522. Diagram of Surcote

A noble lady of the reign of Edward VI is given in Fig. 520.   She wears definitely English dress, in contradistinction to the French with its mahoitered sleeves (see Fig. 524) and the Spanish surcote (see Fig. 521).   The costume is carried out in plain dark velvet, and the sleeves, cut as described under Plate XVI and diagram, Fig. 67, are very tight-fitting on the upper arm, also very much off the shoulders, and are turned back showing the lining of the same velvet as the outer sleeve.   Delicate filigree gold beads, set tubular and spherical alternately, are headed by an edging of cutwork round the square neck of the very décolleté bodice; this edging is drawn in by a black silk lace.   The low-cut neck-line is of the older fashion, as seen in Plate XVII. The false sleeves are of the same material as the underskirt, and on them are placed, not cuttes as usual, but raised pads having pairs of aiglettes at the ends of each.   The skirt has a slight train without folds over the Spanish farthingale, and opens out over an underskirt of silk woven with a large pattern in velvet.   The French hood is wide, and the gauze pleating lies only across the top of the hair.

SPANISH STYLES

The surcote, introduced from Spain and worn by the lady in Fig. 521, is of dark coloured velvet edged with a passamayne of gold.   Notice the lines from the shoulders, which meet the centre lines a little below waist level, forming a W.   The garment is cut to hang from the shoulders, front and back, in a straight line.   In front it is open, being fastened only at the throat, revealing the under-dress of a different colour and material such as is shown worn by the lady in Fig. 517.   Sometimes the surcote and under-dress were

[1] It is curious that there is no curved-out cut at the top of the under-sleeve; also that the lay-out of these patterns does not permit of the same planning in the case of velvet or figured material.

of the same colour and fabric. The short mahoitered sleeves are decorated with wider passamayne. Inside the high collar of the surcote there is another of white lawn: often such collars were embroidered with black silk Spanish work. For the cut of this surcote refer to Fig. 522. A is half the front; B half the back; C one of the mahoitered sleeves, and D half the collar.

This surcote has already been noted under Fig. 516; the differences in the latter are (*a*) the vertical slits on the chest, and (*b*) that the fronts meet all the way down. The under-dress is shaped as shown in Fig. 517. It might be of light coloured silk, with lines of braid on the bodice converging to the point at the waist. The sleeves are braided diagonally, and braid decorates the skirt. From the girdle hangs a pomander.

Fig. 523. The Princess Mary II, 1553

THE LADY MARY II
(*continued from p. 288*)

Fig. 523 is drawn from a three-quarter portrait of the Princess Mary dating about 1551–3. The dress worn by the Princess is of black velvet trimmed with narrow bands of miniver. The arrangement of lines of fur on the mahoitered sleeves is pleasing; the close-fitting braided sleeves and underskirt or kirtle are of white satin braided with black and silver lace, and the embroidered lawn partlet with high turned-down-in-front collar is braided with similar but narrower braid.

The headdress, worn over hair arranged in a double wave around the head, is an amalgamation of the jewelled network cap as seen in Fig. 547, with a wired front edged with pearls. A heart-shaped pomander or purse, attached to a tiny box perhaps containing some relic, is carried in the right hand. The purse, on a larger scale, is inset. The original measures about four inches in width.

(*Continued on p. 438*)

FRENCH FASHIONS

Eleanor, Archduchess of Austria

Queen-Dowager of France, 1547–58

(continued from p. 273)

Eleanor, Queen of Portugal and France, was left a widow for the second time in 1547, and withdrew to Spain where, with her sister Marie, Queen of Hungary, she devoted the rest of her life to her brother the Emperor Charles V.

Roger Ascham, Latin tutor to the Princess Elizabeth, wrote from Augsburg to his friend Mr. Raven an amusing letter which enlightens us on the subject of widows' mourning, dress, manners, etc. Ascham was among those, including Queen Eleanor, Francis I's widow, who attended Mass on the 5th October 1550. He writes:

' . . . the French Queen, the Emperor's sister, was there: she came to Mass clad very solemnly all in white cambric, a robe gathered in plaits [1] wrought very fair as need be with needle white work, as white as a dove. A train of ladies followed her, as black and evil as she was white. Her Mass was sung in prick song by Frenchmen very cunningly, and a gentleman played at the organs excellently. A French Whipit, Sir John, bestirred himself so at the altar as I wished Patrick by to have learned some of his knacks. . . . The Queen sat in a closet above; her ladies kneeled all abroad in the chapel among us. The Regent of Flanders had left at Bruxelles a sort of fair lusty young ladies; they came not out, but were kept in mew [see p. 157] for fear of gosshawks of Spain and France; yet they came to [view] and stood above in windows, as well content to show themselves as we to see them.

'They had on French gowns of black velvet, garded down right from the collar with broad gards, one with another, some of cloth of gold, some of cloth of silver, great chains arranged with precious jewels. On their heads they had glistering cauls of goldsmith work, and black velvet caps above with frills of great agletts of gold, with white feathers round about the compass of their caps. They seemed boys rather than ladies, excellent to have played in tragedies. There was not one well-favoured among them, save one young lady, fair and well-favoured. The Queen went from Mass to dinner; I followed her; and because we were gentlemen of England, I and another was admitted to come into her chamber where she sat at dinner. She is served with no women, as great states are there in England; but altogether with men, having their caps on their heads whilst they come into the chamber where she sits, and there one takes off all their caps. I stood very near the table and saw all.

'Men, as I said, served; only two women stood by the fire-side not far from the table, for the chamber was little, and talked very loud and lewdly with whom they would as methought.

---

[1] Presumably pleats, but a mere man does not know the difference (*see also under* Fig. 554).

'This Queen's service, compared with my Lady Elizabeth's my mistress, is not so prince-like nor honourably handled. Her first course was apples, pears, plums, grapes, nuts: and this meat she began. Then she had bacon and chickens almost covered with *sale* [1] onions, that all the chamber smelled of it. She had a roast caponet, and a pasty of wild-boar; and I, thus marking all the behaviour, was content to lose the second course, lest I should have lost mine own dinner at home.'

Fig. 524. French Noble Lady

In wearing white for mourning, Queen Eleanor was reversing the tradition set by Anne of Brittany (*see* p. 71).

There is at Hampton Court a three-quarter-length portrait of Eleanor in widow's weeds by an unknown artist, from which Fig. 551 showing the headdress has been taken (*see* p. 455). The dress and the wide sleeves are entirely in black, with white under-sleeves and goffered frills at the wrists. The pleated part of the widow's barbe covers the entire front to below the waist, the plain portion passing over the shoulders. She appears to have placed a long black silk scarf, stole-wise, over this.

Eleanor, Archduchess of Austria, Queen of Portugal, and subsequently of France, died in 1558.

Several illustrations of Catherine de' Medici in her widow's weeds are extant, and answer to Ascham's descriptions of Eleanor's except that they are entirely in black; they are of a later date, since Catherine did not become a widow until 1559. Fig. 661 is derived from these illustrations, and should be referred to for comparison with the description on p. 566.

Of Queen Eleanor's maids of honour, 'one young lady, fair and well-favoured,' is shown in Fig. 524. Ascham describes her dress so well that there remains nothing more to explain, except the black velvet cap. This is worn over a gold caul, and is decorated round the crown with laces and golden aiglettes. White plumes rest on the brim on the left side. The costume is of the French fashion, and a little in advance of that worn in England at this time (1550). It shows the latest vogue of sleeve raised on the shoulder. A detail of a rather exaggerated mahoitered sleeve is given in Fig. 820 showing very plainly its humped padding on top and in front of the armpit; it fits close round the arm just above the elbow.

[1] 'Sale' in this case obviously means stale or fermented—considered rather a tasty dish.

CATHERINE DE' MEDICI

Queen-Mother of France, 1547 until 1558

(continued from p. 277)

From the moment it was announced that Catherine de' Medici was to become the wife of the French King's son, the French people manifested their dislike of her, on account of what they regarded as her *bourgeois* extraction. This dislike steadily increased, growing from prejudice to hatred. During her life as Queen, and later Queen-Regent, of France, her every action was misrepresented, and nothing credited save that which defamed her character. Few historical personalities have been so extravagantly vilified as this amiable lady—she has been accused of every conceivable crime it is possible to commit. Modern historians and biographers, however, have had the advantage of a much wider field of research than that open to earlier writers; and during the twentieth century much information has been gleaned, which shows the falsity of previous judgments, and throws a very different light upon the true disposition of 'the Italian woman.' Catherine was a woman of strong character, of pleasing and agreeable manners, and a great stickler for convention. Never at any time during her life did she show a revengeful spirit, or a natural tendency to cruelty. Wise and chaste in the midst of a licentious Court, she was 'an indefatigable peace-maker,' showing great toleration of Protestants and Catholics alike—thus perhaps earning the bigots' accusation of duplicity.

Brantôme, who knew Queen Catherine well, and has always been considered her great admirer, writes of her with some enthusiasm as follows:

'She was of rich and very fine presence; of great majesty, but very gentle when need was; of noble appearance and good grace, her visage handsome and agreeable, her bosom very beautiful, the skin smooth, as I have heard from several of her ladies; of a fine plumpness also, the leg and thigh very beautiful—as I have heard from the same ladies; and she took great pleasure in being well shod, and in having her stockings well and tightly drawn up. Besides all this, the most beautiful hand that was ever seen, as I believe. She always clothed herself well and superbly, often with some pretty and new invention.'

A portrait of Catherine, by Corneille de Lyon, painted about 1549, may be still in existence. It is recorded that in this portrait the Queen is shown 'attired in the French mode [*see* Fig. 255] with a little cap [the French hood] edged with pearls, and a dress with large sleeves of cloth of silver, the latter turned back with lynx.'

While staying at Lyons, in 1574, the Queen-Regent visited this artist in his studio, and there she saw the portrait painted twenty-five years before. It revived memories of the days when, almost a nonentity, she shared the throne of France with her dear, yet not too faithful, husband.

Fig. 525. CATHERINE DE' MEDICI, QUEEN OF FRANCE, c. 1555

In the Uffizi Gallery at Florence is a full-length portrait of Catherine de'
Medici, by Pourbus. In it she is shown wearing the fashionable dress
of this period. Fig. 525 is a drawing made from this portrait. The dress
is of black velvet, entirely covered with a trellis-work of pearls, with sapphires
in gold mounts set at the intersections; the spaces between are embroidered
with a design in gold (Fig. 526).[1] The full-busted bodice is close-fitting at
the sixteen-inch waist, and cut very wide at the neck opening, which is
filled in at the sides with a quilted partlet of gauze set with sapphires and pearls.
A small upstanding collar of gauze, partly goffered and edged with lace, surrounds the sides and back of the neck, leaving the throat bare. The sleeves
are turned back with ermine and have the square effect shown in Fig. 255.
The false sleeves are of pale pink satin, treated in the same manner as the
underskirt, or kirtle, which is of the same colour and material, and decorated

Fig. 526

Fig. 527

with a trellis-work similar to the over-dress, but enclosing embroidery of
silver in a different design (Fig. 527). The kirtle is widely distended over
the Spanish farthingale. A girdle of pearls and sapphires is continued down
the front, emphasizing the decided long point to the waist-line of the bodice,
and terminating in a beautiful cross-ornament of gold set with sapphires and
pearls.

The French hood, decorated with the same gems, but *without* the tubular
part, is worn, and the Queen holds in her right hand a large fan of ostrich
tips, fixed to a rigid handle of gold set with jewels to match her dress.

It is said that this Queen invented the side-saddle, but this is not correct
(*see* vol. ii, Fig. 215). Nevertheless, according to Brantôme, Catherine 'was
very good on horseback, and bold, sitting with ease, and being the first to
put the leg around a pommel, which was far more graceful and becoming than
sitting with the feet upon a plank.[2] Till she was sixty years of age and over
she liked to ride on horseback, and after her weakness prevented her she
pined for it. She was fond of seeing comedies and tragedies; but after
Sophonisbe, a tragedy composed by M. de Saint-Gélais, was very well represented by her daughters and other ladies and damoiselles and gentlemen of

---

[1] Figs. 526 and 527 are not indicated in Fig. 255.   [2] Refer to p. 604.

her Court at Blois, for the marriages of M. du Cypière and the Marquise d'Elbœuf, she took an opinion that it was harmful to the affairs of the king-dom, and would never have tragedies played again. But she listened readily to comedies and tragi-comedies, and even those of Zani and Pantalon, taking great pleasure in them, and laughing with all her heart like any other.'

(Continued on p. 566)

MARY STUART

Queen of Scotland, Dauphine of France, 1542 until 1558

During the course of the period covered by this chapter there was a young girl living at the French Court who was destined to play a prominent part in the politics and affairs of Europe—the Queen of Scotland, Mary Stewart. Born at Linlithgow, 8th December 1542, the only child of James V and Mary, daughter of Claude, Duc de Guise, she succeeded her father at the tender age of six days. The babe was crowned Queen of Scotland by Cardinal Beaton in the chapel of Stirling Castle, 11th September 1543, 'with such solemnity as they do use in this country, which is not very costly.'

At the age of six years Queen Mary was sent to France [1] to be educated as the betrothed wife of Francis the Dauphin, whom she married at Notre-Dame, 24th April 1558. Her husband received the title of King of Scotland, while Mary was created Reine-Dauphine. On the death of Mary, Queen of Eng-land, in the following November 'the title of Queen of England was taken by the Court of France for Queen Mary in a quiet off-hand way.' This was but in accordance with Roman Catholic principles, as Elizabeth Tudor was looked upon as illegitimate, and Mary Stuart was next heiress to the crown, therefore Francis and Mary were styled 'King and Queen of England, Scot-land, and Ireland.' They also quartered the Royal Arms of England with their own.

Of the multitude of portraits of Mary Stuart only about fifteen are genuine. From these, numerous copies and versions have been made during the course of the four following centuries. Apart from these, all others alleged to represent Mary Queen of Scots are spurious.

In appearance Mary Stuart possessed a graceful figure, tall and slender. She had a brilliant complexion, hazel eyes, the upper eyelids rather thick, with arched eyebrows faintly defined; a long straight nose, and a thin mouth with full underlip. Her forehead was high and round, surmounted by yellowish auburn hair in youth: 'si blonds et cendrés' (that hair so beautiful, so fair and *grey*) so much admired by Brantôme. The cheek-bones were somewhat pronounced and her ears unusually large.[2] Her hands were beauti-fully white with long taper fingers. After the death of her first husband she lost her bright colouring and her skin became an alabaster white.

---

[1] According to French orthography the name of her house was now spelt 'Stuart.'
[2] See Plate XXXIII.

MARIA SCOTIÆ REGINA.

Fig. 528. 1558

Fig. 528 represents Mary Stuart at the age of sixteen. The figure above the waist is taken from François Clouet's two drawings, one in the Musée Condé at Chantilly, the other in the Bibliothèque Nationale, Paris. They only show down to the waist, but enough is seen to construct the skirt. The costume was of white satin, the bodice and skirt decorated with wide bands of gold embroidery. The design is shown in Fig. 529. The bodice, rounded at the neck opening, was worn over a partlet of embroidered gauze with an upstanding collar finished in gofferings. The fifteen-inch waist was moulded by a steel corset. The skirt was of moderate proportions compared with that shown in Fig. 525. The sleeves, with puff 'à la ballonnoise' at the shoulders, were ornamented with lines of gold cord caught together with pearls or small gold and jewelled buttons. Her earrings, necklaces, girdle, and pomander were of pearls set with gold. The coif set far back on the head was of gold embroidery, pearls, and jewels (see Fig. 548). This may have been the Queen's wedding gown, for it is recorded that when Henry II led his future daughter-in-law to the altar she was wearing white satin, with a mantle of blue velvet embroidered with lilies in silver. Her coronet was of diamonds valued at half a million crowns, and her whole person glistened with gems.

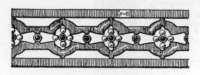

Fig. 529.
Gold Embroidery set with Jewels

(Continued on p. 511)

QUEEN MARY, 1553–8 (continued from p. 430)

Mary, the second child of Henry VIII and Katherine of Aragon, was born at Greenwich, 8th February 1516. Her appearance as a young woman has been set forth on p. 271.

In the year 1553 Queen Mary is described as 'a faded little woman, with a white face, no eyebrows, and russet hair. At thirty-seven an old maid, disillusioned and wearied by years of cruel injustice.'

'She has no eyebrows, is a perfect saint, and dresses very badly,' is an unfair opinion of a Spaniard.

A more favourable pen-portrait of Mary Tudor is given by Soranzo in his report to the Venetian Senate: 'She is of low stature, with a red and white complexion, and very thin; her eyes are light-coloured and large, and her hair reddish; her face is round, with a nose rather low and wide; and were not her

PLATE XXV. QUEEN MARY, 1553: Portrait by Antonio Moro
Prado, Madrid.   *Photo by Mansell*

age on the decline she might be called handsome rather than the contrary.' The kindly disposed Venetian Ambassador also states that 'Her Majesty's countenance indicates great benignity and clemency, which are not belied by her conduct.'

From other sources we learn that Mary's complexion was invariably sallow. During the latter part of her life the Queen was never free from headaches and palpitation of the heart. She was also a great sufferer from melancholy and so short-sighted that she could not read or study anything clearly without placing her eyes quite close to the object.

Giovanni Michiel, Venetian Ambassador Extraordinary 1553, has some pleasant and unbiased things to say about Queen Mary:

'Besides feminine accomplishments, such as needlework and every sort of embroidery, she is very proficient in music, playing especially on the clavichord and lute so excellently, that when she attended to this, which she does but little, she surprised good performers both by the rapidity of her execution and method of playing.'

Of 'Bloody Mary' much that is libellous has been written by champions of the Reformation and others. According to contemporary and unbiased opinion she was 'a most amiable Princess.' Her zeal for the orthodox religion, her implicit faith in her husband's high sense of duty, made her the tool of circumstance. If

Fig. 530.
A Badge of Queen Mary

Mary had not wedded a man whose lifelong obsession was the conversion of heretic Europe, posterity might have remembered her name with greater charity.

On the 30th September 1553 Queen Mary made her triumphal progress from the Tower to the Palace of Westminster, enthroned in a chariot open on all sides save for the canopy, entirely covered with gold tissue; and the trappings of the six horses which drew it were of red velvet and gold. The Queen 'sat in a gown of blew velvet, furred with powdered ermine, having on her head a caul of cloth of tissue beset with pearl and stone, and about the same upon her head a round circlet of gold, much like a hooped garland beset so richly with many precious stones that the value thereof was inestimable.

'After the Queen's chariot came another chariot having the canopy all of one covering, with cloth of silver all white, and vj horses betrapped with the same, bearing the said chariot; and therein sat at the end, with her face forward, the Lady Elizabeth; and at the other end, with her back forward, the Lady Anne of Cleves.' It is obvious from this statement that the Princess Elizabeth had precedence over her stepmother—an interesting point.

The coronation took place the following day at Westminster Abbey, the ceremony being conducted by Stephen Gardiner, Bishop of Winchester. This ceremony is of unusual interest, being the first coronation of a queen-regnant in English history. The procedure adopted was almost identical with that used when a king is crowned.

In her robes of crimson velvet and ermine the Queen entered the Abbey, and was first led by Stephen Gardiner round all four sides of a platform so that all the company might see her, the Bishop crying in a loud voice that all might hear him: 'Sirs, here present is Mary, rightful and undoubted inheritrix by the Laws of God and man to the Crown and Royal Dignity of this realm of England, France, and Ireland, whereupon you shall understand that this day is appointed by all the Peers of this land for the consecration, inunction, and coronation of the said most excellent Princess Mary; will you serve at this time, and give your wills and assent to the same consecration, inunction, and coronation?' All the company shouted joyfully, 'Yea, Yea!' After this Her Majesty went to the altar to hear a sermon preached by George Day, Bishop of Chichester,[1] the subject being obedience due to monarchs from their subjects. At the end the Queen prostrated herself on the ground and received benediction with many prayers. Retiring to the robing chamber, she had her robes removed and returning 'in her corset'[2] she prostrated herself again. At this stage the Queen was anointed with the Holy Oil on her breast, shoulders, forehead, and temples. After this she was clad in the Alb of white taffeta, with the Dalmatic of very rich material over it. Shoes of gold were then put on, and over them golden spurs were strapped. Next came the girding of the Sword, after which the State Mantle of crimson velvet furred with ermine was fastened across the shoulders. This mantle had been specially consecrated; it was not the one Queen Mary was wearing when she arrived at the Abbey.

The Sceptres of the Cross and the Dove were placed in the right and left hands respectively, the Queen changing the Dove over to the right hand in order to receive the Orb. Finally, she was crowned with three crowns, one for England, one for France, and one for Ireland. Thus arrayed, Queen Mary, seated upon the throne, received the homage of all the lords spiritual and temporal. Mass was then performed 'with much solemnity, the Queen kneeling throughout with great devotion and great tokens of religion, which being ended, she entered the aforesaid retired apartment, and speedily came forth with the Orb in her hand and the Royal Sceptre, clad in a mantle of *purple* velvet furred with tufts of ermine, and with the round cap, as monarchs are wont to wear'—the Cap of Maintenance. Thus arrayed, Queen Mary I was acclaimed by the people.

All illustrations of Queen Mary in State robes show that she wore the Royal mantle of velvet with a cape of ermine over a surcote (*see* Fig. 292 and

---

[1] George Day (1501–56) was Master of St. John's College, 1537, and Provost of King's College, Cambridge, 1538. Made Bishop of Chichester, 1543.
[2] A petticoat and bodice.

PLATE XXVI. QUEEN MARY, 1554: After the portrait by Hans Eworth
Original at the Society of Antiquaries. *By kind permission of the Committee*

Plate XLIV). Sometimes the surcote was omitted, as when the mantle was worn over fashionable dress of some very rich material. In full state the Royal crown only was worn: on less formal occasions the crown would surmount the French hood, or the latter would be worn without it.

A portrait of Queen Mary was painted by Antonio Moro about the end of 1553 (Plate XXV) and sent to Prince Philip of Spain. It hung in the gallery of the Prado. There is a copy in the dining hall at Trinity College, Cambridge. In it the Queen wears the usual style of costume in a deep grey-blue velvet, the sleeves turned back with the same velvet; the false sleeves and underskirt are of silk brocade, the large pattern in a lighter shade of the same grey-blue upon a deeper toned ground. The inside of the collar and the wrist-frills are decorated with Spanish work. The girdle, without the customary long end, is a beautiful example of goldsmith's work and jewels (see Fig. 565). From it is suspended by a riband, a jewelled pomander, or reliquary (see Fig. 564). The French hood is reproduced in Fig. 531.

We have a further account of Queen Mary's dresses from Giacomo Soranzo, the Venetian Ambassador, in which he reports that:

'She seems to delight above all in arraying herself elegantly and magnificently, and her garments are of two sorts: the one a *gown such as men wear*, but fitting very close, with an under-petticoat, which has a very long train, and this is her ordinary costume, being also that of the gentlewomen of England. *The other garment* is a gown and bodice with wide hanging sleeves in the French fashion, which she wears on State occasions, and she also wears much embroidery, and gowns and mantles of cloth of gold, and cloth of silver of great value, and changes every day. She also makes great use of jewels, wearing them both on her *chaperon*, and round her neck, and as trimming for her gowns.'

The 'gown such as men wear' refers to the Spanish surcote worn by the lady (Fig. 521). When this was made 'fitting very close,' it formed a bodice and skirt combined and is shown in Fig. 523. 'The other garment' is illustrated in Plate XXVI and Fig. 531. The 'chaperon,' of course, means the French hood.

For her first meeting with Philip of Spain (see p. 410) the Queen was gowned in black velvet over an underskirt of frosted silver. The jewels she wore were magnificent. On the day of her marriage (25th July 1554—the Feast day of St. James the Patron Saint of Spain) Her Majesty 'blazed with jewels to an extent that dazzled those who gazed upon her' as she swept up the nave of Winchester Cathedral (see p. 386) to her chair [1] before the high altar. Her long mantle was of brocaded cloth of gold bordered with pearls and diamonds of great size, and lined with ermine. Her dress, in shape like Fig. 520, was also of gold smothered with the same precious stones, and the underskirt of white satin was embroidered with silver. The French hood in black velvet was surmounted by a double row of large diamonds. On her breast the

[1] Still preserved there. It is said that this chair, originally covered with blue velvet, was blessed and sent to Queen Mary by the Pope.

Queen wore a remarkable ornament—the gift sent to her by her bridegroom. It was a large table diamond mounted in a superb gold setting and valued at 50,000 ducats: from this hung an immense peardrop pearl (*see* p. 461).

Andres Muñoz thus describes two costumes worn by Queen Mary: 'The Queen was clad in a galdres [1] of black velvet, high in the neck, according to the custom over there, without any ornament whatsoever, with a front [2] of frosted silver embroidery, and a chapiron [3] of black velvet with its gold pieces, of great value, gracefully set; and a narrow girdle of very marvellous stones and a collar of the same sort.' Again: 'The Queen came dressed in purple velvet, and the galdres lined with brocade [4] and a front of embroidered frosted gold with very rich precious stones and pearls from the Orient and seed pearls; with chapiron, girdle, and collar of the same stone work.'

It will be interesting to have the opinion of another Spaniard regarding the dresses of English ladies. 'They wear farthingales of coloured cloth without silk,' he says, emphasizing the contrast between these and the more highly decorated and embroidered farthingales of his own country; 'the gowns they wear over them are of damask, satin, or velvet of various colours, but very badly made.'

Another portrait of Queen Mary, painted in 1554 by Hans Eworth, belongs to the Society of Antiquaries of London. The costume is reproduced in Plate XXVI by kind permission of the committee of the society. In it the Queen is seen wearing a very rich dress of yellow cloth of gold of damask over the Spanish farthingale of large size. Here one realizes the great advantage gained by the very wide farthingale in showing off the intricate design of the embroidery on the underskirt. The sleeves illustrate the prevailing fashion for narrow shoulders and tight-fitting tops, the turned-back part being lined with sable. The false sleeves and underskirt appear to be of a pale rose-coloured satin embroidered with two shades of bullion, a gold and a red gold. The design is in the elaborate arabesque style. The large false sleeves, on which the raised-pad effect is well in evidence, help to make the sable turned-back stand out at an angle, an effect aided also by the position of the arms (*see* p. 269). Details to notice are the jewelled collar with the tau cross round the neck; the outer collar of the bodice with an inner one embroidered with Spanish work; the reliquary at the end of a loop of 'ferret' suspended from the waist girdle; and the wide French hood.

In medieval times the term 'ferret' [5] was sometimes applied to the 'lacet' finished at the end with an aiglette. In the sixteenth century it meant a narrow stout band of silk or cotton—a 'riban.' [6] 'Black rybens for lassys.'

In the portrait group (Fig. 531), painted in 1558, the Queen is wearing a dress shaped like that in Plate XXVI, composed of dark blue velvet, with sleeves turned back with squirrel. The false sleeves and underskirt are of gold brocade.

[1] The robe or gown. [2] Refers to the underskirt. [3] 'Chapiron' means the French hood.
[4] The turned-back sleeves were lined with brocade.
[5] Compare the modern use of the word 'ferret,' which is applied to the narrow green ribbon used by the legal fraternity for lacing together the sheets of deeds and other legal documents.
[6] Called in the middle of the sixteenth century a 'ribbon.'

Fig. 531. KING PHILIP II AND QUEEN MARY, 1558

Fig. 532.
Jane, Duchess of Northumberland, 1555

Queen Mary died in London, 17th November 1558. On 13th December the corpse of the late Queen was brought from St. James's to Westminster 'in a chariot with a painted effigy adorned in crimson velvet and her crown on her head, her sceptre in her hand and many goodly rings on her fingers, lying on cloth of gold with a cross of silver. xiiij day her grace was buried.'

JANE GUYLDEFORD

Duchess of Northumberland, 1551–5

Probably the latest example, on a brass, of a noble lady wearing an heraldic mantle is on that to the memory of Jane, sister and heiress of Sir Henry Guyldeford, in St. Luke's, Chelsea. This lady married John Dudley who was created Duke of Northumberland in 1551, and who is notorious for his attempt to place his daughter-in-law, Lady Jane Grey, upon the throne, in consequence of which he was beheaded in 1553. The Duchess was the mother of three famous sons—Ambrose, Guyldeford, and Robert Dudley, and died in 1555. She is reproduced in Fig. 532, her dress and headdress being of the style fashionable in these reigns; her heraldic mantle of state, lined with ermine, is charged with the armorial bearings of the families of Guyldeford, Halden, West, La Warr, Cantelupe, Mortimer, and Grelle.

The brass to the memory of a gentlewoman, Mistress D'Arcy, at Tolleshunt D'Arcy, Essex, is the authority for the costume shown in Fig. 533, which is a style affected by some of this class from, approximately, 1554. The dress shows the French and Spanish influences.

The surcote with deep collar and

Fig. 533. Mistress D'Arcy, 1555

cutte mahoitered shoulder sleeves ties down the front, and is worn over an under-dress with close-fitting sleeves. A front view of the headdress is shown in Fig. 542 from which the design of the cutwork edging to the inside collar, which is repeated on the cuffs, may be seen. A book with an elaborate cover hangs by a narrow riband looped to the girdle underneath the surcote.

The dress of the lady shown in Fig. 534 is of the same period. The drawing is from the brass to the memory of Dame Drury, at Hawstead, Suffolk. Her bodice and sash are similar to those last described, but she has an all-round skirt; the collar of the bodice turns down displaying the frill of cutwork

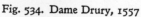

Fig. 534. Dame Drury, 1557   Fig. 535. Dame Brydges, 1558

round the neck. From the mahoitered sleeves hang long tubular ones, and the under-sleeves are banded cambric or lawn with frills of the same cutwork at the wrists. The headdress is an interesting feature and is described on p. 450.

Fig. 535 is a drawing made from the effigy at Ludgershall, Wilts, of Dame Brydges, who died in 1558. The costume is that in fashion during the previous decade and in the true English style. The bodice and sleeves are those which have been described under Figs. 67, 256, and 261, except that the turned-back portions of the sleeves are of soft material and therefore hang in folds. The false sleeves vary slightly in shape from the diagram, Fig. 257. Those in Fig. 535 are decorated with three cuttes and bead ornaments (*see*

III²—F

inset). The square collar is turned back and shows the pleated neckband of lawn. A moderate-sized farthingale distends the trained skirt, and down the front of the underskirt hangs a girdle, terminating in a pomander and fastened at the waist to the narrow sash which is tied in front. The French hood is in its simplest form and of black velvet. The whole figure is interesting as an example of modified fashions worn by an aristocrat.

SECTION II: 1547-58

HAIRDRESSING

Hair close cut to the head was now universal in spite of the fact that the first coronation medal ever struck shows Edward VI wearing longer hair than usual, which might almost be termed bobbed. In all his portraits as King he is nevertheless shown with close-cropped hair. Such a portrait is in the Library of Canterbury Cathedral from which Fig. 536 is drawn. It

Fig. 536. King Edward VI, 1551   Fig. 537. William Parr, c. 1559

represents the King as a boy of about fourteen with hair cut close to the head. This is also seen in Plates XIX and XX.

The hairdressing affected by Philip II in Fig. 497 illustrates the Spanish fashion of this period. The hair is straight, and brushed back off the fore-head and temples.

As far as can be seen from the portrait (Fig. 505) young Lord Maltravers wore his in the same style. After the death of Queen Mary this mode of hairdressing appears to have sunk into oblivion for a time.

Beards of various lengths and shapes were worn by those of mature man-hood, and full beards upon the upper lip. In 1551 this growth of hair was dignified by a special name first referred to in English as 'mowchatowes.' This word derives originally from the Greek 'mustax,' the upper lip:

the modern English form, MOUSTACHE, comes from the French 'moustache,' the alternative MUSTACHIO partly from the Spanish 'mostacho' and partly from the Italian 'mostaccio.'

Very seldom, if ever, was a beard worn without moustaches.

Fig. 538.
Embroidered pattern from doublet of Edward VI, Canterbury

Fig. 537, taken from a drawing of William Parr, Marquess of Northampton, at the age of about forty-five, is an example of the general facial adornment of a middle-aged nobleman.

As mentioned in Chap. II, beards were sometimes worn stiffened with wax. Henry II in the portrait, Fig. 489, clearly does so.

HEADGEAR, 1547–58

There was very little new in the style of headgear fashionable during the eleven years covered by this chapter. Fig. 359 D gives the most up-to-date shape, which was liable to variation in width of brim and its ornamentations.

Fig. 539. Henry II, King of France

Plates XIX and XX show a moderately wide brim turned up or down according to the taste of the wearer. The crowns are flat, and a feather droops over one ear. The hat worn by Edward VI (Fig. 536) is an exceptionally flat bonnet of black velvet with a very shallow brim ornamented with pearls and gold-enamelled beads covering the narrow hatband. A curled feather droops from the left side, and to the quill is fixed a gold ornament. The design down the front of the King's doublet is shown on a larger scale in Fig. 538. It would be carried out in gold embroidery.

The hat worn by the King in Plate XIX is higher in the crown with a gold curled tassel hanging from the quill. Small gold beads are set on the hatband.   It was, however, more general to wear a hat with the brim turned down, a fancy first mentioned on page 317.   As a consequence, the join of the crown and brim was visible, so a narrow hatband was added to make it tidy.   Hatbands were very often decorated with a series of ornaments, buttons, studs, etc., set at intervals.   Brooches and aiglettes were frequently used, and these were set with jewels, pearls, and enamels.   The nobility wore continuous strands of various jewels and ornaments around their hats. The upturned brim as shown in Fig. 365 was still considered smart, and caps without any brim as worn by Henry II (Fig. 488) were much favoured in France.   The King did not limit himself to this style of hat; in fact, that shown in Fig. 539 is the shape he usually wore.   Of black velvet, it has rows of three gold buttons on the under-side of the crown, which probably stiffened it and helped to keep it from sinking down and becoming too flat.   The same arrangement of buttons, of smaller size, is used on the top side of the brim, and an ostrich tip curls over on the right.   Around the King's neck is a double string of gold filigree beads.   The whole suit is of black velvet, closely sewn with small gold cord, and the black silk embroidery on the collar is worthy of notice.

At the middle of this period the crown of the hat was made fuller and larger (*see* Figs. 494 and 505).

HAIRDRESSING—WOMEN: 1547–58

The style of hairdressing favoured by the ladies of this period is shown in Fig. 540.   Most of them parted their hair in the middle, a few drew it back off the forehead, and all puffed or waved it at the sides, so filling the cavity left by the bow of the French hood; and made the remainder into a coil at the back of the head.   This coil formed a substantial foundation on which to fix the French hood or other headdress: frequently it was confined in a caul, which might be made of pearls or goldsmith's work set with jewels (Fig. 549).

Fig. 540

Another method of arranging the hair at the sides of the face is described under Fig. 544.   This style can be traced back to the hairdressing of Joanna of Castile (Plate V).   Fig. 545 shows a slightly different treatment which can also be seen in Fig. 242.   Catherine de' Medici wore her hair at the side closely crimped horizontally (*see* Fig. 543).

HEADDRESSES: 1547–58

THE FRENCH HOOD (*continued from p. 340*)

The latest version of the French hood, in vogue during the six years Edward VI was on the throne, is exemplified in Fig. 515 and in profile, Fig. 541. The front piece of black velvet is curved and finishes *behind* the

ear, and the edge is decorated with a band of gold set with emeralds faceted in points between groups of three pearls. Behind this is a second curved piece of white satin edged with a flat roll of velvet, on which are set groups of three pearls and single rubies in gold mounts giving a decided 'coronet' effect. The points of these crescent-shaped pieces all radiate from behind the ears. The black velvet hood itself is fixed behind the second crescent, and the part that falls down the back (*see* Fig. 590) is now definitely a flat tube, as first mentioned under Fig. 405, but without the folds in the nape of the neck as seen in Fig. 407, these being now obsolete.

The headdress of Dame Drury (Fig. 534) is but the French hood in its original form, like that of Dame Brydges (Fig. 535), but the former has achieved the fashionable line by adding a roll

Fig. 541. Lady Jane Grey

of material bound with gold cords over the front. This style could also be carried out in white linen, as is shown in Fig. 542, or in black velvet: it is of the usual shape as seen in the diagram, Fig. 163. The front is wired to give the bow effect, and a piece of silk, placed at the nape *under* the tube, is tied round the head with a knot on top.

The French hood worn by Catherine de' Medici is mentioned under Fig. 525. A narrow goffering of gold gauze edges the front of the hood, and is here used to break the hard line between the hood and the much crimped hair. It is the first example of a French hood without the tube at the back; this was often dispensed with as it was found somewhat inconvenient when worn with a

Fig. 542. Mistress D'Arcy, 1555

stand-up collar. Nevertheless, Catherine sometimes appeared with the tubular attachment in spite of the fact that she has at the same time a stand-up collar. She is wearing such a hood in a miniature of Clouet's now in the Uffizi, reproduced in Fig. 543. In this portrait the front is of pale pink silk or satin studded with pearls; both the front edge and the ridge are outlined with rubies in gold mounts separated by groups of three pearls.

The French hood as worn in Queen Mary's reign made its appearance just before she came to the throne, as proved by the portrait of Lady Jane Grey from which Fig. 516 is taken. Fig. 544 gives a three-quarter view of Mary herself wearing it. The ridge of jewels or coronet marked B now takes a different line (compare with Fig. 407). It is almost flat and wider at the top, and descends in a slight curve *inward*, finishing behind the ears. The black velvet front part,

Fig. 543. Catherine de' Medici, 1547
(*after Clouet*)

which lies on the hair, also becomes flatter and wider. Particular notice should be taken of the dip over the forehead and of the big curves at the sides which are rectangular at the bottom (*see at* A).

Queen Mary

Fig. 544. 1553   Fig. 545. 1555

What was originally the turned-back lining is now represented by a shaped piece of white or coloured silk or satin (*see at* C), a further development of that seen in Fig. 541. The tube is fixed to the back part of the ridge by pleats—a single box-pleat or sometimes a double one. The front part of the hood is severely plain, the only portion ornamented being the ridge: the jewels seen in Fig. 544 are three pearls, two with one on top, alternating with an enamel and gold ornament set with a ruby or diamond in the centre. The hair, like that in Figs. 515 and 541, is parted in the middle and lies smooth on the forehead, a portion being brought round from the back to form a puff which fills the cavity left by the side curves of the hood. This portion is carried backwards under the hood over the top of the head.

Fig. 546. The Attifet

The profile portrait of Queen Mary, from a medallion struck in 1555, reproduced in Fig. 545, explains the side construction of a somewhat similar French hood. It is wide and flat across the top like Fig. 544, but the piece of silk or satin, C, is reduced in size. The tube is pleated into the back with a piping, the superfluous material being arranged in folds to form a bag which contains the back hair, the tube itself falling over it. In front, braided plaits in place of puffs fill the cavities of the side curves.

The French hood worn by Lady Jane Grey (Fig. 516) has neither ridge nor ornamentation. This also applies to the headdress in Fig. 521, which, however, shows the dip on the forehead.

The price of a French 'whood,' according to the Princess Elizabeth's household accounts for 1553, was perhaps exorbitant. Two of them cost £2 8s. 9d, which sum, of course, does not include the gold and jewels; but as one had to pay in those days 20s. to 30s. per yard for velvet, not much was left for the lining or the making.

Shortly after the middle of the century a contrivance called an ATTIFET came into vogue (*see* Fig. 546). This was a wire of brass inserted in the edge of the front part of the hood or headdress and formed a curve on each side of the temples with a point on the forehead—in fact, it gave a bow or top-of-a-heart shape to the front.

Fig. 546 illustrates the use of the attifet with the French hood. The back portion comprises a roll from which the flat tube hangs down the back.

A suggestion of a wire is visible in the headdress of the lady (Fig. 521). The Princess Mary (Fig. 523) wears a very up-to-date headdress. It is the

ESCOFFION (*see* Fig. 547) to which an attifet front, edged with pearls, has been added. This style of headdress was quite popular with the ladies of both England and France.

Wire is definitely used in the cap worn by Queen Eleanor (Figs. 551 and 554).

Milan had long been celebrated for its wonderful headgear (*see* p. 313), besides fancy goods such as ferrets or ribands, gloves and pouches; and the vendors of Milanese wares began to be known as 'milliners.' A *fashion note*, recommended by French milliners in order to achieve the fashionable curve of the headdress, was to insert a wire of brass at the edge—the attifet, in fact.

OTHER FRENCH HEADDRESSES
(continued from p. 337)

Fig. 547 is made from a portrait of Jeanne d'Albret, born 1528 at Fontainebleau

Fig. 547.
Jeanne d'Albret, Queen of Navarre

Fig. 548. Mary Stuart, 1559

and only child of Henry II, King of Navarre. In 1548 she married Antoine, Duc de Bourbon, known as 'l'Échangeur,' because he could not be true to any faith. Her son Henry was born in 1553, and on the death of her father in 1555 she became Queen of Navarre in her own right. The headdress shown in Fig. 547 is known as an 'escoffion,' and was fashionable in France for a decade or so. It was a round cap of gold network and jewels mounted on a foundation of gold or silk. This particular one is shaped like a low hassock, cross-barred at the sides, and edged with a band of jewels. The back is plain with a row of pearls down the centre. The hair is brushed back off the forehead, slightly puffed over the ears, and confined by a band of gold round the head, having a jewel in a gold mount set on top. The cap is worn over this right off the back of the head, and encloses the remainder of the hair. The Queen of Navarre was left a widow in 1562, and in a drawing by François Clouet dated 1570 she wears widow's weeds in exactly the same style as those shown in Fig. 884. Queen Jeanne died suddenly in Paris, to which city she had come to attend the marriage of her son with Marguerite de Valois, 1572.

Fig. 549

The escoffion worn by Mary Queen of Scots in Fig. 528 is reproduced in Fig. 548. In shape it is similar to the last, except that it is wider on top of the head than at the sides. The front part is of gold tissue, cross-barred with gold and having pearls at the intersections and centres. On the front and back edges are set jewels in gold quatrefoil mounts alternating with pearls. Where the front rests on the hair there is a narrow goffering of gold gauze. The oval-shaped back, either of plain gold tissue or coloured silk, has a band of the same jewels down the centre. The hair is waved off the temples with a puff over the ears, the remainder being confined within the cap. The large jewel on the forehead, perhaps, serves the purpose of securing the cap more firmly on the head.

A network caul was often used to cover the coil of hair dressed at the back of the head, and was much favoured by English and French ladies. It is seen worn by the ladies in Figs. 550, 524, 549, and many others. It has its origin in the network caps worn in Italy.

Up to this time ladies had no hats of their own to use as an extra head covering, so during the reign of Henry II they adopted the velvet cap worn by gentlemen as described under Headgear of this chapter. Fig. 550 is one of the earliest examples, worn over a caul of gold and pearls. The lady is dressed in a Spanish surcote like Figs. 516 and 575.

Another such hat or cap is worn by the lady (Fig. 524) and, together with the caul, was known as a 'chapeau à l'Italienne,' and is often referred to in writings of the period. It is distinctly Italian in character (*refer to* Fig. 662), and is usually carried out in black velvet, although coloured velvets or silks were sometimes used. The brim resembles that of a man's hat, the whole effect

Fig. 550. A French Hat

being, in fact, decidedly masculine. The full crown is pleated into the brim, the join being covered by a narrow band to which are fixed aiglettes at all angles. Several small plumes are coquettishly set at the back on one side. The hair is rolled off the forehead, and confined at the back under a caul of gold network.

The widow's headdress as worn by Eleanor, Queen-Dowager of France, is shown in Fig. 551. First of all the widow's barbe is placed under the chin and tied up to the coil of hair fixed just below the cranium. Over her hair she wears a gauze cap finely gathered to a wire edging covered with white stitchery. This wire, the attifet, is bent to bow down on the forehead and curve round at the temples to the level of the mouth. At this point the wiring is bent into goffered or nebulée folds which continue up the side of the face. On top a lawn veil twenty-four by eighty inches, but folded in two as shown

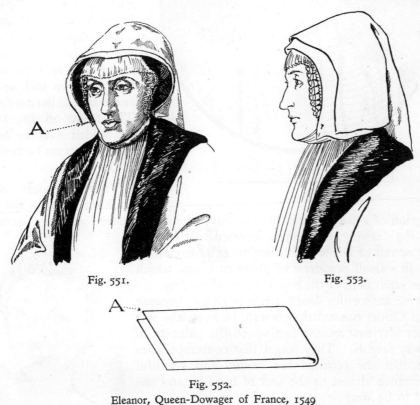

Fig. 551.

Fig. 553.

A

Fig. 552.
Eleanor, Queen-Dowager of France, 1549

in diagram, Fig. 552, is placed round the head as described under Fig. 164; a corner of the outer fold is marked A, and the inner corner is pinned to the band of the barbe. The folds are then pinned together in the nape of the neck and the remainder hangs down the back. A black silk scarf is placed round the neck over the barbe, the plain part of the latter falling over the arms as far as the elbows. A side view of this headdress is given in Fig. 553.

A similar type of widow's headdress is to be seen in the sculptured portrait bust of Queen Eleanor in the Prado. In the drawing (Fig. 554) the pleated under-cap is clearly shown, as are also the second cap with attifet front and the lawn veil, and these more distinctly than in Fig. 551. The barbe hangs from beneath the collar, which is possibly part of the barbe itself.

LA REINE ELEANOR.

Fig. 554

The interest of the sculpture lies not merely in its representation of the Queen - Dowager in advanced years, but more particularly in the robe she is wearing, which is of white *pleated* material, such as is referred to by Roger Ascham (*see* p.431). The sculpture definitely portrays narrow tucks, about half an inch deep and about an inch apart, and arranged horizontally. The fronts of the robe are folded over to form stole-effects on both sides of the barbe.

To the readers of a book on costume the description of a lady in her bath can have no interest, nevertheless the accompanying drawing, Fig. 555, is inserted. It is from the portrait of Diane de Poitiers in her bath, clothed only in a small headdress of gauze ruchings, which is the equivalent of the boudoir cap of to-day.

Some authorities doubt if this is Diane, because when Clouet painted the portrait, in 1549, she was in her fifty-first year, a fact which the painting in no way reveals. They forget that contemporaries state that she retained her beauty and youthful appearance almost to the end of her life, and she lived to be sixty-seven.

At Chantilly there is a painting identical with this in the main composition, but the head is that of Gabrielle d'Estrées.

Fig. 555. Diane de Poitiers
(*after Clouet*)

FOOTGEAR, 1547–58

By the time Edward VI ascended the throne footgear had begun to assume a more natural shape in the toes. This shape is first seen in Fig. 280 and in the first sole plan, Fig. 556. These show that the toe is rounded but somewhat clumsy in appearance. Fig. 504 illustrates a modification, and in it one sees that eventually the toe not only became quite natural, but at the same time elegant (*see also* the second sole plan, Fig. 556).

Cuttes on shoes were reintroduced from the Continent, and they are first seen worn by Prince Philip (Fig. 497). Although the sole follows the outline of the foot the cuttes, intended as ornaments, give an ugly bulging appearance.

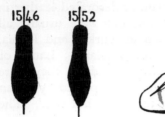

Fig. 556

Fig. 557

Fig. 558

Shoes treated in this manner are said to be 'razed.' Fig. 557 is the shoe in question. Over the joints of the toes on the uppers are three long cuttes, and a series of small ones surrounds the heel. Across the instep are three rows of ornamental stitching, and all round the edge of the shoe are very small loops. These shoes nearly always matched the hosen in colour if not in material, which was either velvet, silk, or satin.

Fig. 558 gives a shoe cut higher at the heel and on the instep; from the centre of the latter a V-shaped piece has been cut, although a round-topped upper was also in vogue. The decoration consists of a series of very small cuttes which greatly improves the appearance of the shoe as compared with that in Fig. 557.

Nothing new in long boots is noticeable in England at this period: the shape of the toe becomes natural as with the shoe. The boots worn by Lord Maltravers (Fig. 505) are good examples.

Fig. 559

The 'botte à genouillère' or 'jack-boot' made its appearance in France at the end of this period, as seen in the portrait of Henry II (Plate XXI). The latter name is perhaps due to the leather being 'jacked,' i.e. beaten or pommelled hard. This boot is reproduced in Fig. 559. The narrowness at the ankle would be found inconvenient for passing the foot through, although it must be more pliable in this part than at the top because creases or folds are shown. The ridge at the top is triangular in section; the toe is rounded and the heel rather square.

Common sense forewarned the careful, well-dressed man that to put his legs, clothed in silk hosen, into the rough interior of long leather boots would ultimately ruin delicate leg wear. A lining of linen, shaped like a stocking,

Fig. 560. Chopine

was therefore devised, and drawn up over the hosen for protection before pulling on the boots. These linen stockings were called 'boot-hose,' but at this early period were unseen.

CHOPINES were clogs of cork covered with plain or decorated leather in various colours; these could be slipped on and off, but were usually all in one with the shoe (Fig. 560). They were used in Turkey and Persia, adopted in Italy, and found their way, via Venice, into England. Ladies of quality and fashion used chopines to give them height; and, as they were awkward to walk in, it was necessary for the wearer to be supported by a man or woman, usually by the arm, 'to the end that they may not fall.' The Spanish lady (Fig. 248) is wearing chopines.

It was in 1557 that the cordwainers received their second charter from Philip and Mary.

JEWELLERY, 1547–58

Edward VI naturally inherited most of his father's enormous store of personal jewels and articles of jewellery and, of course, the English Crown Jewels. The juvenile King was not too young to realize the advantages gained by these inestimable assets, and appears to have followed the example set by his grandfather as a means of speculation. Like other monarchs and persons of great wealth, he not only locked up money in jewels, but also found them a universally accepted security when he wished to raise a loan. In his journal we have several memoranda bearing on this subject, and the following is a very good specimen:

25th April 1550. 'A bargain made with the Foulcare [the Fuggers] for about 60,000*l*., that in May and August should be payed for the defraying of it. (1) That the Foulcare should be put off for 10 in the 100. (2) That I should buy 12,000 Marks weight, at 6*s*. the ounce, to be delivered at Antwerp, and so conveyed over. (3) I should pay 100,000 Crowns for a very fair Jewel of his, four Rubies marvelous big, one Orient and great Diamond, and one great Pearl.'

And again:

29th February 1551. 'Paiment was made of 63500*l*. Flemish to the Foulcare, all saving 6000*l*. which he borrowed in French Crowns by Sir Philip Hobbey.' His allusion to the Fuggers as Foul-care is not without a certain exquisite appropriateness.

COLLARS

It is an interesting point that no sovereign of the House of Tudor was painted showing the Collar of the Order of the Garter.[1] Queen Mary was spared the embarrassment experienced by a much later Queen-Regnant

[1] If one is in existence the author would be glad to know of it.

because she wedded shortly after she ascended the throne. As King Philip was joint sovereign, it was ordained that he had the right to wear the full Insignia as Sovereign of the Order, so that it was not essential for the Queen to do so.[1]

The collar of four petalled roses and rectangular links, worn by Edward VI in Fig. 536, is not that of the Order of the Garter and, it should be noticed, it carries the pendent Lesser George.

In the same drawing is seen a new mode, copied from abroad, of suspending a jewelled ornament like a tassel over the quill of the feather in the bonet. This is seen also in Plate XIX. Whether these new ornaments were native made or not, it is a fact that from this time onwards new kinds of jewellery were produced in England.

PENDANTS

The decoration of pendants and pectoral ornaments consisted, as previously, mainly of enamel; sometimes they were entirely without jewels, in which case jewels were introduced into the frame. The pendant, with part of the chain by which it is suspended, worn by the King in Plate XIX is reproduced in Fig. 561. It is quite small, not more than three inches in length; the ruby, enclosed in an acanthus leaf of gold, supports a 'proof' set in a coronet, and from the pendant hangs a pearl. The ornaments which make up the chain are of gold studded with pearls, and in the centres of the connecting chains are single ball-shaped motifs of goldsmith's work.

Plate XX shows how lavishly King Edward spread emeralds set in beautiful gold mounts over his whole costume of black satin braided with gold. There was an idea prevailing until quite recently in the minds of

Fig. 561.
Pendant of Edward VI

Fig. 562.
Pendant of Henry II

most people that the Court of this godly young King of the Reformed Faith was devoid of Tudor magnificence, but, as stated earlier, portraits of both men and women and inventories of the period prove the contrary.

The two drawings of Henry II of France (Figs. 489 and 539) show some articles of jewellery worth noticing. The pendant hung from the collar is typically Franco-Italian in design. The cartouche framing has a grotesque

[1] See vol. vi, p. 99.

head at the top and a smaller one at the bottom, and encloses a figure of St. Michael in enamel (Fig. 562). The collar is crescent-shaped, and composed of pearls set close together like corn on the cob, bound with bands of gold, and suspended round the neck by linked golden balls. In Fig. 539 the neck-chain is entirely of filigree gold balls, and is wound twice round the neck, hanging half-way down the front of the doublet. The *upper* side of the bonet brim is now besprinkled with tiny flower-shaped gold ornaments, which are repeated in groups of three on the under-side of the crown.

The *enseigne* continued to hold its place in bonet or hat in England because it was the mode in France, where, according to an inventory of Henry II, Cellini made most of the jewellery worn by this monarch. Below are given some items as an example of the elaborate nature of such headgear ornaments:

Fig. 563. Sword of Edward VI

'A golden enseigne, representing several figures, garnished all around with small rose-diamonds; an enseigne of gold, the ground of lapis lazuli, the figure representing a Lucretia; an enseigne with a gold setting, the figure being a Ceres on an agate, the body of silver, the dress of gold; an enseigne of a David and a Goliath, the head, arms, and legs of agate.'

Jewels were extensively introduced into the decoration of the sword, especially on the handle. Fig. 563 is a fair specimen, taken from the drawing of Edward VI referred to under Fig. 536. The design is carried out in gold and jewels, the grip and scabbard having a background of velvet. At the side is shown one of the hooks by which the waist and sword belts are fastened.

The jewellery worn by Royal and noble ladies was as splendid as that of the previous reign.

The drawing of Lady Jane Grey (Fig. 515) shows her dressed in a sumptuous manner, and with jewels which can compare with those worn by the ladies of Henry VIII's Court. In Plate XXIV her upper abillement is of pearls and diamonds. Both Figs. 515 and 541 show a pendant of similar design to that in 463. She wears a girdle of engraved gold beads, and many jewels round her neck and on her French hood. In Figs. 544 and 545 we see the type of pendant so familiar in the portraits of Queen Mary. From early days, Princess and Queen, she was fond of beautiful jewels, and had a large number, among them 'The Three Brothers,' inherited from her father. The history of this jewel up to this date is obtained from the Latin work of Peter

Lambeck,[1] a grandson of Johann Jacob Fugger, Count Kirchberg (1516–75). Lambeck used as his authority the written description of it made about 1555 by his grandfather. In the Count's description he expresses the pious hope that 'The Three Brothers' might 'by the will of Providence' return into the possession of the House of Austria through the marriage of Queen Mary with Philip of Spain. However, the Count's desire was not realized.

Before his marriage, that is early in 1554, Prince Philip sent the Queen, by the Marqués de las Navas, a present of some wonderful jewels, including a remarkable diamond. This is described as 'a great table diamond mounted in a superb gold setting, and valued at 50,000 ducats; a necklace of eighteen brilliants worth 32,000 ducats; a great diamond, with a *fine pearl* pendant from it, worth 25,000 ducats, and other jewels, pearls, diamonds, emeralds, and rubies of inestimable value, for the Queen and her ladies' (19th June 1554).

Fig. 564.
Pendant worn by
Queen Mary

The 'fine pearl' has an interesting history which is worth relating here. It was found by a slave in the Pearl Islands in 1513. Vasco Nuñez de Balboa (1475–1517), the discoverer of the Pacific Ocean, annexed this great pear-shaped pearl, and in return gave the slave his freedom. Having fallen out of favour with his sovereign, Ferdinand V, Balboa endeavoured to propitiate the King by sending this pearl amongst other presents. Its beauty was at once recognized, and the pearl became one of the most prized of the Spanish crown jewels. After Ferdinand's death it came into the possession of the Emperor Charles V, who handed it over to his son Philip, and the portrait of Queen Mary (Plate XXV), which hung in the Prado, shows her wearing this pearl and pendant. At the Queen's death the pearl was returned to Spain, where it remained for two hundred and fifty years.[2] Fig. 564 is a drawing of this historic jewel. The pendant of gold is set with a table

---

[1] Peter Lambeck was born in Hamburg in 1628 and died in 1680 in Vienna, where he had been librarian to the Emperor. During this time he made a comprehensive catalogue of a number of documents in the Imperial archives. This was published in 1669. From the same source comes the description of Charles le Téméraire's famous ceremonial hat shown in Plate XVIII F. Details are given on p. 121.

[2] Its subsequent history is of even greater interest, and at a later date this celebrated pearl received the name of 'La Pelegrina'—the Wanderer: it was worn by all the queens-consort until 1808, when Napoleon took Spain and placed his brother Joseph on the throne. When the latter fled, he took La Pelegrina with him amongst other treasures, and at his death left it to his nephew, Prince Charles Louis Napoleon, afterward Napoleon III. Being in somewhat distressed circumstances while in exile in England, Prince Napoleon took La Pelegrina to the 2nd Marquess of Abercorn and asked his advice about a purchaser. Without any hesitation, and without asking the price required, he wrote a cheque for a sum which has not been divulged. The pearl had always been set in a socket, and being very heavy frequently fell from its setting. Twice the Duchess lost this peerless pearl: once at a drawing-room at Buckingham Palace, where three hours later it was recovered riding upon a lady's velvet court train, and again at Windsor, much to the consternation of Queen Victoria *and* the Duchess, where, after three weeks, it was found in the squabbing of a sofa. The second Duke had it bored to make it more secure, but this impaired its value. However, succeeding duchesses have enjoyed its possession, and the last the author heard of it was in March 1931 when it was seen worn by the Duchess of Abercorn.

Fig. 565.
Portion of
Girdle

diamond, surrounded by scrolls in goldsmith's work and flanked by satyrs in white enamel; it is hung from a smaller diamond set in gold.

The girdle (Fig. 565) in the same portrait is of a beautiful design of sapphires in gold mounts alternating with leafy scrolls and pairs of pearls. At the end hangs a circular reliquary of gold (Fig. 566). The ground-work is dark enamel, and the gold cross of sapphires and diamonds has figures in white enamel seated between the limbs. The hinge and clasp for opening it can be seen in the drawing. The Queen's jeweller was named Robert Raynes.

When Philip came to England he brought 'a chest upholdered with red velvet six spans long, two spans high and three spans broad . . . filled with precious stones and other regal gold finery, jewels and neckchains.'

Another pearl, a beautiful white Indian and a perfect sphere in shape, twenty-eight carats in weight, is in the Museum of Zosima, Moscow. This is also known as 'La Pellegrina.'

The drawing (Fig. 525) shows Catherine de' Medici wearing a large pectoral cross set with large sapphires, with round and peardrop pearls hanging from its limbs. To this is attached a chain, composed of clusters of pearls something like large mulberries alternating with sapphires in gold mounts. The chain is draped over the shoulders in the approved manner. Round the throat is a small carcanet of rows of pearls with sapphires in gold mounts at intervals; pear-shaped pearls hang from the sap-

Fig. 566. Reliquary

phires. The girdle, and the cruciform ornament hanging from it, are likewise in sapphires and pearls. The dress is covered with a close trellis-work of pearls: Catherine had an insatiable mania for pearls of great price—one wonders if the thousands used on her dress were of this kind.

The carcanet worn by Catherine in Fig. 543 has jewels set in rose mounts linked by what appear to be a D and a D reversed, joined together. This is the monogram of Diane de Poitiers. It is seen again on her stomacher, which gives the impression that this lady friend of the King was very much esteemed by the Queen.

A handsome carcanet is worn by the French lady (Fig. 550), and another by Queen Jeanne (Fig. 547), with a pendant in the form of the head and shoulders of a woman in enamels holding a pear-pearl. The lace of pearls

Fig. 567. Reliquary

round the shoulders is looped up on the front of the bodice, which clearly shows this recently introduced fashion. The jewels on the headdress are lozenge shape, with pearls on the sides alternating with circular stones in goldsmith's work, all set close together on a band of gold—a billement.

Mary Stuart's pendant and lace of pearls should be noticed, Fig. 548.

Fig. 567 shows a rather unusual cruciform *reliquary* displaying the five wounds of Our Lord. The Heart, a ruby surrounded by a Crown of Thorns in white enamel and gold, covers some small but precious relic, most likely a particle of the Blood of Our Lord, and is surmounted by a scroll inscribed 'I.N.R.I.' The wounded Hands and Feet are in white and red enamel and the cross is of gold with guttée de sang in red enamel. Pearls are set in the four angles, and a larger one hangs from the base.

The revival of Catholicism under Queen Mary may have brought such *objets de piété* again into favour; the actual example comes from a portrait by Holbein, and may very well be of his own design.

RINGS

Edward VI refers to one of his finger rings in his *Journal* as follows: 'Monsieur le Mareschal dined with me. After dinner saw the strength of the English Archers. After he had so done, at his departure I gave him a Diamond from my finger, worth, by estimation, 150l., both for Pains, and also for my Memory' (26th July 1550).

When the Venetian Ambassador saw Queen Mary in 1554, she was wearing two rings which attracted his attention. 'On her finger the Queen has two rings, with which she was espoused twice, first on her accession when she was crowned and confirmed the Treaty with France, and secondly when she became the wife of the present King of Spain.' During this period the wedding ring was changed from the right hand to the third finger of the left.

GUILDS AND TRADE (*continued from p. 374*)

The governorship of the Merchant Adventurers was, in 1553, under Sebastian Cabot, and trade with rediscovered Muscovy began that year through the energies of Richard Chancellor, who was received at Moscow in a very friendly manner by the Tsar Ivan IV (1530–84) known as 'the Terrible.' The Tsar, eager for the 'search of new trades and countries,' wrote to Edward VI declaring that he was 'willing that you send unto us ships and vessels. And if you send one of your Majesties Council to treat with us, whereby your merchants may with all kinds of wares, and where they will, make their markets, they shall have their free mart with all liberties through my whole dominions, to come and go at their pleasure.'

This letter was received by Queen Mary on Chancellor's return in 1554, and commerce with Russia began under favourable conditions. This same year the Russia Company received its first charter, and two years later the first ambassador from the Tsar was honourably received in England. This agreement was not at all approved of by the merchants of the Hanseatic League, who were already established at Novgorod, 'the chiefest mart in all Muscovy,' but who were not held in very high esteem by the Russians.

WEAVING, COLOURS

During the short reign of Edward VI an Act was passed for preventing frauds in the woollen manufacture in England, wherein was set forth that 'some for lack of knowledge and experience, and some of extreame covetousnes do daylie more and more studdye rather to make monye then to make good clothes,' and many restrictions were made.

According to another Act of the same reign, English dyers were limited in the variety of colours to the following: scarlet, red, crimson, murrey, pink, brown, blue, black, green, yellow, orange, tawny, russet, marble grey, sad new colour (a dark tone), azure, watchet (light blue), sheep's colour, motley, and iron grey.

The general reader may have the impression that the colours used for costume in the past were crude, but if he will turn to p. 386, and read and digest the quantities of shades of colour used in the weaving of tapestry, he will realize that the art of the dyer, if not in England, certainly in foreign lands, had reached an exceedingly high standard. If numerous shades, delicate tints, subtle hues and gradations of tone could be dyed for the use of tapestries, they must also have been used in dyeing velvets, satins, silks, and cloths.

PATTERNS

Nothing new in patterns or designs is noticeable during this short period, except that known as the arabesque. This is to be seen on the underskirts worn by the lady (Plate XVI), and Queen Mary (Plate XXVI).

(Continued on p. 787)

VEHICLES (*continued from p. 377*)

Coach, Char

By Act of Parliament, 1555, two surveyors of roads were appointed in each parish to repair and maintain in good order the most important highways of England. Their energies (or lack of them) could only have been crowned with a minimum amount of success, for roads in general continued in a very bad state throughout the sixteenth century.

The origin of the word 'coach' is not absolutely certain. One authority suggests that the French first applied the word 'coche' to the char; others that it is derived from the town of Kocs in Hungary where coaches were first made. Charles VII of France received a coche from Hungary as a present in 1457. However, the name means a conveyance with a roof forming part of the frame of the body. The Queen of Francis I, Diane de Poitiers, and a corpulent nobleman, René de Laval, were the only people who then owned 'coches' in France.

The first Englishman to be called a coachbuilder was one Walter Rippon, who is said to have built the first coach in England for the Earl of Rutland in 1555, but what this was like is uncertain. He also built one for Queen Mary in 1556. A few particulars of Queen Mary's coach are given on p. 439.

There is extant a letter of the privy seal to the clerk of the Queen's stables, dated 1557, which gives some particulars relating to a char or wagon. This is inserted as it may interest the practical mind:

'By the Queen
'Marye the Queen,
'We will and commaunde you forthwithe uppon the sight hereof ye deliuer or cause to be deliuered to our trustie and well beloved servaunte Edmonde Standen Clarke of our Stable, one Wagon of tymbre work for Ladies and Gentlewomen of our Prevye Chamber with wheeles and axeltrees, stakes, nayles, clouts, and all maner of work thertoo apperteyninge; fine red cloths to kever and line the same wagon, fringed with redde sylke and lyned with redde buckeram paynted with redde colours; collars, drawghts of red lether, hamer clothes with our arms and badges in our colours; and all other things apperteininge unto the same Wagon.
'xxviii^th daye of Aprill in the Thirde and fourthe Years of our Reign.'

A 'charriot'[1] or decorated wagon, such as has just been described, is illustrated in the book of drawings referred to on p. 485, and is reproduced in Fig. 568. Although the book dates 1559, the design of the three charriots shown is as old as the early days of the Tudors. All three are unoccupied, but were for the use of maids of honour or ladies-in-waiting who followed the Royal litter in the coronation procession of Queen Elizabeth. The ladies

---

[1] This spelling is used by the official of the College of Arms, who describes the figures in the procession of which he was an eye-witness.

themselves ride behind these charriots on palfreys, sitting side-saddle with
their legs at right angles to the animals' bodies with their feet on planks.
Obviously it was considered more dignified to appear on horseback than in
a carriage, so that the ladies in question would ride in the charriot during a
journey from one town to another, and transfer to their palfreys for the
state entry. On this occasion, the presence of the empty charriots is purely
formal.

Fig. 568. A 'Charriot'

The canopy of some rich material is supported by ornamental columns,
which in the case of the front charriot have plumes at the top. The original
pen-and-ink drawing is not coloured, but quite possibly the frame-work was
entirely covered with gold, and lined inside with some colour, or it may have
been decorated as set forth in the above letter, which possibly describes this
very charriot.

Each vehicle is drawn by six horses, tandem-wise; the teams have no drivers,
but footmen walk at the sides. The shaft horse of each is saddled, as shown
in Fig. 568; the others have a saddle or hammer-cloths only. The leading
horse alone carries plumes on his head.

(Continued on p. 796)

CHAPTER IV

THE REIGN OF QUEEN ELIZABETH

1558—1603

CONTEMPORARY SOVEREIGNS

	ENGLAND	SCOTLAND	FRANCE	GERMANY	SPAIN	SWEDEN	DENMARK
1558	Elizabeth	Mary	Henry II	Ferdinand I	Philip II	Gustavas Vasa	Christian III
1559			Francis II 1559-60 Mary Stuart				Frederick II 1559-88 Sophia of Mecklenburg
1560			Charles IX 1560-74 Elizabeth of Austria			Eric XIV 1560, deposed 1568 Karren Mannsdatter	
1564				Maximilian II 1564-76 Marie of Austria			
1567		James VI 1567-1625 Anne of Denmark					
1568						John III 1568-92 1. Catherine of Poland 2. Guinilla Bulk	
1574			Henry III 1574-89 Louise de Vaudemont				
1576				Rudolph I 1576-1612			
1588							Christian IV 1588-1648 Anne Catherine of Brandenburg
1589			Henry IV 1589-1610 1. Marguerite de Valois 2. Marie de' Medici				
1592						Sigismund of Poland	
1598					Philip III 1598-1621 Margaret of Austria		

1558. Accession of Elizabeth and the Reformation Settlement in England and Scotland.

1559. Peace between England, France, and Spain, at Congress of Cateau-Cambrésis.

The Third Act of Uniformity restores the second Prayer Book, and another Act of Supremacy severs the connection with Rome.

1560(?). Robert Greene born. 'An author of plays and penner of love pamphlets.' Died 1592.

1562. Religious wars in France, lasting until 1598.

First religious war in France. The Huguenots.

Second religious war followed in 1567–8, and a third in 1569–70.

1563. Sir Robert Naunton born at Alderton, Suffolk. Educated at Trinity College, Cambridge. Author of *Fragmenta Regalia*, Secretary of State to James I. Died 1635.

1564. Christopher Marlowe born. Poet and dramatist. Died 1593.

William Shakespeare born at Stratford-on-Avon. Died 1616.

Queen Elizabeth visits Cambridge, and witnesses three plays given by the students in King's College Chapel.

1567. The Duke of Alba sent to quell the insurrection in Flanders. Established the 'Bloody Council' 1568.

1568. The persecutions of the Protestants in the Netherlands under the Duke of Alba (1567–73) drove many refugees into England.

1570. Queen Elizabeth excommunicated by Pope Pius V.

Henry Clifford born. Writer in service of Lady Jane Dormer who was born in 1538.

Richard Tarlton (born at Condover, Salop), had made a reputation as a comic actor by 1570. One of Queen Elizabeth's actor-servants, with whom he remained until his death. He is credited with the power of diverting the Queen when her mood was least amiable. Died 1588.

1571. The Ridolfi Plot discovered, and execution of the Duke of Norfolk in 1572.

1572. Peaceful times for England, until 1577.

An alliance formed between England and France. Philip II schemes to restore Mary Queen of Scots.

Massacre of St. Bartholomew, 24th August.

1573. Inigo Jones born in London. Architect. Studied in Italy. Returned to England in 1605. Designed many settings and costumes for the Court masques of James I. Died 1652.

Ben Jonson born. Poet and dramatist. Poet Laureate 1619. Died 1637.

1574. Patent granted to James Burbage authorizing the Earl of Leicester's players. Date of birth unknown: actor, and first builder of theatres in England—Shoreditch and Blackfriars. Died 1597.

His son, Richard, born 1562, also an actor of repute, built the Globe Theatre, Southwark, 1599. Died 1619.

1576. Formation of the Holy League for the defence of the Holy Catholic Church in France.

Commedia dell' arte first given in England at Kenilworth.

1577. Thomas Coryate born at Odcombe, Somersetshire. A great traveller and author of *Coryats Crudities*. Died 1617.

Francis Drake's voyage round the world began; returned in 1580.

Raphael Holinshed's *Chronicles* published. Born about the beginning of the sixteenth century, wrote the *Chronicles of England, Scotland, and Ireland*, which furnished Shakespeare with materials for his historical plays. Died about 1580.

1579. John Fletcher, poet and dramatist, born. Died 1625.

1580. The Jesuits come to England.

John Taylor born in Gloucester, who later styled himself 'The King's Majesty's Water Poet.'

1582. Pope Gregory XIII (1572–85) reformed the calendar. Adopted by Italy, Spain, and Portugal immediately; France and the Catholic parts of Switzerland, Germany, and the Netherlands soon followed. Not used in England until 1752.

1583. The Throckmorton conspiracy.

The Anatomie of Abuses by Philip Stubbes published.

Sir Humphrey Gilbert, the pioneer of English colonization, endeavoured to establish a settlement in Newfoundland.

1584. Francis Beaumont, poet and dramatist, born. Died 1616.

1585. Sack of Antwerp by the Duke of Parma; many Flemings sought refuge in England. More craftsmen arrived.

Sir Walter Raleigh and Sir Richard Grenville settled Virginia.

1586. The Babington conspiracy.
Expedition under the Earl of Leicester to the Netherlands to assist the Dutch. Battle of Zutphen. Death of Sir Philip Sidney (born 1554).

1587. 'The Tragedy of Fotheringay.'

1588. The Armada, sent to invade England, shattered in the English Channel and destroyed by a gale in the North Sea and Atlantic. Death of the Earl of Leicester.

1592. *Henry VI* written by William Shakespeare. There is no authentic proof which definitely shows in what order his plays were written or produced.

1596. The Cadiz expedition.

1598. Edict of Nantes: Henry IV of France granted perfect toleration to all Protestants.
Love's Labour's Lost published. The first play with Shakespeare's name attached, 'may reasonably be assigned priority in point of time of all Shakespeare's dramatic productions.'

1601. Rebellion and execution of the Earl of Essex.

1603. Death of Queen Elizabeth. Accession of James VI of Scotland as James I of England.

SCULPTURE, MONUMENTAL EFFIGIES (*continued from p. 385*)

WITH the influx of Protestant refugees from the Low Countries came architects and sculptors who had achieved a reputation throughout the Continent as tomb designers. All the same, the Gothic touch in their work executed in this country was not entirely eliminated. Figures are now found in reclining positions, lying on one hip with the head resting on hand and elbow. Rush matting now covers the table tomb, being rolled up to form a pillow when the figure is recumbent.

Noble ladies, and sometimes their husbands, when lying on their backs, often have one corner of the mantle arranged in graceful drapery across the lower part of the body.

Kneeling figures make their appearance, usually with a faldstool in front of them, or, if there are two figures—husband and wife—they face each other with the stool between them: their prodigious family is ranged behind them, the boys after their father, the girls after their mother. Or the family might be arranged in rows below their parents, still maintaining their order of precedence.

Into the decoration of the altar tomb, which is of no special interest to us except for its weepers and heraldic devices, are introduced, during the latter part of the century, various coloured marbles.

Decadence in the treatment of portrait sculpture in effigies is noticeable at the end of the century, in such points as globular eyeballs, receding chins, elbows stiffly bent, and legs weak-kneed and long. Another blemish, useful as a detail of identification of the period: towards the end of the century the alabaster used for the figures is often discoloured by red veins.

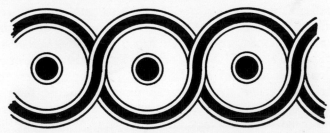

Fig. 569. Guilloche Ornament

MEMORIAL BRASSES (*continued from p. 385*)

Many more brasses were laid down during Queen Elizabeth's reign, and there was a decided improvement, both in technique and in the style of engraving employed.

During the early years of this reign, attempts were made to produce at home the necessary supplies for the growing trade in material for memorial brasses;

and, for the first time, plates of brass—'latten' or 'laton'—were manufactured in England. A 'copper and brasse myll near Thistleworth' (or Isleworth) is mentioned in a description of Middlesex at this time. The earliest English-made laton was inferior in quality to the imported material; it was thinner, and consequently wore out quicker by constant traffic.

Mural brasses now came into fashion. They were usually rectangular in shape; simple in style in the early examples, although by degrees the backgrounds of the figures were filled in with classical architectural details and heraldic designs.

Brasses executed during this reign often depicted the deceased kneeling at a prie-dieu or litany stool, which was sometimes covered with drapery. Also, a man and his wife were sometimes shown facing each other, and kneeling at such stools, and accompanied by representations of their family— the sons and daughters grouped on either side according to sex, behind or beneath their parents.

Inscriptions were engraved in English or Latin, with Roman or Gothic lettering.

TAPESTRY (*continued from p. 386*)

The Renaissance period in tapestry continues during this reign, but the year 1570 marks the date of the commencement of its subdivision known as 'Late Renaissance.'

The figures representing gods and goddesses, Biblical characters, Classic heroes and heroines, and early historical personages which are found in tapestries of the second half of the sixteenth century, are nearly always garbed in costume of a fanciful nature. This being so, they are useless for the study of period costume. They do suggest, however, the type of dress worn in stage plays, disguisings, and masques of the sixteenth century, and represent almost the first intentional use of what we term to-day 'fancy dress.'

The skill of the Flemish weavers held first place among tapissers all through the sixteenth century, and Flanders continued to be the centre of manufacture until the troublous times of the Spanish oppression under the Duke of Alba. After this period many Flemish tapissers sought their fortunes in foreign countries. Many masterpieces of the tapisser's art decorated the walls of the English aristocracy. At Chawton Manor, the home of the Lewkenor family, there hung some tapestries made in 1564.

Robert Dudley, Earl of Leicester, has left some panels at Drayton House, Northamptonshire, and there were many beautiful pieces hung upon the walls of Kenilworth previous to the visit of Queen Elizabeth in 1575. (The earl's expenses incurred on that memorable occasion amounted to £60,000.)

William Cecil, Lord Burleigh, acquired much fine tapestry, which ultimately ornamented Hatfield House, though this was not actually completed until the early years of the seventeenth century.

Queen Elizabeth was not a monarch to be outdone by her subjects, or **even** by contemporary sovereigns. She possessed many beautiful examples of tapestry weaving, and we are told that the apartments of the Royal palaces shone with tapestries of gold, silver, and silk of different colours. Her private chapel at Hampton Court was hung with rich tapestries. In her bedchamber she had some very fine pieces, and many of the rooms in Hampton Court were adorned with tapestry of gold, silver, and velvet, some representing historical events. In other rooms oriental subjects were portrayed, and special mention is made of tapestry depicting Turkish and American scenes, 'all extremely natural.' 'In one chamber are several excessively rich tapestries which are hung up when the Queen gives audience to foreign ambassadors.'

A visitor to this country writing in 1589 mentions tapestry of silver cloth, on which various animals were embroidered in gold. 'This tapestry is suspended on the wall behind the Queen.' The presence chamber at Greenwich where 'she generally resides, particularly in summer, for the delightfulness of its situation' was hung with rich tapestry; and, as late as 1598, the floor, 'after the English fashion,' was strewed with rushes.

English Tapestry

Practically all tapestries used in England, including those enumerated in the various household and wardrobe accounts of Queen Elizabeth, and of the nobility, were woven in the Netherlands.

The first tapestry-weaving factory was established in England as a result of the great interest in the art taken by a Warwickshire gentleman, William Sheldon. He sent a certain Richard Hyckes, of Barcheston, to the Netherlands in order to study the craft, and, on Hyckes's return to England, looms were set up at Barcheston and at Sheldon's country seat at Western, about the year 1558.[1] Some tapestries were woven at these places, but there is to-day no evidence of their existence.

In the year 1567 some Flemish weavers settled in Canterbury, Maidstone, Sandwich, Norwich, and Colchester. Two Dutch arras-weavers followed in 1570, and took up their abode in York. The amount of work turned out by these tapissers during the sixteenth century is unknown, neither does any undoubted specimen of their work exist to-day.

French Tapestries

Tapestry produced in France during this time does not compare with the Flemish, although Francis I and Henry II made great efforts to establish a factory at Fontainebleau. Whatever success this factory achieved, the ultra-discriminating Catherine de' Medici did not deign to place an order with a firm in her adopted country, or even in her native land, but commissioned the tapissers of Brussels.

---

[1] A hundred years later, this factory became famous for its tapestries representing maps of the English counties.

The set she requisitioned took five years to complete, and was woven to commemorate the reception of the Polish Ambassadors at the Tuileries in 1573 and the departure of Henry, Duc d'Anjou, to assume the crown of Poland. These tapestries, finished by 1580, are now in the Museum of Florence, and are most useful for the study of French costume and other details of the Court of Charles IX (1560–74) and Henry III (1574–89).

Italian Tapestries

Tapestry was made in Italy about the middle of the fifteenth century, but it is not of any appreciable importance.

About 1536, two Flemings, the brothers Hans and Nicolas Karcher, emigrated to Italy and were employed at a tapestry factory at Ferrara, presumably to raise the prestige of the business.

In 1546, a tapestry factory was established at Florence by Cosimo I, later Grand Duke of Tuscany, and in this year Nicolas Karcher left his brother in Ferrara to supervise it. He was joined in 1553 by a tapisser named Stoadamus, a native of Bruges, who designed cartoons and supervised the weaving. His work, however, was typically Flemish, characterized by burly Flemings of the middle and lower orders in *Italian* dress engaged in various pursuits, such as hunting, husbandry, etc.

This factory developed into what was known as the 'Arazzeria Medicae'; Jean van Roost was another Flemish tapisser in the firm.

Angelo Bronzino (1502–72) and afterwards Salviati, Italian artists, became designers of cartoons in this establishment which flourished until Cosimo's death in 1574.[1]

ILLUMINATED MANUSCRIPTS (*continued from p. 148*)

Some of the Illum. MSS. produced in the reign of Elizabeth are of first-rate workmanship, and in the early part followed the traditional style. For instance, the miniature of the Queen at prayer, mentioned on p. 493, in the library at Lambeth, is a very beautiful and finished painting.

Later Illum MSS. lose the decorative treatment which was the great charm of those of earlier times; the figures now become simply water-colour drawings, such as were in vogue until the beginning of the twentieth century.

Documents still retained the method of showing a portrait in the initial letter, as in earlier works. There are many showing Queen Mary, some alone and some with Philip of Spain, and many more of Queen Elizabeth.

Later, the manuscript artist turned his attention to painting portraits on a small scale. Now that the printing press was in general use the demand for Illum. MSS. became less and less until the end of the century, when it may be said that the art of the manuscript writer and illuminator had almost completely died out.

[1] After this date its fame gradually diminished, and can be said to have ended when the House de' Medici became extinct in 1737. Many specimens of these Medici tapestries are to be seen to-day in the Royal collection at Florence.

PORTRAITS AND PAINTERS (*continued from p.* 388)

During the reign of Queen Elizabeth portrait painting became more general, as evidenced by the number of portraits of all kinds still extant.

FRANÇOIS CLOUET (or JANET) held the office of painter to the Court of France, 1541–72, and his works depict very accurately the French modes of his period.

FRANS POURBUS, son of Pieter Pourbus, was born at Bruges in 1545, and died at Antwerp in 1581. His son FRANS POURBUS II, born at Antwerp in 1569, was an eminent portrait painter who spent the best part of his life in portraying crowned heads. In 1610 he became painter at the French Court. He died in Paris in 1622.

NICHOLAS HILLIARD, born at Exeter in 1537, son of Richard Hilliard, who was High Sheriff of Exeter in 1560. Nicholas was the first Englishman to attain fame as a painter of portraits in miniature. It is not known whose pupil he was, but he says himself that he took Holbein's work as his model, though his own is very different from that of Holbein. He was also a goldsmith and jeweller. Queen Elizabeth appointed him her goldsmith, carver, and limner—'a painter in little.' He died in 1619, leaving a son, Laurence, who was also a miniature painter.

FEDERIGO ZUCCARO, an Italian born in 1542, was an eminent portrait painter who worked in England between 1574 and 1582. He died in 1609.

One of the most important portrait painters of this era, whose portraits of the nobility are numerous, is MARCUS GHEERAERTS THE YOUNGER, born at Bruges in 1561, son of Marcus Gheeraerts the Elder (born Bruges, 1525), who came to England with his father in 1568. He is also known as MARK GARRARD. His portraits can often be recognized by his habit of concealing one of the sitter's hands; evidently he found difficulty in painting these, and having laboured over one, shirked the other. He died in London in 1635–6.

PETER PAUL RUBENS, born at Siegen in Nassau 1577, son of Jan Rubens, an eminent man of law. In 1588 the family removed to Antwerp, where young Rubens received his education. He learned his craft from 1591 to 1600 under Tobias Verhaeght, Adam van Noort, and Otto van Veen. It was during this time that he received kind and appreciative support from the Archduke Albert and his wife, the Archduchess Isabella Clara Eugenia, Governess of the Netherlands.

Rubens went to Italy to study art in 1600, and to Spain in 1603.

JUAN PANTOJA DE LA CRUZ, born in Madrid in 1551, was a disciple of Sanchez Coello whom he succeeded as Court painter to Philip II. As such he painted numerous Royal portraits, some of which are mentioned in this book. 'All that he did is of admirable composition, being very definite and finished.' He died in his native city in 1610.

DON DIEGO RODRIGUEZ DE SILVA Y VELAZQUEZ, of supreme importance in the next century, was born in 1599.

EL GRECO—DOMINICO THEOTOCOPULI. Painter, architect, and sculptor. Born in Crete between 1545 and 1550. He studied first in Venice, then in Rome (1570). His first portrait, of Giulio Clovio, was painted between 1570 and 1578. In 1577 he went to Spain and settled at Toledo and became painter to Philip II from 1590. He painted thirty-two portraits besides other works. He died 7th April 1614.

Canvas was used for large portraits about this time much more generally than hitherto. Examples are the portraits of Charles IX by Clouet (Janet), 1569, at Vienna, and nearly all the works of Marcus Gheeraerts.

By the middle of Elizabeth's reign picture frames were carved and gilded, and towards the end of the century a vogue for painting them in addition came into use.

Among English *miniature painters* the two OLIVERS, father and son, were the most important. ISAAC OLIVER, born about 1566, was the son of a French refugee named Pierre Olivier, and was a pupil of Nicholas Hilliard. He died in 1617, leaving a son, PETER OLIVER, who became miniature painter to Charles I.

Serjeant-paynters working during the reign of Queen Elizabeth were:

NICHOLAS LYZARD, who died in 1570.

GEORGE GOWER, who flourished 1575–85, was appointed to the office of serjeant-paynter to the Queen in 1584. He was granted the monopoly of making portraits of Queen Elizabeth, in oil, on boards, canvas, copper, and in woodcut.

LEONARD FRYER held the same office from 1598 to 1605.

The first Englishman who is known to have practised copperplate engraving was WILLIAM ROGERS. Plate XXXIX reproduces an example of his craft. He came into prominence about 1580 and worked until his death in 1610.

AUGUSTIN RYTHER was another engraver of repute. He was a native of Leeds, Yorkshire, and died in 1590.

CRISPIN VAN DE PASS THE ELDER, born at Armuyden about 1560, was an eminent draughtsman and engraver. There is no English print by him dated later than 1635.

CRISPIN VAN DE PASS THE YOUNGER, born at Utrecht in 1585, flourished during the first half of the seventeenth century.

In the eighteenth and nineteenth centuries any portrait of an elderly lady, painted with ruff, long stomacher, and farthingale, was inevitably labelled 'Queen Elizabeth,' quite irrespective of the lack of corroborative evidence, and frequently in the absence of any details for the identification of the period.

Many such portraits have been recognized in recent years as representing other well-known ladies; but unfortunately the false attributions are still so numerous that they have misled many students and others, and even to-day it is only too easy to be deceived into thinking one is contemplating the features of Queen Elizabeth instead of some lady of the Court, a noble lady, or a parvenu of the later part of the sixteenth century or of the reign of James I.

As early as 1563 it was found expedient to check the circulation of spurious portraits of Her Majesty, and a proclamation was issued forbidding ' . . . all paynters and gravers from drawing the picture of the Queen, till some cunning person meet therefor shall make a natural representation of Her Majesty's person, as a pattern for other persons to copy.'

In 1584 a licence grants the monopoly of making 'all maner of purtraictes and pictures of our person . . . in oyle cullers upon bourdes or canvas, or to grave the same on copper,' to 'George Gower our officer, maker, paynter . . . and we doe strictly forbydd and prohibit . . . all and every other persone or persons whatsoever, Englishmen or straingers . . . to entermeddle with the making, paynting or pryntinge . . . except only one Nichas Hilliard.'

It has been suggested that there was in the sixteenth century a factory for the reproduction of portraits of eminent people. This probably accounts for the existence of the large number of spurious portraits which is encountered to-day.

To enable the student to visualize the appearance of Queen Elizabeth at different periods, so far as she is represented by portraits and figures in this book, the following chronological list is inserted.

Chapter II

1546. Fig. 313   1547. Fig. 314

Chapter IV, Section I   Chapter IV, Section II

1559.	Fig. 571	1585.	Plate XXXII D
1559.	Fig. 575	1588.	Fig. 705
1559.	Plate XXVII	1588.	Plate XXXVIII
1560.	Plate XXIX	1588.	Plate XXXIX
1564.	Fig. 576	1588.	Plate XXXVII
1569.	Fig. 574	1589.	Plate XL
1569.	Plate XXVIII	1589.	Plate XLI A
1569.	Plate XXX	1590.	Fig. 698
1570.	Fig. 578	1592.	Plate XLI B
1570.	Plate XXXI A	1592.	Plate XLI C
1575.	Fig. 873	1594.	Plate XLI D
1575.	Fig. 579	1597.	Fig. 880
1575.	Plate XXXI B	1598.	Plate XLII
1575.	Plate XXXI C	1600.	Plate XLV
1575.	Plate XXXI D	1601.	Plate XLIII
1578.	Plate XXXII A		
1579.	Plate XXXII B		
1580.	Plate XXXII C		

SECTION I: 1558–80

QUEEN ELIZABETH, 1549–80

'Elizabeth, Queen of England, France, and Ireland, Sovereign of the Most Noble Order of the Garter.   She was the Delight of her own subjects, the Terror of Europe.' [1]

INTRODUCTION

Queen Elizabeth is one of the best-known characters in history, so any description of her in these pages may be considered superfluous.   The few remarks given here, however, may include some new details of interest to readers.

Appalling misrepresentations of 'Gloriana' have appeared frequently, upon the stage, in pageants, and at 'fancy-dress balls,' to say nothing of 'period' pictures and films—as defective in their lack of discrimination and accuracy as many of her so-called 'portraits'—sufficient, indeed, to grieve her departed spirit beyond endurance.

The recent controversy about her sex and parentage need not concern us; the odds favour a Tudor and a woman.

Elizabeth was born at Greenwich, 7th September 1533; the only child of Henry VIII and Anne Boleyn.

This Princess was named after her grandmother and her great-grandmother.

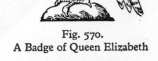

Fig. 570.
A Badge of Queen Elizabeth

There have been ten Princesses in the English Royal family bearing the name of Elizabeth.   Elizabeth Tudor was the fifth, the others being:

1. Elizabeth, daughter of Edward I.
2. Elizabeth, daughter of Thomas of Brotherton.
3. Elizabeth, daughter of John of Gaunt.
4. Elizabeth, daughter of Edward IV, afterwards queen.
6. Elizabeth, daughter of James I.
7. Elizabeth, daughter of James II.
8. Elizabeth, daughter of George III.
9. Elizabeth, daughter of William IV.
10. Elizabeth, daughter of George VI.

[1] From a cartouche on an engraving of the Queen.

The following notes are intended as supplementary to those given with the various portraits of the Queen reproduced here.

APPEARANCE

Some interesting descriptions of Elizabeth's appearance, at various times, are given below—some extracts from contemporary writings, and others by eminent historians:

1549 (16).   Frederick Chamberlin describes the picture referred to on p. 287 (Fig. 313), '. . . full rounded wide forehead, eyes full and wide, long nose, long oval face.'

Fig. 571. Queen Elizabeth, 1559.   After an engraving by Cock
(*British Museum*)

1558 (25).   Queen Elizabeth was twenty-five years old at the time of her accession.   A description of her appearance at this time is as follows:

'She was of a commanding personality, her forehead was high and open, her nose aquiline, her complexion pale, and her hair a deep yellow, verging to red.   Her features were good, but the length and narrowness of her face prevented her from having any just pretensions to beauty.'

1559 (26).   The accuracy of this description may be judged from the contemporary engraving dated 1559 from which Fig. 571 is made.

1564 (31). Referring to a series of portraits of about this date, Chamberlin summarizes his conclusions as follows:

'Nose long, almost straight, just a suspicion of aquiline, long face, complexion that of a dark brunette, with pale white skin, destitute of any ruddiness.'

The Scottish Ambassador of this date, Sir James Melville, tells us:

'Elizabeth had hair reder than yellow, curlit apparently of nature.' A sceptical gentleman!

1565 (32). When Elizabeth was thirty-two, an emissary from the Emperor Maximilian II, in conversation, quoted to her that the French Ambassador had 'pronounced Mary Stuart a very beautiful woman'; but Elizabeth of England retorted that she was 'superior to the Queen of Scotland.'

The remark contrasts oddly with another, made at the age of sixty-four, to another holder of the Ambassadorship of France: 'I was never beautiful, but I had the reputation of it thirty years ago.'

(*Continued on p. 595*)

CHARACTER

Of her character much has been written. She possessed many faults; she was but human. She loved her England and passionately maintained its interests. She was majestic and dignified, but without the arrogance of upstarts, while her affable disposition is well known. Bishop Aylmer (tutor to Lady Jane Grey) affirms on the authority of Elizabeth's Italian tutor that she possessed in her youth two qualities, 'a singular wit and a marvellous meek stomach.'

William Thomas, Clerk of the Closet to Edward VI, who wrote in 1546, says that 'the Lady Elizabeth, which is at this time of the age of fourteen years, or thereabouts, is a very wittye and gentyll yonge lady.'

Stubbes,[1] whose virulent prejudice against sartorial magnificence predisposed him to anything but kindly criticism of so magnificent a person as the Queen, yet says: 'Yea, so affable, so lowly and humble is her Grace, as she will not disdaine to talk familiarlie to the meanest or poorest of her Grace's subjects upon special occasions.'

Elizabeth was always easy of access by her people of all classes, and would give personal attention to the complaints or petitions presented in the most informal manner to her. Her frequent promises of attention to affairs brought, however, uncouthly, to her notice were always fulfilled. This kindly and good-natured accessibility won all hearts and endeared her, perhaps more than any other attribute, to her people.

---

[1] Author of *The Anatomie of Abuses*, 1583.

This is not the place to deal with Elizabeth's love affairs, most of which had some ulterior motive of statecraft behind them. 'She is a princess who can act any part she pleases,' said the French Ambassador, and the only men for whom she appears to have had any real regard were Leicester, Alençon, and Essex. While the matrimonial speculations of her unfortunate rival, Mary Stuart, terminated in lamentable tragedies, those of Elizabeth degenerated into farce.

As a modern schoolboy once said: 'Queen Elizabeth refused to marry anybody. She was one of the wisest queens that ever reigned.'

Although Queen Elizabeth's passion for dress is proverbial, as a young woman, and at the time she ascended the throne, her dress was quite normal. Roger Ascham, her tutor, tells us in 1549 that: 'In adornment she is elegant rather than showy.' She was then aged sixteen, and in 1557 Bishop Aylmer exhorts his pupil, the Lady Jane Grey, to emulate her kinswoman, the Lady Elizabeth, 'who goes clad in every respect as becomes a young maiden. And yet, no one is induced by the example of so illustrious a lady, and in so much gospel light, to lay aside, much less look down upon gold, jewels, and braidings of the hair.'

(Continued on p. 599)

ACCOMPLISHMENTS

Like her father, Elizabeth was a great lover of music; in fact, a modern author [1] informs us that 'a tune on the virginals had always been more to Elizabeth's mind than a prayer.'

The envoy of the Emperor Maximilian II, writing to his sovereign in 1565, states that 'I had also seen her dancing in her apartments, some Italian dances, half Pavanne and half Galliard, and she also played very beautifully upon the clavichord [Fig. 572] and the lute [Fig. 573].'

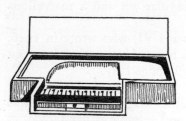

Fig. 572. Clavichord

Queen Elizabeth retained on her Royal establishments four sets of singing boys who belonged to the Cathedral of St. Paul, Westminster, St. George's Chapel, and the Household Chapel. She formed these boys of the Royal Chapel into a company of theatrical performers under the superintendence of Richard Edwards, the poet and musician. Shortly after this date she formed a second society of players, 'Children of the Revels,' and by these two companies all Lyly's plays, and many by Shakespeare and Ben Jonson, were first performed.

It is interesting to know Queen Elizabeth's favourite tune, and we have it definitely stated in a letter dated 10th July 1564 from the Spanish Ambassador. At a supper party we hear that 'the meal was attended with the usual cere-

[1] Lytton Strachey.

monies. Nothing could be more handsome than the entertainment. She [the Queen] made the band play *The Battle of Pavia*,[1] and declared it was the music that she liked best in the world.'

An amusing story was current at this time concerning Dr. Tye (*see* p. 156), a peevish and humoursome old man, especially in his latter days, who died in 1572. It shows how punctilious Elizabeth could be in the matter of music. On one occasion the doctor was playing to the Queen on the organ in the Chapel Royal. Much music was there, but it contained little to delight the ear. Elizabeth sent the verger to tell him that he played out of tune: whereupon he sent word that her ears were out of tune.

Thomas Tallis (*see* p. 156), died 1585, and William Byrd (1538–1623) were pre-eminent musicians and composers who received a special grant from Queen Elizabeth in 1575 for the monopoly of music printing.

The supreme master of Catholic Church music was Giovanni Pierluigi da Palestrina (1525–94). Many of his Masses were dedicated to Philip II.

Elizabeth was an unusually proficient linguist in both senses of the word. In her girlhood she was taught Greek, Latin, French, Italian, and Spanish. To speak six languages fluently would be a remarkable achievement for any one, and is doubly so in the case of a young woman who must have had hitherto scant opportunity for airing these accomplishments. So apt a pupil must have been a great joy to her tutors.

Fig. 573. Lute

As to the oaths she was in the habit of using when she wished to assert herself very emphatically, they were numerous and well known, and probably caused less sensation to her contemporaries than they would have done in the nineteenth century.

As a needlewoman and embroideress Elizabeth's work was of the highest order. At an early age she made garments of excellent workmanship for her small brother.

In 1555 when Queen Mary had hopes of an heir, Elizabeth showed her sympathy in her sister's happiness by working, while a guest at Ashridge, a full set of baby garments. These were never required, and remained in the Brownlow family until a few years ago when they came under the hammer.

After she came to the throne her time was occupied with more important matters which left little for needlework. She found time, however, for a gamble at cards, as there are records of her winnings at play amounting to anything from £25 to £100.

The Queen was a good horsewoman at a time when all women could ride,

---

[1] *The Battle of Pavia* was a polyphonic vocal composition written by Clément Jannequin, and published in Paris in 1528. Curiously enough, Jannequin was in the service of Francis I, but the piece was composed to commemorate the victory of the Emperor Charles V over Francis I in 1525.

having been taught the manage by that master of the art, Claudio Corte. She was also a good hunter and spent many joyous days in her early woman-hood at this sport.   On occasion she was driven in her coach, a luxury which was fast finding favour with the aristocracy, and it is on record that once, having been driven too fast in her coach over the appalling roads, she was so knocked about that she suffered many aching pains and bruises as the result and had to retire for several days.   As the historian aptly remarks: 'No wonder that the Great Queen used her coach only when occasions of State demanded.'

(*Continued on p.* 600)

As the occupant of the throne of England is a woman and, moreover, a woman of strong personality, the costume of women is described first in this chapter.

QUEEN ELIZABETH'S WARDROBE, 1558–80

Queen Elizabeth was so fond of her clothes that she would never part with any of them, and it is said that at her death there were three thousand dresses and 'head-attires' in her wardrobe.   It is not possible to describe them all because a complete record of them is not extant.   The following chrono-logical accounts must therefore suffice; they are based on portraits, miniatures, engravings (many of which are from portraits now unknown), and con-temporary descriptions.

With regard to the portraits, reference should be made to the paragraph on p. 477.   In the case of portraits of Elizabeth which are definitely dated, no difficulty arises; but the others have necessitated much consideration of points such as the circumstances under which they were painted, some special reference in the painting, or some item about the costume or other details.   By such methods the author has been able in most cases to allocate the period within a space of about five years.

For the costumes worn by Elizabeth as Princess see Figs. 313 and 314.

STATE ROBES

For her progress through London to the Tower on 28th November 1558 it is recorded that Queen Elizabeth's robes were of purple velvet and ermine. They would consist of a close-fitting bodice, with sleeves and a skirt bordered with ermine shaped like Fig. 517, and over them a mantle cut on the oval

PLATE XXVII. QUEEN ELIZABETH IN CORONATION ROBES, 1559
Portrait by Gwillim Stretes
Warwick Castle. *By kind permission of the Earl of Warwick*

plan and lined with ermine, and a cape of the same fur.   Although the fact
is not mentioned, it is more than probable she wore a black velvet French
hood like that in Fig. 544.

The College of Arms possesses a very interesting book of pen and ink drawings made by one of the officials of the College who was an eyewitness of the
coronation procession on its way back from Westminster Abbey, 15th January
1559.   Death had overtaken the Archbishop of Canterbury, and Dr. Heath,
Archbishop of York, positively refused to crown Elizabeth as Supreme Head
of the Church.   Five Roman Catholic bishops declined for the same reason,
but Dr. Owen Oglethorpe, Bishop of Carlisle, was prevailed upon at the last
moment.   He wore his own mitre and borrowed more splendid vestments
than his own from Edmund Bonner, Bishop of London.   The ceremony was
almost the same as described for Queen Mary.

Part of this drawing is reproduced in Fig. 956, and shows the Queen borne
in her litter.   The drawing, crude though it is, accurately delineates the dress,
crown, and sceptre, but *without* the Royal mantle as described below.

Two gentlemen selected from the large number in attendance on the
Queen are shown in Figs. 609 and 610.

By kind permission of the Earl of Warwick the portrait of Queen Elizabeth
in coronation robes, said to be by Gwillim Stretes, is reproduced in Plate
XXVII.   The bodice, sleeves, and full skirt are of a golden yellow silk
ground, the Renaissance pattern being worked in dull silver and seed pearls.
The point of the stomacher is very long and outlined by a girdle of gold set
with rubies, sapphires, pearls, and diamonds.   A narrow band of ermine
edges the cuffs of the close sleeves, and there is, no doubt, a deep border of
the same fur surrounding the hem of the skirt.   A small goffered ruff edged
with gold, high at the back and narrow in front, encircles the face.   The
State mantle is very gorgeous.   It is of cloth of gold covered with embroidery
in coloured silks incorporating red roses, grey-green leaves, and *silver* fleurs-
de-lys and lined throughout with ermine; a deep collar or cape of the same
fur is attached at the throat by long cords and tassels of gold.   This cape is
a substitute for the official hood, the latter being dispensed with on account
of its bulk at the back of the neck; though it may be represented by a false
hood lying flat on the back (*see* p. 418).   The neck collar, shoulder collar or
carcanet, girdle, orb, sceptre, and very beautiful arched crown worn over her
flowing hair, are set with rubies, sapphires, pearls, and diamonds.

In nearly all illustrations of Elizabeth in State dress dating the first half of
her reign her hair is worn parted in the middle, slightly waved on the temples,
and flowing over the shoulders.

In an inventory of the Queen's wardrobe taken in 1600, her coronation
robes are stated to have consisted of a dress with a long train of gold tissue
lined with white sarcenet and bordered with ermine, and worn over the
Spanish farthingale.   The mantle was of cloth of gold tissued with gold and
silver, furred and powdered with ermine.   The veil of fine transparent silk
was interwoven with gold threads, and had cutwork superimposed upon it.

Fig. 574. QUEEN ELIZABETH IN STATE DRESS (*see* Plate XXVIII)

PLATE XXVIII. QUEEN ELIZABETH WITH GODDESSES, 1569: Painting by Hans Eworth
Hampton Court Palace.   *By gracious permission of H.M. the King*

The border was composed of small gold buttons and tassels at intervals. The foregoing description suggests that these coronation robes might be the same as those shown in Plate XXVII.

The parliamentary robes worn by Queen Elizabeth were of the same shape and colour as worn by previous sovereigns, and are entered in one of the Royal wardrobe accounts thus:

'Item, one mantle of crimson velvet, furred throughout with powdered ermines, the mantle lace [cord] of silk and gold, with buttons and tassels to the same.

'Item, one kirtle and surcote of the same crimson velvet, the train and skirts furred with powdered ermines, the rest lined with [white] sarcenet, with a Cap of Maintenance (see vol. ii, Fig. 390) to the same, striped down-right with passamayne lace of gold, with a tassel of gold to the same furred with powdered ermines' (see Plate XLIII).

The robes of estate were the same as the above in detail but in purple velvet.

The picture painted by Hans Eworth in 1569, now at Hampton Court (Plate XXVIII), represents Queen Elizabeth greeted by Juno, Minerva, and Venus with Cupid. It is, of course, allegorical, but the costumes worn by the Queen and her two ladies-in-waiting are of the fashion of the early years of her reign. The Queen is wearing full state dress, which is reproduced in Fig. 574. The whole costume is in black velvet, with a tight-fitting long pointed bodice edged at the waist-line with small tabs and cut square at the neck. The skirt, open up the front, is edged with gold embroidery and rubies in gold mounts, the surface of the skirt being cutte in a set pattern to show silver underneath. The under-bodice, with high collar and close-fitting sleeves, and the underdress are of silver tissue covered with gold embroidery and pearls. The surcote, with a long train and short puffed sleeves, is of black velvet having a pattern in gold all over it and a gold embroidered border. A close ruff and wristlets, a ruby and gold carcanet, and a jewelled girdle complete this rich and dignified dress. The Royal Crown is worn over hairdressing as seen in the portrait (Fig. 571), and the Sceptre and Orb are carried.

The ladies-in-waiting are dressed, one in black velvet and gold, the other in scarlet velvet, and both wear French hoods.

It is interesting to note the costumes of the Goddesses Juno and Minerva, as they are excellent examples of the Elizabethan idea of the classic Greek. The coiffure of Venus is noted under Headdresses (p. 737).

Many illustrations of Queen Elizabeth in robes of state are to be found attached to statutes and documents. In all of them these robes consist of a close-fitting long stomachered bodice with close-fitting sleeves on the fore-arm; a full skirt over the Spanish farthingale; and ermine-lined mantle fastened by long cords and tassels, and having an ermine cape which represents the official hood. A close ruff and a jewelled collar, the Crown, Sceptre and Orb, complete this Royal outfit.

ELISABETH DEI GRATIA REGINA ANGLIÆ.

Fig. 575. 1559. From engraving by Cock. (*By courtesy of the British Museum*)

PLATE XXIX. QUEEN ELIZABETH, 1560-70: *Portrait by an unknown artist*
Private collection

OTHER COSTUMES, FULL DRESS, AND EVERYDAY DRESS

In Fig. 575 we see the new Queen ready to receive some Ambassador in private audience. Her Majesty wears a surcote of a dark-coloured damask similar in shape to that in Figs. 516 and 521, and cut as shown in diagram, Fig. 522. This garment, known as a costume à l'Espagnole, is made to be worn closed over a dress for extra warmth. It is lined throughout with fur, ermine or miniver, of which edgings show round the collar, down the front (where it is fastened with laces and aiglettes), round the hem, slits on the breast, and openings and bottom of the very short mahoitered sleeves. A narrow gold passamayne edges the openings of the garment. A small band, or ruff, of lawn is mounted on the upstanding collar of the under-dress and encircles the face. A diagram of the cut of the bodice and skirt of the dress worn underneath the surcote is given in Fig. 518. A jewelled carcanet with pendant is worn, and the French hood completes the everyday costume. This surcote, of Spanish origin, was very popular with great ladies in England and on the Continent, and it appears in varying forms and methods of decoration in many portraits of the time. The French hood is referred to on p. 741.

The costume illustrated in Plate XXIX is derived from a three-quarter-length portrait formerly at Clopton House, Stratford-on-Avon, and said to be Queen Elizabeth. Whether it is the Queen or some other lady of the period—1560–70—is immaterial; the costume depicted is that which was worn at this time by noble ladies of the realm for everyday use, in fact, such as Her Majesty would wear on ordinary occasions both indoors and out. The surcote is of black velvet, open up the front and edged with a band of ermine. The long sleeves attached to it are slightly raised upon the shoulders—the mahoitered sleeve is now going out of fashion with smartly dressed women—trimmed vertically with narrow bands of ermine with aiglettes set at intervals. A similar band edges the opening at elbow level, and these cross the hanging part. The underdress, made like that shown in Fig. 517, is of black silk or satin; the lines of the bodice being defined by narrow gold passamayne which also edges the opening of the skirt and the hem. A gold-edged escallope surrounds the pointed waist-line. The cloth of gold underskirt edged with gold embroidery is worn over the Spanish farthingale, and a gold girdle, with pomander, hangs down the front. The ruff of lawn is edged with fine lines of gold, and a carcanet of rubies, pearls, and diamonds is worn *under* the surcote encircling the neck twice and terminating with a large pendant. The French hood is worn and brown leather gloves are carried.

Fig. 576 is a drawing of the Queen as she appeared when she visited Cambridge in 1564. She stayed the night of 4th August at the house of Mr. Worthington at Haslingfield. The next afternoon, accompanied by divers ladies and gentlemen and her Gentlemen Pensioners, she set out for Cambridge, passing through Grantchester and arriving at Newnham about five o'clock. Robert Lane, Mayor of Cambridge, supported by the aldermen

Fig. 576. QUEEN ELIZABETH AS SHE APPEARED WHEN ENTERING CAMBRIDGE,
SATURDAY, 5TH AUGUST 1564

and all the burgesses, with the recorder, Robert Shute (afterwards one of the barons of the exchequer), all on horseback, met Her Majesty, a little above Newnham. Here the Mayor, according to custom, delivered the mace to the Queen together with 'a fair standing cup,' and Her Majesty returned the mace to him.

When she came to Newnham Mills she dismounted in the yard, and retired for a space into the miller's house—to titivate, we presume. After a while she remounted her horse, and entered Cambridge by Newnham Bridge. The Queen stayed at King's College, the best chambers and galleries being devoted to her use.

The drawing of Elizabeth's riding costume (Fig. 576) worn on this occasion is founded on contemporary descriptions. It was of black velvet, pounced or cutte all over in a design, and worn over an underdress of white satin. The bodice and sleeves were braided with narrow gold. Her hair was rolled off the face, the knob being enclosed in a gold network caul set with precious stones and pearls, and over it the Queen wore a flat cap of black velvet—the bonet—with gold embroidery round the brim and crown: a white ostrich-tip drooped over the left side. A touch of colour was supplied by a sky-blue silk suspending the Lesser George in enamels set with diamonds. A 'riding-rod,' or whip, might be carried, but it was not necessary as a groom would be in attendance. If one was used by the Queen, the handle would be covered with crimson velvet and studded with jewels.

The rich horse furniture of the period was of vermilion velvet embroidered and embrossed with gold.

Queen Elizabeth is following the example set by Catherine de' Medici of riding side-saddle with a pommel, although on full State occasions it was customary for the Queen to use a plank or footboard as evidenced by her seal, 1586 (see Fig. 705). Elizabeth was, like her father, a good judge of horse-flesh and her mount was a thorough-bred Arab.

The next day being Sunday, the Queen went in great state to King's College Chapel. 'Then Mr. William, Master of King's College, orator, making his three curtesies, kneeled down upon the first greece [1] of the West door.' The Queen entered during the Litany under a canopy [2] carried over her head by four Doctors of Divinity, 'and going into her travys [3] . . . and marvellously revising at the beauty of the Chappel, greatly praised it above all other in her realme.' [4]

This same Sunday evening Her Majesty witnessed a play, the *Aulularia* of Plautus, acted by certain selected persons chosen out of the colleges. On Monday at nine o'clock the play *Dido*, written by Edward Halliwell, Fellow of King's College, was presented before the Queen. Thomas Preston,

---

[1] A step.
[2] According to custom . . . 'which the footmen as their fee claimed: and it was redeemed for £3-6-8.' This canopy may be the one in the possession of the Fitzwilliam Museum.
[3] Travys, the specially erected chair of state, with dais, and dorsal, probably similar to those shown in Fig. 292.
[4] Other actual words used by Queen Elizabeth were 'O domus antiqua et religiosa.'

later Fellow of King's College and afterwards Master of Trinity Hall, played so well in this tragedy, and 'did so genteely and gracefully disporte before her' that the Queen gave him a pension of £20 a year.   On Tuesday, the 8th, the play called *Ezechias* by Nicholas Udall was performed by the King's College.

Elizabeth left Cambridge for Ely on Wednesday, 9th August, two days earlier than was anticipated.   Frankly, Her Majesty was rather bored by the innumerable Greek and Latin orations made to her.   One delivered by Mr. Dodington, a Greek professor of Trinity College, occupied 'the space of a quarter of an hour, and was considered very short.'   However, on her departure she remarked to the university professors with all her usual charm and graciousness that, if a larger provision of beer and ale had been made, she would have stayed until Friday.   We are not told if the day was wet or fine. Queen Elizabeth was habitually indifferent to the weather.   'A most extreme rain' would not prevent her mounting her horse, or ordering her coach to be ready at the appointed time.

In September 1564 the Queen in order to impress Sir James Melville— that Franco-Scot with his courtly foreign graces—wore a different dress every day, one day English, another French, and a third Italian; and was delighted when he announced that the Italian style suited her best, as it showed off her golden hair to advantage wearing a caul and bonet 'as they do in Italy.'   At Christmas in the following year, spent at Westminster

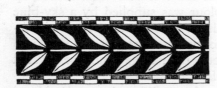

Fig. 577

Palace, Elizabeth was very richly apparelled in a gown of purple velvet, embroidered with silver very richly set with jewels.   She wore a carcanet of gold and many precious stones.

On 31st August 1566 Queen Elizabeth visited Oxford and stayed at Christ Church.   The preparations for the event were not so elaborate as at Cambridge, and the reception itself was far less imposing.   The Queen travelled 'in a rich chariot' to Wolvercote, and three miles on the Woodstock Road she was met by the heads of the houses in their gowns and hoods. The days of her stay were spent, as at Cambridge, in hearing orations and plays, or in attending the exercises of the university.

On 6th September after dinner Her Majesty mounted her horse and set out for Rycote.

A full-length portrait said to be of Queen Elizabeth is in the possession of the Earl of Buckinghamshire at Hampden House.   It has been attributed to Zuccaro, but it is more probable that Hans Eworth was the artist.   The features, especially the nose, are not those of Elizabeth; but the presence of the Royal armorial bearings, embroidered upon the dorsal, favour the likelihood of its being by Eworth's hand.   The costume dates 1565–73, and is similar in style to that shown in Fig. 579.   It is reproduced by kind permission of the Earl in Plate XXX.   The bodice, sleeves, and circular skirt,

PLATE XXX. QUEEN ELIZABETH, 1570
After a portrait attributed to Federigo Zuccaro.
Original at Hampden House. *By kind permission of the Earl of Buckinghamshire*

worn over the Spanish farthingale, are of deep rose velvet decorated with two bands of gold embroidery designed in two rows of leaves on a central stalk (*see* Fig. 577) having a heavy edging of gold passamayne top and bottom. The moderately mahoitered sleeves are decorated with bands of the same embroidery on a smaller scale, between which are puffs fixed with rubies in gold mounts; there are also puffs or cuttes set at an angle on the plain part of the sleeves between the groups of bands.   Short sleeves mahoitered on the shoulders are now giving place to slightly tapering sleeves still padded on the shoulders and pleated or gathered into the armholes.   The neck of the bodice is rounded upwards in front, and is filled in with a partlet of gauze banded with narrow gold and open at the throat; a stand-up collar supports a small gold-edged ruff.

A small detail to be noticed is that the skirt of velvet is woven or embroidered with small gold Greek crosses per saltire having tiny cuttes between them, whereas the bodice is of plain velvet embroidered.

A handsome jewelled carcanet is draped around the shoulders and suspends a square ruby and pendent pearl.   A mirror in a gold frame hangs at the end of the twisted pearl girdle.   The headdress consists of a front piece surrounded by two rows of pearls and a roll of rose and gold tissue, but there is no tube hanging therefrom.   An exotic flower is fastened on the left side.

In the original painting the background is very ornate, the dorsal and chair being covered with elaborate embroidery, but in Plate XXX both are shown in purple velvet.

It should be noticed that the Queen grasps the knob of the chair and her forearm rests on a cushion *placed over the arms*.   This is a little unusual, for the method of posing the arm in this manner was not adopted by painters until a later period and is referred to under Fig. 731.

The library at Lambeth Palace possesses a book of *Christian Prayers* printed in London in 1569.   In it is a miniature of Queen Elizabeth at prayer, and she wears a dress almost identical with that shown in Plate XXX.   It is of crimson velvet, the bodice and sleeves being decorated in the same manner; but the skirt is divided, by bands of gold embroidery or passamayne in which are set rubies, emeralds, and pearls, into tapering panels of gold scroll work upon crimson velvet.

A painted panel was discovered at Little Gaddesden House, Hertfordshire, depicting Lord William Howard and other gentlemen about to arrest the Princess Elizabeth at Ashridge House for suspected implication in Wyatt's rebellion, 1554.   Elizabeth's costume (Fig. 578), and those of the gentlemen, date about 1570, a positive proof that the panel was painted at this date or even later.   The dress in Fig. 578 is simple in shape.   It consists of a tight short-waisted bodice open and turned back at the throat forming revers and lined with a contasting colour: close-fitting sleeves raised on the shoulders: and a semicircular skirt worn over the Spanish farthingale.   It is made of a red material having two lines of narrow fancy braid which form horizontal stripes.   A zigzag border of braid surrounds the skirt and descends the sides of the open front.   The underskirt of white is elaborately ornamented with rows of braid and embroidered motifs on alternate bands.   A small ruff attached to the top of the high collar of the under-garment closely encircles the face.   The hat is either of black velvet or blocked felt, and is of a new shape modelled on the lines of those worn by gentlemen at this time.   This type of costume was worn by the Queen, noble ladies, and gentlewomen as a smart out-of-door everyday dress, and, so it appears, when mounted.

In George Turbervile's *The Noble Arte of Venerie*, published in 1575, there are woodcuts of Queen Elizabeth wearing a very similar dress.   The only differences are that the bodice, rounded at the top, shows the partlet and close ruff; and that the sleeves are open up the front and tied in three places.   Although she has been riding to the hunt, her all-round skirt is distended by the Spanish farthingale.   The high hat with ostrich feathers is shown in Fig. 873.

Fig. 578. Queen Elizabeth, 1570

Other illustrations in the same work show the Queen hawking and mounted, and also on foot; in each case she wears a dress almost identical in shape, but not decoration, with the portrait, No. 190, in the National Portrait Gallery (*see* Plate XXXI B).

The 'Darnley' three-quarter-length portrait of Queen Elizabeth (Plate XXXI A), now in the National Portrait Gallery, No. 2082, has been dated at 1570.   The name of the artist is uncertain.   The dress worn by the Queen consists of a close-fitting bodice with a normal waist-line edged with small tabs.   The neck is high with a stand-up collar to which the ruff, a little larger than hitherto, is fixed goffered into deep nebulée sets.   The sleeves are leg-of-mutton shape, with a small roll and puffs on the shoulders.   The same decoration is placed on the lower part of the sleeves about four inches from the wrists, and suggests cuffs.   The full all-round skirt is worn over the Spanish farthingale.   The whole dress is composed of white silk brocaded in a floral scroll design in gold.   The front of the bodice is frogged with gold passamayne intermixed with rose-coloured floss silk which is fluffed at the extremities forming tiny tassels.   Pearls and rubies set in gold encircle the waist, but there is no pendant end.   On the right side a jewel, set in a very beautiful mount composed of six human figures and scroll work in gold, is suspended by a black ferret from the waist-belt.   Two rows of pearls hang round the neck and are looped to form a circle on the right side.   A fan of

A

B

C

D

PLATE XXXI. QUEEN ELIZABETH

A. The 'Darnley,' 1570.   B. and C. *c.* 1575: Portraits by unknown artists
National Portrait Gallery.   *By kind permission of the Directors*

D. The 'Pelican,' 1575: Portrait by an unknown artist
By kind permission of E. Peter Jones, Esq.

natural-tinted ostrich tips set in a gold mount and handle is carried in the right hand. The headdress is a network cap of jewels and pearls set at the back of the head like the ridge on the French hood: a gauze veil arranged behind as shown in Fig. 579 hangs from it.

Fig. 579 gives the outline of the garments worn by Queen Elizabeth between the years 1570 and 1580. It is photographed from a crayon drawing made in London by Zuccaro in 1575. This dress is shaped on the same lines as that shown in the 'Darnley' portrait, in fact, in a whole series of portraits, obviously painted about this time because the lines of the dress and headdress are very similar in all of them. There are very slight differences, such as the method of filling in the neck and the decorative treatment of the whole costume, but in general style all these dresses are identical. Other examples may be seen in Plate XXX, the Lambeth Palace Prayer Book, Nos. 190 and 200 in the National Portrait Gallery (Plate XXXI B and C), one of Turbervile's woodcuts, and the 'Pelican' and 'Portland' portraits. In Fig. 579 the bodice is short-waisted and the sleeves fit moderately close and are raised on the shoulders. The skirt is worn over the Spanish farthingale. The headdress shown is of special interest because a back view of it is also drawn. It is an embroidered veil, and the edge goffered where it is attached to the head. At the back the lines of the goffering suggest an escallop shell; in front a series of loops or 8's surrounds the head behind a cap or band of jewels like a coronet.

To this period—1575—must be assigned the two head-and-shoulder portraits of Queen Elizabeth in the National Portrait Gallery, London, just referred to. In the former Elizabeth wears a dress of the same shape as that shown in Fig. 579, carried out in black velvet elaborately embroidered with a leaf design in gold, cross-barred, and set with pearls. The sleeves, however, are in the older fashion as seen in Plate XXX. The skirt is open up the front showing a white satin underskirt worn over the Spanish farthingale. The Queen holds a red rose in her right hand and a white feather fan in her left.

In the second portrait, No. 200 (Plate XXXI C), the Queen wears a dress of white satin decorated with bands of gold embroidery with cuttes outlined with gold, and jewels in gold mounts between them. The sleeves are not so much raised on the shoulders and are finished round the armholes with cutte rolls. A bunch of pansies, Elizabeth's favourite flower, is held in the right hand. The Lesser George is suspended by a black riband surrounding the neck. The ruffs and headdresses in both portraits are similar to those described under Fig. 579.

In the 'Pelican' portrait (Plate XXX D) dating the same period Elizabeth is wearing a similar shaped dress in deep red velvet. The rolls over the shoulders are very pronounced, and the sleeves and partlet are embroidered with Spanish work. Two red roses are tucked into the side of the bodice, and the whole dress is much bejewelled. The pelican in enamels worn as a pendant has given its name to the portrait.

There is a drawing in the British Museum of a procession of the Knights

Fig. 579. ZUCCARO'S DRAWING OF QUEEN ELIZABETH, 1575
(*By courtesy of the British Museum*)

of the Garter, dated 1576, in which the Queen is the principal figure. As Sovereign of the Order, she wears the crimson velvet surcote over her farthingaled dress. The mantle is, according to this drawing, of white, which contradicts a former statement made in vol. ii, p. 241, to the effect that the mantle was of purple velvet. The Collar of the Order encircles the shoulders rather low down, and the hood is omitted. Neither does the Queen wear the headdress, which at this time was nothing more than a gentleman's fashionable hat (*see* Fig. 623); this remained the official headgear of the Order during the course of the sixteenth century.[1]

In place of a hat the Queen is wearing a veil arranged as described under Fig. 579. Other innovations are the large ostrich fan carried in the hand, and the omission of the hood, sword, and garter. It is curious that Elizabeth, so punctilious with regard to official ceremony and tradition, should not have dressed the part correctly. Later queens have, however, been guilty of the same offence.

The portrait in the Accademia delle Belle Arti, Siena, by Cornelius Ketel was painted in 1578 (Plate XXXII A). The dress is made on similar lines to that shown in the 'Darnley' portrait, but is of black velvet. The Queen holds a colander in her left hand and as in the 'Portland' portrait a group of courtiers is seen standing in the background; one of these is Sir Christopher Hatton.

A three-quarter portrait dating about 1579 or 1580 finds its place here. It is No. 2471 in the National Portrait Gallery, bequeathed by Sir Aston Webb (Plate XXXII B). There are other portraits very similar; one in the National Maritime Museum, another at Arbury Park. They all show the Queen in everyday dress, consisting of black velvet with a band of gold embroidery set with jewels in gold mounts down the front. In the Arbury portrait the girdle of pearls and jewels is very rich. The full sleeves in all three are of white linen heavily embroidered with black silk; a detailed drawing of the Arbury sleeve is given in Fig. 686. The circular ruff edged with cutwork is *supported* by a wide circular collar of black velvet. The veil, put on the head as described under Fig. 579, is very voluminous and is decorated with bands of cutwork. A fan of ostrich feathers in a rigid jewelled handle is seen in both the Arbury and the National Portrait Gallery portraits, though there are slight differences in the decoration. In the Maritime she holds a sceptre.

The full-length portrait of Queen Elizabeth painted by Gheeraerts and owned by the Duke of Portland was exhibited at the Queen Elizabeth Exhibition, 1933 (Plate XXXII C). On the modern label was the date 1580. The dress in this portrait is shaped like that shown in Fig. 579; it has rolls, set with jewels round the armholes of the sleeves, but at the waist there are no tabs and the dress appears to be fastened down the front of the bodice and skirt with frogs of gold set with jewels. The material of which this

---

[1] In the seventeenth century it became more elaborate, with a higher crown of black velvet pleated into the brim and surmounted by numerous white ostrich plumes, exactly like that worn by Queen Elizabeth for riding (*see* Fig. 623).

dress is made is rich white silk embroidered in colours and gold, with groups of flowers and leaves on stalks diaper-wise with a conventional design in gold. A very fine carcanet of jewels with a pendant surrounds the shoulders, and a double row of pearls is draped round the neck in the same manner as shown in the 'Darnley' portrait; except that it hangs towards the left, and a pendent jewel hangs from the waist on the right. The large circular ruff is of starched lawn edged with deep cutwork. A voluminous green mantle, bordered and covered with gold embroidery and lined with white silk, hangs from the shoulders, but without a cord fastening. The headdress is elaborate; it is in the form of a French hood and covered in pearls, surmounted by an upstanding coronet of goldsmith's work, jewels, and pearls. A fan hangs from the girdle on the left side, while gloves are carried in the left hand, a branch of myrtle in the right. The Sword of State lies at her feet accompanied by a small dog of the spaniel breed. Three courtiers stand in the background.

Fig. 580

FURNITURE

The surroundings of a great personage always excite the interest of the public, and the beauty and lavishness of Queen Elizabeth's homes—Windsor, Whitehall, Greenwich, Hampton Court, etc.—were household words all over Europe. Foreigners who visited Elizabeth's Court were greatly impressed by the magnificence they beheld, and many have, fortunately, written detailed descriptions.

'I have seen,' says a German, writing home in 1559, 'several very fine summer residences that belong to her, in two of which I have been myself, and I may say that there are none in the world so richly garnished with costly furniture of silk adorned with gold, pearls, and precious stones. Then she has some twenty other houses, all of which might justly be called Royal summer residences.'

As this description was written in the first year of her reign it is clear that she inherited these numerous palaces from her father with the Crown.

The following details are taken from other written descriptions:

At Windsor the Royal apartments consisted of magnificent halls, chambers, bedchambers, and bathrooms. The banqueting hall was said to be seventy-eight yards long by thirty yards wide. The bedchambers contained the four-

A

B

C

D

PLATE XXXII. QUEEN ELIZABETH

A. The 'Siena,' 1578: Portrait by Cornelius Ketel
Accademia delle Belle Arti, Siena. *By kind permission of the Director*
B. 1579–80: Portrait by an unknown artist.   National Portrait Gallery
By kind permission of the Directors
C. The 'Portland,' 1580: Portrait by Marcus Gheeraerts
Welbeck Abbey. *By kind permission of the Duke of Portland*
D. The 'Ermine,' 1585: Portrait by Nicholas Hilliard
Hatfield House. *By kind permission of the Marquess of Salisbury*

post beds used by Henry VII, Henry VIII, and Edward VI, all of them eleven feet square, with hangings of silks glistening with gold and silver.

Elizabeth's own bedchamber was hung with tapestry taken from a palace of the French King during the English occupation early in the fifteenth century. The bed, not so gigantic as that of her forbears, had curious coverings of embroidery, and the cushions were 'curiously wrought' by Elizabeth's own hands. A table of red and white marble occupied an important position. Two bathrooms were close at hand, so there is no reason why the glorious 'Gloriana' should be accused of having a bath *only* when her physician commanded it. These had the walls and ceiling covered with looking-glass.

Fig. 581. Draw-table

Bathrooms leading out of bedrooms began to be built in all the best houses towards the end of the sixteenth century. One for the Countess of Northumberland cost the Earl £400. He protested, and gave vent to his opinion that a bathroom 'this 15 yeare before was never miste nor wanting.'

Queen Elizabeth caused the Terrace Walk to be made on the north side of the castle, from which there was a pleasant view of the surrounding country. It was her favourite promenade.

Furniture in general consisted of draw-tables which had portions to draw out at both ends, with bulbous legs joined at the base by a foot-rail; also tables of other kinds.

The Court cupboard was also important; and coffers, as before mentioned, were common. 'Chests with drawers,' just coming into use, were composite pieces of furniture, the top being a coffer with a hinged lid as of old; the lower portion contained two or more drawers.

Seats comprised square oak chairs, with solid backs and arm-rests, on which cushions were placed, besides types of chair already described under Fig. 215, chairs of the later style as shown in Figs. 674 and 731, and innumerable

Fig. 582. Oak Chair

stools such as that shown in Fig. 756. All these seats would be upholdered in velvet, silk, damask, or embroidery. The decoration of the wood-work consisted of elaborate carving of polished oak, and towards the end of the century marquetry was first introduced. Often the carved oak was painted with the patterns picked out in colours, the more raised motifs being gilded.

The following are some items from an inventory of furniture dated 1590.

> 'Bed steads of walnuttre and Markatre
> Chares of walnuttre and Markatre
> Stools of walnuttre and Markatre
> Fourmes of walnuttre
> Tables of walnuttre and Markatre
> Tables of marble
> Stooles of nedlewoorke cruell.'

With what joy one would have attended a sale of furniture in Tudor times when items fetched such convenient prices for small purses:

'Item two damask chaires iii low stooles of damask & two long quishions of damask priced and valued 1ˢ.'

'Item two long drawinge tables of Walnottree one folding table of wainscott and a little table of wainscott price vˡⁱ.'

'Item two fyne merketree cupbords & two liverey cupbords price xiiiˡⁱ.'

'Item 6 wallnottree formes & 24 stooles of wallnottree price Lˢ.'

'Item 6 walnottree chaires price xxxˢ.'

'Item three other pictures vidzᵗ Quene Maries. Queene Elizabeths & Constantynes the Great. price xˢ.'

The floors of rooms in palaces, where a great deal of company was admitted, were strewn with rushes or hay, a method which continued until the end of the reign. Even in the Presence Chambers this was done. 'Only where the Queen was to come out and up to her seat were carpets laid down worked in Turkish knot.' Towards the end of the century, however, carpets were more generally used in the private apartments of Royalty and the nobility.

In the palace of Whitehall the Presence Chamber was a large lofty room with a gilded ceiling on which were painted important battle scenes. A very beautiful fireplace adorned the Council Chamber; on this the Royal Arms, supported by two lions, were cut in the stone 'as clear as crystal.'

Among the many paintings which hung upon the walls of the numerous rooms were portraits of Henry VI, Richard III, Edward IV, the Emperor Charles V, the Duke of Saxony, Katherine of Aragon, Philip of Spain—and of Zwingli and many other divines. Two of special interest were the portrait of Elizabeth at the age of sixteen, now at Windsor (a drawing of it is given in Fig. 313), and in the corridor overlooking the tilt yard 'a picture of King Edward VI, representing at first sight something quite deformed till, by looking through a small hole in the cover which is put over it, you see it in its true proportions.' This painting now hangs in the National Portrait Gallery, No. 1299.

Along the walls of the corridor leading to the River Gate were hung the armorial shields with mottoes of those knights who solicited Her Majesty's permission to take part in the tournaments. If the Queen accorded permission, the bearers of these shields presented them to her, and they made a very imposing array.

The ceiling of the Queen's bedchamber was entirely gilded, but the room had only one window. The Royal bed was ingeniously composed of woods of different colours. One sometimes sees in national museums these Tudor beds with the cornice, back, posts, etc., elaborately inlaid with all kinds of woods. The coverlids or quilts were of silk, velvet, gold, silver, and embroidery.

Elizabeth kept all her jewellery and other things of special value and sentiment in a little chest ornamented all over with pearls, and her writing table consisted of two pedestal cabinets of exquisite silversmith's work. Another was of ebony inlaid with silver, and had two boxes of silver—one for ink and the other for dust or sand. The writing board lifted up and formed the lid of a receptacle for papers, etc., and had a mirror set inside it.

In this room was 'a piece of clockwork, an Ethiop riding upon a rhinoceros, with four attendants, who all make their obeisance when it strikes the hour.'

The palace at Greenwich dates back to the reign of Edward I, and successive kings resided there occasionally until Henry V granted the manor to Thomas Beaufort, Duke of Exeter, and later to Humphrey, Duke of Gloucester. This Duke rebuilt the palace and called it 'Placentia' or a 'Manor of Pleasaunce.' He enclosed the park and erected within it a tower on the spot where the Observatory now stands, and at his death the domain reverted to the Crown. Edward IV bestowed much cost in finishing and enlarging the palace, and granted it to his Queen Elizabeth Wydeville for life. Henry VII often resided at this place, and beautified the palace by the addition of a brick front toward the water-side; Henry VIII spent much money to make Greenwich 'a pleasant, perfect, and princely palace.' During his reign it became one of the principal scenes of those festivities for which his Court was celebrated. Here Edward VI died, and Mary and Elizabeth were born, the latter spending a great deal of her time at her favourite summer residence.

In the palace we learn that the Presence Chamber overlooked the river, and here was set the usual Chair of Estate on a dais under a canopy with plumes at the corners, 'where the Queen sits in her magnificence.' It also contained a positive organ.

Most of the rooms at Greenwich were hung with tapestries wrought in gold and silver (see p. 474).

The Chapel Royal was hung with cloth of gold; the font of silver was raised three steps high, and the pulpit was covered with gold-embroidered red velvet. Almost half of the chapel was taken up by a large high altar of gold; and there, divided off from the rest, was a recess entirely of cloth of gold out of which the Queen came when she was about to receive the Sacrament.

In 1598 we get some details of Hampton Court from Paul Hentzner, a German, who, unfortunately, is not quite correct in some of his descriptions.

He writes: 'We were led into two chambers, called the Presence, or Chamber of Audience, which shone with tapestry of gold, and silver, and silk of different colours, and a small chapel, richly hung with tapestry, where the Queen performs her devotions.' The windows are said to have been glazed with crystal.

In the Great Hall hung many portraits, those of Henry VIII, Edward VI, Charles V, Philip II, and Mary Queen of Scots, and a painting of the Battle of Pavia, being the most conspicuous. Several musical instruments were noticed, made entirely of glass except the strings, and a great number of cushions were lying about all elaborately embroidered with gold and silver.

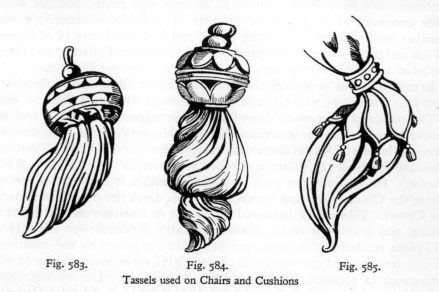

Fig. 583.   Fig. 584.   Fig. 585.
Tassels used on Chairs and Cushions

'All the other rooms, being very numerous, were adorned with tapestries of gold, silver, and velvet'—in short, the whole palace shone with precious metal.

In the Royal Chamber the bed 'costers' or hangings, the 'sparver' (top of tester), and the 'stranets' or curtains were of very costly silk; and in another chamber, not far distant, was a bed the tester of which was embroidered by Anne Boleyn and presented by her to Henry VIII. Even the warming-pan was of gold garnished with small diamonds and rubies, with two ragged pearl pendants.

Many of the counterpoynts and coverlids were of rich silk or velvet, and lined with ermine.

Nonesuch Palace, a wonderful fairylike place according to contemporary prints, was begun by Henry VIII near Cheam, Surrey, but he did not live to see it finished. Queen Mary sold it to the fourteenth Earl of Arundel, and Queen Elizabeth bought it back from the then possessor, Lord Lumley.

In an inventory made at this time is set forth a wealth of magnificent furniture of English and foreign manufacture, including some special beds. The 'counter-poynte' of one was of velvet, embroidered with two horses and a man riding upon one of them.   Another had a 'cieler' on top of the four posts, and 'tester' (back) of white Turkey silk, a counterpane of white sarcenet, the whole embroidered with popinjays.   Another bed was hung with purple Nimeguen [1] silk embroidered with dolphins.   The tapestries enumerated in this inventory were very numerous and of great beauty.

In this same inventory there is mention of chairs being upholdered in purple velvet fringed with purple silk; of cloth of gold having a raised pattern of crimson velvet; and some with a pattern in black velvet.   One set was covered in cloth of gold with a pattern of wreaths and flowers in cloth of silver and crimson velvet.

So vast a concourse accompanied Elizabeth on the elaborate progresses which to the end of her life she insisted on making that even the long cavalcade of coaches, chariots, and waggons was sometimes insufficient.   Such progresses entailed the conveyance of the whole Court and officers of the household and all their servants, and, in addition, a large staff of menials to minister to their wants.   The Queen's wardrobe of personal necessities alone sometimes occupied as many as three hundred baggage waggons, and on one occasion, when she was visiting 'The Vine,' near Basingstoke, in September 1601, not only was much furniture brought from Hampton Court, but 'the willing and obedient people of the County of Southampton' brought, at two days' warning, seven score beds and the furniture (i.e. bedding) thereof —so great was their love for the Queen.

Those who wish to know more about domestic matters will find a great deal of useful information in *Elizabethan Life in Town and Country*, by M. St. Clare Byrne.

NOBILITY—WOMEN: 1558–80

Having reviewed the current fashions as exemplified in the descriptions of Queen Elizabeth's costumes, an explanation of the details and other items is necessary.

The Farthingale (*continued from p. 199*)

The farthingale as first described in Chapter II, p. 65, continued to be worn during the periods covered by Chapter III and this section of Chapter IV.

---

[1] The name of the town in Guelderland, Flanders, where this silk was made.

As worn by French Royal ladies and the nobility its circumference at the hem was often abnormal as seen in Fig. 525. Queen Elizabeth varied the size of her farthingale according to circumstances, as evinced in her costumes illustrated in this section; and ladies of fashion followed her example.

(Continued on p. 618)

THE CORSET (continued from p. 223)

The type of corset worn by fashionable women during this period was the same as described on p. 222, and shown in Figs. 242 and 261.

(Continued on p. 622)

THE RUFF OR BAND

In Chapter II it has been pointed out that cutwork or lace edging decorated the neckbands of gentlemen's shirts. Next, a small frill appeared on the top of the neckband, as noted on p. 167; and by the time of Edward VI this neck frill had developed into a small ruff. The process of development can be traced in the illustrations throughout Chapter III.

The ladies of Edward VI and Mary's reigns adopted this frill to finish off the collars of their partlets. It became more pronounced during the early years of this reign and was worn by both sexes. It was but a mere frill about an inch to an inch and a half wide, and became what we know as the 'ruff'; but the more correct name is the 'band,' so called because it was made as a *band* or long strip of linen or lawn, varying in width according to the period of its development; its length might be anything from one and a half to six yards. It was hemmed on both edges, one edge being ornamented with stitchery, gold-thread, or cutwork. A string was inserted in the other edge, by means of which it was all drawn up tight into many folds. This string was also used to tie it round the neck, and its tasselled ends hung down in front.

Fig. 862 illustrates this method of forming a small ruff. On the lady's neck, left, the ruff is seen correctly set, the inside edges being tacked to the top of the high collar of the bodice. On the right side, the ruff is purposely left unattached to the corner of the collar, which is turned down: and the band is shown drawn out along part of the length of the band string. At first these bands were narrow, as it was not possible to stiffen them: but the introduction of starch paved the way for astounding changes.

Starch, called by the Puritans 'the Devil's liquor,' was known and manufactured in Flanders; but the practice of clear-starching did not reach England until 1560. In this year William Boonen, a Dutchman, was appointed as Queen Elizabeth's coachman, and his wife monopolized in England the knowledge of clear-starching. The Queen availed herself of Mistress Boonen's services until 1564, when a rival artist appeared upon the scene in the person of one Mistress Dingham van der Plasse, a Fleming. This lady became a professional starcher of ruffs and cuffs—a service for which she charged high prices. The flutes of the goffering were called the 'set,' generally nebulée, and to accomplish them the laundresses used setting-sticks of wood, later of bone, which were heated and then thrust into the folds of the linen or lawn. This somewhat primitive method could only produce ruffs of a minimum size, but in 1573 'began the making of steel poking-sticks,' and with the use of these implements work was made easier and the result more satisfactory.

Cuffs at the wrist usually matched the ruff and a 'suit of ruffs' means a ruff and a pair of cuffs.

(*Continued on p. 623*)

THE VEIL

The first appearance in England during the sixteenth century of gauze drapery hanging from the back and fixed to the headdress is seen in the 'Darnley' portrait of Queen Elizabeth, 1570. This veil is of plain transparent material. In Zuccaro's drawing, 1575 (Fig. 579), the gauze is patterned all over with needlework, *not* lace, and the edge is goffered over the top of the head. The veil now becomes a more important item of costume and, according to the drawing, is worn enveloping the sides of the figure as well as the back.

In the National Portrait Gallery, No. 190 (Plate XXXI B), the veil is again of transparent gauze with smaller yet higher gofferings around the head; but it is more elaborate in No. 200 (Plate XXXI C) in the same gallery. It is composed of black net or gauze, cross-barred with narrow black velvet having large pearls at the intersections and at the apex of each goffering. This veil is somewhat similar to one described in a Royal wardrobe account: 'One vale of blacke networke, florished with Venice silver like flagon worke, and embrodered all over with roses of Venice gold, silver, and silk, of colours of silk-woman's worke.'

The 'Siena' portrait, 1578, shows the veil arranged in a different way, as described under Fig. 721, Section II.

(*Continued on p. 626*)

THE FAN (*continued from p. 224*)

The Italian banner-shaped fan continued in general use during the remainder of the sixteenth century, but chiefly among the women of Italy and especially the ladies of Venice. They were sarcastically termed 'fly whisks' by Westerners.

A beautiful Italian feather fan is shown in Fig. 586, composed of five straight and uncurled ostrich feathers rising from a group of curled tips, with a rigid handle of ivory and gold. Such a fan formed the model of those used by the great ladies of Europe during the second half of the sixteenth century, and in England throughout Queen Elizabeth's reign.

On the Queen's accession, she artlessly let it be known that the most acceptable gift that she could receive from her subjects was a fan—although she did
not decline presents of other kinds.   The City Fathers did not need a second
hint: on every New Year's Day they brought their Royal mistress, with becoming humility, a rich and beautiful fan.   In such gifts they wisely did not
stint themselves.

In many portraits of the Queen she is seen holding a feather fan in her hand,

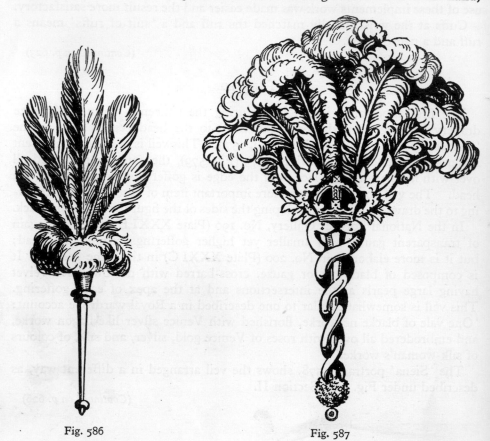

Fig. 586   Fig. 587

attached by a narrow ferret or riband to the girdle at her waist.   Her wardrobe
contained many such fans, and a few are described below.   A fan belonging
to the Queen in 1577 was of 'flowers of sylke of sundry colours, the handill
of an inbrawdry worke set with small sede perle.'   A fan presented to Her
Majesty for a ''Newyers-tyde' gift had the handle studded with diamonds.
'A fanne of white feathers, with a handle of gold, having two snakes wyndinge
about it, garnished with a ball of diamonds at the ende, and a crowne on each
side within a paire of wings garnished with diamonds' was in the Queen's
possession in 1600.   This description has inspired Fig. 587.

'One fanne of feathers of divers colours, the handle of golde, with a bare and a ragged staffe on both sides [obviously a gift from some member of the Dudley family] and a looking glasse on thone side' proves that, contrary to report, Elizabeth actually *carried* a mirror.

Another example had 'one handle of golde enameled, set with small rubies and emerodes, with a Shipp under saile on thone side.'

In the inventory of her wardrobe made in 1603, no fewer than thirty-one beautiful fans of great worth are enumerated. Some of these were of feathers and others of the new folding type. As much as £40 was sometimes given for a fan in Elizabeth's time.   (*Continued on* p. 628)

Fig. 588. Embroidery on Cushion of the Period

Elizabeth set the standard in her realm of a thoroughly well-dressed woman, so that it was natural for the ladies of the Court and other ladies of quality to follow her lead. A general similarity therefore exists between the wardrobes of these ladies and those of their Royal mistress. Thus the noble lady in Fig. 589 is wearing a costume which, although fashionable under Henry VIII and Mary, continued to be popular during the first half of Elizabeth's reign, especially with the more sedate women of the aristocracy. It should be noticed that the turned-back sleeves no longer assume the angular effect which was so modish in Henry VIII's time. The partlet of fine lawn entirely covers the shoulders and is high round the throat, finishing in a small ruff. Also the overskirt is divided down the front and folded back on itself, being held by laces sewn to the skirt beneath the folded portions; the tagged ends pass through holes in the latter, and tie in bows of one loop and two ends.

Fig. 589. A Noble Lady, 1560
(Lady Maud Vernon, Bakewell)

The back view of the lady (Fig. 590) explains three important features of sixteenth-century costume: first the effect produced by the wide turned-back sleeves in vogue for many years, and first seen in Plate XVI; secondly, the definite English mode of the Spanish farthingale worn under a *trained* skirt, with the bulk of the material arranged at the back; and thirdly the regulation tube hanging at the back of the French hood.

The dress just described will serve as a type of those worn by the ladies of the Court on most occasions during the earlier part of Elizabeth's reign; and William Harrison, with his usual disarming frankness, has much to say about the occupations of these same ladies when not in attendance. Thus: 'Ancient ladies of the Court do shun and avoid idleness, some of them exercising their fingers with the needle, others in caulwork, divers in spinning of silk, some in continual reading either of the Holy Scriptures, or histories of our own or foreign nations about us, and divers in writing volumes of their own, or translating of other mens into our English and Latin tongues.' Again: 'Many of the eldest sort also are skilful in surgery and distillation of waters, besides sundry other artificial practises pertaining to the ornature and commendations of their bodies.' The 'younger sort,' however, engaged in mere amusement instead of such useful employment: who 'in the mean time apply their lutes, citharnes, pricksong, and all kind of music; which they use only for re-creation sake, when they have leisure, and are free from attendance upon the Queen's Majesty, or such as they belong unto.'

Fig. 590. La Mode, 1550–80

The beauty of Englishwomen always attracted the admiration of foreign visitors. Such a one was Herr Johann Jacob Breuning von Buchenbach, who spent some time in England between 1592 and 1595. 'At no other Court,' he writes—and he had been at many, including the Imperial, 'have I ever seen so much splendour and such fine clothes. This holds good both of the men and of the Countesses and other Noble Ladies, who were of rare surpassing beauty and for the main part in Italian costume with breasts bared. In their hands they held large black plumes or other fans wherewith to cool themselves.'

Fig. 591. Gold embroidered Border

The Spanish surcote, fashionable during the first twenty years of this reign, is shown in Fig. 592. The only differences from those already illustrated are the sleeves and the treatment of the back: this is cut wide enough across the shoulders to form pleats from twelve to fifteen inches long. It has buttons and loops of fine cord part of the way down the front, and the collar is high and upstanding at the back. The sleeves, cut on the leg of mutton plan, hang behind the arm, but they could be worn over the arm since buttons and loops are provided for that purpose.

A similar garment (an original one) was shown at the Elizabethan Exhibition of 1933. It is made of deep claret-coloured velvet decorated down the open fronts, round the hem, up the side-seams, and on the shoulder rolls with a design worked with very small white opaque beads. Fig 593 gives two of the chief motifs of the design, which measures four inches from the lowest line to the highest point. The buttons (Fig. 594) are of claret velvet mounted on metal shanks, bound with fine white silk and studded with white beads.

Fig. 592. The Spanish Surcote

The dimensions of this surcote are of interest. The two fronts are forty-four inches each at the hem; at the back the hem is eighty inches; the fronts are

Fig. 593. Pattern in Beadwork

fifty-four, and the centre back fifty-eight inches long. It is made up of twenty-one-inch velvet, all the widths being joined with a straight seam—

III ²—K

selvage to selvage. The leg-of-mutton-shaped hanging sleeves are twenty-nine inches at the front seam and thirty-two at the back; they widen from ten round the wrist to eighteen at elbow level; the shoulder rolls are formed of loops.

The garment in the condition when examined had no lining; this originally must have been of silk in the same or contrasting colour.

Fig. 594. Button

The effigy in Hereford Cathedral, to the memory of the wife of Sir Richard Denton, who died in 1566 at the age of eighteen, is excellent study for the costume worn by the provincial aristocracy in the early years of this reign (*see* Fig. 595). The dress with bodice and skirt, which appear to be cut all in one, is of black velvet: the high collar and mahoitered sleeves with long hanging panels behind are banded with gold passamayne. The skirt is short in front, an arrangement sometimes seen in illustrations of this period, and falls over an underskirt of vermilion silk mounted on the farthingale. The tight sleeves are of the same material, having gold embroidery down both seams. White lawn is used for the partlet with high collar, and for the small ruffs and cuffs. The carcanet and girdle are gold chains; and the pendent waist ornament and pomander are in goldsmith's work. This effigy affords a good side view of the French hood, which is referred to on p. 743. A cloak of crimson with a high collar spreads its ample folds over the altar tomb upon which Lady Denton rests.

Fig. 595. Lady Denton, 1566

MARGARET DOUGLAS

Countess of Lennox, 1515–78

The everyday outdoor dress of a great lady of the 1560's is depicted in Fig. 596. It is taken from a three-quarter portrait of Margaret Douglas, Countess of Lennox (born 1515), daughter of Margaret Tudor, Queen-Dowager of Scotland, and her second husband, Archibald Douglas, Earl of Angus. She married in 1544 Matthew Stewart, fourth Earl of Lennox,

Regent of Scotland, and was the mother of Henry Stewart Lord Darnley, and Charles Stewart. Although of Scottish nationality this lady spent a great deal of time at the English Court. The historian, Camden, has some-something interesting to say about her. 'She was,' he says, 'a matron of singular piety, patience, and modesty; who was thrice cast into the Tower (as I have heard her say herself) not for any crime of treason, but for love matters; first, when Thomas Howard, son of Thos. Howard the first Duke of Norfolk of that name, falling in love with her, died in the Tower of London [1536]; then for the love of Henry, Lord Darnley, her son to Mary Queen of Scots; and lastly for the love of Charles, her younger son, to Elizabeth Cavendish, mother of the Lady Arabella.'

Lady Lennox's costume is representative of the fashion worn at this time.

Fig. 596. The Countess of Lennox, 1560

The velvet gown is woven or embroidered with a gold spot (compare with Plate XXX), and is made in the prevailing style of close-fitting bodice, with rolls on the shoulders and moderately full sleeves of mottled cloth of gold. The high collar supports a small ruff, and the skirt opens over an underskirt which matches the sleeves, mounted over the Spanish farthingale. The Countess wears a hat over a network caul (compare with Figs. 576 and 597), and carries a beautiful fan of the usual design, and a large lawn handkerchief with a deep border of lace and insertion in reticella.

Margaret appears to have been a bit troublesome to her kinswoman, Queen Elizabeth. She suffered from ill-health owing to the severity of her imprisonments. She died at Hackney in 1578, having survived her eight children and left her affairs so involved that Elizabeth had to pay her funeral expenses.

MARY STUART

Queen of Scotland and Queen-Dowager of France, 1559 until 1580

(continued from p. 438)

For a portrait of Mary Stuart as Queen-Consort of France, from July 1559 to December 1560, reference must be made to the miniature now in the Uffizi, Florence. This miniature is framed with those of other members

Fig. 597. Mary Stuart, 1560

of the French Royal family, which are said to have been sent by Catherine de' Medici to her relatives at home.[1]

In the National Portrait Gallery, London, is a head-and-shoulders portrait (eight by eleven inches), No. 1766, of Mary, precisely similar to this miniature. Undoubtedly this is a close copy, on a larger scale, of the miniature: probably made in France after she had become a widow, and perhaps before she returned to Scotland.

Fig. 597 is made from the painting in the National Portrait Gallery. The style of the dress would be like that shown in Fig. 596, but perhaps more elaborate. The bodice is black velvet with pointed oblong cuttes in two lines radiating from the shoulders to the waist: narrow shoulder-pieces surround the armholes: the undergarment seen through the cuttes is white, probably linen, embroidered with Spanish work.

Plate XXXIII is a reproduction of a portrait of Mary Stuart in the Victoria and Albert Museum, itself an enlarged copy of a miniature painting in the Royal Library at Windsor, and dates 1560-1. Experts pronounce it to be an excellent likeness. The dress is of incarnadine satin—a satin which goes

Fig. 598

almost crimson in the shadows and a faint lilac-pink in the high lights—made on simple lines as shown in Fig. 517. The whole dress is covered with perpendicular double rows of fancy silver braid, with groups of three tiny silver ball buttons set closely in the intermediate spaces. The sleeves are slightly gathered at the shoulders and fit the forearm close, ending in lace cuffs. No ruff is worn; and the very high collar, edged with silver thread from which oval spangles of jet hang, is turned back with white showing a bare throat. Round the neck, knotted and hanging in front, is a cordon of some of Mary's famous black pearls 'like black muscades'; the earrings, being pear-shaped white pearls, do not match, which seems rather

Fig. 599. Mary Stuart, 1560

[1] Marie de' Medici may have sent them to Florence at a later date.

PLATE XXXIII. MARY STUART, QUEEN OF SCOTLAND AND FRANCE, 1560–1
Victoria and Albert Museum. *By kind permission of the Directors*

unusual. The coif or escoffion is of a dull black mesh, perhaps very narrow black velvet network; it has a border of silver loops containing groups of three minute granules of white (*see* Fig. 598) and there is a row of white pearls at the front edge. A richly jewelled escoffion worn by the Queen of Scotland, Fig. 599, is described on p. 751.

There is reason to believe, according to the following excerpt from Brantôme, that on some occasion while Mary Stuart was in France she must have appeared in the costume of her native country. He says: 'See what virtue there was in such beauty and grace that they could turn coarse barbarism into sweet civility and social grace. We must not be surprised, therefore, that being dressed (as I have seen her) in the barbarous costume of the uncivilized people of her country, she appeared, in mortal body and coarse ungainly clothing, a true goddess. Those who have seen her thus dressed will admit this truth; and those who did not see her can look at her *portrait, in which she is thus attired.* I have heard the Queen-Mother, and the King, too, say that she looked more beautiful, more agreeable, more desirable in that picture than in any of the others.'

The portrait mentioned, depicting the Queen in Scottish dress, has not yet been discovered, if still in existence. Should it come to light in the future, perhaps in some secluded country manor, the find could not fail to prove a discovery of the utmost importance.

The only description we have of Mary Stuart's Scottish costume concerns the long loose cloak of damask worn over the under-

Fig. 600. A Highland Gentlewoman

dress. The Queen had three more of these Highland mantles, one of black frise trimmed with gold and lined with black taffeta, another of blue and a third white.

'The Queen, the Parliament now ended, hath made her Highland apparel for her journey into Argile,' 1563.

Fig. 600 is given to help the reader to visualize the rest of the dress, based upon that generally worn by a Scottish gentlewoman. Her rectangular cloak was less rich, and striped in colours, in fact, a tartan; two corners were fastened on the breast by a brooch or buckle, the material behind forming a kind of burnous. The brooch was of silver or brass according to the quality of the person, and had a crystal or some other semi-precious stone in the centre surrounded by smaller ones. This mantle, cloak, or PLAID

Fig. 601. Mary Stuart, 1561

(*see* vol. i, p. 88) was gathered high in the waist by a leather belt ornamented with silver, and having a mordant some eight inches long engraved in a characteristic Celtic design, often intermixed with stones or coral. The underdress was a close descendant of the gwn (*see* vol. i, p. 18), of some bright coloured cloth, with close sleeves perhaps having gold buttons at the wrist and down the front of the body part. The headdress was a kerchief of white linen, folded corner-wise and tied under the chin over hair worn loose and long, but bound by a snood. Shoes were of old Celtic pattern, as worn by the woman in Fig. 40 (vol. i).

Mary Stuart-Valois was left a widow at the age of eighteen, 5th December 1560.

There are several portraits of her by Clouet and his school known as the 'Deuil Blanc' portraits. One of these, not a good example, is in the National Portrait Gallery (No. 555). Another is in the Wallace Collection. The most authentic is the drawing in the Bibliothèque Nationale, Paris. Fig. 601 is made from this. The black velvet dress worn with this headdress is made like that shown in Fig. 517.

If the drawing in the Musée Condé, Chantilly, of the school of Clouet, is really Mary Stuart, then we have a portrait of her at the age of nineteen, made in 1561 before she left France. The costume is very simple and rather austere, as can be seen from Fig. 602, and consists of a dark underdress, showing a lawn partlet and small frill, and having a girdle at the waist. Over this is a light-coloured robe turned back with lynx: the full sleeves are pleated and slightly padded on the shoulders (*see also* Fig. 823). The coif of white lawn is without the peak, and round the back of it is set in horseshoe shape a band of jewels.

Fig. 602. Mary Stuart, 1561

Having been a widowed queen nine months, Mary left France and landed at Leith, 19th August 1561, and took up her residence at the 'Palace of Halyrudhous.'

The next seven years of her reign as Queen of Scotland were crowded with incident—her marriage with Lord Darnley in 1565, the murder of Rizzio and the birth of her son James in 1566. The tragedy of Kirk-o'-Field, her marriage with James Hepburn, Earl of Bothwell (born c. 1536, died 1577), the defeat at Carberry Hill, her captivity at Loch Leven, and abdication 24th July, kept her busy during 1567. In May 1568, after two previous attempts, she escaped from Loch Leven, and was recaptured at Carlisle, all within a space of sixteen days. Henceforth, Mary Stuart was the State prisoner of the English Government, being shifted from one place of residence to another—eight in number.

Of her wardrobe during this hectic time there is plenty of information contained in the inventory made in 1562. This includes sixty dresses, chiefly of cloth of gold, of silver, velvet, satin, and silk: five cloaks in the Spanish fashion, and nine others, and two Royal mantles of velvet and ermine. Thirty-four corsets known as vasquines (*see* p. 222); sixteen foreparts, which might mean stomachers and under-skirts, chiefly of cloth of gold, cloth of silver, and satin; and a 'vertugade' or farthingale 'expanded by girdles of whalebone.' It is a foregone conclusion that her apparel, regulated by State functions and the routine of everyday life, was of the French fashion, simple but rich, and mainly of white silk or satin, or black velvet.

One entry in the above inventory is of special interest—a sunshade. 'Item a little canopy of crimson satin of three quarter long, furnished with fringes and tassels made of gold and crimson silk, many little painted buttons, all serving to bear, to make shadow for the Queen.' Surely this is the first mention of a sunshade since Greek and Roman days (*see* vol. i, p. 41).

During her later years Queen Mary wore widow's weeds on only two occasions.

Both her marriages, with Darnley, 29th July 1565, as with Bothwell, 15th May 1567, were celebrated in the old chapel at Holyroodhouse, and for both of them she wore widow's deep mourning robes. To have worn mourning as a bridal dress must have been a decidedly unusual experience, and in the second case at least definitely superfluous.

On ordinary occasions she probably wore a dress under an outer robe with large sleeves, like Fig. 602 or 823, such garments being worn by great ladies in their homes. The Queen is seen gowned in this fashion in the Blairs College painting.

As early as 1561 Mary wore PERUKES according to an inventory of that date. Her hair gave her much concern; perhaps it was getting thin, although at the age of nineteen this seems very improbable. It is much more likely that these perukes were only fashionable additions. An important piece of information on the subject is given by Claude Nau, the Queen's French secretary, who states that in her flight from Langside (May 1568) she had her head shaved; no doubt for purposes of disguise. Consequently there was every excuse for her to use as many perukes as she liked from that time onwards. We know she possessed such a number of changes of wig, chiefly dark auburn, that her favourite lady-in-waiting, Mary Seaton, could deck the head of her Royal mistress with a different one every day. She was the finest 'busker,' as Mary admitted, and Sir Francis Knollys, writing to Sir William Cecil in 1568, mentions the art in which Mary Seaton was so proficient—'whereof we have seen divers experiences since her coming hither; and among other pretty devices, yesterday and this day, she did set such a curled hair upon the Queen, that was said to be a PEREWYKE—that showed very delicately, and every other day she hath a new device of headdressing without any cost, and yet setteth forth a woman gaily well.' Nicholas White, who had an interview with Mary Stuart at Tutbury in February 1569, says with unsophisticated surprise that 'her hair of itself is black, and yet Mr. Knollys told me that she wears hair of sundry colours.'

On top of her coiffure the Queen usually wore a white coif (Fig. 875) with an attifet front edged with lace, and over it a fine transparent veil also edged with lace—a headdress evidently inspired by her widow's weeds.

The four Marys—Mary Livingston, Mary Beton, Mary Fleming, and Mary Seaton—who had accompanied the young Queen to France and had returned to Scotland with her would, like their mistress, be much influenced in their attire by French fashions of the 1550's. The costume worn by the Queen's ladies-in-waiting was undoubtedly similar to that shown in Fig. 589, which exemplifies the dress worn by the ladies of the Scottish aristocracy of the 1550's and 1560's.

An excellent horsewoman, Queen Mary possessed suitable garments for riding. Plate XXXIV is a suggestion of what she would wear when entering Edinburgh in state, or on some similar occasion. The riding costume is of fine white silk or cloth braided with gold, the bodice and sleeves being almost covered with braid set in oblique and perpendicular lines. There are four cuttes on the front, and groups of three loops surround the armholes; a green ribbon suspends the Badge of the Thistle.

The cut of the skirt is that generally adopted for ordinary wear—half or two-thirds of a circle; skirts were not specially shaped for saddle and pommel like a riding-habit of the nineteenth century. A blue velvet cloak with a border of gold embroidery hangs from the shoulders, and a blue bonet, decorated with jewels and a small white feather, might be worn over a network caul. The mount is a cream French hackney with black points.

Although the Queen of Scotland owned a litter, covered with crimson velvet and fringed with silk and gold, 'and two little chairs in it,' with harnessing thereto, besides a coach, she seldom used either, much preferring the saddle. Besides, she showed to great advantage on horseback, loving horses as much as she did dogs.

At Carberry Hill 'she gathered an army of those whom she thought her most faithful adherents, leading it herself—at its head, mounted on a good

PLATE XXXIV. MARY STUART, QUEEN OF SCOTLAND. 1562

horse, dressed in a simple petticote of white taffetas, with a coif of crêpe on her head.' 'Petticote' means the riding dress, and was obviously untrimmed: the taffeta must have been of a substantial texture for hard wear on horseback. The coif of crêpe with veil was like that shown in Fig. 875.

It is also recorded that in time of war Mary Stuart wore a 'steel bonet,' but more likely the morion, and carried a pistol at her saddle-bow. Randolph writing to Cecil in 1562 reports that the Queen, during the siege of Lord Gordon's

Fig. 602A.   Fig. 603.   Fig. 604.
Three Society Ladies, 1578

castle in Inverness, expressed the regret that 'she was not a man to know what life it was to lie all night in the fields, or to walk upon the Causeway with a jack [coat of mail], and a knapscull, a Glasgow buckler, and a broadsword.'

On 14th April 1568 the Queen attempted an escape from Loch Leven disguised as her laundress, but heavily veiled; however, her beautiful white hands, such as no washerwoman ever had, betrayed her identity. The costume of a laundress, though not very different in shape from the dress worn by others of the lower classes, is seen in Fig. 719.

(Continued on p. 634)

The three ladies of the English aristocracy (Figs. 602A, 603, and 604) are attending a funeral in 1578. They are not mourners, otherwise they would be wearing mourning robes: they are 'Diuers other gentlewoemen not in black cloth'—just smart Society people who like an interment and have come out of pure curiosity.   The lady (Fig. 602A) wears a walking dress of black silk trimmed with black velvet and golden crowsfeet.   The bodice, with full leg-of-mutton sleeves, is cutte six times on the chest; it buttons down the front and has shoulder pieces of black velvet.   A gold chain is wound round the neck, across the front, and under the left arm.   At the waistbelt a chain suspends a bag.   The black hat with high crown, worn at a jauntish angle, is decorated round the band with gold, and two black ostrich feathers set with gold crows-feet cover the crown at one side.   The lady with her (Fig. 603) wears a dress of brown velvet with partlet and sleeves of lighter brown silk covered with a trellis-work of narrow brown velvet.   The shoulder pieces and skirt are braided with grey, and the latter opens over a black satin underskirt having black velvet bows and tiny roses up the front.

The third lady (Fig. 604) wears cinnamon-brown cloth or silk banded at different angles on the bodice, sleeves, and skirts with velvet of a deeper shade. Down the entire fronts of the overskirt a wider band of velvet is criss-crossed with fine gold.   The last two ladies wear the French hood, and all three have the Spanish farthingale, but of moderate proportions.

The Baldachin, Sunshade, Umbrella

Sunshades were used by the Greeks and Romans as described in vol. i, page 41.

The ecclesiastic *baldachin* was a canopy over an altar or bishop's throne, and was usually made of very rich material such as baudekyn; a portable baldachin was carried on four rods over a monarch in coronation processions.

In the second half of the sixteenth century a small baldachin supported on a single rod—a sunshade, PARASOL, UMBRELLA—was used by persons of rank in Italy and Spain as a protection from sun or rain.   Henri Estienne is the first to make reference to the use of such a sunshade in his *Dialogues* (1578).

That Mary Stuart should have possessed 'a little canopy' (*see* page 515) as early as 1562, or even earlier, is remarkable.

It is true that Daniel Defoe, writing one hundred and fifty years later, states that Queen Elizabeth used an umbrella to keep the rain off when walking on the terrace at Windsor; but we have only his authority for this!

Possibly the earliest representation in England of a sixteenth-century sunshade or umbrella is to be seen in the portrait of Sir Henry Unton, No. 710 in the National Portrait Gallery, which was painted after his death in 1596. He is shown surrounded by pictures of episodes in his life; and in Italy, when mounted on horseback, he carried an all-white sunshade, including the stick.   The frame is obviously constructed on the same principle as the Greek sunshade shown in Fig. 17, vol. i.

MOURNING ROBES

The Countess of Surrey officiated as chief mourner at the funeral of Lady Lumley, 1578, and Fig. 605 shows her in mourning robes of heavy black. The underdress is of the prevailing fashion as shown by the lady (Fig. 604), but plain and of black cloth. The up-to-date *barbe* takes the form of a pleated white lawn front tied round the neck and waist; and over her head is a black

Fig. 605.   Fig. 606.

Mourning Robes

hood, cut semicircular and bordered and lined with white. From the shoulders hangs a mantle with a train, the length of which was regulated. The train-bearer in this instance was 'Mrs Coote the Queen's woman' (Fig. 606), lent for this occasion by Her Majesty as a special favour. She wears the usual dress of a gentlewoman in black cloth with a barbe, a white lawn close-fitting cap gathered into a band round her face, and over this a starched lawn veil fastened V.A.D. fashion.

FRANCES SIDNEY

Countess of Sussex, 1531–89

Frances, the daughter of Sir William Sidney of Penshurst, was born 1531. In 1555 she married, as his second wife, Thomas Ratcliffe (born 1525), 'a goodly gentleman,' who succeeded as third Earl of Sussex in 1557. He was invested a K.G. the same year, and held many official posts, among them that of Lord Chamberlain of the Household, 1572. He died 1583. The Countess of Sussex (Fig. 607) was the foundress, under her will, of Sidney Sussex College, Cambridge (1596). This drawing is adapted from her full-length portrait by Hans Eworth in the dining hall of the college, by kind permission of the Master and Fellows. It shows the full dress of a noble lady

Fig. 607. THE COUNTESS OF SUSSEX. After Hans Eworth
(*Sidney Sussex College, Cambridge*)

of the 1570's. It is carried out entirely in black velvet, embroidered all over with gold quatrefoils (*see* one inset below heraldic lozenge). In the original portrait these are about one inch in diameter, and set two and a half inches apart.

The costume consists of an underdress with bodice worn over the Spanish farthingale which slopes outward at the hem. The overdress fits at the waist, and is edged up the fronts with white fur—ermine or lynx. Narrow bands of the same fur outline the back seams of the sleeves and the edge of the shoulder pieces; these are decorated with three patches of fur and the sleeves with five. Narrow fur also edges the hem of the skirt and train. It appears to be the mode at this time for the turn-back of the fronts of the over-robe to widen considerably where it passes over the shoulders, and so form a high upstanding collar round the back of the head. This is seen in Figs. 607 and 867. The effect of this collar was to minimize the combined length of the head and neck, which had been artificially increased by the height of this headdress, contrary to the vogue at the end of the following period. The wearer thus appears to have neither neck nor shoulders. The ruff and cuffs are of goffered cambric, having a narrow black satin binding set with pearls at intervals along the edge.

A rich jewelled carcanet with pendant is partly hidden by the long fur, and a jewelled girdle worn *underneath* the overdress has an elaborate pomander at the end. The French hood is small and close-fitting, and in her left hand she holds a sable skin. The armorial bearings are displayed on a lozenge, Ratcliffe impaling Sidney, surmounted by a countess's coronet.

The Countess-Dowager died 9th March 1589; her effigy in St. Paul's Chapel, Westminster Abbey, shows her in robes of estate and wearing a rather large circular ruff and a coronet over a headdress something like Fig. 879. Many portraits of ladies of the 1560's and 1570's show them wearing an overdress similar to that described above.

Fig. 608. Gold Embroidery

Sumptuary laws regulating feminine dress did not affect the maids of honour or the ladies of the Court, who were granted exemption.

So much attention did women pay to raiment at this time that their vanities provoked the wrath of their ecclesiastical advisers. Things were rather worse in France than in England: so much so as to rouse the anger of a Franciscan friar, who in 1570 published an entertaining work entitled, *A Charitable Remonstrance to the Dames and Damoyselles of France touching their dissolute Adornments*. Such wholehearted condemnation was nothing new: as long ago as the eighth century B.C. Isaiah (iii. 18–24) had complained of much the same

excess amongst the Jewish women.   Listen then to the pious father giving
vent to his indignation:

'Look you, then, I pray you, whether there be no harm; and, first of all,
let us consider what are your habiliments.   In brief, they are: false hair,
wigs, curls, plaits, earrings, attifets, hair-nets, chaplets of jewels, masks,
wirings, low-cut and open bodices garnished with fringes and braids, and
others that are called burnouses; chains, jewels, bracelets, collars of diverse
kinds and shapes, panaches, fans, busks, mahoitered sleeves with robes of
velvet, satin, damaske, and taffata, altogether shameless and deeply cut back
and front, as well as being cut square even below the armpits; peliçons and
petticotes enriched with excessive embroideries, passamaynes, outrageous
farthingales, hauts de chausses, shoes, and vests; stockings of silk and estamet
of divers colours, with openwork seams, clocks and garters of the same; high-
heeled Venetian slippers and pantoufles, and an infinity of other vanities.'

For denunciation of eccentricity of dress in England we turn again and
again to *The Anatomie of Abuses*, published in 1583.   The author, Philip
Stubbes, was born about 1555, and though educated at both universities
graduated at neither.   His interest lay in people rather than in books; and so
we find him travelling all over the country 'to see fashions, to acquaint
myselfe with natures, qualities, properties, and conditions of all men.'   By
the time his great work appeared he had developed pronounced Puritan sym-
pathies, and to him all ordinary items of attire were extravagant and to be
condemned.   His book thus throws interesting light on the manners of the
times, though some of his statements must be gross exaggerations and require
the proverbial grain of salt.   His *Anatomie* was virulent enough to provoke
a reply (*The Anatomie of Absurditie*), and of his other considerable work,
A Christal Glasse for Christian Women, published in 1591, no fewer than
seven editions were called for.   Philip Stubbes, who must not be confused
with his reputed brother John, the Puritan pamphleteer, died about 1610.

The Franciscan friar and Puritan fanatic, disagreeing violently on most
matters, agreed on at least one, for Stubbes is no whit behind in his dis-
approval of women painting, or rather 'trimming,' their faces and dyeing
their hair.   Thus he complains that 'the women of England use to colour
their faces with certain oils, liquors, ungents and waters made to that end,
whereby they think their beauty is greatly decorated.'   Further: 'In a man
three ounces of lust, in a woman nine: for what meaneth else their outward
tricking and dainty trimming of their heads, the laying out of their hairs,
the painting and washing [with coloured water or dye] of their faces, the
opening of their breasts, and discovering them to their waists, their bents
[shapes] of whalebone [1] to bear out their bumes, their great sleeves and bum-
basted shoulders, squared in breadth to make their waists small, their coloured
hose, their variable shoes?'   Amongst special names for such preparations
in use at this period we may mention 'fard,' white paint for the face, and
'slibbersawces,' washes and unguents kept in small boxes.   The same

[1] Probably their corsets or perhaps farthingales.

pernicious habit of painting the face and wearing false hair by fashionable women of London, good and bad alike, surprised and disgusted gentlefolk up from the country.

It is only fair to mention the contrary opinion of Samuel Kiechel in 1586–9, who refers to the resplendently fair and beautiful women of England, who did *not* paint, and who saluted all stranger-guests with a kiss and an embrace, 'for this is their custom and ettiquette, and any demur in conforming to it would be misconstrued as a sign of ill-breeding and a want of sense.'

Thomas Nashe in 1593 gibes at the effects of the elderly to restore their youth:

'Gorgeous ladies of the Court, never was I admitted so near any of you, as to see how you torture poor old Time with sponging, pinning, and pouncing; but they say his sickle you have burst in twain, to make your periwigs more elevated arches of . . . Why dye they and diet their faces with so many drugs as they do, as it were to correct God's workmanship, and reprove Him as a bungler, and one that is not his craftsmaster? Why ensparkle they their eyes with spiritualized distillations? Why tip they their tongues with *aurum potabile*? Why fill they age's frets with fresh colours? Even as roses and flowers in winter are preserved in close houses under earth, so preserve they their beauties by continual lying in bed.'

Many were the devices adopted to revive the complexion: and to soften wrinkles, night-masks 'well plastered within' were worn in bed.

MASKS

'When they use to ride abroad they have invisories made of velvet, wherewith they cover their faces, having holes made in them against their eyes, where out they look.' Some masks had glass inserted in them. Queen Elizabeth often wore a mask while riding in her coach or on horseback, and even while hunting. This she sometimes removed, especially when addressing any one. Ladies wore masks also when walking and when attending the play.

In France ladies wore them to preserve their complexions and when they rode or walked. In fact a mask was considered so important an item of outdoor costume that to be seen without one was decidedly *en déshabillé*.

Gentlemen wore masks chiefly to conceal their identity during escapades and in the gaming houses.

'Masks of Medyoxes' were used chiefly in masques. They were divided down the centre, usually into good and bad halves, such as one side the human face, the other a skeleton, or an angel impaled with a devil.

NOBILITY—MEN: 1558–80

The differences in social grade during the Elizabethan era are so clearly expressed by William Harrison that his own words are better than any modern description.   Thus he writes: 'We in England divide our people commonly into four sorts, as gentlemen, citizens or burgesses, yeomen, and artificers or labourers.   Of gentlemen the first and chief (next the King) be the prince, dukes, marquesses, earls, viscounts, and barons, and these are called gentlemen of the greater sort, or (as our common usage of speech is) lords and noblemen: and next unto them be knights, esquires, and last of all they that are simply called Gentlemen. '   He disapproves, however, of young men going abroad to sow their wild oats. 'Noblemen's and mean gentlemen's sons are foolishly sent to Italy, from whence they bring home nothing but mere Atheism, infidelity, vicious conversation, and ambitions and proud behaviour, whereby it commeth to pass that they return far worse men than they went out.'   No wonder that when later on some of them became courtiers, although they were most learned knowing many languages and writing well, they had the reputation of being the biggest liars out.

Fig. 609.   Fig. 610.
Noblemen, 1559

From another source we learn that 'the nobles and yeomen willingly intermarry, and so do the burghers and nobility according to their wealth and rank.'

Many nobles and gentlemen attending on Her Majesty are shown in the drawings of Queen Elizabeth's coronation procession referred to on p. 485. Two are given in Figs. 609 and 610 as being examples of the style fashionable at this time.   The costume worn by the gentleman (Fig. 609) is, in many respects, similar to that shown in Fig. 505, and can be said to be contemporary with it.   The decoration of the doublet consists of six cuttes of varying length on the chest and three on each of the four tabs which form the basque: the large puffs on the shoulders are also decorated with them.   The close-fitting sleeves are similarly treated with rows of very small cuttes. An upstanding collar is now an essential part of the doublet.

In the last chapter it was noticed that slops were gradually increasing in size; they first appear in Plate XIX, and are noticeably larger in Fig. 487. Those worn by young Courteney (Fig. 504) are much more in evidence, and the latest (Fig. 505) are even more pronounced. In Fig. 609 they are equally large, but the panes are narrower and consequently more numerous. The fashionable contour of slops is a slope from the waist to their widest at the base, where they turn up under, and surround the thigh.

Fig. 496 illustrates the shape of a pair of slops of this period. The full material and panes are fixed to a hip-yoke, which is covered by a basque, to ensure a sloping line on the hips.

When the full material which formed slops was covered with panes, they were said to be 'pansid.'

The other gentleman (Fig. 610) wears the same kind of suit underneath a short coat cut on the semicircle plan. The coat has a wide open collar and puffed sleeves with rectangular false sleeves hanging from under the arm, the complete garment fastening with one button at the throat. Both gentlemen wear the same kind of hat as described under Fig. 359 D, as also hosen, shoes, and swords slung by hangers from the waist-belt.

Henry Stewart

Lord Darnley, 1545-67

Henry 'Stewarde,' by courtesy Lord Darnley, son of the Earl of Lennox and grandson of Margaret Tudor, Queen-Dowager of Scotland, was born in 1545. Tall of stature with a graceful bearing, he had the youthful attraction of a fair smooth face, broad forehead, and auburn hair. By nature he was arrogant, petulant, and self-willed, and had a weak sense of moral responsibility. His mother very carefully educated him in England, though only in accomplishments and seeming good manners, in the hope that he would some day occupy an important position. This was thrust upon him at the age of nineteen, but he entirely failed to justify expectations.

Fig. 611 is taken from a portrait of Lord Darnley painted by Hans Eworth in 1563. He was just eighteen at the time, and as he was a very dressy young gentleman we may be sure that his clothes were of the latest and best English cut.

In the original portrait at Holyroodhouse Palace, the entire suit is painted in a very dark warm grey to suggest black silk braided with plaited black silk braid. This descends the doublet and side-seams both front and back (see Fig. 612) and both the seams of the sleeves, with a double row of cuttes on the outside. The edges of the panes of his slops are also outlined with braid.

III ²—L

Fig. 611.
Henry, Lord Darnley, 1563.

Darnley made his exit from this world on the night of the tragedy of Kirk-o'-Field, amid exquisite surroundings befitting an ancestor of Great Britain's Royal family.

The house consisted of a hall built over an arched crypt, a cabinet and a chamber on the ground floor, with another built above it. These were all sumptuously furnished for the occasion, the hall with a set of beautiful tapestries (looted from the Gordons, by the way!), a chair of estate covered with leather, on a dais in front of a dorsal, both of black velvet fringed with black silk.   In the chamber on the ground floor occupied by the Queen was placed a new bed of black figured velvet, enriched with passamaynes of gold and silver and fringed with the same.   It had lately come into the Queen's possession with other spoils from Strathbogie.

In Darnley's room, the upper one, also hung with tapestry (of inferior quality we presume), a bath was provided, and a wondrous state bed erected, with hangings of violet-brown velvet ornamented with cloth of gold and silver and embroidered with ciphers and flowers in needlework of gold and silk. There were three coverlets, the uppermost of quilted blue taffeta.   On the floor was a Turkey carpet, and the furniture included a high chair covered with purple velvet and fringed, three or four red velvet cushions, and a little table with a cover of green velvet.

During the evening of 10th February, some valuable tapestry, a fur coverlet, and the Queen's bed were removed, the latter being replaced by another of meaner sort hung with seedy purple velvet; and beside it were stacked quantities of gunpowder ready for the fatal moment.

Having sung Psalm V, and drunk a cup of wine to his servants, one of whom only, Taylor, slept in his chamber, Darnley retired to his velvet-hung bed wrapped in a velvet and sable nightgown or dressing-gown, and all was ready for the tragedy—two of the clock, Monday, 11th February 1567.

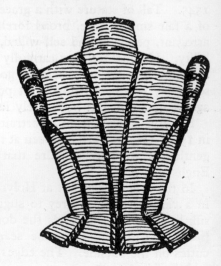

Fig. 612

Darnley's small brother, Charles, aged six, is shown in Fig. 613 taken from the same painting before mentioned. Most small boys of all periods were dressed like their fathers or big brothers, but in miniature; however, young Charles wears a distinctive costume of black silk braided with black, and consisting of a long gown with close-fitting sleeves raised on the shoulders, a 'suit of ruffs' edged with black stitchery or Spanish work, a gold girdle, and a flat black velvet cap with white ostrich feather. A gold key and ring are suspended by a black ferret from his neck. Lord Charles married in 1574

Fig. 613.
Lord Charles Stuart, 1563

Fig. 614.
Lord Edward Seymour, 1563

Elizabeth, daughter of Sir William Cavendish and his wife Elizabeth, better known as Bess of Hardwick. He died in 1576 leaving an only child, the Lady Arabella Stuart, who was born in 1575.

LORD EDWARD SEYMOUR, 1561–3

Lord Edward Seymour at the age of two is shown in Fig. 614. He is taken from the three-quarter-length portrait of himself and mother (Katherine Grey) painted by Hans Eworth in 1563. She was the second daughter of Henry Grey, Duke of Suffolk, and his Duchess, Frances Brandon, daughter of Mary Tudor I, and therefore, like her sister Lady Jane Grey, in close succession to the throne. Contrary to regulations concerning persons of Royal blood she secretly married in 1560 Edward Seymour, Earl of Hertford, which offence so angered the Queen that both Lady Katherine and her husband were confined as State prisoners in the Tower. There, in 1561, was born her son Edward, who one day might have been King Edward VII. Her second son, Thomas, was also born there in 1562–3.

His young lordship wears a black velvet gown braided with fine gold. It has a long skirt attached and the sleeves are puffed in the fashionable manner on the shoulders, whence hang long tubular sleeves. The underdress with

Fig. 615.
Scottish Nobleman, 1567

Fig. 616. Fig. 617.
Noblemen, 1570

close-fitting sleeves is of white silk. Under his chin is pinned an embroidered bib, and a biggen is worn under a bonet of black velvet studded with gold and jewelled buttons, a white ostrich tip curling over the right side.

Fig. 615 is from a portrait, dated 1567, of a member of the Lennox family. It is interesting because the style fashionable in the previous reigns is at this time worn by a nobleman of Scotland. The black velvet jerkin edged with strands of gold bullion worked at right angles to the edges is caught at the throat by a jewelled ornament, showing that the jerkin is worn immediately above the embroidered shirt. The sleeves of rose-coloured satin are fixed to the outer garment and, with the slops of the same colour, are decorated with cuttes bound with gold showing white underneath; the slight padded ridge at the shoulders simulating the roll is somewhat unusual. The hosen

and cap feather are also rose-colour, the cap and shoes black; the sword is
carried in a hanger of simple construction.

Figs. 616 and 617 are taken from the painted panel referred to on p. 493.
The figures of Lord William Howard (Fig. 616) and Sir Edward Hastings in
the original are extremely crude, but the shape and decoration of their costumes are sufficiently clear to enable them to be reproduced in black and white.
The fashions depicted are of the period
1570–5.   Fig. 616 wears a PEASCOD
DOUBLET with moderately full
sleeves and a deep basque, also the
new kind of breeches, lately introduced
from Venice, called VENETIANS.
Both doublet and venetians are profusely decorated with braids and
cuttes: so also are the garments worn
by Sir Edward (Fig. 617).   His doublet is of the older shape, with larged
puffed sleeves; and to the paned slops
are attached canions tied at the knee.
The hats of both gentlemen have high
crowns and moderately wide brims,
and one has an ostrich tip drooping
over the left side. It should be noticed
that these gentlemen are carrying
staves and not swords.   Courtesy apparently demanded that the latter
should not be used when arresting a
lady, above all, the Lady Elizabeth.

Two gentlemen from Turbervile's
work are shown in Figs. 618 and 619.
They represent the fashions of the
1570's. The elder is wearing a plain

Fig. 618.   Fig. 619.
Gentlemen, 1575

suit of velvet, silk, or cloth, consisting of a doublet with no basques,
shoulder pieces, plain sleeves, and the latest thing in breeches known
as GALLYHOSEN. At each knee is a row of small tabs, and down
the front of the doublet are buttons with worked button-holes—the sole
decoration.

The younger man has chosen a suit of cloth banded with a silk braid. The
slops, when compared with those of Fig. 611, slope more from the hips to
their lowest extremities, a feature which is gradually prevailing.

JAMES VI

King of Scotland, 1566 until 1580

Lord Darnley's son now makes his appearance on the scene. Born in
Edinburgh Castle, 19th June 1566, he, James Stuart, became King of Scotland
on his mother's abdication, 24th July 1567, and was crowned on the 29th
of the same month. The drawing (Fig. 620), made from the portrait in the
National Portrait Gallery, No. 63, shows King James VI, at the age of eight,
in 1574; and like all other children, Royal or otherwise, he is dressed like a

Fig. 620. James VI,
King of Scotland, 1574

Fig. 621. La Mode, 1576

grown-up man. He wears a peascod doublet of soft pale-ochre leather,
stitched up the front and round the sleeves. Small WINGS surround the
armholes, and the collar is high to support the band. The doublet fastens
with three gold buttons only, and around the waist is a narrow crimson
velvet belt carrying the dagger, sword-belt, and sword all covered with the
same velvet. The wide, full gallyhosen in moss-green velvet with loops at
the knee are worn over pink stockings and pale buff shoes. The bonet of
black velvet has several ostrich tips in natural colourings, and the hatband
is composed of a string of pearls. His Small Majesty has at this early age
already developed a love of falconry, and upon his gauntleted wrist he carries
a favourite bird, with jess and bell attached to its leg. Later he became a
very keen hunter, although a remarkably poor horseman.

The fashionable line has not changed much during this period, as may be seen by comparing Fig. 621 with either 611 or 619; the only appreciable difference is in the shape of the slops, which have become less pumpkin-shape than those in Figs. 609, 611, and 617.

The nobleman (Fig. 621) carried the Sword of State immediately in front of the Queen when walking in procession with the Knights of the Garter (1576). On all occasions of State or semi-State the Sword-bearer preceded the Sovereign. The suit is of light colouring and covered with stitchery in black silk. The puffs on the shoulders are obviously dispensed with because they would produce bulkiness in the Spanish cloak, whereas it hangs in radiating folds from the shoulders. It is made of satin or silk, has bands of black velvet of varying width, and is lined with brocade.

Fig. 622. German Cloak, 1576

Fig. 622 shows a cloak of German fashion worn by a nobleman in the same procession. It is made of silk cut on the circular plan, having sleeves that *could* be worn, but which usually hung empty outside. The cloak is bordered with bands of black velvet diminishing in width as they ascend. Two bands of black velvet border the lining, which is turned back forming revers, and having a step where the flat false hood meets them.

A Knight of the Garter taking part in the procession before mentioned is shown in Fig. 623. Additions and alterations to the Insignia of the Order are to be found in vol. ii, pp. 238 and 241. As there stated the original hood gave place to the chaperon in the reign of Edward IV. In Fig. 623

Fig. 623. A Knight of the Garter, 1576

it should be noticed that the chaperon is still laid over the right shoulder, and that the circular roll is much reduced in size, the diameter measuring not more than six or seven inches. The chaperon in turn was superseded in the reign of Henry VIII by the flat black velvet bonet with one small feather. This knight (Fig. 623), dating 1576, is wearing the fashionable hat. The mantle of the Order in 1515 was of violet velvet (see p. 161), but at this date was of white cloth with the Garter embroidered as usual upon the left shoulder. Later Elizabeth changed the white mantle back again to purple velvet. The surcote, worn over a suit like that shown in Fig. 621, and the chaperon were of crimson velvet, the latter placed very low down on the back under the Collar, with the cape part spread out as shown in the back view.

PERSONAGES OF DISTINCTION ABOUT THE COURT

WILLIAM CECIL
Lord Burleigh, 1520 until 1580

Fig. 624. William Cecil
Lord Burleigh, 1579

The most important man in the kingdom at the beginning and during the greater part of the reign was William Cecil. He was born at Bourne, Lincolnshire, 1520, and served both Edward VI and Mary. On her accession, Elizabeth made him Secretary of State, which post he held until 1572 when he was made Lord Treasurer of England—'a person of most subtle and active spirit . . . wholly intent on Her Majesty's service.' William Cecil married in 1541 Mary, sister of Sir John Cheke (tutor of Edward VI), and mother of Thomas Cecil, born 1542 and created Earl of Exeter in 1605. Secondly, in 1546, he married Mildred, daughter of Sir Anthony Coke, and they were the parents of Robert, born 1563, who, in 1605, became the first Earl of Salisbury of the Cecil family.

William Cecil was raised to the peerage as Baron Burleigh in 1571 and received the Garter in 1572. Twelve times Lord Burleigh entertained Queen Elizabeth in his home, each time for several weeks together, and each visit cost him approximately £3,000. Burleigh House in the Strand was his town residence.

A portrait in the National Portrait Gallery, No. 604, shows Sir William Cecil at about the age of forty. Many other portraits exist showing him at different ages; and Fig. 624, made from some of these, represents him at the end of this period when he was Lord Treasurer and K.G. As befitting the dignity of his position Burleigh always dressed soberly but richly. His suit is of black silk banded with black velvet, over it being a black velvet gown reminiscent of the Middle Ages, lined with sable. He wears the Collar of the Garter, and in his official capacity a black velvet 'coif,' dating from Henry III's reign (*see* vol. ii, p. 176), under his black velvet hat.

(*Continued on p.* 642)

Robert Dudley

Earl of Leicester, 1532–88

Most famous among the ostentatious courtiers who surrounded the Queen was Robert Dudley. He was born about 1532, the fifth son of John, Duke of Northumberland. His chief assets were his goodly person (which won Elizabeth's admiration), showy dress, and skill in the tactics of the courtier. His paternal grandfather was Edmund Dudley, the extortioner favoured by Henry VII, who came to the block in 1510. Of Robert's antecedents the uncharitable said that 'he was the son of a duke, the brother of a king, the grandson of an esquire, and the great-grandson of a carpenter, that the carpenter was the only honest man in the family, and the only one who died in his bed.'

Lord Robert Dudley, as he was known during 1551–3 and 1558–64, was gentleman to the Privy Chamber to Edward VI. He married in 1549 Amy or Anne, heiress of Sir John Robsart, Kt., of Cumnor Place. This lady died in 1560, under somewhat suspicious circumstances. His rise in the Royal favour was nevertheless rapid; in 1559 the Garter was conferred upon him; in 1564 he was created Earl of Leicester; and he entertained the Queen most lavishly at Kenilworth in 1575. His portrait, No. 447 in the National Portrait Gallery, dates about this time (1560–70), and No. 105 in the same gallery shows him at a later date. The Queen's strong attachment to Dudley is notorious, and there was some anxiety at the time lest she should marry him.

Fig. 625. Robert Dudley, Earl of Leicester, 1578

Having abandoned in course of time all expectations of becoming King-Consort, he secretly married the Dowager Lady Sheffield, but in the end (1578) married bigamously Lettice Knollys, widow of Walter, Earl of Essex, much to the Queen's displeasure.   The Earl was appointed Lieutenant- and Captain-General of the Queen's armies and companies, 24th July 1588.

Fig. 625 is drawn from a portrait taken at the end of his life, though he is wearing a costume fashionable in the 1570's.   His peascod doublet is of white silk banded with gold; and in place of the ruff a turned-down linen collar edged with reticella is worn and matches the cuffs; the venetians are of grey and gold brocade; over them is placed a padded roll of white silk as described under Fig. 634, the panes decorated with a black velvet pattern (Fig. 626).   White openwork stockings are drawn up over the venetians at the knee.   This fancy treatment of the netherstocks, much the mode at this time, is the shocking indecency complained of by the puritanical Mr. Stubbes. A new fashion in shoes is worn.   They are of white satin and have narrow upstanding tongues.   The short surcote of black velvet lined with sable has full sleeves of black and gold brocade, with a row of gold ornaments set with jewels down the sides.   The hat is black velvet with an osprey and jewel.   The Earl carries his white rod of office in his right hand.   To the great regret of every one, especially the Queen, Lord Leicester died 3rd September 1588 at the age of fifty-four.

Fig. 626. Pattern on Panes

Ambrose Dudley, born about 1528, was Robert's elder brother and known as Lord Ambrose Dudley, 1551–4; he was restored in blood 1558, and became Earl of Warwick in 1561.   He married three times: first, Anne, daughter and co-heiress of William Whorewood; secondly, Elizabeth, daughter of Gilbert, Lord Talboys, before 1553; and thirdly, Lady Anne Russell, eldest daughter of Francis, second Earl of Bedford, in 1565.

In 1576 Lord Warwick fitted out two ships of twenty-five tons burden, and sent Frobisher to search out the North-west Passage.   This is all that is worth recording of him, except that his portrait painted about 1560 in the Wallace Collection, No. 534, shows him wearing a very elaborate doublet with high collar; the shape of the 'wings' is shown to good advantage.   His jewels are also worth noting.

The Earl of Warwick died in 1590; and his effigy, unaccompanied by any of his three wives, is to be seen in St. Mary's, Warwick.   His lordship is dressed in full armour and wears an earl's coronet.

Sir Christopher Hatton, 1540 *until* 1580

Another courtier and 'a man of real capacity' was Christopher Hatton, the youngest son of William Hatton, Esq., of Holdenby, Northants. Born in 1540, he went to Oxford in 1555, but took no degree. On his admission to the Inner Temple in 1559 he became 'the first great exampler of England's Barristers.' It was in 1561 that he attracted the attention of the Queen while dancing a galliard in a masque in which Lord Robert Dudley also took

part. 'He came . . . to the Court in a mask [masque] where the Queen first took notice of him, loving him well for his handsome dancing, better for his proper person, and best of all for his great abilities.'

In 1564 the Queen took him into her band of fifty Gentlemen Pensioners, and 'for his modest sweetness of condition . . . made him Captain of the Guard' in 1572. Hatton was Member of Parliament for Higham Ferrers in 1571, and for Northants the year following. Knighthood was conferred upon him in 1577.

Sir Christopher's costume, as shown in his portraits, was smart and of the latest fashion. Fig. 627 is reconstructed from these portraits and depicts him as he appeared between 1570 and 1580. There is a head-and-shoulders portrait of him in the National Portrait Gallery wearing the same dress, but dated 1589: the portrait is, however, a little earlier than this. The doublet

Fig. 627. Sir Christopher Hatton, 1589

is white with braidings of red and gold, and gold buttons down the front: between the braidings is a row of perpendicular pinkings. The venetians are red and gold brocade, with white fancy-woven stockings and French pantoufles. The cloak and hip-roll are of black velvet, diapered with pearls set in three leaves of gold.

The Italian bonet is of the same material; it has a row of gold jewelled ornaments round the hatband, a brooch, and tuft of feathers. Sometimes Hatton is shown wearing a goffered ruff, and sometimes a lawn collar of Spanish work edged with lace which matches that on his cuffs, as shown in Fig. 627.

The courtier standing in the background of the painting (Plate XXXII C) is said to be Sir Christopher. (*Continued on p.* 643)

The insertion of a note from Harrison on the subject of knighthood is opportune here:

'When a man is made a knight, he kneeling down is striken of the King, or his substitute with his sword naked upon the back or shoulder, the Prince saying, "Soyes Cheualier au nom de Dieu," and when he riseth up the King saith: "Aduances bon Cheualier."   This is the manner of dubbing knights at this present time, and the term *dubbing* is the old term for that purpose and not *creation*, howbeit in our time the word *making* is most in use among the common sort.'

EDWARD DE VERE

Earl of Oxford, 1550–1604

A very dashing and fashionable young man of this era was Edward de Vere, born at Castle Hedingham, 1550, and the son of the sixteenth Earl of Oxford.   Precocious in youth, he matriculated at Cambridge at the age of eight—an effort never equalled before or since.   Young Edward succeeded to the title and the office of Great Chamberlain of England in 1562, and took his M.A. degree in 1564.   In 1571 he married Anne Cecil (who died in 1588), daughter of Lord Burleigh.   Naturally the seventeenth of a long line of earls of the de Vere family, dating back to 1155, was a great Society catch, as the following excerpt from a letter written by Lord St. John shows. He says:

'The Earl of Oxenforde hath gotten him a wyffe, or at the least a wyffe hath caught him.   This is Mistress Anne Cycille, whereunto the Queen hath given her consent, the which hath caused great weeping, wailing, and sorrowful chere of those that hoped to have had that golden daye.'   No long time after his wedding, he toured the Continent, like most young men of the nobility, without his wife we may assume.   On his return in 1574, it was noted that: 'My Ld of Oxforth is lately growne into great credite; for the Q. Matie delitithe more in his parsonage & his dauncing & valientnes then any other . . . if it were not for his fyckle hed, he would passe any of them shortly.'

In 1575 he sat for his portrait—a head and shoulders, from which Fig. 846 has been drawn.

Yet Lord Oxford was by no means a mere Court gallant.   'At his own charge and in pure love of his country, he hired ships and joined the Grand Fleet sent to oppose the Spanish Armada.'   He was, moreover, a poet and a wit of no mean order; but in spite of these admirable qualities, he was already a spendthrift, and in later life dissipated the greater part of his fortune.   His second Countess was Elizabeth, daughter of Thomas Trentham, Esq., whom he married about 1591.   His death took place in 1604; he was buried at Hackney, and Castle Hedingham passed into the hands of Lord Burleigh.

SIR PHILIP SIDNEY, 1554–86

Philip Sidney, the pattern of chivalry, was born at Penshurst, 29th November 1554, son of Sir Henry Sidney, Lord Deputy of Ireland and President of Wales. The child was named after the husband of Queen Mary. To Shrewsbury he was sent to school so that he might be under the charge of Thomas Ashton, equally renowned as courtier and schoolmaster. He left Oxford in 1571 without taking a degree, and at eighteen, the usual age, obtained the requisite licence, dated 1572, to travel abroad, witnessing in Paris the massacre of St. Bartholomew. On his return to England he joined the Court at Kenilworth in 1575. An excellent portrait of him as a young man of twenty-three is in the National Portrait Gallery, No. 2096, and in this he wears a suit of the same cut as that shown in Fig. 655.

At Shottesbrooke Park is a very beautiful full-length portrait of Sir Philip Sidney painted about 1580 by Pantoja de la Cruz (1551–1610). He is shown at the age of twenty-six, wearing demi-armour, i.e. cuirass, armpieces, and tassets, of steel damascened with gold. The remainder of his equipment is of a pale buff colour; the slops are of soft leather with panes decorated with cuttes, and long round-tied boots turned down at the top are attached to the slops by inverted V-shaped straps (*see* Fig. 908).

A later portrait, dated 1585, will be found in the National Portrait Gallery, No. 1862. It is referred to on p. 547.

Although he was in temporary disgrace with the Queen for airing his opinions on her proposed French marriage, as also for quarrelling with the Earl of Oxford, he soon recovered the Royal favour and was knighted in 1583, and in the same year married Frances, daughter of Sir Francis Walsingham. So attached did Elizabeth become to her handsome young courtier that she prevented him from accompanying Sir Francis Drake to America, and even, it is said, disappointed him of the Polish throne. Sir Philip Sidney, 'a person of great parts,' 'a noble and matchless Gentleman,' was mortally wounded at Zutphen, 1586, and is buried in St. Paul's. For many months after his death it was counted indecent for any gentleman of quality to appear, at Court or in the city, in light or gaudy apparel.

SIR JOHN HAWKYNS, 1532 *until* 1580

John Hawkyns was born at Plymouth in 1532. Chief of the 'Sea Lions' of the Elizabethan era he was knighted by Queen Elizabeth the year she ascended the throne. His seafaring expeditions were important; but what is more so to most men and women of to-day, he has the credit for introducing tobacco into England in 1565. 'Tabaco' was the native name for a leaf of the plant, rolled like a tube, through which the Indians inhaled the smoke. The name was adopted by the Spaniards for the leaf. In 1573 we have a statement made by Harrison the chronicler to this effect: 'In these daies, the taking-in of the smoke of the Indian herbe called "tabaco" by an instrument formed like a litle ladell, wherby it passeth from the mouth into the hed and stomach, is gretlie taken-up and used in England, against Rewmes and some other diseases ingendred in the longes and inward parts, and not without effect.' Of his slave-trading activities the less said the better.

Sir John was elected Member of Parliament for his native city in 1572, and became Treasurer and Controller of the Navy from 1573 onwards. Fig.

Fig. 628. A Young Gentleman, 1581

Fig. 629. An Overcoat, 1580

851 is taken from his portrait in the Plymouth City Museum. In it, a three-quarter, he wears a peascod doublet with narrow hip-roll, venetians, and an embroidered cloak all in black.

The gentleman (Fig. 628) is taking the air at Brightstowe,[1] for the drawing is taken from a map of that place dated 1581. The costume is of the type worn by the aristocracy in ordinary life. It is a bright dress according to the original, the doublet being red cloth and the slops yellow braided with red. The cloak is of black cloth bound with black velvet, the hat also of black velvet, the hose yellow, shoes black, and gloves brown. Should the weather be cold or stormy, he would don the very comfortable overcoat shown in Fig. 629. This would be made of cloth, the best being of velvet faced with fur and often lined throughout with the same. Its hanging sleeves could be

[1] Bristol, 'the place of the bridge.'

Band tied with
Band strings.

Wings

Jerkin

codpaunch
Dubblet.

Picadils

Sword carriage

Upper stocks or
Canions

Fringed garters
above knee.

os covered
e panes in
ulte-work.

her stocks

Quirkes.

soled shoes

HN.
25.

Fig. 630. GENERALIZED ELIZABETHAN MODE FOR GENTLEMEN

worn if required, the tabs at the wrists forming a protection for the hands even though gloves are carried.   The hat is of velvet, cloth, or blocked felt, with a small plume.

The general survey of men's costume which follows applies not only to the period covered by Section I, but also to that of Section II.   The subject has been concentrated in this place instead of being divided as has been done for women, because gentlemen's costume was not so varied during the Elizabethan era as that of the ladies.

Fig. 630 gives a practical illustration of all items of dress which, with slight differences, constituted fashionable attire during the whole period of Elizabeth's reign.   The young man himself actually dates about 1580.   The details of his costume which show affinities with both earlier and later styles are now described.

THE DOUBLET

The doublet was a close-fitting body garment cut in four sections as shown in the diagram, Fig. 631.   A is half the front, B half the back, C half the high upstanding collar, and D and E are the outer and inner parts of a sleeve.   It has been noted in describing the drawings in the previous chapter that a little padding was inserted in the front of the doublet just above the waist-line. By the year 1577 this padding, known as 'bombast,' became very pronounced.

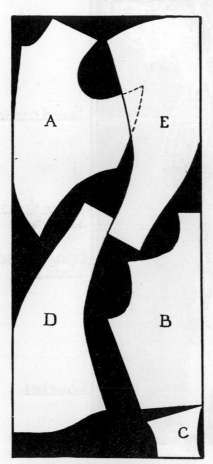

Fig. 631. Man's Doublet

The doublet was generally fastened with buttons, and the centre line down the front, where it opened, gradually protruded from the chest into a curve at the waist suggesting a peascod in shape.   This was known as a 'peascod paunch.' Later, whalebone busks were inserted behind the seams, or parchment glued together in layers was used as a foundation to make the fronts of the doublet stiff and stick out.

The peascod paunch appeared about 1574 and assumed its largest proportions between 1580 and 1590.

Fig. 632 shows a military gambeson of canvas covering diamond-shaped steel plates mounted on a lining of canvas. It has a peascod paunch and undoubtedly is constructed in much the same manner as the peascod-paunched doublet. A is half the front, which laces down the centre, and to it is attached a hip piece, D. B is half the back. The projecting portion C passes round the back under the arms, where it is laced to the corresponding part.

To the waist-line of the doublet a row of tabs was sewn, but when the front of it was cut in two, sometimes three, sections, these sections continued below the waist-line and formed one tab to each section, the seams being usually overlaid with braid or embroidery. This braiding of the seams is to be seen in several earlier drawings, for instance Figs. 492, 493, and a back view, Fig. 612. Loops or scallops sometimes took the place of tabs.

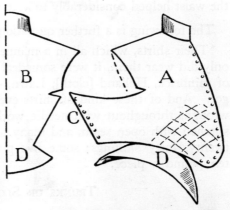

Fig. 632. Gambeson

Any decoration of this kind acquired the name of PICADILS, derived from the Spanish 'pica,' a spear, diminutive 'picadilla,' meaning a *little spear-head*. At first the name was applied to the pointed edgings of the ruff (*see* p. 632) which suggested spear-points. Later—during the second half of this reign—it was given to any fancy-shaped edging. Those surrounding the armholes were generally termed 'wings.' Collars were finished off in this manner to help support the ruff or 'neck whisk.' Picadils reached their greatest development about the year 1595. Master Higgins, the tailor, who introduced the fashion of picadils into England, made a small fortune, and owned quite a large estate north of St. James's Palace. It is said that the road leading to his house was, in compliment to him, called 'Piccadilly.'

Stubbes, in a long rigmarole, gives some interesting details of the doublets as worn in the 1580's: 'They are no less monstrous than the rest of their garments; for now the fashion is to have them hang down to the middest of their theighs, being so hard-quilted, and stuffed with four, five, or six pounds of bombast at the least, and sewed, as they can neither work, nor yet will play in them, through the excessive heat; therefore they are forced to wear them loose about them.' This accounts for the doublet being often seen in portraits unfastened up the front, otherwise they could hardly stoop to the ground or give a gracious low bow. Some doublets were made of 'satin, taffeta, silk, grogram, chamlet, gold, silver, and what not.   Slashed, jagged, cutte, carned [tabbed] pincked and laced with all kinds of costly lace of divers and sundry colours.'

THE JERKIN

The jerkin, cut to fit closely over the doublet, was very popular, and was made of leather, velvet, satin, or silk.   The waist-line and arm-holes were finished off with picadils.   It had no sleeves to be worn on the arm, but sometimes had long hanging ones, whence emerged the sleeves of the doublet underneath.

CORSETS

Corsets were worn by fashionable men as well as by women.   Confining the waist helped considerably to accentuate the size of the slops.

The following is a further quotation from Stubbes:

'Their shirts, which all in a manner do wear (for if the Nobility or Gentry only did wear them, it were somedeal [somewhat] more tollerable) are either of cambrick, Holland [cloth], Lawn, or else of the finest cloth that may be got.   And of these kind of shirts every one now doth wear alike. . . . and wrought throughout with needle work of silk, and such like, and curiously stitched with open seam, and many other knackes besides.   Shirts cost ten, twenty, forty shillings; some five pounds, some twenty nobles, and some ten pound a piece.'

TRUNKS OR SLOPS, AND HOSEN

Slops gradually increased in size between 1565 and 1575, often reaching vast proportions, and were in shape like a pumpkin with the greatest width in the middle, each leg being separate from the fork downwards.   These later slops sprang from a narrow waistband, the hip yoke being omitted. Panes elaborately embroidered and decorated, and often with many cuttes, were still the fashion.   The under part or lining was 'pulled through' in a manner which verged on the eccentric.   Shakespeare refers to these cutte slops as 'short blistered breeches' in *Henry VIII*, Act I, Sc. III, where Sir Thomas Lovel remarks: 'They must either (for so run the conditions) leave those remnants of fool and feather, that they got in France [meaning the German fashion of slashes, and long feathers in their hats, which were so fashionable at the Field of the Cloth of Gold] . . . renouncing clean the faith they have in tennis, and tall stockings, short blister'd breeches. . . .'

To make these slops stand out, busks of whalebone were used by the fashionable and wealthy; the less expensive alternative being bombast, i.e. a padding of wool, cotton, flock, horse-hair, bran, sawdust, or even rags. Slops were no longer attached to the lower edge of the doublet, in the manner shown in vol. ii, Fig. 314, but to the doublet lining or a canvas inner belt; eyelet holes and laces were, however, still employed.

The following directions from Richard Onslowe's letter to Sir William Cecil, Kt., February 1565, may be useful in the making of slops:

'. . . lyne a sloppe-hose not cut in panes with a lynyng of cotton stytched to the sloppe, over and besides the lynnen lynyng, and the other lynyng straight to the leg: and that any loose lynyng not straytt to the leg was not permytted, but for the lynyng of panes only: and that the hole upperstock being in our sloppe uncutt, could not be sayd to be in panes.'

The stages in the development of the proportions of slops and TRUNK-HOSE worn during the reign of Elizabeth have been so excellently summarized by Mr. Francis M. Kelly, that we cannot do better than reproduce his own words from the *Connoisseur*:

'1555–60. Reaching to about mid-thigh (the normal length) and moderately wide.

1560–5. Gradually swelling, length about same.

1565–75. Often of vast circumference, without appreciable lengthening.

1575–95. The older forms still seen, but the modish world either prefers venetians, or curtails the trunks till they are often no more than a padded roll barely covering the buttocks. (Trunk-hose are either worn with long cloth stockings sewn to them, or—from about 1570—they are equipped with canions.) For a while they appear to have lost favour with fashionable folk.

1595–1600. Revival of their vogue.'

Spanish trunk-hose broadened downwards to a square base.

Long hose, covering the leg from thigh to foot, continued in use, but about the 1560's an alternative divided form came into fashion. The upper portions covering the thigh were called UPPER STOCKS or CANIONS (a revival of tonnelets), and Fig. 633 is a drawing of one. It has a point in front attached to a strap and buckled above or below the knee. Canions appeared about 1570. The lower portions were called NETHER STOCKS or stockings, and were usually secured above the knee by garters with fringed ends. The following method of cross-gartering the knee was also adopted. The band of silk was placed first *above* the knee, crossed behind, and brought round and tied at the side *below* the knee. This method of tying could be reversed. Another way is shown in Fig. 793. Here the band of silk is first placed under the knee-cap, crossed behind, brought up above the knee, and tied in a loop and two ends on top.

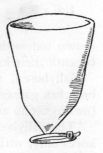

Fig. 633. Canion

Nether stocks were 'curiously knitte with open seam down the leg, with "quirks" and CLOCKS about the ankles and sometimes interlaced with gold and silver threads as is wonderful to behold.'

'These worsted stocks of bravest dye,
And silken garters fringed with gold,
These corkēd shoes [1] to bear them high.'

[1] See p. 758.   [*Poem dated* 1595.]

Other materials besides worsted were used for making stocks (*see* p. 545).

'Venetians' was another name for canions which originated in Venice; they were really peg-top breeches. Some were moderately padded on the hips, others outrageously so. In Fig. 616, among others, the gentleman is wearing venetians. Sometimes they were very rich and ornate, and Stubbes says that some cost as much as £100 per pair. On top of venetians or canions a roll, or pansid slop on a smaller scale, was often worn (*see* Fig. 658). Fig. 634 shows half of one of these rolls and is drawn from one in the London Museum. The original measures thirteen inches round the thigh. The panes are composed of blue silk with a pattern in pale raw-sienna velvet; the under padding is covered with white silk woven with lines of gold and silver and a pine design. A patch of white silk brocaded with sprigs of light and dark blue flowers and green leaves was inserted in the eighteenth century.

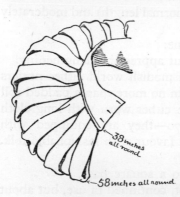

Fig. 634.
Half a Roll or Pansid Slop

Again the informative yet carping Stubbes is useful: 'Then they have hosen, which as they be of divers fashions so are they of sundry names. Some be called French hose, some gally hose, and some Venetians. The French hose are of two divers makings, for the common French hose containeth length, breadth, and sidenes sufficient, and is made very round. The other containeth neither length, breadth, nor sidenes, being not past a quarter of a yard wide, whereof some be paned, cutte, and drawn out with costly ornaments, with canions annexed reaching down beneath their knees.'

Gallyhosen, GALLIGASKINS, or galliegascoignes were large, wide breeches gathered or pleated at the waist and reaching down to the knees (*see* Figs. 620 and 807). They were introduced from Gascony.

'The gallyhosen are made very large and wide, reaching down to their knees only, with three or four gards a piece laid down along either hose.

'The Venetian hosen, they reach beneath the knee to the gartering place of the leg, where they are tied finely with silk points, or some such like, and laid on also with rows of lace or gards as the other before. And yet not withstanding all this is not sufficent, except they be made of silk, velvet, satin, damask, and other such precious things besides. Yea, every one serving men and other inferior to them, in every condition will not stick to flaunt it out in these kind of hosen, with all their other apparel suitable thereunto.'

STOCKINGS (*Chausses*): WOMEN AND MEN

At 'Newyers-tyde,' 1561, Mrs. Mountague, one of Queen Elizabeth's gentlewomen, presented Her Majesty with a pair of knitted silk stockings. It had taken quite ten years to discover the secret of making them, even with Edward VI's cast-off silk stockings as a model.

Mrs. Mountague told the Queen that she had had them made on purpose, and would set some more in hand at once if they pleased her. 'Do so,' said the Queen, 'for indeed I like silk stockings so well because they are pleasant, fine, and delicate, that henceforth I will wear no more cloth stockings.'

The stockings shown at Hatfield House (Fig. 635), said to have been worn by Queen Elizabeth, are knitted by hand, but look much more like crochet, in a silk thread almost as coarse as string. The stitch is plain-stitch, and over the whole surface are lozenges with open-work borders. These stockings are of a deep sulphur yellow, and bands of silk of the same shade two and a half inches wide are sewn to the tops, most likely to roll round the garters.

In a wardrobe account of about this time the following entry appears:

'To Alice Mountague, the Quene's Majestie's silk-woman, for sondryie nescesaries by her dilivered to her Majestie's use—£702 11s. 0¾d.'

It is not clear if the whole of this vast sum was spent on stockings. The salary of Henry Herne, the Queen's hosier, was only £11 7s. 10d. per annum.

Silk stockings formed an acceptable present to Elizabeth, e.g.: 'One peire of silk stockings and a peire of garters of white sypres, by Mrs. Vaughan.'

Fig. 635

Of course, the news of Her Majesty's latest acquisition of attractive silk hosiery gradually leaked out—or was it given voluntarily? Most certainly her ladies-in-waiting had every opportunity of a close inspection, and who knows but that many gentlemen-in-waiting may have been treated to a more distant view?

It was not long, however, before the ultra-fashionable of both sexes wore hand-knitted silk stockings, and the reputation of English-made hosiery attained a high standard. A stocking-maker of the time was known as a gordner or gradner. The ordinary person, and even the best-dressed, still used worsted, as silk stockings were very expensive. In 1564 an acute London apprentice named William Rider chanced to see a pair of knit worsted stockings in the lodgings of an Italian merchant from Mantua. He borrowed them—most likely without permission—and caused others to be made like them. These were the first hand-knitted stockings made in England since early medieval days.

Fancy knitted stockings are seen worn by gentlemen in Figs. 625 and 627.

(Continued on p. 630)

CLOAKS

Cloaks were circular, or shaped like that shown in diagram, Fig. 507. Some were short; others reached to the feet, and being ample resembled mantles.

Collars were usual, but a few cloaks were without them. The German cloak (see Figs. 622 and 654) was in reality a large jacket, with sleeves not intended to be worn but hanging, so giving width to the figure.

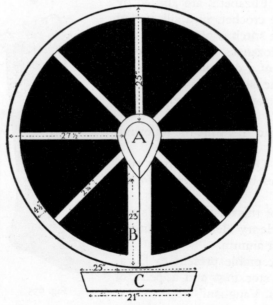

Fig. 636.
Diagram of Cloak

Fig. 637.
Embroidery on Cloak

The diagram (Fig. 636) is drawn from a cloak in the London Museum: A is the hole for the head, B the front, and C the collar. It is of crimson velvet having gold embroidery in a scroll design round the circumference and along the radii, shown white in the diagram. This design is reproduced in Fig. 637, and forms part of the four-and-a-half-inch border: the main scrolls are in gold silk appliqué edged with gold cord or twisted bullion, as are also the minor decorations. The edge is finished with a looped fringe of crimson silk and gold thread, and the cloak is lined throughout with a small patterned crimson and gold brocade.

A later version of the Spanish hooded cloak or muceta, described and figured in Chapter III, p. 417, is shown in Fig. 638. This muceta dates at the end of the century. The patterns, cut for a bishop by an eminent Spanish tailor of the period, are laid out on a length of cloth doubled. The reader should be able to puzzle out the construction for himself.

A hood of different shape, to be attached to a cloak, is given in Fig. 639, in which AB is the opening for the face, and BC surrounds the neck.

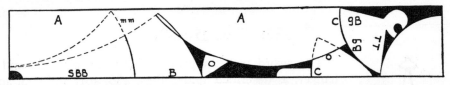

Manteo y museta de paño para obispo.

Fig. 638

A cross between a cloak and a jerkin, known as a MANDILION, was worn towards the end of the period covered by Part I. It was a loose short coat similar in shape to the journade (*see* vol. ii, Fig. 564), but sometimes slit up the sides. It was made of all kinds of material and often richly braided. It had sleeves which were seldom worn, the coat itself being used as a cape, or more frequently draped around the shoulders. The manner of wearing the mandilion askew, or 'Collie - Westonward' as this mode was termed by Harrison, is to be seen in the portrait of Sir Philip Sidney, No. 1862 in the National Portrait Gallery.

Stubbes tells us that the fashionable of the 80's and 90's 'have clokes . . . of diverse and sundry colours, white, red, taunie, black, green, yellow, russet, purple, violet, and infinite other colours: some of cloth, silk, velvet, taffata, and such like, whereof some be of the Spanish, French, and Dutch fashions. Some short scarcly reaching to the girdlestead, or waist, some to the knee, and othersome trayling upon the ground (almost) liker gowns than clokes. Then they are garded with velvet gardes, or else laced with costly lace either

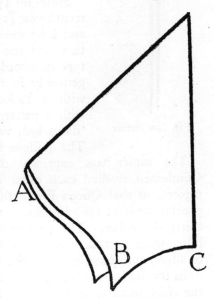

Fig. 639. Diagram of Hood

of gold, silver, or at least of silk three or four fingers broad down the back, about the skirts and everywhere else. And now of late they use to gard their clokes round about the skirts with bables, I should say bugles, and other kinds of glass, and all to shine to the eye. They are sometimes so lined as the inner side standeth almost in as much as the outside: some have sleeves, othersome have none, some have hoods to pull over the head, some have none; some are hanged with points and tassels of gold, silver, or silk, some without all this.'

He also mentions that 'some be made with collars and some without; some close to the body, some loose, which they call mandilians, covering the whole of the body down to the thighs, like bags or sacks that were drawn over them, hiding the demensions and lineaments of the same.'

SWORDS AND DAGGERS

Fig. 640. Rapier

The sword was slung on the left hip by belts and a hanger, as described under Figs. 486, 501, and 502, and types of hilt can be seen in many of the previous drawings in vol. iii, especially Fig. 503. In the reign of the Emperor Charles V, the RAPIER was introduced from Italy into Spain, and brought to England in the entourage of Prince Philip. The rapier was also known in France and Germany, and became a fashionable weapon in England during the early years of Elizabeth's reign.

Stow in 1578 tells us that 'shortly after the thirteenth year [1571] of Elizabeth began long tucks [swords] and long rapiers, and he was held the greatest gallant that had the deepest ruffe and longest rapier.' This type of sword (Fig. 640) had a long thin narrow blade, generally four-sided, the best being forged at Toledo, with a basket or cup-hilt either solid or perforated with a pattern, the smartest being of silver or silver gilt 'damasked, varnished, and engraven marvellous goodly.' The quillons were straight or curved, and the handle long.

The rapier was expressly designed for thrusting. Gentlemen rivalled each other in the length of their rapiers, so that Queen Elizabeth was forced to issue a proclamation in 1580 limiting the length of the blade to thirty-six inches. The scabbards were as ornate as the hilts, being often covered with velvet decorated with gold or silver, and sometimes set with jewels.

In the Italian mode of fighting, the rapier was held in the right hand to attack, and the dagger in the left to defend, and divert the thrusts of the adversary.

The dagger, originally stuck through the pouch and later (in the reign of Henry VIII) slung by a cord from the waist sash, was during the Elizabethan era passed through the waist-belt on the right side, the handle or dudgeon projecting in front so as to be readily grasped. This fashion of

Fig. 641. Dagger

carrying the dagger was introduced by the Spaniards in the last reign, and in this volume Lord Darnley is the first to be shown wearing it (Fig. 611). The top of the hilt is just visible. Probably the first Englishman's portrait to show the dagger stuck through the waist-belt is that of Ambrose Dudley (1560) in the Wallace Collection.

Fig. 641 shows an ordinary dagger of this period. When carried by the nobility, the handle was often elaborately decorated. The length of the blade varied, and daggers are usually referred to as long or short; but in 1562 the length of blade was limited to twelve inches.

The term 'bilbo' meant a sword blade made in Bilbao, and noted for the fine temper of its blade. It is frequently used humorously for the sword of a braggart.

THE HANDKERCHIEF (*continued from p. 261*)

During the reign of Elizabeth, handkerchiefs were universally used by ladies and gentlemen, and generally carried in the hand. They were made of very fine linen, lawn, cambric, or silk, about twelve or fifteen inches square—very large by modern standards—and edged with embroidery or lace of various widths, and sometimes both.

The useful yet dainty handkerchief often had a picot edging, and ornaments worked in white thread are sometimes seen hanging from the corners in portraits. Fig. 642 shows one kind in use.

Fig. 642

The estimation in which handkerchiefs were held is evidenced by the mention of them in wills and bequests, and many details are found in wardrobe

Fig. 643. Embroidered Border in Handkerchief

accounts. A set of six handkerchiefs edged with passamayne of gold and silk was a New Year's gift to Queen Mary, and Queen Elizabeth frequently received such gifts.   The following is a typical entry of 1578: 'Six faire handkerches of camerike of black Spanish worke edged with a brode bone lace of gold and silver.'   A handkerchief belonging to Queen Elizabeth was left behind after one of her visits to Warwick Castle, and can be seen there for the asking.   It is of deep cream linen (possibly with age) having a border two inches wide embroidered with red roses and green leaves in silks and gold thread.   Fig. 643 is a drawing of the border.   The handkerchief measures thirteen inches square.

Borders embroidered with blue thread of Coventry—a very vivid blue— were fashionable during the later part of the reign.   At this time also handkerchiefs were often made of tiffany.

The historian Stow tells us that 'maydes and gentlewomen gave to their favourites, as tokens of their love, little handkerchiefs of about three or four inches square, wrought round about, with buttons at each corner.'   The best were edged with gold and silver lace.   The fortunate recipient wore these favours tucked into the band of his hat, and on this account they were of diminutive size.

A few lines from a poem of this time proves the handkerchief to be a very important item of dress even among the lower classes:

'Nor imitate with Socrates,
to wipe thy snivelled nose
Vpon thy cap, as he would doe,
nor yet upon thy clothes.

But keepe it cleane with handkerchiffe,
provided for the same,
Not with thy fingers or thy sleeve,
therein thou art too blame.'

The handkerchief was the most general item of dress for the medium of perfumery.   When used by fashionable men and women it was scented with some delicious perfume.   Certain scents had disinfecting properties, which none the less had a pleasant smell and were very necessary.

The modern handkerchief sachet had its prototype in the 'sweete bagges' of Elizabethan days, which were dainty accessories much appreciated by both ladies and gentlemen.   Such articles were often presented to the Queen: 'A sweete bagge all over ymbrodered, and six handkerchers'; '24 small sweete bagges of sarsenett of sundry cullors, and six handkerchers of camberick wrought with black silk, and edged with a passamayne of gold, given by Mrs. Huggens.'

THE GLOVE (*continued from p. 261*)

Gloves used by ladies and gentlemen of this period had cuffs or gauntlets larger than before and richly embroidered in silks, bullion, and often spangles. Silk fringe, sometimes mixed with gold thread, finished off the bottom edge. A characteristic feature of Elizabethan gloves was the two, or perhaps three, loops also embroidered, which connected loosely the two edges of the gauntlet. Those of the very best quality were imported from Venice.

Fig. 644 shows one of these embroidered gloves as worn by the fashionable. It is made of light buff leather. The embroidery consists of roses in silk of two shades of pink and blue, with green trees linked by half-circles of silver wire gimp. A fanciful bird appears twice in the border. Below the gauntlet is a narrow binding of pink silk finished with silver fringe. The loops are also of pink silk embroidered with silver. This glove once belonged to Mary Queen of Scots, and is now in the Saffron Walden Museum. It measures fourteen and a half inches from finger-tip to base of fringe.

Shakespeare's gloves can be seen in the museum at Stratford-on-Avon. They are

Fig. 644. Glove of Mary Stuart

about the same length, but cut in one with the cuff. Fancy braids and a narrow fringe finish off the edge, and on the back is a braided design. Several Elizabethan gloves are to be found in museums. A beautiful pair, of white embroidered kid, was presented to Queen Elizabeth by the University of Oxford, but inadvertently left behind; they now repose in the Ashmolean. On the occasion of another visit to Oxford: '6th Sept. 1566. This day, the Commissary and Proctors in the name of the whole University, presented unto the Queen's Majesty six pairs of gloves, that were very fine; and to divers of the Noblemen, and to the Officers of the Queen's House, some two pair, some one; which were accepted thankfully.'

Fig. 645. Cutte Glove

The man of fashion was very fastidious about his gloves; so that the author of *A Briefe Conceipte of English Pollicys* writes in 1581: 'There is no man can be contented now with any other gloves than is made in France or in Spain nor Kersey, but it must be of Flanders dye.' However, Duke Frederick of Württemberg considered English-made gloves good enough for him, as he commissions his secretary while travelling in this country to purchase some. 'Six pair English gloves, of equal quality at 8s., making 48s. = 12 Gulden 12 Batzen,' are included in his account for goods bought.

Fig. 646. Mitten

Gloves with a series of cuttes round the fingers to show the rings were still fashionable, and an excellent example is to be seen in the portrait of the Empress Maria by Antonio Moro in the Prado. Fig. 645 is a drawing of them. Holes in gloves were made also to prevent any ill effects from confined perspiration: 'White prick seamed gloves of kid.' It is stated that on more than one occasion Queen Elizabeth wore gloves of kid having five air-holes, rather larger than melon seeds, stamped in the palms. Gloves were also made of chicken-skin, not necessarily of a chicken but the prepared skin of a very young animal, and ornamented in various ways.

Perfumed gloves were very little used during the first years of the reign of Elizabeth. In 1573 the young Earl of Oxford, returning from his travels on the Continent, brought some from Italy, including many other 'pleasant things' such as 'sweet-bags,' and perfumed leather jerkins. He presented Her Majesty with 'a payre of perfumed gloves, trimmed onlie with foure tuftes of roses in culler'd silk. The queene took such pleasure in those gloves that she was pictured with those gloves upon her hands.' So deliciously smelling were they that she christened the scent 'The Earl of Oxford's perfume.' Gloves of this odour came to be known as 'Oxford gloves'—'two pairs of Oxford gloves' cost 2s. 4d.—although they were not necessarily made in Oxford.

In 1578 when the Queen again visited Cambridge the Vice-Chancellor presented her with 'a pair of perfumed gloves garnished with embroiderie and goldsmiths-wourke.' These cost the University 60s. '15 paires of perfumed gloves' were given by different people to the Queen as New Year's gifts in 1599.

White gloves were worn at weddings—'innocent white wedding gloves'—

and the custom of winning a pair of gloves by kissing a person when caught sleeping originated in the sixteenth century.

Mittens (*see* vol. ii, p. 93). In the sixteenth century this term is applied not only to a bag for the fingers and a separate compartment for the thumb, but also to *warm* gloves with separate fingers. They were made of many kinds of material: leather, linen, or velvet mittens with stitched or fancy ornament, or knitted wool.

Fig. 646 gives one of a pair of mittens which belonged to Queen Elizabeth. They measure sixteen inches in length, and are of crimson velvet embroidered on the backs with a design (*see* inset) in gold, and edged with gold cord. The cuffs are covered with white satin cut in panels at the bottom, and worked in a design of flowers, leaves, etc., in various coloured silks, gold and silver thread and spangles; the whole background is besprinkled with tiny beads.

According to Shakespeare (*Winter's Tale*) gloves [1] were sold by milliners: 'No milliner can so fit his customers with gloves' (*see* p. 453).

PERFUMES AND POMANDERS AND ROSES (*continued from* p. 272)

Edmund Howes tells us that perfumes were not made in England until the early years of Elizabeth's reign. At this time very strong aromatics, such as musk and civet, formed the basis of most preparations. Sweet-smelling waters were distilled from roses, lavender, rose-mary, and juniper, and were used to scent hand-kerchiefs, clothes, and bed-linen.

Floors were perfumed with sweet-smelling rushes or sprinkled with scented waters. For fumigating the atmosphere of stuffy rooms, perfumed bellows were brought into use. 'The smoke of juniper is in great request with us to sweeten our chambers.'

A pomander of the time of Elizabeth is shown in Fig. 647. It takes the form of a vase two inches in diameter, and is of gold and enamels. There are six sections, each containing space for one kind of perfume; these are hinged at the bottom and fall when the catch at the top is released, like the pomander shown in Fig. 304. The ladies (Figs. 679 and 595) are carrying pomanders at the ends of their girdles.

Fig. 647. Pomander

'Perfumes of sundry kyndes bought and provided by John Wynyarde and John Doden £68 7s. 11d.' is a heavy item which occurs in the Queen's accounts for 1568.

That gentlemen used pomanders is not certain, but most likely. It was,

[1] The Glovers' Company was not incorporated until 1638.

however, the correct thing for both ladies and gentlemen to carry on their persons a 'casting-bottle' with a perforated top and containing scent.

The scent of flowers was also much appreciated, especially by the ladies, for we are informed that they 'will carry in their hands nosegays and posies of flowers to smell at, and which is more, two or three nosegays sticked in their breasts before.'

That Queen Elizabeth was passionately fond of flowers is well known. As before mentioned, pansies were much in the Royal favour, even perhaps taking precedence over roses; though in some of her portraits the Queen is shown with one in her hand, and in others she wears a full-blown rose, such as are familiar to us to-day, fastened to her ruff. She liked also to be surrounded by flowers, and her chambers were made cheerful with the presence of cut blooms in large bowls and vases. Even in her progresses through the country she indulged in her love of flowers: so that as much as £182 5s. 5d. was so spent by Francis Cornwalles, groom-porter, for the privy chamber of presence 'for flowers and bowes [bowers].'

The cult of the rose had now developed since Dr. Linacre's introduction (*see* p. 294) owing to the perseverance and skill of John Gerard, the celebrated English herbalist and surgeon. He was born at Nantwich in 1545 and lived in Holborn, where he had a garden in which he devoted a great deal of his time to the cultivation of rare plants, especially those for medicinal use, and nine different varieties of roses. He also became an expert in the laying out of gardens, including those of Lord Burleigh's house in the Strand and at Theobalds, Hertfordshire. He died in 1611, and is buried in St. Andrew's, Holborn, but no monument is erected to his memory.

Fig. 648. Embroidered Border

It will have become apparent to the reader of the foregoing descriptions that the garments clothing English men and women were a medley drawn from many nations: thus the same man might one day appear dressed entirely as a Spaniard, and on the next in a variety of garments each characteristic of a different country. Harrison makes a strong point of this foible of his countrymen, saying that it is very difficult to describe pure English dress as the numerous fanciful follies, culled from all over the known world, displayed in gentlemen's attire are astonishing. To-day it is the Spanish style and to-morrow the French fashion or the German guise. 'By and by the Turkish manner is generally best liked of, otherwise the Morisco gowns and the Barbarian sleeves, the mandilion worn to Collie weston ward (*see* p. 547) and the short French breeches (*see* Figs. 658 and 751).'

This was even more obvious to foreigners: a Dutchman visiting England during this period remarks that 'the English dress in elegant, light, and costly garments, but are very inconsistent and desirous of novelties, changing their costumes every year both men and women.'

The sartorial mind of the average Englishman of Tudor times is well expressed in the woodcut (Fig. 649). Here is the story: 'Yea, many men are become so effeminate, that they care not what they spend in disguising themselves, ever desiring new toys, and inventing new fashions. Therefore, a certain man, that would picture every countryman in his accustomed apparel, when he had painted other nations, he pictured the Englishman all naked,

Fig. 649. He 's an Englishman

unto whom he gave a pair of sheares in the one hand, and a piece of cloth in the other, to the end he should shape his apparel after such fashion as himselfe liked, sith he could find no kind of garment that could please him any while together.'

Underneath the picture is written this soliloquy:

> 'I am an Englishman, and naked I stand here,
> Musing in my mynde what rayment I shal were;
> For now I wyll were thys, and now I wyl were that;
> Now I wyl were I cannot tel what.
> All new fashyons be plesaunt to me;
> I wyl haue them, whether I thryue or thee.'
>
> ANDREW BOORDE.

The authors of the *Church Homilies*, published in 1562, eagerly seized upon such an attractive weakness for their fulminations. In the homily *Against Excess of Apparel* they refer with approval to the Israelites who 'were contented with such apparel as God gave them, although it were base and simple. And God so blessed them that their shoes and clothes lasted fortie years.'

The Elizabethans were not so well favoured by the Almighty, nor were they by any means so careful and contented. 'Most commonly he that ruffleth in his sables, in his fine furred gown, corked slippers, trim buskins, and warm mittens is more ready to chill for cold, than the poor labouring man, which can abide in the field all the day long, when the north wind blows, with a few beggarly clouts about him. We were loth to wear such as our fathers have left us; we think not that sufficient or good enough for us. We must have one gown for the day, another for the night; one long, another short, one for winter, another for summer; one through furred, another but faced; one for the working day, another for the holy-day; one of this colour, another of that colour; one of cloth, another of silk or damask. We must have change of apparel, one afore dinner, and another after; one of the Spanish fashion, another Turkey; and to be brief, never content with sufficient.'

It is to be regretted that such excellent advice fell upon deaf ears, and the sermons evidently had little effect. For at the beginning of the seventeenth century the good work was continued by Thomas Dekker, who, in his *Seuen Deadly Sinnes of London*, hurls further caustic remarks at the fashionable Englishman. His suit, he says, 'is like a traitors body that hath been hanged, drawn, and quartered, and is set up in several places; his codpiece is in Denmark, the collar of his doublet and the belly in France: the short waist hangs over a Dutch Botchers [a mender, a patcher] stall vtrich: his huge slopps speaks Spanish: Poland gives him boots: the block for his head alters faster than the feltmaker can fit him, and thereupon we are called in scorn "blockheads."'

One of many examples of cosmopolitan fashion can be illustrated by Figs. 655, 664, 673, 737, and description of Fig. 665; the same gentleman might wear any of the slops there shown, be they English, French, German, Italian, or Spanish.

FRENCH FASHIONS, 1558–80

The special reason for treating the costume of English women before that of men does not apply to foreign countries, so that in dealing with France, Italy, and Spain, we shall return to the normal order, and give precedence to the gentlemen.

KING CHARLES IX, 1550–74

An excellent example of the height of fashion in France is illustrated in Plate XXXVI. This is taken from the full-length portrait group of Catherine de' Medici with her three surviving sons and daughter (Plate XXXV), which has been reproduced by kind permission of the owner, Miss Oswald-Smith, from the original at Shottesbrooke Park. Of the school of François Clouet, it was painted in 1561 when Charles IX (the subject of Plate XXXVI) was eleven years of age, in spite of which his costume is that of a full-grown man. The three brothers are dressed alike in suits of amber satin decorated with silver passamayne in perpendicular and oblique lines. The doublet is slightly padded at the waist, the lines of decoration converging from shoulders to the waist and surrounding the tabs. The left wing is clearly defined in

·ANNATA·SVÆ·XI·

PLATE XXXV. CATHERINE DE' MEDICI AND HER FAMILY, 1561
Shottesbrooke Park.   *By kind permission of Miss Oswald-Smith*

shape, and is finished back and front in points like that shown in Fig. 630. The sleeves are close-fitting and the slops are decorated in the same manner as the doublet, as is also the velvet cloak. This and the hosen and shoes match the dress in colour; a pendant hangs from a blue cordon, while waist and sword belt, and scabbard, are of amber velvet. The hat, of amber velvet, is decorated with triangles of clustered pearls, and carries a natural-coloured ostrich feather. Brown gloves turned back at the wrist to show the grey lining are carried. Charles, Duc d'Orléans, second son of Henry II and Catherine, was born 27th June 1550 at Saint-Germain-en-Laye. He ascended the throne of France in 1560, on the death of his brother Francis II, as Charles IX.

In appearance as a young man he was tall and slim like his younger brother Henry, but feeble and sickly, his demeanour being spoiled by a habit of

Fig. 650. Charles IX, 1569 (*after François Clouet*)

stooping and an awkward way of holding his head on one side. His complexion was fair and pale, his hair dark brown, his countenance haggard and unpleasing, his eyes glassy and listless except when he became excited, when they flashed like fire. In disposition he was indolent and without moral courage, and easily influenced by his dominating mother. Poetry and hunting were his chief amusements, and he was particularly fond of dogs, which swarmed all over his apartments, an Italian greyhound being his constant companion. Fig. 844 is made from a drawing of this King at the age of nineteen in the Bibliothèque Nationale, Paris.

A year later we have the well-known portrait (Fig. 650) of Charles IX at the age of twenty. The original is by François Clouet and is in the Kunsthistorisches Museum, Vienna. The King has now grown a small moustache,

Fig. 651   Fig. 652

and his costume consists of a black velvet jerkin with basques which are in the fashion of twenty years earlier. It is banded with wide bands of gold embroidery of a delightful and complicated pattern. The black velvet cloak has two bands of embroidery all round the edge. The design of this is not shown in Fig. 650, but Fig. 651 is a detailed drawing of it. A duplicate portrait by the same artist is in the Louvre; it is identical except for the embroidery, the different pattern of which is shown in Fig. 652.

The underdress is of white silk or satin, thereby carrying out the same scheme as was adopted by his father. The chair upholdered in crimson

Fig. 653. François de Lorraine,
Duc de Guise, 1560

Fig. 654.
Odet de Coligny, 1569

velvet is a typical French one of the period. Many portraits of Charles IX in later life are extant.

Death struck terror into the heart of this young king. Overcome with remorse for the reluctant consent he was made to give under moral pressure to the Massacre of St. Bartholomew (1572) and the murder of Coligny, he died, 30th May 1574.

The French nobleman (Fig. 653) is dressed entirely in white except the hat and cloak which are of black velvet, the latter edged with wide gold lace. The edgings of the bands of white on the doublet and slops are of a narrow fancy gold braid.

Fig. 654 is made from a drawing of the three brothers Coligny, all of whom

PLATE XXXVI. CHARLES IX, KING OF FRANCE, 1561

met with violent deaths—two being poisoned and one a victim of the massacre
of St. Bartholomew. The figure represents the eldest, Odet (1517–69),
Cardinal de Chastillon. Although French he wears a German fashion in
cloaks. It has practical sleeves with wings or shoulder pieces, but these were
not usually worn on the arm but
hung from the shoulders, giving an
effect of breadth to the figure. The
garment itself is cut as a semicircle
like an ordinary cloak; sometimes it
was much less than a semicircle.
It is elaborately braided, having
cuttes or pinking between braids,
and fastens down the front, if desired,
by buttons and frogs. Another German cloak is seen in Fig. 622. The
dress worn underneath the cloak in
Fig. 654 is a doublet with trunk
hose, not paned, but decorated with
horizontal bands of braid.

The three-quarter-length drawing
(Fig. 655) is made from a portrait in
the Louvre of a French gentleman
dating about 1568. The very attractive suit is carried out in soft buff
leather, most probably chamois; the
peascod doublet is elaborately pinked,
and the decoration of the pansid slops

Fig. 655. A French Gentleman, 1568

is a cut steel braid outlined with vermilion silk. The venetians are of plain
leather. Cut steel buttons fasten the doublet, and a line of steel braid overlies
the seams. A black waist- and sword-belt, scabbard, and dagger tucked in the
waist-belt at the left back, buff nether stocks, and shoes complete this very
smart costume.

HENRY, DUC D'ANJOU, 1551 until 1580

Henry, Duc d'Anjou, third son of Henry II and Catherine, was born 19th
September 1551 at Fontainebleau. He is seen at the age of ten in the
portrait group (Plate XXXV) standing on the right, dressed in the same manner
as his brother Charles.

When he reached manhood Henry is described as tall, slim, and elegant,
although it was said he looked like a walking spectre. His eyes were sunken,
his mouth always twitching, and his gaze unsteady. He wore a small satanic
moustache and a narrow pointed beard.

When the Polish Ambassadors came to Paris in 1573 to offer the Crown of
Poland to Henry, the fêtes given in their honour were most lavish and magnificent; and to commemorate this auspicious event the Queen-Mother

commanded several panels of tapestry to be made by Flemish tapissers. Fig. 656 is reconstructed from the portrait of the Duc d'Anjou depicted in one of the panels.

His dress appears to consist of a peascod-paunched doublet of light-coloured silk, braided and pinked, with venetians of the same material but untrimmed; a moderate-sized ruff, a short black velvet cloak draped over the left shoulder, and a very characteristic Italian hat.   His stockings and shoes

Fig. 656. Duc d'Anjou, 1573   Fig. 657. Duc d'Alençon

match the rest of this dress.   A black ribbon surrounds his neck, and he is fingering some jewel or the badge of St. Michael suspended therefrom. Henry is credited by some with being intensely effeminate, 'weaker than woman and worse than harlot,' nevertheless, a man of keen intelligence and cultivated mind, who during his command in the religious wars showed great courage, for which he won golden opinions.

The Duc d'Anjou succeeded to the Crown of France as Henry III on the death of his brother Charles in 1574.   (Continued on p. 654)

FRANÇOIS, DUC D'ALENÇON, 1554 until 1580

The small figure in the left-hand corner of the group (Plate XXXV) is François, Duc d'Alençon, at the age of eleven, the youngest son of Henry II

and Catherine, who was born in 1554. He was not a normal child; rather
deformed, he had smallpox while still young which left his not-too-beautiful
face deeply pitted. However, in some of his later portraits he is depicted
as a quite good-looking young man. In 1572 the Queen-Mother suggested
François as a suitable husband for Queen Elizabeth—he was just eighteen
while she was thirty-nine.

Elizabeth was full of admiration for her young lover—from hearsay only,
most likely through his Ambassador Jean de Simier, Baron de Saint-Marc,
whom he sent over in 1579 to do his wooing for
him. Always astute, the Queen did suggest 'the
absurdity that in the general opinion of the world
might grow' if she married this ill-favoured, pock-
marked boy after refusing so many suitors of great
worthiness. At the end of this year François rushed
over to England, heavily disguised, to see the
Queen. She then admitted to him that 'he had
been represented to her as hideous, hump-back,
and deformed, but she found him the reverse and
most handsome in her eyes.' Love is blind, they
say! England was much opposed to this marriage
of their Queen and Alençon, since (1576) Duc
d'Anjou, but the matrimonial negotiations and the
courtship of the young couple waxed and waned
at intervals.

A miniature of Alençon, painted about 1574, and
showing the whole figure, can be seen in the Victoria and Albert Museum. Fig. 657 is made from
it. The slightly peascod doublet, with straight
basque and full sleeves, and the short slops are of
white silk covered with delicate gold embroidery.
An ample cloak of black velvet, banded with a fancy
jet trimming and lined with black fur, swings from the
shoulders. The black velvet Italian hat has diamond

Fig. 658.
A Nobleman, 1570

ornaments around the brim, with a large ruby surrounded by diamonds and
surmounted by black fronds. A small ruff, white and gold sword-belt, white
hosen, and black shoes with red ties are worn. In his right hand, resting
upon a green velvet gold-fringed table-cloth, Alençon holds a portrait of
Queen Elizabeth.

A nobleman of the 1570's is shown in Fig. 658. The usual peascod doublet
is cutte in six places, and has sleeves with spiral bands of cuttes: a paned
hip-roll and venetians ornamented up the fronts with embroidery are worn
under a long cloak. This is of fine material, cut on the semicircle, and
gathered in groups to a deep band which looks like a collar. The garment is
tied by cords and tassels over the left shoulder and under the right arm.

Fig. 659. ELIZABETH OF AUSTRIA, QUEEN OF FRANCE

NOBLE LADIES, 1558–80

ELIZABETH OF AUSTRIA

Queen of France, 1557–92

The First Lady in the Land—at least, the most important leader of feminine fashion—was Elizabeth or Isabella of Austria, second daughter of the Emperor Maximilian II and his cousin Marie, daughter of the Emperor Charles V. This Archduchess, who was born in 1557, married Charles IX of France in 1572.

'She was very beautiful, having the complexion of her face as fine and delicate as any lady of her Court, and very agreeable. Her figure was beautiful also, though it was of only medium height,' thought Brantôme; very devout, she always had a 'night-lamp filled with wax which she kept lighted on her bed to read and pray to God, though other Queens and Princesses kept theirs upon their sideboards.'

The Queen's costume, shown in Fig. 659, is similar in many respects to that worn by Mary Stuart (Fig. 528). The sleeves have the same character, and are trimmed with spiral puffings fixed with jewels. The bodice and skirt are of a delicate patterned brocade edged with embroidery; and the skirt is open up the front to show an under-skirt of plain silk. A profusion of jewels ornaments the coif, neck, bodice, waist, and sleeves.

Elizabeth was so devoted a wife that when Charles IX died in 1574, she could 'not forget her husband in a second marriage . . . Such was the great constancy and noble firmness of this virtuous Queen, which she kept to the end of her days, towards the venerated bones of the King her husband, which she honoured incessantly with regrets and tears.' Fig. 884 is made from a drawing by François Quesnel and shows Elizabeth of Austria in widow's weeds.

On her death-bed the Queen 'felt especial longing for a sight of His Majesty, her most beloved brother [the Emperor Rudolph II]. His Majesty had arrived the previous night by *mail-coach* with but a few horses. His arrival caused the Queen no little joy in her great suffering before the end.' She died in January 1592 at the age of thirty-five.

LOUISE OF LORRAINE

Queen of France, 1575 until 1580

At the time Henry, Duc d'Anjou, was on his way to Poland, 'he saw at Balmont in Lorraine, Mademoiselle de Vaudemont, Louise de Lorraine, one of the handsomest, best, and most accomplished princesses in Christendom, on whom he cast his eyes so ardently that he was soon in love.' On his return to France, and soon after his accession, he sent for the lady, and married her in 1575.   She is described by Brantôme as 'wise, chaste, and virtuous,' and 'delicate and loveable'; but she did not have a very happy time as Queen-Consort of France, owing to her very decadent husband and strong-minded mother-in-law.

Nearly all the portraits of Louise of Lorraine show her wearing the same style of dress and coiffure.   In Fig. 660 the Queen wears a robe of deep-toned velvet that recalls the style fashionable during Francis I's reign; indeed, it is entirely so except for the up-standing ruff and the hairdressing.   The presence of bands of jewels on the upper arms above the white fur suggests that these sleeves of old-fashioned shape are faked and are *not* turned back as described under Fig. 254: while the under-sleeves are not nearly so large as their predecessors.   The skirt is edged with fur up the fronts and at the hem, and the under-skirt is of a light colour with an embroidered border in gold.   From the bejewelled girdle hangs a handsome ornament ending in a peardrop pearl.

Fig. 660. Louise de Vaudemont, Queen of France

The chief feature of this costume, however, is the ruff, which is distinctly French, and is a development of that worn by Catherine de' Medici (Fig. 543), but simpler.   The shaped plain transparent collar part fits into the décolletage of the bodice and folds back in crescent form around the neck.   To the edge is fixed a pleated frill of the same lawn, in this particular case doubled; although lace and insertion might be used, pleated or put on plain.   Similar examples of this kind of ruff are seen in Figs. 755 and 757.

(Continued on p. 662)

MARGUERITE DE VALOIS [1]

Queen of Navarre, 1553 until 1580

The costume of a young girl of this period is seen in Plate XXXV.   This is Marguerite de Valois, the third daughter of Henry II and Catherine.   She was born in 1553 and therefore aged eight in the painting.   Her gown is of

---

[1] It should be borne in mind that there were two other princesses bearing the same name—Marguerite de Valois—of note in the sixteenth century: (1) The authoress of the *Heptameron* and of many poems was Marguerite, daughter of Charles, Duc d'Orléans and Comte d'Angoulême, and sister of Francis I.   Born in 1492, she married first, in 1509, Charles, Duc d'Alençon, who died

grey-blue velvet, and has a wide band of gold passamayne round the neck of the bodice and up the fronts and at the hem of the all-round skirt. The underdress is of cloth of silver, and a beautiful network cap—an escoffion —is worn composed of bands of jewels—rubies, diamonds, emeralds, and pearls. The collar and girdle are composed of the same jewels, the pendant being a pomander in the form of a gold vase.

She was considered a great beauty. Pierre de Ronsard (1524–85), whose prolific poems delighted all Europe, describes her features thus: 'Waving hair more dark than blond' (her hair was very black, having been derived from her father, so Brantôme tells us, though the painting (Plate XXXV) shows it as dark chestnut), her eyebrows like 'ebony bows,' brown eyes, tilted nose, and shell-like ears, 'teeth like rows of pearls,' slim, tender hands, and little feet.

Her future mother-in-law, Queen Jeanne of Navarre, was sceptical about her charms, for she admits, 'as for her beauty, I confess that she is well made, but she laces extravagantly; her face is arranged with so much art that it angers me, but at this [French] Court paint and powder are almost as common as in Spain.' Later on, the Queen states that 'she is fair to see, and well instructed, and of happy manner, but brought up in the most abandoned and loose company.'

Marguerite was very learned, and had some claims to be considered an authoress; and it is not surprising to learn from the aforesaid statement that she was also famous for her licentious manners, even in those days. She lived before her time: her place is the twentieth century.

Her ambitious mother evolved many plans for her daughter's marriage, and would be satisfied by nothing short of a Royal diadem. Don Carlos of Spain, Rudolph of Austria, and the King of Portugal were all approached without success; so, after a liaison with Henry, Duc de Guise, Marguerite eventually wedded Henry of Navarre, 18th August 1572. Thus she secured an insignificant crown, little dreaming that it would lead to the crown matrimonial of France.

Her wedding dress is described by Marguerite herself: 'I myself was in Royal splendour, with crown and mantle of ermine, all ablaze with jewels, and with my great blue train four ells long, borne by three princesses.'[1]

Another report of her wedding costume mentions that it was of cloth of gold, the bodice so closely covered with pearls as to look like a cuirass; over this was a blue velvet mantle nearly five yards long embroidered with fleurs-de-lys. Her dark hair was loose and flowing, and studded with diamond stars. After the marriage ceremony she heard Mass alone without her husband—he was a Huguenot. As a wedding present from her family and her bridegroom, quantities of jewels were given her amounting to £100,000.

in 1525. Her second husband, married in 1527, was Henry d'Albret, titular King of Navarre. Their only child, Jeanne d'Albret, later Queen-Regnant of Navarre, was the mother of Henry IV. Marguerite de Valois I died 1549. (2) A second Marguerite de Valois (II), niece of the above and daughter of Francis I, was born in 1523. She married in 1559 Emmanuel Philibert, Duke of Savoy, and died 1574.

   Marguerite de Valois III, described in the text, was niece of No. (2) and great-niece of No. (1)

[1] Is this the first appearance of bridesmaids?

The five following days were devoted to splendid entertainments, until the 23rd—the eve of St. Bartholomew.

As Queen of Navarre Marguerite spent much time at the French Court where 'La Reine Margot' was a supreme leader of fashion. Whatever she appeared in she was the envy of all the Grandes Dames who desired to be a à la mode. At the suggestion of her mother, whom she greatly feared, she arrayed herself one day while at Cognac most gorgeously in the fine and superb apparel that she was accustomed to wear at Court for great and magnificent pomps and festivals. If her desire was to give pleasure to the noble ladies of the district, she succeeded beyond her utmost expectations, so great was their amazement when she appeared in a gown of silver tissue of dove colour, à la Bolonnoise, and hanging sleeves, and a rich headdress with a white veil.

'The Queen-Mother said to her: "My daughter, you look well." To which she answered: "Madame, I begin early to wear and to wear out my gowns and the fashions I have brought from Court, because when I return I shall bring nothing with me, only scissors and stuffs to dress me then according to current fashions." The Queen-Mother asked her: "What do you mean by that, my daughter? Is it not you yourself who invent and produce these fashions of dress? Wherever you go the Court will take them from you, not you from the Court." Which was true; for after she returned she was always in advance of the Court, so well did she know how to invent in her dainty mind all sorts of charming things.' [1]

From the same author we learn that at the fête at the Tuileries for the Polish nobles in 1573 'she was robed in a gown of rose-coloured Spanish velvet covered with spangles, with a bonet of the same adorned with plumes and jewels.' He says that she was painted in this dress: but where is the picture? He also tells us of another splendid costume worn by Queen Marguerite: 'I have seen her dressed in a robe of white satin that shimmered much, a trifle of rose-colour mingling in it [et un peu d'incarnadin meslé] . . . her head was adorned with quantities of pearls and jewels, especially brilliant diamonds, worn in the form of stars. . . . Her beautiful body, with its full, tall form, was robed in a gown of crinkled cloth of gold, the richest and most beautiful ever seen in France.' This material was a gift specially manufactured at Constantinople, and was fifteen ells long, costing one hundred crowns per ell.

(Continued on p. 665)

CATHERINE DE' MEDICI
Queen-Mother of France, 1558–89
(continued from p. 436)

On Queen Catherine's widowhood, in 1559, she set aside her rich attire, and wore heavy mourning, modelled on the prevailing fashionable lines, with a black veil attached to the front of her 'attifet'—the wired-out front of the headdress referred to on p. 452.

[1] Translated from Brantôme.

After an interval of ten years, however, her costume became more elaborate and rich, but always black.

There are several well-known portraits of her in widow's weeds. Fig. 661 is made from a contemporary drawing of the Queen-Mother a few months after she had become a widow. The dress is probably made of black silk, the bodice plain, very pointed in the stomacher, and buttoned up the front. A plain hemstitched white cambric collar surrounds the throat on top of the high collar of the bodice.

In most portraits the skirt is plain, but in others it is very finely pleated, almost like modern accordion pleating: it has a short train, and is worn over the Spanish farthingale of moderate dimensions.

The close-fitting cap of black gauze has an attifet front, and to this and the sides of the cap is gathered a portion of one corner of a voluminous square black veil. The veil is gathered again into the nape of the neck and wired out in curves over the shoulders, being fixed to the bodice just in front of the sleeve seam, thence falling in small pleats down the back and over the arms (see diagram, Fig. 721).

The figure of Catherine in the portrait group (Plate XXXV) is not very discernible, the dress being all in black against an almost black background. She

Fig. 661.
Catherine de' Medici, Queen-Mother of France

is represented at the age of fifty-two with chestnut-brown hair, looking many years older than in either the portrait by Pourbus at fifty (Fig. 525), or the original from which Fig. 661 is taken showing her in her fifty-first year. In Plate XXXV the dress of black silk is severely plain. The bodice, pointed at the waist, is fastened up the front with small silk buttons: the collar is high, and the pointed white collar is worn inside the ruff. The sleeves are moderately close-fitting, and of leg-of-mutton shape. The skirt is gathered into the waistband, and no farthingale is worn. The headdress is rounded, not pointed, on the forehead, the veil hanging straight from it: both are of black crêpe, a new kind of transparent material produced in Italy chiefly at Bologna. The veil was not always pleated, and there were other ways of attaching it to the cap (see Fig. 883).

Brantôme, still an invaluable source of information, writes:

'The Queen-Mother wished and commanded her ladies always to appear in grand and superb apparel, though she herself during her widowhood never clothed herself in worldly silks, unless they were lugubrious, but always properly and so well fitting that she looked the Queen above all else. It is true that on the days of the weddings of her two sons, Charles and Henry, she wore gowns of black velvet, wishing, she said, to solemnize the event by

Fig. 662.   Fig. 663.
Italian Gentlemen (*after Moroni*)

so signal an act. While she was married she always dressed very richly and superbly, and looked what she was.'

When Catherine reached middle age she became somewhat corpulent; but still, at sixty, 'her complexion was fresh, and she had not a wrinkle on her full round face.'

In 1581, Catherine, at the age of sixty-two, appears in the painting of the ball given in honour of the marriage of the Duc de Joyeuse, wearing widow's weeds of black satin. A head-and-shoulders portrait at the Louvre is interesting as showing how the depth of the attifet point varied. In this case it extends almost to the top of the nose.

Catherine de' Medici died at the Castle of Blois, 5th January 1589, at the age of seventy.

A few details relative to widows' weeds as worn by noble ladies in France are found in the writings of Brantôme. Colours, we are not surprised to learn, were forbidden to widows, 'though their skirts and petticoats, and also their hosen they may wear of a tan-gray, violet, or blue. Some that I see emancipate themselves in flesh - coloured red and chamois colour, as in times past, when as I have heard said, all colours could be worn in petticoats and stockings, but not in gowns. . . . Our widows of to-day dare not wear precious stones, except on their fingers, on some mirrors, on some Book of Hours, and on their belts; but never on their heads or bodies, unless a few pearls on their neck and arms. But I swear to you I have seen widows as dainty as could be in their black and white gowns, who attracted quite as many and as much as the bedizened brides and maidens.'

ITALIAN INFLUENCES, 1558–80

NOBILITY: MEN

The description of characteristic costumes of Italy is made difficult by the fact that the country was divided into numerous principalities and dukedoms. Their styles differ somewhat, so that although portraits are fairly plentiful, it is not easy to select representative examples. Venice was the chief of the Italian states, and it was a common thing for Venetians to visit France and England during the whole of the sixteenth century.

An attempt has been made to interpret the costume in the portraits of the two Italian gentlemen (Figs. 662 and 663) by Moroni, at Bergamo, in the most explicit manner possible. As they are both garbed entirely in black it is not an easy task.

Doublets with moderately close sleeves, padded pumpkin-shaped slops, and, in Fig. 662, venetians, hosen, and shoes are of the fashion which was general throughout Europe during the 1570's and 1580's. The hats are definitely Italian, with bag crowns pleated into a brim

Fig. 664. (after Moroni), 1560–70

or a rouleau. The most important detail is the manner in which these gentlemen wear their cloaks.

Fig. 662 has taken the right corner and draped it over the right shoulder, and it should be noticed that the edge of the cloak is finished with tiny black buttons. Fig. 663 has caught the right-hand corner and holds it with the forearm, grasping the left side of the cloak with his right hand. The cloak is bordered with bands of black satin.

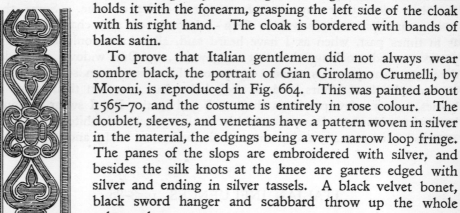
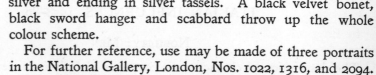

Fig. 665

To prove that Italian gentlemen did not always wear sombre black, the portrait of Gian Girolamo Crumelli, by Moroni, is reproduced in Fig. 664. This was painted about 1565–70, and the costume is entirely in rose colour. The doublet, sleeves, and venetians have a pattern woven in silver in the material, the edgings being a very narrow loop fringe. The panes of the slops are embroidered with silver, and besides the silk knots at the knee are garters edged with silver and ending in silver tassels. A black velvet bonet, black sword hanger and scabbard throw up the whole colour scheme.

For further reference, use may be made of three portraits in the National Gallery, London, Nos. 1022, 1316, and 2094.

An exceptionally fine three-quarter-length portrait of an Italian nobleman is to be seen at Shottesbrooke Park. It represents a member of the Medici family and was painted by Bronzino about 1565. The costume worn by this nobleman is in shape and colour exactly the same as that of the French gentleman (Fig. 655) except the decoration of the slops. These are of white satin; the panes, about two and a half inches wide, are set close together, and are of brick-orange velvet or cloth cut out in a pattern of which Fig. 665 is a drawing, and outlined with a very small cord of a golden yellow colour. The waist- and sword-belts are of black edged with gold, the latter being passed under three panes in the same manner as shown in Fig. 673. A glimpse of this appears through the openwork design, which is very effective.

This portrait is but another example of the similarity of fashion prevalent throughout Europe at this time, and referred to by many contemporary writers.

Fig. 666.
Dr. Jerome Capivacio

Fig. 666 is taken from a portrait of Dr. Jerome Capivacio, who died at Padua in 1589. His black velvet hat is full in the crown and pleated into the band, and the brim is fairly wide.[1] Similar hats were worn in England, and may be seen in many of the drawings in Chapters II, III, and IV (Part I).

---

[1] This type of hat formed the model for the headgear worn by later doctors of various arts and sciences; especially it will be recognized as that worn by doctors of music.

The doctor is wearing *spectacles* of the latest type. The frames of these are made of bone, though copper, lead, iron, and even wood were in use for this purpose: the best qualities were of gold or silver. In Fig. 666 the frame is attached by leather straps round the ears. Spectacle lenses were still made in Venice, though in Queen Elizabeth's time this craft was practised in London, where it had already reached a high standard. Coloured glasses to protect the eyes had come into use during the last century, when they were made in Germany; for the best quality lenses beryl was used.

Fig. 667.
An Italian Lady (*after Moroni*)

NOBLE LADIES

In England, as in France, the Italian vogue became that most sought after. Queen Elizabeth herself, on her own confession (*see* p. 492) favoured Italian fashions, and her ladies made haste to follow her example. It will, therefore, be useful to show a few examples of the costume worn by Italian noble ladies.

After minute investigation, the conclusion is reached that there is really very little difference between the costume of the leading nations of Europe, Germany, perhaps, excepted. Here and there one finds a detail or two which are decidedly national: otherwise the similarity is more or less general.

The chief distinctions are that Italian ladies, as a rule, ignored the farthingale, both Spanish (Fig. 242) and wheel (Fig. 243), but distended their skirts, possibly by the aid of the bolster (Fig. 713), to give the line of a modified farthingale.

The Italian ruff was small compared with the English, French, and Spanish, being either close to the neck and circular, or standing up from the shoulders in the Venetian (*see* Fig. 764) or the Florentine fashion (*see* Fig. 763).

The international exchange of headgear and headdresses is complicated, but it will be found that when a headdress of foreign origin is shown in any of the drawings the fact is mentioned.

Fig. 668

The Italian lady (Fig. 667) is taken from the seated portrait in the National Gallery, No. 1023, painted by Moroni in the 1570's. She is said to be one of the Fenaroli family. The dress is of rose-red satin with all edges of the cuttes and the garment rolled and bound over by a sort of blanket stitch in fine gold metal. The inside turned-back collar and small close cuffs are of transparent lawn, having a charming yet simple pattern (Fig. 668) embroidered round the hem in red silk. The underdress with sleeves is of gold-coloured satin or perhaps one of those exquisite materials woven by the expert Italian craftsmen: gold high lights with red-gold shadows, secured by a mixture of metal and silk, yet soft in texture, the prototype of which was woven at Constantinople centuries before, and originally known as baudekyn (see vol. ii, p. 123).

Fig. 669. A Lady of Pisa, 1580

Without doubt the shape of this distinctive Italian costume formed the model for the wardrobes of the western nobility—the high collar seen in England in Queen Mary's reign, stiff corsage, sleeves puffed on the shoulders and close on the arm, as seen in the drawings of Mary Stuart (Fig. 528) and Elizabeth of Austria (Fig. 659), the full trailing skirt open up the front and hanging in graceful folds from the waist, and, in this example, undistorted by the solid farthingale. The flat fan of five sticks is plaited with ochre-coloured straw and has a rigid handle.

Quite a different style of dress is worn by the Italian lady (Fig. 669), taken from a plan of the city of Pisa and dated 1580. The original is coloured, showing that the short over-robe with hanging sleeves is red and banded with gold. The robe worn under this is blue, with bands of black having cuttes between them, as also round the sleeves and at the hem. The under-robe is a pinkish mauve, forming an artistic combination with the red and blue. The Italian fan opens and closes, but is fixed to a rigid handle.

SPANISH STYLES: 1558–80

NOBILITY: MEN

After the death of Queen Mary, there was no longer a vogue in England for new fashions of Spanish origin. During her reign such styles had become incorporated in the fashionable attire of both men and women. Under Queen Elizabeth their place was taken, both in England and France, by those of Italy.

Most of the Spaniards who had come to England were very unpopular there.   Many of the middle class, tradesmen and artisans, had settled in England, thinking that the marriage of their Prince ensured complete domination of the kingdom.   There were numerous conflicts between the shopkeepers of both nationalities, compelling the English authorities to take stringent measures by ordering all shops kept by Spanish tradesmen to close down. Nothing remained for their disgusted proprietors but to return to their native land.

Despite the restrictions issued in the pragmatic of 1537 ingenious tailors devised a method of ornamenting the clothes of the upper classes by cutting out patterns in coloured cloth, and sewing them on to garments and overlaying them with delicate lace-like snippet work of applied cloth.   In face of this abuse, the Cortes of Valladolid begged the Emperor Charles V to forbid the use of any and every sort of trimming, lace, or adornment on garments both of men and women, which might give excuse for the scheming tailors to charge exorbitant prices.

Fig. 670. Philip II, 1559

Charles thought this too drastic; but in 1552 he issued a further pragmatic prohibiting this applied work, as well as the manufacture of gold and silver lace and ornaments, and also rigidly limiting the weaving and making of velvets, silks, and satins.   A ruinous policy!

PHILIP II

King of Spain, 1558 until 1580

Philip as a young man was as splendid in his dress as his father, and for his forthcoming marriage with the Queen of England great preparations were made as described in Chapter III; but still a severe check was kept upon the clothes worn by the people in general.   Such were the conditions existing in Spain during the years 1552 to 1560.

Fig. 670 is taken from a portrait of 'His Catholic Majesty' at the age of

III²—O

thirty-two in 1559, shortly after he had become a widower for the second time, and was in consequence particularly amiably disposed towards Elizabeth. Through his Ambassador he proffered his assurances of friendship and good-will, having, indeed, intentions of marrying her.

Fig. 671 is an example of the costume affected by the nobles, including the hidalgos,[1] of the period covered by Part I.   It is entirely of black; the jerkin with high collar and the wings are of velvet, and the sleeves, paned slops, and hosen of black silk.   The shoes are of black Spanish leather.   A new feature is seen in the sleeves: they are slightly gathered along the front seam, producing folds around the arm.   This Spanish fashion will be observed in some of the later English and French figures.   It is mentioned in the introduction to Part II that the English ignored Spanish fashions.   Rucked sleeves must therefore have come to England via France.

Fig. 671. Spanish Noble
(after Antonio Moro)

Philip II married for the third time in 1559 his gifted and amiable bride, Isabel or Elizabeth de Valois, eldest daughter of Henry II and Catherine, who was the mother of two daughters, Isabella Clara Eugenie and Catherine Michela (see pp. 678, 680).   A drawing of Philip, taken from a miniature painted about this time, is given in Fig. 835.

Owing to the influence of the new Queen, who introduced some French ideas, Spanish costume became richer, more ornate and colourful; but by 1563 it was thought advisable to issue another pragmatic, ostensibly re-enforcing that of 1537 but really relaxing the regulations for the benefit of the upper classes only.   Silk weaving was revived, and great extravagance in dress and living followed during this period: in fact, weavers, tailors, dressmakers, and embroiderers were allowed a free hand in all their departments.

Noteworthy amongst tailors, these very important craftsmen of both ladies and gentlemen's apparel, was Juan de Alcega, who is represented in Fig. 672. He was a smart little citizen of Madrid, and published in 1589 a very useful and interesting book on patterns of garments and the best methods of cutting them out.   Presumably he always worked in his pinked and cutte doublet, which shows the style worn by the middle classes during the period about

[1] In Spain 'hidalgo' signifies a member of the class immediately below the highest in the land. The title 'don' gave the necessary distinction.

1565–89, and reminds us at once of Moroni's portrait of an Italian tailor, No. 697 in the National Gallery, London. His scissors and dividing compasses are much the same as are used to-day.

In the nine years of his married life with Elizabeth de Valois, Philip perhaps for the first time experienced anything like real happiness. Much of it was occupied in the erection of the Escorial in fulfilment of a vow to commemorate St. Lawrence in gratitude for his victory gained at St. Quentin on that saint's day, 10th August 1557. The first stone of this palace-monastery was laid in 1563, and here is the best opportunity for introducing an excerpt from Martin A. S. Hume's *Philip II of Spain*, which gives an entirely different idea of Philip from that usually held.

Fig. 672. Juan de Alcega, 1588

'Even in his home life his care for detail was as minute as it was in public affairs. The most unimportant trifle in the dress, management, studies, or play of his children came within his purview. The minutiae of the management of his flower-gardens, the little maladies of his servants, the good or ill temper of his dwarfs and jesters did not escape his vigilance. The furnishing and decoration of his rooms had to be done under his personal supervision, and the vast task of building the stupendous piles of the Escorial on an arid mountainside, and adorning it with triumphs of art from the master hands of all Christendom, was performed down to the smallest particulars under his unwearied guidance.

'His favourite place for work was at the Escorial, where, said the Prior, four times as many dispatches were written as in Madrid. As soon as a portion of the edifice could be temporarily roofed in, the monks were installed, and thenceforward Philip passed his happiest moments in the keen, pure air of the Guadarramas, superintending the erection of the mighty monument which forms a fitting emblem of his genius—stupendous in its ambition, gloomy, rigid, and overweighted in its consummation. Here he loved to wander with his wife and children, overlooking the army of workmen who for twenty years were busy at their tasks, to watch the deft hands of the painters and sculptors—Sanchez Coello, the Carducci, Juan de Juanes, the Mudo, Giacomo Trezzo, and a host of others—whom he delighted to honour.

'As a patron of art in all its forms Philip was a very Maecenas. He followed his great father in his friendship for Titian, but he went far beyond the Emperor in his protection of other artists. Illuminators, miniaturists, and portrait painters were liberally paid and splendidly entertained. The masterpieces of religious art, the cunning workmanship of the Florentine goldsmiths and lapidaries, the marvels of penmanship of the medieval monks, the sculptures of the ancients, were all prized and understood by Philip, as they were by few men of his time.'

When the King became a widower for the third time in 1568, his grief was such that he retired from the world into the monastery of St. Jerome, and his hair and beard became quite white.   But 'his task in the world was greater to him even than his sorrow or his love.'   His gloom, deepened by fanaticism, influenced the whole Court and Society, and henceforth he and his attendant nobles dressed simply, and wholly in black: even the middle and lower classes followed the example set by the nobility.   It must, however, be remembered that the King kept most of the nobles aloof, surrounding himself only with his personal attendants.   The usual costume of the King was a suit fashioned on modified prevailing lines in black velvet or silk, and in his most sombre moods without any ornamentation.   When he was in a more cheerful vein, jet or black bugles edged the cuttes and panes of his dress.   On all occasions he wore the Badge of the Golden Fleece suspended on a gold chain.

In 1570, at the age of forty-three, Philip took as his fourth wife, Anne, daughter of the Emperor Ferdinand I, who was the mother of Philip III of Spain.   These ten years of domestic life gave Philip a second period of happiness, and Queen Anne's death in 1580 caused him the deepest grief, from which he never recovered although he lived another eighteen years. Costume and social life relapsed into their former austerity and dreariness.

(Continued on p. 673)

THE IDOL OF EUROPE

Don Juan of Austria, the natural son of the Emperor Charles V and Barbara Blomberg of a Flemish noble family, was born 24th February 1546.   There is a three-quarter portrait by Coello[1] in which he appears about twelve years of age wearing a doublet like that in Fig. 768 with moderate-sized paned slops. After his father's death he was acknowledged by his half-brother Philip II, who sent him, at the age of sixteen, with his son, Don Carlos, and his nephew, Alexander Farnese, to the university at Alcalá.   He was given the Golden Fleece in 1566, and took up his first naval command (1566–8) in defence of the coast against African pirates; in 1570 he crushed the Morisco rebellion at Granada.   When only twenty-five, he reached the summit of his remarkable naval and military career, by inflicting so crushing a defeat upon the Turks that their naval power in the Mediterranean was completely destroyed.   As 'Captain-General of the Holy League,' he had under his command no fewer than three hundred galleys and eighty thousand men, the combined fleets of Spain, Venice, Genoa, Malta, and the Papacy; and this victory at Lepanto, near Corinth, on Sunday, 7th October 1571, won him the praise, gratitude, and affection of the Christian world.

He excelled in all manly sports, had no rival in the management of horses

[1] Reproduced in the *Connoisseur*, vol. 102, p. 62.

or in jousting, and often played 'tennis five or six hours together . . . and in the pursuit of these exercises he is unwearied.'

This brilliant illegitimate Hapsburg with golden hair and without the family jaw is described in 1575 as follows: 'He is of middle stature, well made, of a most beautiful countenance, and of admirable grace. He has little beard, but large moustache of a pale colour; he wears his hair long and turned upward, which becomes him greatly; he dresses sumptuously, and with such nicety that it is a marvel to see him.'

Unfortunately he is painted in all his portraits wearing a steel cuirass or a leather doublet over richly embroidered slops. Fig. 673 is made from the portrait by Antonio Moro in the Prado, in which the panes of the slops are somewhat narrow; a noticeable feature is the method of carrying the dagger slung by a chain from the waistbelt and passed behind three of the panes. The swordbelt also passes behind the panes on the opposite side. There is, however, one record of his appearing in ordinary clothes. This was when he was reviewing his fleet before Lepanto when he

Fig. 673. 'Pansid Slops' of Don Juan

made a most picturesque figure, 'saluted by volleys of musketry. The young Prince, gallant in white velvet and gold, stood erect in the stern castle of his gilded barge, with the sacred banner of the Pope fluttering over him.' During the battle he was in complete armour.

His later successes were the siege of Tunis in 1573, the Stadholdership of the Netherlands in 1575, and the victory of Gemblours in 1578. Scarcely had Queen Elizabeth offered him the crown matrimonial of England, when fever cut short his life at the siege of Namur, 1st October 1578. The hero of Lepanto is introduced here mainly because the method of dressing his beautiful golden hair became the rage of masculine Europe. His portrait showing this fashion is reproduced in Fig. 843.

ELIZABETH DE VALOIS

Queen of Spain, 1545–68

The Queen of Peace and Kindness—'la reyna de la paz y de la bondad.'

Elizabeth de Valois, Queen of Spain, sometimes referred to as Isabel or Isabella,[1] was the eldest daughter of Henry II and Catherine, and was born in 1545. A political marriage with Philip II was arranged for by her father, and took place at Notre-Dame, 21st June 1559, the Duke of Alba acting as proxy

[1] The name of Elizabeth was Hispanicized into Isabella.

Fig. 674. Elizabeth de Valois, Queen of Spain

for the bridegroom. Her wedding dress is described as being of cloth of gold interwoven with pearls, and her mantle of blue velvet with a border of gold bullion twelve inches wide was borne by her sister Claude, and her sister-in-law, Mary Stuart. A much-bejewelled imperial crown 'cast a halo of light around her as she walked,' and from her neck were suspended Philip's portrait and a great pear-shaped pearl, the most prized treasure of the crown jewels of Spain—La Pelegrina.

It is said that this French Princess adopted Spanish dress after her marriage, and that she had no patience with the rigid puritanism and petty interference of stern authority which had prevailed in former times. She also introduced French fashions among her Court ladies so that the mixture of styles — Spanish and French — seen in portraits of many of them is explained.

Fig. 674 is made from a painting of Queen Elizabeth by Pantoja de la Cruz (1551–1610). If this portrait is the work of the artist to whom it is attributed, it must have been painted at the end of her life, since he was only seventeen when she died. The dress is in black velvet or some deep rich colour, having the bodice cut to fit the normal figure well in at the waist and finishing in a point in front. There are three rolls on the shoulders, and three rows of jewels in gold mounts descend from neck and shoulders and converge to the point of the waist where the belt of jewels encircles it. The hanging sleeves are in true Spanish type and are first illustrated in Fig. 592; they are a little more shaped on the curve at the back, and are caught together at the wrist and finished with small tabs. On these sleeves and down the front of the skirt distended by the Spanish farthingale are set loops of silk with two elaborate jewelled aiglettes on each (Fig. 675 and also Fig. 936). This type of decoration became most popular during the second half of the sixteenth century and is seen in many portraits of all nationalities. The close-fitting under-sleeves are of light-coloured satin, probably matching the silk loop decorations, and have small cuttes alternating with groups of pearls. At the

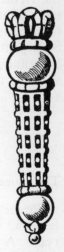

Fig. 675.
An Aiglette

LA REINE ELIZABETH DE VALOIS.

Fig. 676.   After Antonio Moro

wrist the sleeve is cut into a series of small tabs. Attention is drawn to the sable skin with head and feet garnished with goldsmith's work and jewels carried on the right forearm ready to place round the shoulders. A ring is passed through the golden nose of the animal to which is attached a gold and often jewelled chain (*see* Fig. 709). The chair is similar in shape to that shown in Fig. 650.

Elizabeth de Valois was pronounced a very beautiful and gifted princess,

Fig. 677

though judging by our modern standards of beauty her sister-in-law, Elizabeth of Austria, was decidedly the prettier. Brantôme, who knew her intimately, thus describes her: 'Her face was handsome, her hair and eyes so shaded her complexion and made it the more attractive. . . . Although she had had the smallpox after being grown-up and married, they had so well preserved her face with poultices of fresh eggs (a very proper thing for that purpose) that no marks appeared. . . . Her figure was very fine, taller than that of her sisters, which made her much admired in Spain, where such tall women are rare, and for that the more esteemed. And with this figure she had a bearing, a majesty, a gesture, a gait, and grace that intermingled the Frenchwoman with the Spaniard in sweetness and gravity.'

Extremely well dressed, this young Queen-Consort was the model for the great ladies of the Spanish Court.

'She never wore her gowns a second time, but gave them to her ladies and maids; and God knows,' remarks Brantôme, 'what gowns they were, so rich and so superb that the least was reckoned at three or four hundred crowns; for the King, her husband, kept her most superbly in such matters; so that every day she had a new one, as I was told by her tailor, who from being a very poor man became so rich that nothing exceeded him, as I saw myself. She dressed well, and very pompously, and her habiliments became her much; among other things her sleeves were slashed,

Fig. 678. Cut of sleeve

with scallops which they call, in Spanish, *puntas*; her headdress the same, where nothing lacked. Those who see her thus in painting admire her; I therefore leave you to think what pleasure they had who saw her face to face, with all her gestures and good graces. As for pearls and jewels in great quantity, she never lacked them, for the King, her husband, ordered a great estate for her and for her household.'

Extravagant young woman! Yet, ignorant of the tricks of tailors and dressmakers, a mere man may have been deceived, and her dresses were most likely altered and refurbished beyond recognition. And although those who now look at her portraits may not share Brantôme's opinion of her beauty, they cannot fail to notice the quantities of marvellous pearls and jewels that she habitually wore. The slashes to which he refers may be seen in Fig. 676. There are several versions of this dress shown in her portraits. Some are in black or rose velvet, others in white satin or brocade, and one, in the Fitz-william Museum, Cambridge, in rose-coloured satin. In Fig. 676, taken from

a three-quarter portrait by Sir Antonio Moro, the whole dress is of white satin with a gold-embroidered border (Fig. 677) down the front and round the hem. The bodice finishes with tabs at the normal waist-line, and there are slashes on the breasts surrounded by groups of pearls. A diagram of the delightful sleeves with 'puntas' is given in Fig. 678. They are cut in two separate semicircles joined to-gether at AB and EF. BC is gathered or pleated into the armhole, and the length CD is folded back to the broken line when worn, to show a lining of contrasting colour. DE is the wrist, and from F to A the sleeves are cut as shown, forming straps which hang in a most attractive manner from behind the arm. As seen in the drawing, either arm might be passed through the wrist opening, or the whole sleeve might hang behind; the most chic manner was to have only one arm through the wrist opening.

Fig. 679.
A Spanish Lady, 1560 (*after Antonio Moro*)

The close-fitting under-sleeves were braided, often in zigzag lines. The surface of the skirt is cutte, and the usual ornaments of loops and jewelled aiglettes are placed in various positions about the dress. The headdress, something like the jewelled coif shown in Fig. 599, collier, and girdle are set with very fine jewels and pearls. A plain handkerchief is held in the right hand; the left, wearing one glove and holding the other, rests on a pedestal table covered with a velvet cloth buttoned up the edges.

To the great regret of the whole nation, Elizabeth de Valois died 1568.

Fig. 679 is from a three-quarter portrait by Antonio Moro of a noble lady, dating from 1550 to 1570. The dress is in a medium shade of velvet, with bands of very narrow white fur set on the mahoitered sleeves, at the divisions of the small tabs at the waist, and down the front openings of the skirt. The close-fitting sleeves and under-skirt are of silk, or they could be of a damask or brocade. The partlet is white lawn, embroidered with fine gold in a trellis-work design. The cap is similar in shape to that shown in Fig. 548, but this lady has puffed out her hair at the sides. She wears a ruff at the throat and small cuffs to match, with jewelled bracelets, a fine carcanet with pendant, girdle, and pomander. This lady carries a sable skin in her right hand.

ANNE OF AUSTRIA
Queen of Spain, 1549–80

Anne, daughter of the Emperor Ferdinand I, and fourth wife of Philip II, was born in 1549: a very homely soul, a great needlewoman, and rather over-

Fig. 680.
Anne of Austria, Queen of Spain

whelmed by the 'vastness and majesty of the mission confided by Heaven to its chief.' She had five children, all of whom died in infancy except her fourth son, who succeeded as Philip III. This drawing (Fig. 680) is made from the portrait of Queen Anne by Coello. The original is at Vienna. The velvet dress has two rows of gold embroidery (a detail of which is inset as a heading to the drawing) down the front of the normally shaped bodice and skirt, along the hem of the skirt, and also round the new-shaped long hanging sleeves. These are cut on a similar plan to diagram, Fig. 67, but much longer from wrist to point; and the front seam is left open, the edges being caught together on the forearm. The close under-sleeves are of a light-coloured satin embroidered with bands of gold. Loops of silk with jewelled aiglettes are everywhere in evidence. (See Fig. 936.)

This Queen died at the age of thirty-one in 1580.

For some particulars of widow's weeds worn by Spanish ladies of noble birth we have Brantôme's authority. On one occasion he met Jeanne of Austria, the widow of the Infante Jean of Portugal: 'I approached the princess,' he says, 'and kissed her gown in the Spanish manner. . . . I thought her very beautiful according to my taste, very well attired, and wearing on her head a Spanish coif of white crêpe coming low in a point upon her nose, and dressed as a Spanish widow, who wears silk usually.'

Fig. 681. Arms of the Broderers' Company

EMBROIDERY (*continued from p. 419*)

Queen Elizabeth greatly encouraged the art of embroidery, and in the year of her accession the Broderers' Company of London were granted a coat of arms. The Company bore: Paly of six argent and azure, on a fesse gules, between three lions passant guardant or, two broches in saltier, between two trundles or. Crest, on a wreath, a dove displayed argent, encircled with gold all proper. Supporters, two lions or, guttée de sang (drops of blood). Motto: 'Omnia de Super.' (Fig. 681.)

Fig. 682 shows two kinds of broches. These were instruments used by embroiderers. An empty trundle, or quill, is shown in Fig. 683. Trundles

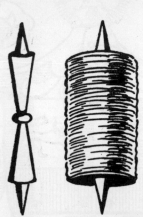

were used for winding silk, wool, or gold thread. A full trundle is seen in Fig. 684.

In 1561 the Broderers' Company of London received their first charter from Queen Elizabeth, and in her reign domestic embroidery began to flourish.

During the second half of the reign broderers introduced a variety of quaint conceits into their work—humorous animals, insects, reptiles, even certain species of vermin, and other curious objects which it is surprising to find interwoven in embroidery for costume — equalled only, perhaps, by the comic decorative detail used by illuminators of fourteenth-century manuscripts.

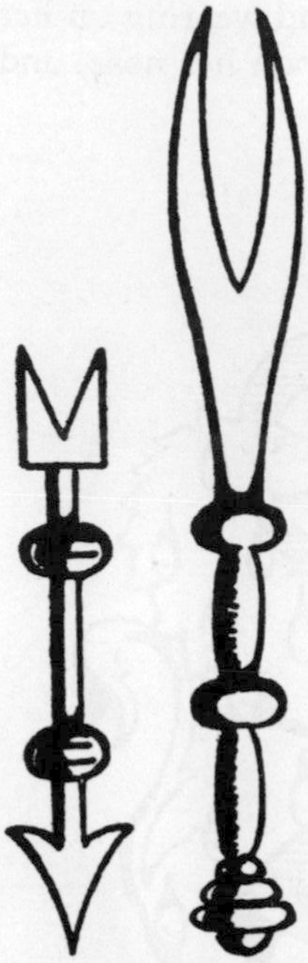

The following list of objects suitable for embroidery is taken from a contemporary work:

Birds' eyes; divers personages; esses (ss); pomegranettes; roses; honiesocles; acorns; wild fernbrakes; pillars; essefirmes; wormes of silk of sondrie colours; like a dead tree; artichokes; caltroppes (a four-pointed iron instrument used in war to maim horses); antiques (figures in *ancient* dress); flies; snails; rainbows, clouds, and droppes and flames of fire; spiders; birdes of Arabia (birds of paradise); sondrie beasts and fowle; allover verie fair like seas, with divers devyses of rocks, shippes, and fishes; fountains; frutidge (clusters of fruit); butterflies; dogges of silver; birds in a cage.

Fig. 682.
Broches

Fig. 683.

Fig. 684.
Trundles

All flowers then cultivated were employed, usually treated in the most naturalistic manner (*see* Fig. 685).

In a well-known portrait of Queen Elizabeth her dress is embroidered with eyes, ears,

Fig. 685. Coloured Embroidery upon Linen

and serpents—the first two, no doubt, symbolized her vigilance, the last, her subtilty. (Plate XLI D.)

Rows of obelisks flank the front and hem of one of her white satin gowns (Plate XL). The surface of this dress is embroidered all over with interlaced knots and scrolls in gold, and small pearls, intermixed with leaves, carnations, lilies, pansies (her favourite flower), butterflies, and worms.

Suns in splendour, made up in diamonds set in embroidery, cover the front of a petticoat, and Jove's thunderbolts and flames, in gold and rubies, decorate an apricot satin skirt (Plate XLII).

In the Hardwick portrait by Gheeraerts (Plate XLI C) of Her Majesty the white satin petticoat has, besides

Fig. 686

ordinary flowers, frogs, serpents, swans, ostriches, sea-horses, rabbits, and whales. The Queen stands upon a Turkey carpet.

Fig. 686 is a drawing of part of a design embroidered in black silk upon a white linen sleeve worn by Queen Elizabeth in a portrait at Arbury Park dating about 1590.

The Queen possessed many pairs of gloves. One pair was embroidered with frogs and flies.

Spanish Work (*continued from p. 226*)

The chief characteristics of Spanish work of the time of Elizabeth are first, that the surface of the linen ground was decorated, as previously, with scrolls; these were in silk, but now worked in knot stitch, producing a thicker line than that used in the rest of the design. These scrolls or stems were frequently worked in gold thread instead of silk.

Secondly, all kinds of flowers, chiefly roses, carnations and honeysuckle, and fruits—less conventional in form than the patterns used earlier — sprang from these scrolls: birds, beasts, fishes, and other objects were encircled by them.

Fig. 687

As the sixteenth century proceeded, stems and scrolls became less prominent, and the flowers, fruit, and objects more realistic (Fig. 687).

In addition to its use for the decoration of various items of costume, Spanish work was employed on bed hangings, coverlets, sheets, and 'pillow-beers,' [1] and, for such purposes, usually embroidered in black silk upon linen, or, as is sometimes specified in inventories, 'fine Holland cloth.'

Spanish work remained popular throughout the sixteenth century, but gradually disappeared from use during the reign of James I.

In modern times the type of needlework known in Tudor days as 'Spanish work' is generally referred to as 'Old English work.' It is still made; but,

Fig. 688. Half an Embroidered Collar

while the designs used for it to-day are very similar to the patterns of Elizabeth's period, a variety of additional stitches has been incorporated.

A good pattern embroidered in black silk upon a linen collar edged with lace of simple design is reproduced in Fig. 688, which shows one side of it. It is taken from a head-and-shoulders portrait (in the Music School, Oxford) of Dr. John Bull. This musician and composer was born in 1563, became Mus.Bac., Oxon, in 1586 and Mus.Doc. in 1592. He died in 1628 at Antwerp where he was organist at the cathedral. In the portrait is seen the upper part of a black robe and over it a white hood edged with white fur, with the head-part thrown back, leaving the head bare. The collar, of course, is worn outside the hood.

STUMPWORK (*continued from p. 227*)

Stumpwork was not extensively carried on in England during the reign of Elizabeth; it was much more popular upon the Continent. In England, however, occasional references are found, which prove that some ladies occupied themselves with this kind of embroidery.

---

[1] A cover spread over the pillow during the daytime.

PETIT POINT

A type of needlework which became very popular during the seventeenth and eighteenth centuries, and is commonly associated with that period, really made its first appearance in England during the reign of Elizabeth. It is known as 'petit point' (Fig. 689), and resembled tapestry, but was worked on a very much smaller scale, upon canvas, in coloured silks, or silks and wool, the whole surface being covered with needlework. Sometimes the work on the canvas ground was cut out and mounted on some plain material, chiefly velvet. It was used generally for wall panels, cushions, and the coverings of stools and chairs.

Fig. 689. Petit Point

HALLINGS

For late sixteenth-century 'hallings' an embroidery which comes under the heading of 'Opus Consutum' was much used.

Figures, flowers, patterns, and arabesques, etc., on a large scale, were worked in silks, wools, and gold thread, on backgrounds of velvet, silk, or brocade, probably with a linen or close canvas foundation. These were cut out and sewn to a ground of velvet, silk, or cloth, with every known variety of stitch. Subjects such as allegorical figures, standing under arches ornamented in the favourite Renaissance manner; shields of arms, sometimes surrounded by conventional wreaths of flowers and leaves; the whole design often framed with pilasters supporting a frieze of elaborate design — all this was

Fig. 690. Wall Hanging

appliquéd or worked with the needle on a dark-coloured velvet background or curtain.

In some of the great houses of the land this type of decorative needlework was much prized, and examples are still extant.

Fig. 690 shows a part of a hanging. It is composed of deep red velvet and golden yellow silk appliqué. The parts of each material cut away for the ground are used in the next row for the pattern, and vice versa. Silk

Fig. 691. Part of a Dorsal

gold cord, used double, covers the lines of the patterns where velvet and silk join.

A section, to be repeated, of gold embroidery upon a dark velvet ground is shown in Fig. 691. This design is a development of the interlaced work mentioned in Chapter II, p. 228. It is used as a dorsal, or hanging, in a portrait of Queen Elizabeth dating about 1590.

FLOOR COVERINGS

References to carpets have been made on p. 229.

By the year 1575 'Turkey' carpets (i.e. Oriental, Persian, etc.) were used in the houses of the nobility and wealthy. The unenterprising and more conservative middle classes, although in some cases they might have been able to afford carpets, still retained the old custom of strewing the floors with rushes or 'grise.'

At the end of the sixteenth century carpets were in general use in the households of the wealthy.

Matting coverings for floors were quite usual after the middle of the century. At first this material was imported from Holland, but later on matting was made in Bedfordshire. A household account dated 1578 mentions: 'Item. Matting 3 Chambers with Bedfordshire mats, vd. a yard.'

It is useful to remember that in most portraits painted during the latter part of Queen Elizabeth's reign the figure stands upon an oriental carpet. By the dawn of the seventeenth century men are usually depicted standing on matting and women on carpets.

LACE (*continued from p. 420*)

The art of the lace-maker had already made considerable progress at the time of Queen Elizabeth's accession, and thereafter thrived as a modest industry. It was not until many Flemish lace-makers had settled in the Midlands, after the Duke of Alba's persecutions in the Netherlands (1567),

Fig. 692. Lace—first half of reign

that lace was made, with their co-operation, in sufficient quantities to become an article of commerce. Since that time pillow lace-making has been practised continuously by women in the counties of Buckingham, Bedford, and Northampton.

During the first twenty-five years of her reign, Queen Elizabeth and the great ladies of her Court used a number of different kinds of lace as the edging to their narrow lawn bands or ruffs, and to cuffs, as seen in many contemporary portraits.   These included the following:

Cutwork and *Spanish work*.   These have been already described.

Venys gold or *passament*.   Fine threads of gold, woven in imitation of white thread lace.

Italian point, needlepoint, or *punto in aria*, as already stated, was worked on a pillow with the needle—made in Italy.

Bone lace.   The original name for fish-bone, and, later, pin-made lace.

Fig. 693.
Cutwork worn by Queen
Elizabeth in the 'Ermine'
Portrait. Plate XXXII D

Fig. 694.
Cutwork worn by
Marguerite de Valois

When made with slightly coarser thread it was often called *bobbin lace*. *Gimp* was a heavier bobbin lace.   Price of bone lace varied between 40s. per dozen yards and 11s. 6d. per yard.

Fig. 692 gives an example of the design in lace used to edge the small band or ruff worn during the first part of Queen Elizabeth's reign.   It is taken from an effigy dating about 1565–70 and measures one and a half inches in width.

It was not until the 1580's that lace was used on a lavish scale.   By this time the band or ruff had greatly increased in size, owing to the introduction of starch and poking-sticks.

The laces used to border these bands were of great variety; among others were:

Billement.   The exact type of lace called billement has not yet been determined.

Bone or *bobbin*.   Already described.

Buckingham lace, made of extremely fine thread, the ground and pattern being worked simultaneously.

Crown lace had the pattern worked on a succession of crowns, sometimes intermixed with acorns and roses.

Cutwork, of Flanders, Italy, and Spain; was much used by Queen Elizabeth on her ruffs, cuffs, foreparts, veils, smocks, nightcaps, cushions, and tooth cloths.   See Figs. 693, 694.

Diamond lace.   A lace woven of silver in lozenge design.

Fig. 695. Reticella worn by Queen Elizabeth in the 1580's.
Plate XLII

Genoa lace.   Needlepoint, sometimes referred to as 'lace of Jeane.' Very rare, but used by Queen Elizabeth.

Parchment lace had the thick raised pattern formed of small pieces of parchment or vellum, called cartisane, cut out to the required shape, and worked over with thread.   This same method applies to *guipure.*

Point lace. Needlepoint, of Genoa, Venice, Flanders, and England. Price, 6s. 8d. to 50s. per yard.

Point coupé.   Another name for cutwork.

Point tresse.   Lace made of human hair, with the needle.

Reticella.   Another name for cutwork (*see* Fig. 693).

Spanish chain. This explains itself.

Spanish black point lace. Used occasionally for edging ruffs and cuffs.

Venys gold, passament, or *passamayne.* Already noted.

Fig. 694 shows a pointed edging and an insertion of the same kind of lace. The edging measures two and a half inches and the insertion two inches in width.

Fig. 693 is a detail of one section of the lace which edges the band or ruff and cuffs worn by Queen Elizabeth in her portrait (*see* Plate XLII) by Marcus

Fig. 696. Reticella edging and insertion—second half of
sixteenth century

Gheeraerts. It measures about four inches in depth and is of Italian workmanship known as reticella.

Some interesting items from wardrobe accounts of the period are here given:

'1 yd. of double Italian cutwork, ¼ yd. wide. 55s. 4d.

'1 yd. of double Flanders, worked with Italian purl. 33s. 4d.

'3 suits (ruffs and cuffs) of good lawn cutwork, ruffs edged with good bone lace, at 70s. £10 10s.

'3 yards broad needlework lace of Italy, with the purl of similar work, at 50s. per yd. £7 10s.

'A veil of white cutwork, trimmed with needlepoint lace. . . .'

NEEDLES AND PINS

As the art of the broderer has now reached such a high standard of efficiency one may inquire what sort of needles were used.

The needle is of great antiquity, as proved by its discovery in burial places all the world over. Those used by the Egyptians were of bronze or gold. These metals, as well as polished iron, were used for making needles during the early periods in Europe. In the earlier Middle Ages steel needles were made in Antioch, Damascus, and Adrianople, and the Moors introduced them into Europe. The industry was being carried on in Nuremburg by the middle of the fourteenth century and at Cordova and Milan during the sixteenth. Steel needles were first produced in England in 1545, by a native of India whose daughter married an Englishman named Greening. Their son, Christopher, established a workshop in 1560 at Long Crendon, Bucks, which existed there as a needle factory until the middle of the nineteenth century, when most of the workers emigrated to Redditch.

Fig. 697. Needle-case

The cases in which these needles were kept usually hung from the girdle by a cord. The cover was flat and rectangular, and made of stiff embroidery, wood, metal, or even ivory or crystal: the ornamentation was often very rich. The actual booklet which carried the needles could be pulled down out of the case on a cord. Here is a sixteenth-century needle-case (Fig. 697) made of embroidered velvet, the booklet being covered with a piece of brocade.

Before the sixteenth century the case was lozenge-shaped. 'A nedell case of cristall garnysshed with silver gilt, with twoo thymbles in it' was a New Year's gift to Queen Elizabeth.

Thimbles of metal, bone, or leather were used as early as the twelfth century; in the thirteenth they were made of latten and later of silver.

Pins of bronze were made at Nuremburg as early as 1365. Those made in England during the fourteenth century were of brass and highly esteemed, and in the following century their manufacture became so extensive that import was prohibited in 1483. In the sixteenth century France also manufactured them. Pins have always been a very important item of costume and dressmaking, and an order of the late-fifteenth century is still extant, in which the following items occur: '6,000 large white pins, 6,000 lesser, 3,000 neete or polished, 1,000 great white, and 1,000 black,' while in an account for a trousseau dated 1494, 8,000 needles, 9,000 pins, and 6 silver thimbles are mentioned.

In a statute passed in 1543, entitled 'An Act for the True Making of Pynnes,' the price was fixed not to exceed 6s. 8d. per 1,000.

In Elizabeth's reign, the value of the annual importation of pins amounted to nearly £4,000.

Brass pins discovered during recent excavations at Baginton Castle, near Coventry, are unique, in that they are enclosed in protective sheaths, and must therefore be large ornamental pins.

A 'minikin' was a very small pin.

PLATE XXXVII. QUEEN ELIZABETH, 1587: Portrait by Marcus Gheeraerts
University Library, Cambridge. *By kind permission of the Syndics*

SECTION II: 1580-1603

QUEEN ELIZABETH, 1580-1603

APPEARANCE (*continued from p. 481*)

Queen Elizabeth's pride in her appearance lasted throughout her life, and at sixty she might easily have passed for twenty years younger—at a short distance.

1581 (48). Even at forty-eight 'she still retained a measure of her good looks. . . . If silver threads glistened among her once auburn locks, only tirewomen were wiser, for a periwig covered all deficiencies.'

1588 (55). The head-and-shoulders portrait of Queen Elizabeth by Marcus Gheeraerts, in the University Library, Cambridge (Plate XXXVII), shows her at about the age of fifty-five; it is pronounced by authorities to give the most accurate idea of the Queen's appearance. The complexion is pale, the shadows being painted in a cold grey; the eyes are brown, and the hair a dark auburn tinged with gold. This portrait, painted on a panel twenty-four inches by nineteen inches, was presented to the library by Vincent Skinner in 1588. The method of painting the face adopted in this portrait had the full approbation of Her Majesty, and it was used in many other likenesses of the Queen; hence the lack of modelling apparent in most of them. As Elizabeth matured in years her features became more pronounced and, conscious of this, she would not permit those who painted her to add *shade* to her portraits. 'Shade,' she said, 'was an accident, and not naturally existent in the face.' Pursuing the same theory, she preferred to give audience by daylight, and frequently in the open air, as the shades had then less force.

An onlooker, Samuel Kiechel, writing of a visit to England at the time of the Armada, said: 'The Queen sitting all alone in her splendid coach appeared like a goddess such as painters are wont to depict.'

1585 (52)   Writing some years after her death, Sir Robert Naunton,
  to   Secretary of State to James I, describes the appearance of
1590 (57). Queen Elizabeth between these dates: 'She was of person tall,
            of haire and complexion faire, and therewith all well favoured,
            but high nosed; of limbs and feature neate, and, which added
            to the lustre of these externall graces, of a stately and majestick
            comportment.'

            Fig. 698 is a drawing made from a cameo representing the
            Queen about 1590.

Fig. 698. Queen Elizabeth, c. 1590

1595 (62). At sixty-two, a German visitor, Jacob Ratgeb, with a gallantry
            borrowed from his Gallic neighbours, recorded that 'the Queen,
            despite her age, can in grace and beauty vie with a maiden of
            sixteen years.'

1598 (65). Another German, Paul Hentzner, writing of a journey into
            England in this year, gives a graphic account: 'Next came the
            Queen, in the 65th year of her age (so we are told), very majestic;
            her face oblong, fair but wrinkled; her eyes small, yet black [1]

            ⎯⎯⎯⎯⎯⎯⎯⎯⎯⎯⎯⎯⎯⎯⎯⎯⎯
            [1] An error for 'brown.'

and pleasant; her nose a little hooked, her lips narrow, and her teeth black (a defect the English seem subject to, from their too great use of sugar). She had in her ears two pearls with very rich drops; her hair was of an auburn colour but false; upon her head she had a small crown, reported to be made of some of the gold of the celebrated Luneberg [1] table; her bosom was uncovered, as all the English ladies have it till they marry; and she had on a necklace of exceeding fine jewels; her hands were slender, her fingers rather long, and her stature neither tall nor low; her air was stately, her manner of speaking mild and obliging. That day she was dressed in white silk bordered with pearls of the size of beans, and over it a veil of black silk shot with silver threads; her train was very long, and the end of it borne by a marchioness; instead of a chain she had an oblong collar of gold and pearls.'

1599 (66). Elizabeth was very proud of her small, beautifully shaped hands, with long, delicate, nervous fingers. When giving audience, especially to any foreign potentate or ambassador, she would call attention to them by *unconsciously* drawing on and off her gloves and toying with her finger-rings. De Maurier, in his *Memoirs of Holland*, says: 'I heard from my father, who had been sent to her Court, that, at every audience he had with her, she pulled off her gloves more than a hundred times to display her hands, which were indeed very white and beautiful.'

1600 (67). 'It was commonly observed this Christmas [1600] that Her Majesty, when she came to be seen, was continuously painted not only all over her face, but her very neck and breast also, and that the same was in some places near half an inch thick.'

1602 (69). Sir John Harington, a godson of Elizabeth, writes: 'There is almost none that waited in Queen Elizabeth's Court and observed anything, but can tell, that it pleased her very much to seem, to be thought, and to be told that she looked young. The majesty and gravity of a sceptre borne 44 years could not alter that nature of a woman in her.'

In connection with the above the following story, although of an earlier date, may not be out of place.

Dr. Rudde, Bishop of St. David's, preached before her in Lent, 1596, and 'wishing in a goodly zeal, as well became him, that she should think sometimes of Mortality, being then sixty-three years of age, he took this text fit for that purpose out of the Psalms: "O teach us to remember our days, that

[1] The famous Luneberg table served as an altar in the Church of St. Michael at Luneberg. Whatever may have been the basis of the writer's comment (in 1598), it is an odd coincidence that, in 1598, a great part of the golden ornament and of the jewels which adorned the altar were stolen by a notorious robber, Nickel List, who was brought to justice early in 1599. The remains of the altar are now in the Provincial Museum, Hanover.

we may incline our hearts unto wisdom," [1] which text he handled so well, so learnedly, and so respectfully, as I dare undertake, and so should I if I had not been somewhat better acquainted with the humour, that it would have well pleased her, or at least no way offended her.   But when he had spoken a while of some sacred and mystical numbers . . . she perceiving whereto it tended began to be troubled with it.   The Bishop discovering all was not well, for the Pulpit stands there *vis-à-vis* to the Closet,[2] he fell to treat of some more plausible numbers, as of the number 666 making Latinus,[3] with which he said he could prove the Pope to be anti-Christ, also of the fatal number of 88 [the year of the Armada] which being so long before spoken of for a dangerous year, yet it hath pleased God that year not only to preserve her, but to give her a famous victory against the united forces of Rome and Spain; and so he said there was no doubt but she should pass this year also and many more, if she would in her meditations and soliloquies with God, as he doubted not she often did, and would say thus and thus.   So making indeed an excellent prayer by way of Prosopopoeia [4] in her Majestie's person acknowledging God's great graces and benefits and praying devoutly for the continuance of them, but withal interlarding it with some passages of Scripture that touch on the infirmities of age, as that of Ecclesiastes xii. 3, "When the grinders shall be few in number, and they wax dark that look out of the windows, etc., and the daughters of singing shall be abased," [5] and more to like purpose, he concluded his sermon.   The Queen, as the manner was, opened the window [of her pew], but she was so far from giving him thanks or good countenance, that she said plainly he should have kept his arithmetic for himself, but I see, said she, the greatest Clerks are not the wisest men, and so went away for the time discontented.'

'The Queen [March 1602] is still . . . frolicly and merry, only her face showeth some decay, which to conceal when she cometh in public she putteth many fine cloths into her mouth to bear out her cheeks, and sometimes as she is walking she will put off her petticote, as seeming too hot when others shake with cold.'

1603   (70).   The effigy of Queen Elizabeth in Westminster Abbey is considered to be an excellent portrait of her in old age.   It is taken from a death mask.

See also section on Portraits and Painters, p. 477.

[1] In a Bible dated 1569 this excerpt reads thus: 'Make us to know so our days that we number them: and we will frame a heart unto wisdom.'—Psalm xc. 12.

[2] The Royal pew.

[3] A distinctive epithet of that branch of the Catholic Church which acknowledges the primacy of the Bishop of Rome and uses the Latin tongue in its rites.

[4] A figure by which an imaginary or absent person is represented as speaking or acting.

[5] In the 1569 Bible it is written thus: *The Book of the Preacher* xii. 4 and 5.   'When the milners [teeth] stand still because they be so few, and when the sight of the windows [eyes] shall wax dim.   When the doors [mouth] in the street shall shut, and when the voice [chawes] of the milner shall be laid down, when men shall rise up at the voice of the bird [cockcrow—because they cannot sleep] and when all the daughters [ears] of music shall be brought low.'   The words in brackets are from notes in the margin.

CHARACTER (*continued from p.* 482)

As she grew older Queen Elizabeth still retained that charm of manner which so struck every stranger coming into her presence for the first time.

'Her Majesty spoke most graciously to every one, even to those of the vulgar who fell upon their knees in homage,' states an eyewitness (1595).

Her godson, Harington, writing some time after her death, said: 'Her speech did win all affections, and her subjects did try to show all love to her commands. . . . When she smiled, it was a pure sunshine, that every one did chose to bask in; but anon came a storm from a sudden gathering of clouds, and the thunder fell, in wondrous manner, on all alike.'

Not until she had been Queen of England for at least twenty years did Elizabeth indulge in the great extravagance of finery with which her name is associated.   The Queen firmly believed in the principle that it was necessary to be 'most Royally furnished both for her person and for her train, knowing right well that in pompous ceremonies a secret of government doth much consist, for that the people are naturally both taken and held with exterior shows.'

Her lavish taste for dress and her vanity did not pass uncriticized, for Sir John Harington tells us that 'one Sunday my Lord of London preached to the Queen's Majesty, and seemed to touch on the vanity of decking the body too finely—Her Majesty told the Ladies that if the Bishop held more discourse on such matters she would fit him for Heaven, but he should walk thither without a staff, and leave his mantle behind him; perchance the Bishop hath never sought Her Highnesse's wardrobe, or he would have chosen another text.'

Yet the same writer elsewhere declares that Elizabeth 'did love rich clothing, but often chid those that bought more finery than became their state.'

The ingratitude and fall of Essex in 1601 had a great effect upon Elizabeth and almost drove her to frenzy.   Sir John Harington's letters give us instances of her temperamentality in old age.   He writes: 'She is much disfavoured and unattired and these troubles waste her much.   She disregardeth every costly cover that cometh to her table and taketh little but manchet [1] and succory pottage.[2] . . . She walks much in her privy chamber, and stamps much at ill news: and thrusts her rusty sword at times into the arras in great rage.'   Again, 'The dangers are over and yet she keeps a sword by her table.' 'So disordered is all order, that Her Highness has worn but one change of raiment for many days, and swears much at those that cause her griefs in such wise.'

So late as 1602 Elizabeth would not admit to any sign of physical weakness; she suffered sorely from gout (only no one dared to call it gout), so that the coronation ring, which she had worn night and day since her accession, had to be filed off her finger.

---

[1] The best kind of white bread.   [2] Succory, a form of chicory.

ACCOMPLISHMENTS (*continued from p. 484*)

Elizabeth's health was never very robust, but during the latter part of her life she kept herself fit by taking bodily exercise, chiefly riding and dancing.

A visitor at Court during the Christmas festivities of 1589 wrote that it was the Queen's habit to dance six or seven galliards every morning. No small effort for a woman of fifty-six!

Even towards the end of her days she indulged in her favourite pastimes of music and dancing. De Maisse, Ambassador from France, writes in December 1597: 'I departed from her audience at night and she retired half dancing to her chamber, where is her spinet which she is content that every one should see.' '24th December. The same day I went to see the Queen and she sent me her coaches. I found her very well and kindly

Fig. 699. Pentagonal Spinet, 1552

disposed. She was having the spinet played to her in her chamber, seeming very attentive to it; and because I surprised her, or at least she feigned surprise, I apologized to her for diverting her from her pleasure. She told me that she loved music greatly and that she was having a pavane played. I answered that she was a very good judge, and had the reputation of being a mistress of the art. She told me that she had meddled with it divers times, and still took great pleasure in it.'

Again, on 31st December: 'She takes great pleasure in dancing and music. She told me that she entertained at least sixty musicians; in her youth she danced very well, and composed measures and music, and had played them herself and danced them. She takes such pleasure in it that when her Maids dance she follows the cadence with her head, hand, and foot. She rebukes them if they do not dance

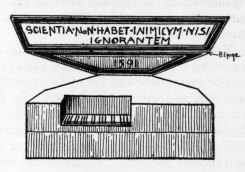

SCIENTIA·NoN·HABET·INIMICVM·NISI·IGNORANTEM

1591

Hinge

Fig. 700. Virginal, 1591

to her liking, and without doubt she is a mistress of the art, having learnt in the Italian manner to dance high. She told me that they called her "the Florentine."'

The minuet, 'menu pas,' and called by the Italians the 'passe-mezzo,' appears to have been known at the French Court. Brantôme describes seeing Elizabeth de Valois and Mary Stuart 'dance the Italian pazzemeno' in these words: 'Now advancing with grave port and majesty, doing their steps so gravely and so well; next gliding only; and anon making most fine and dainty and grave passages, that none, princes or others, could approach, nor ladies, because of the majesty that was not lacking.'

Fig. 699 is a pentagonal spinet or virginal dating 1552. The name 'virginal' was in earlier days restricted to the smaller forms of the instrument, pentagonal or rectangular: it was kept in an ornamental case, and taken out and laid on a table for use. A virginal in the Gruuthuse, Bruges, which measures sixty inches in length is shown in Fig. 700. It has a lid hinged in two places, on which is a Latin inscription and the date 1591. There are twenty-seven white and eighteen black notes.

The following excerpt throws an interesting light on the subject of orchestras at this time. At a masque given by the Earl of Hertford at Elvetham in 1591 'the Fairy Quene and her maides daunced about the garden singing a song of sixe parts, with musicke of an exquisite consort wherein was the lute, bandora,[1] base-violl, citterns,[2] treble violl, and flute.'

Fig. 701. Rebec   Fig. 702. Harp

On 28th April 1602, eleven months prior to her death, Queen Elizabeth opened a ball with the Duc de Nevers, dancing a galliard 'with a disposition admirable for her age,' says de Maisse. Two months later she kept the Scottish Ambassador waiting when he called to see her. He was led into a room adjoining her own, and seated where, by peering around a curtain carefully turned back for the purpose, he could see the Queen dancing to a lively tune from a small fiddle or rebec (Fig. 701). This was the last time she ever danced. A modern painting illustrates this incident.

Fig. 703. Trumpet

The Queen's skill in languages became more famous as time went on, and was a continual surprise, not only to the university professors, but to ambassadors of foreign powers whom she often addressed in their native tongues.

---

[1] *Bandora, bandurria,* a small kind of Spanish guitar of deeper pitch than the mandoline. *Mandora,* a lute with four strings.

[2] *Cittern,* a lute-shaped instrument, though with a flat back, having wire strings, usually four pairs.

De Maisse remarks that 'she spoke to me of the languages that she had learned, for she makes digressions very often, telling me that when she came to the Crown she knew six languages better than her own; and because I told her that it was great virtue in a princess, she said that it was no marvel to teach a woman to talk; it were far harder to teach her to hold her tongue.'

Although Elizabeth frequently drove in her coach, and she had many, she did not in her latter years give up riding on horseback, and was still very fond of hunting. We hear that in her old age, and as late as August 1602, the 'Queen hunteth every second or third day, for the most part on horseback, and showeth little decay in ability.' Not bad for an old woman of sixty-nine!

Queen Elizabeth's Wardrobe, 1580–1603

This period opens with the end of one of Elizabeth's many political love affairs. 'Froggy [Elizabeth's pet name for the Duc d'Anjou] would a-wooing go' no longer—he died 10th June 1584, and his 'forlorn widow,' as the Queen called herself, wept for three weeks on end. In six months Majesty completely recovered herself and we are assured that during the Christmastide festivities, 1584, when all her ladies- and gentlemen-in-waiting were very gorgeously apparelled, the Queen, as complimentary mourning for the Duc d'Anjou and the Prince of Orange, was dressed in black velvet sumptuously embroidered with silver and pearls. From her headdress to the hem of her skirt fell an ample veil of diaphanous silver. On either side of her crisp crimped hairdressing hung a great pearl about as large as a hazel-nut.

The 'Ermine' three-quarter-length portrait by Nicholas Hilliard, now at Hatfield (Plate XXXII D), is dated on the sword handle 1585, a fine example of the goldsmith's art. The lines of the black velvet dress, pounced all over with cuttes and engraved gold buttons, headdress, and circular ruff, suggest that the style is of the same make as described under the 'Portland' portrait on p. 497. The cutwork, of which the circular ruff and cuffs are composed, is a very beautiful specimen of the lace-makers' craft, and is reproduced in Fig. 693. The jewels worn are diamonds, rubies, emeralds, and pearls. An ermine climbing up the Queen's left wrist and peering into her face has given the title to the painting. As an emblem of chastity, the ermine was an especially appropriate compliment to the Virgin Queen.

'The Queen of England wears mourning for the Queen of Scotland' is stated in a letter bearing date, 'March 27 1587.'

The end of the year 1585 finally brought about friction between Spain and England: the breach widened—although both Philip and Elizabeth had an intense aversion to war. Disquieting news of the Spanish Armada under the command of the Duke of Medina Sidonia, waiting at Lisbon, reached England in the spring of 1588, and on the 12th July 'the Kinge of Spaines Navy was Abroad,' sailing up the Channel in crescent form on the 19th. On the 29th the English fleet under Lord Howard of Effingham, supported by

Fig. 706.

Fig. 705.

Fig. 704.

TILBURY, 8TH AUGUST 1588. 'LORD BLESS YOU ALL.' 'MY LOVING PEOPLE'

Drake, Hawkyns, and Frobisher, inflicted a final blow on the 'Invincible' off Gravelines, after which the mighty Spanish galleons rounded the north of the British Isles, and so the remnants returned home.

The Earl of Leicester was in command of the land forces stationed at Tilbury to intercept the advance of the Spaniards if they landed, and to this army Elizabeth resolved to appeal.

On 8th and 9th August, 'she passed like some Amazonian Empress through all her army,' mounted on a richly caparisoned war-horse. For this occasion the astute Elizabeth adopted a semi-military outfit and Fig. 705 is a conjectural drawing, but made partly from contemporary descriptions. The dress is of cloth of gold, and the under-skirt of white stain embroidered with emblems, in which the rose and fleurs-de-lys are important features of the design. A cuirass of polished steel, damascened with gold and surmounted by a large circular ruff, the Crown poised upon an immaculately dressed auburn wig, a marshal's truncheon in her hand, and quantities of gems and jewels, are all calculated to increase Her Majesty's regal appearance and impress the loyal hearts of her devoted people. The military helmet, with crown and plumes of white ostrich feathers, is too cumbersome for the Queen to wear, so it is carried by a gentleman-in-waiting or a page (Fig. 706), who is dressed in sleeves, trunks, and hosen of green with a white jerkin—the Tudor livery colours. A similar costume is worn by the groom, who in Fig. 704 is leading the white charger which the Queen rode on this occasion. The horse is drawn from its portrait, painted in 1594, which now hangs on the staircase at Hatfield House. It should be noticed that the feet of the Queen rest upon a footboard, as was her usual custom when riding in full dress and on State occasions. A lady riding side-saddle with a pommel is seen in Fig. 714.

Another good illustration of this notable event is to be found in the mid-nineteenth-century picture by Sir John Gilbert, R.A., and made familiar in many history books.

By this time Elizabethan costume had reached the stage of elaborate development so familiar to every one. Queen Elizabeth in 1588 is shown in Plate XXXVIII. This is reproduced from the delightful brown ink and thin water-colour drawing by Isaac Oliver preserved in the Royal Library at Windsor Castle. The original measures twelve by eight inches, and was made in that year. The photograph is published by gracious permission of His Majesty the King. It is considered by authorities to be an excellent likeness of Queen Elizabeth, and is said to represent the dress in which she went in State to St. Paul's, to return thanks for the defeat of the Armada. It is the earliest portrait of the Queen showing her dressed in full band or ruff, long stomacher, veil, and wheel-farthingale. The farthingale in this picture shows the cart-wheel effect described on p. 618. The bodice, long hanging sleeves, and over-skirt are composed of white satin brocaded or embroidered with a gold scroll design. The full sleeves, stomacher, and under-skirt with cart-wheel arrangement on top are of cloth of gold, covered

PLATE XXXVIII. QUEEN ELIZABETH, 1588: Water-colour drawing by Isaac Oliver
Royal Library, Windsor. *By gracious permission of H.M. the King*

PLATE XXXIX. QUEEN ELIZABETH, 1588: Engraving by William Rogers
British Museum. *By kind permission of the Governors*

with diagonal puffings of fine white silk: alternate intersections are decorated with groups of five pearls each, and rubies set in gold mounts, and a large pearl poses in the centre of each lozenge of the gold foundation.

Down the front of the stomacher and skirt, and round the hem, is a line of larger puffings, interspaced by larger jewelled ornaments of the same character, but including emeralds. Diamonds are liberally besprinkled over the whole costume. A gold band, set with groups of four pearls, interspaced alternately by rubies and emeralds, edges the stomacher, the over-skirt, and the long hanging sleeves.

Other important items to be noticed are the much-becurled wig, ornamented with groups of pearls mounted on pins and with clusters of jewels; the festoon of pearls, finishing in a peardrop pearl on the forehead; the crown surmounting all; the girdle; the earrings, lace, ropes of pearls, sceptre, and orb. The ruff and veil are described on pp. 623, 626. Note the glimpse of a white satin petticote, the gold fringe of which just clears the ground.

Fig. 707. Burse

The print shown in Plate XXXIX is a rare one, engraved by William Rogers. He took the details from Isaac Oliver's drawing (Plate XXXVIII).

Working some years after Oliver, Rogers has made the Queen look older, and many of the other details differ. The crown is much more open, and its design less reliable than that shown in Plate XXXVIII; the hair is differently adorned; the neck pendant is not the same; the rope of pearls, instead of being caught and festooned, hangs only from the shoulders to the point of the stomacher; jewels set in mounts are introduced on the ruff; no single pearls are placed between the puffings; a gold fringe edges the hem of the skirt; and the orb is jewelled. The details of the chair are interesting, and should be compared with those in Figs. 354 and 571, vol. ii, and with Fig. 215 in this volume.

The order in which the Court progressed and precedence prescribed is always interesting and often useful. The following composite description is based upon various accounts of eyewitnesses at Court. When the Queen processed in State or semi-State in the precincts of the palace or in public, the Lord Chamberlain walks first, being followed by all the nobility, ladies and gentlemen (the latter bare-headed), who are in the Court; and after them, near the Queen's person, walk the Knights of the Order of the Garter that are present, such as the Earl of Essex and the Admiral Lord Howard of Effingham (born 1536, Earl of Nottingham, 1596; died 1624). After come the six heralds who bear maces before the Queen. Immediately in front of Her Majesty comes the Lord Chancellor, bearing the seals in a red silk embroidered Burse or bag (Fig. 707), between two noblemen, one of whom carries the Royal Sceptre, the other the Sword of State, in a crimson velvet scabbard, studded with golden fleurs-de-lys, the point upward. Then comes the Queen's Majesty. She is guarded on each side by the Yeomen of the Guard, and the Maids of Honour follow, 'very handsome and well-shaped, and for the most part dressed in white.' After her march fifty Gentlemen Pensioners, also with halberts.

Plate XL is reproduced from a portrait said to be Queen Elizabeth, and dating some time between 1582 and 1589. It is one of a set of four portraits by the same artist, two of which are of Lady Southwell née the Lady Elizabeth Howard and the remaining one of Kate Carey, the celebrated Countess of Nottingham. Three of these portraits may have been painted at the time of the Lady Elizabeth's first marriage in 1582. In any case Plate XL shows the salient features of the height of fashion during the 1580's and onwards.

The entire dress is of white satin covered with embroidery in gold, silver, and coloured silks, obelisks forming an important item in the pattern on the skirt. It should be noticed that the embroidery on the bodice and sleeves is of a different design. The ruff, its surface powdered with jewelled brooches representing arrows, and the veil of gold and silver gauze, are described on pp. 626, 778. The headdress, which dominates the curled auburn wig, comprises seven upstanding points of flashing jewels finishing in pearls. These points are fixed to a band which fits round the head behind the front puff of the wig.

The three-quarter portrait at Woburn Abbey was painted in 1589–90 by Marcus Gheeraerts to commemorate the defeat of the Armada. A similar portrait in which the costume is the same but the background omitted is in the National Portrait Gallery, No. 541 (Plate XLI A). This latter shows the Queen in full dress such as she wore when giving audiences or on any other ceremonial occasion. The bodice with long sleeves hanging behind (see Plate XLII) and the skirt are of black velvet with borders of rows of pearls between narrow gold lines. These borders have, set at right angles to the borders, loops of silk in three shades each—pale yellow, rose, and grey, with rubies and emeralds in the centres. The sleeves and under-skirt are of white satin embroidered with red roses and pearl centres set in squares, and golden flowers of ten petals with ruby centres set in hexagons. A circular ruff of elaborate reticella, seven ropes of pearls and many other jewels, and a Royal crown set upon the usual auburn wig stuck with singularly large pearls complete the effect.

The 'Ditchley' full-length portrait, bequeathed by Viscount Dillon to the National Portrait Gallery, No. 2561, is dated 1592 and painted on canvas; it shows Queen Elizabeth at the age of fifty-nine (Plate XLI B). Her costume is not unlike that shown in Plate XXXVIII, of white satin diagonally cross-barred with white silk puffings, having roses superimposed with ornaments of goldsmith's work set at the intersections. These gold ornaments vary in design; some have groups of four pearls, others oval rubies, and others again rectangular sapphires. The long-pointed bodice and sleeves are decorated

PLATE XL.   QUEEN ELIZABETH, 1589: *Portrait by an unknown artist*
Private collection

in the same manner, but the long-hanging sleeves have these ornaments set along the edges. The wired-out portions are the only parts of the veil visible. The headdress of crown-shape is a mass of rubies, pearls, and some spherical jewel of a brilliant red, with a pearl apex surmounting the whole structure. Other interesting details are the ropes of pearls hanging from the neck and the pearls on the wig, the pink rose set on the ruff, the decorated brown leather gloves in the left hand, and the Chinese fan, made to open and shut, attached by a coral-coloured riband to the waist girdle.

At Hardwick Hall is a full-length portrait of Queen Elizabeth, painted on canvas ninety by sixty-six inches, by the same artist (Plate XLI C). The Queen is shown wearing a dress of black velvet worked with gold and an under-skirt of white satin embroidered with many wonderful objects (see p. 585), the general style being similar to that just described.

On the 22nd September 1592 Queen Elizabeth paid her second visit to Oxford and, as on the first occasion, was housed at Christ Church. Long, tedious orations and elaborate productions of impossible plays were her chief entertainment. 'Hir Highnes departed from the University this day [28th September] about eleven of the clock in the forenoon, in hir open and princely carriadge.' Unfortunately no descriptions of the Queen's costumes, worn on her first or second visit to Oxford, are to be found in the docu-ments relating to these events. From which it may be inferred that the Cambridge reporters of the day were more observant than their Oxford contemporaries.

To this same period may be assigned the portrait of Queen Elizabeth reproduced in Plate XLII and painted on canvas, seventy-six by forty-three inches, by Marcus Gheeraerts. It hangs in the drawing-room of the Master's Lodge at Trinity College, Cambridge, and represents the Queen at about sixty years of age.

Her costume is particularly interesting as it is exceptional in colouring. The bodice, long hanging sleeves, and back-skirt with train are all of a rich purple velvet. The long hanging sleeves and skirt have a border consisting of two lines of gold passamayne edged with pearls both planted upon the purple velvet. Between these lines are rubies in gold mounts set alternately with pink five-petalled roses in silk embroidery with seeded gold centres. The hanging sleeves are lined with white damask; the long pointed stomacher and the large leg-of-mutton sleeves are of white satin embroidered with a beautiful design in gold and pearls. The under-skirt mounted on the wheel farthingale is of apricot satin covered with a diaper design of conventional roses and flames. The roses, alternately rose colour and green, are worked in shaded silks outlined with gold and pearls, each having a large pearl centre. The flame ornaments are worked in gold and pearls, with ruby centres. The border at the bottom of the skirt is composed of two double rows of gold passamayne enclosing a design of connected squares and ovals carried out in gold lines, the centre of each feature being alternately rubies and emeralds surrounded by pearls. A beautiful pendent jewel (see Fig. 929) hung on a mauvish-pink riband is attached to the point of the stomacher, and caught up on the right side. (The 'Darnley' portrait in the National Portrait Gallery, London, shows the same detail).

The unseen headdress would be either a French hood, without tube, or a network caul enclosing the hair at the back, and to this is attached the up-standing jewel and feather. Pairs of pearls, mounted on pins, are stuck at intervals into the outside edge of the orange-golden wig. Seven ropes of pearls hang from the neck to the waist. A detail drawing of the lace which edges the band is given in Fig. 695. Other items of interest are the jewelled collar (Fig. 922), fan handle (see Fig. 937), and shoes (see Fig. 906), but no earrings are worn. A similar dress is worn by the Queen in a portrait at Jesus, and in yet another at Christ Church, Oxford.

The chair, upholstered in scarlet velvet, has elaborately carved arms, and is of French make. The design of the arm includes a figure whose headdress is in the style of those worn in the reign of Francis I. The cover of the table is green velvet edged with gold and fringe. Her Majesty stands upon a foot carpet of vermilion velvet fringed with gold.

A three-quarter portrait on canvas of Queen Elizabeth at the age of sixty-one, belonging to the Marquess of Salisbury and known as the 'Rainbow' portrait, was painted by Marcus Gheeraerts in 1594 (Plate XLI D). It is somewhat emblematic, which accounts for the rainbow—possibly referring to the prosperity which her skilful statecraft had brought about (suggested by Genesis viii. 22 and ix. 14, 15), though the words 'Non sine sole iris' (No rainbow without the sun) on the background may indicate the imper-sonation of the sun by the Queen. The serpent is symbolical of subtle wisdom ('wise as serpents'), and the eyes and ears on the orange drapery or lining of the fawn outer robe imply that Her Majesty saw and heard every-thing. The Crown mounted upon a turban-like headdress is suggestive of the heart-shaped headdress of the early fifteenth century; and the bodice of linen, embroidered with floral designs, is the first example of a vogue very popular during the following reign. Contrary to her usual custom, the Queen is wearing her hair in ringlets, perhaps to give the illusion of youth, while the chin ruff serves to mask her sinewy neck.

A description of the Queen, given by a German gentleman who had an interview with her in 1595, states that on this occasion she was seated upon a throne under a canopy of cloth of gold. Her dress was a silver robe, adorned with magnificent gems and jewels beyond compare, and on her head a Royal crown of pearls.

Later in the same year the aforesaid gentleman was present at Court during a meeting of the Knights of the Garter, awaiting an audience:

'Then Her Majesty stepped out of the Privy Chamber, arrayed in silver cloth. On her robe were embroidered two obelisks crossed, which in lieu of a button had at the top a beautiful oriental pearl. The robe was further adorned with rare costly gems and jewels. On her head she wore a very costly royal crown. Her Majesty was escorted on either side by Knights and

A  B

C  D

PLATE XLI. QUEEN ELIZABETH

A. *c.* 1589.   B. The 'Ditchley,' 1592: Portraits by unknown artists
National Portrait Gallery.   *By kind permission of the Directors*

C. The 'Hardwick,' 1592–4: Portrait by an unknown artist
Hardwick Hall.   *By kind permission of the Duke of Devonshire*

D. The 'Rainbow,' 1594: Portrait by Marcus Gheeraerts
Hatfield House.   *By kind permission of the Marquess of Salisbury*

PLATE XLII. QUEEN ELIZABETH, 1590: Portrait by Marcus Gheeraerts
Trinity College, Cambridge. *By kind permission of the Master and Fellows*

Earls.   Her train was borne by a Maid of Honour.   On stepping out of the chamber Her Majesty greeted all present.'

In the autumn of 1597, when receiving certain foreign officials, Queen Elizabeth wore a dress of red interwoven with threads of gold.   On her head was the usual crown of pearls, from which hung a long openwork veil; but what astonished one of the onlookers was a hideous large black spider which sat upon it and looked so natural and alive that many might have been deceived by it.   One is shown in Fig. 935.

The French Ambassador, De Maisse, who was much interested in Elizabeth's wondrous robes, tells us that on one occasion, in 1597, when he had an interview with the Queen in the privy chamber she was standing by the window.   'She looked better in health than before.   She was clad in a dress of black taffeta, bound with gold, and like a robe in the Italian fashion with open sleeves and lined with crimson taffeta.   She had a petticoat of white damask, girdled, and open in front, as was also her chemise, in such a manner that she often opened this dress and one could see all her belly, and even to her navel. . . . She had bracelets of pearl on her hands, six or seven rows of them.   On her head-tire she wore a coronet of pearls, of which five or six were marvellously fair.   When she raises her head she has a trick of putting both hands on her gown and opening it insomuch that all her belly can be seen.'

Evidently there was something wrong with De Maisse's powers of observation on this particular occasion or else he has a very coarse way of explaining some characteristic movements adopted by ladies at this time.   In Elizabeth's reign such indelicacies as those he describes could not possibly have been indulged in by any ladies of the Court, much less the Queen.   Obviously he was speaking metaphorically.   The two statements refer to the action of taking the sides of the open overdress and parting them with a graceful movement of the hands so as to display the underdress to full advantage.

A little later De Maisse tells us that 'she was strangely attired in a dress of silver cloth, white and crimson, or silver gauze as they call it.   This dress had slashed sleeves lined with red taffeta, and was girt about with other little sleeves that hung down to the ground, which she was for ever twisting and untwisting.   She kept the front of her dress open, and one could see the whole of her bosom, and passing low, and often she would open the front of this robe with her hands as if she was too hot.   The collar [ruff] of the robe was very high, and the lining of the inner part all adorned with little pendants of rubies and pearls, very many, but quite small.   She had also a chain of rubies and pearls about her neck.   On her head she wore a garland of the same material and beneath it a great reddish-coloured wig, with a great number of spangles of gold and silver, and hanging down over her forehead some pearls, but of no great worth.   On either side of her ears hung two great curls of hair, almost down to her shoulders, and within the collar of her robe, spangled as the top of her head.'

On 24th December 1597 when De Maisse surprised the Queen when playing the spinet, 'She was clad in a white robe of cloth of silver, cut very low and *her bosom uncovered*. She had the same customary head attire, but diversified by several kinds of precious stones, yet not of any great value. She had a little gown [1] of cloth of silver of peach colour, covered and hidden, which was very fair.'

'Bosom uncovered' seems to have struck the gentleman as unusual. All unmarried women had their bosoms, that is their throats and necks, exposed. Some portraits of Elizabeth show this, especially those painted in later life, although there are some in which she is covered right up to the circular ruff.

On New Year's Eve of the same year, De Maisse informs us that 'this day she was habited, as is her custom, in silver tissue, or gauze as we call it in French; her robe was white and the over-vest of gold and silk of violet colour. She wore innumerable jewels on her person, not only on her head, but also within her collar [ruff], about her arms and on her hands, with a great quantity of pearls round her neck and on her bracelets. She had two bands, one on each arm, which were worth a great price.'

For the description of a costume worn by the Queen in 1598 see p. 597.

When giving an audience in 1599 Elizabeth was, we are told, 'most lavishly attired in a gown of pure white satin, gold-embroidered, with a whole bird of paradise for panache, set forward on her head studded with costly jewels, a string of huge round pearls about her neck, and elegant gloves over which were drawn costly rings. In short she was most gorgeously apparelled, and although she was already seventy-four [she was only sixty-six], was very youthful still in appearance, seeming no more than twenty years of age.'

On the 16th June 1600, Queen Elizabeth honoured the Earl of Bedford with her presence at the wedding of his daughter, the Lady Anne Russell, with Lord Herbert, son of the Earl of Worcester (*see* Plate XLV).

The Queen is carried in a litter shoulder high by four gentlemen and is very gorgeously gowned all in white, the style and decoration being much the same as shown in Plate XXXVIII, and in the 'Ditchley' portrait. The hairdressing is very lofty, much bejewelled, and surmounted by a Crown. An elaborate jewelled ornament is fixed high up on the left sleeve.

A portrait head of the Queen is in the Library of the Master's Lodge, St. John's College, Cambridge. It appears to have been painted at this time as the hairdressing and ruff are almost the same as in Plate XLV, but the Crown is omitted, and she does not wear so many jewels.

Queen Elizabeth gave audience to the Persian Ambassador in February 1601. It is recorded that 'the Queen, though very feeble and tottering on account of her illness, nevertheless appeared on this occasion adorned and bedecked with great pomp and right royally.'

The British Museum possesses an engraving of Queen Elizabeth opening her last Parliament on 27th October 1601. Plate XLIII is a reproduction of it. Her robes consist of a long pointed bodice and an all-round skirt of

[1] This is an erroneous translation from the French. It refers to the under-skirt.

PLATE XLIII. QUEEN ELIZABETH IN PARLIAMENT,
1601: Engraving by an unknown artist.   British Museum.   *By kind permission of the Governors*

brocade open over an under-skirt of a different-patterned brocade and colour with the Spanish farthingale beneath.   Over them is the parliamentary mantle of crimson velvet with a cape and lining of ermine fastened in front by long cords and tassels.   A headdress,[1] like the French hood, but with a rolled front, and a circular ruff of moderate proportions, are worn, and the sceptre and orb carried.   It is recorded that the weight of these Royal robes caused Her enfeebled Majesty to stagger on this occasion.   The chair of State with crown fixed to it just above the Queen's head, dorsal, and cushions of brocade are other interesting features of the engraving.

So late as 6th February 1603, a little more than a month before her death, Elizabeth gave an audience to an envoy from Venice.   In spite of her years, she still made a regal figure dressed in silver and white taffeta embroidered with gold: the Royal diadem surmounting hair 'of a light colour never made by nature,' and multitudes of pearls, rubies, diamonds, and other gems scintillating from all parts of her person.

Examination of the effigy of Queen Elizabeth, erected in Westminster Abbey by order of James I, will enlighten the student on some practical points of detail of the Queen's costume as worn by her during her last years.

The following is a list of garments taken from the Queen's wardrobe account dated 1600:

Robes	99	Foreparts	136	Juppes	43
French gowns	102	Peticoats	125	Dublettes	85
Round gowns	67	Cloakes	96	Lappemantles	18
Loose gowns	100	Cloakes	31	Fannes	27
Kirtells	126	Saufegards	13	Pantobles	9

Apparell, Jewelles, Kirtells, Coronation Robes, Mourning Robes, Parliament Robes, For Order of Garter.   Sondrie P'cells.

The following descriptions of some of these garments are taken from the same wardrobe account:

'One Frenche gowne of russet stitched cloth, richlie florished with gold and silver, lyned with orange colour taphata, and hanginge sleeves, lyned with white taphata, embrodered with *antiques* of golde and silke of sonderie colours, called China-work.'[2]

'One rounde gowne of white cloth of silver, with workes of yellow silke, like flies, worms, and snailes.'

'One rounde gowne of Isabella colour[3] satten, cut in snippes and raised up, set with silver spangles.'

'One rounde gown of heare coloured raised *mosseworke* embroidered all over with leaves, pomegranets, and men.'

---

[1] The Cap of Maintenance was not generally worn after coronation.
[2] 'China work' refers to the pattern.   China was a country vaguely known in the Middle Ages under the Tartar name of 'Cathay.'   In the sixteenth century the Indian name of 'Chin' was latinized by the Spanish and Portuguese adventurers into 'China.'
[3] See List of Colours, p. 133.

'One loose gowne of Ladie-blushe satten, laide with bone-lace of Venice golde and silver, with spangles, with buttons downe before of the same lace.'

'One loose gowne of white tillyselge [tinsel] like grograine, bounde aboute with a small lace of golde, the hanging sleeves beinge cutt and bounde with the like lace and tufts of golde threede, and some golde spangles.'

Fig. 708. A Snoskyn

'Kirtells' refer to the under-skirt: 'foreparts' were equivalent to stomachers.

'One peticoate of white satten, embroidered all over with black flies, with a border of fountaines and trees, embroidered rounde aboute it, and waves of the sea.'

'One cloake of heare-colour raised mossworke, embrodered like stubbs of dead trees, set with fourteen buttons embrodered like butterflies, with fower pearls and one emerode in a pece, lyned with cloth of silver, prented.'

'One juppe and saufegarde of orenge-colour, or marigolde-colour vellat, cut and uncutt, the sleeves and downe before garnished with a lace of Venice silver, like essefirmes, and laide aboute with twoe plate laces of Venice silver.'

Safeguards were outward petticoats put on to protect an elaborate dress in bad weather. This name was also applied to the surcote since it had sleeves and made of rich material. The same may be said of loose gowns.

'One lappemantle of white plush, with a pane [a breadth] of redd swanes downe in the middest.'

'Lapmantle' was another name for apron.

Other items of dress which appear in different wardrobe accounts and inventories follow:

MUFF, *snoskyn* or *snuftkin*, an item of costume introduced towards the end of this reign. The shape of these muffs is obvious. Unfortunately,

Fig. 709. Sable skin

representations of them in portraits of this period are scarce and the only example known to the author appears in a miniature of the 1590's in a private collection. It is of brown fur, rectangular in shape, and well padded, yet soft like a feather cushion as shown in Fig. 708.

'One snoskyn of crimson saten, laide upon with perfumed leather cut, embrothered with Venice gold, silver, and silk,' was a New Year's gift to the Queen in 1600. At the same date a pair of snoskyns was given to Her Majesty—one for each hand. They were 'of cloth of silver, embrothered all over with flowers and braunches of Venice, silver and silk of sondry colors.'

Sable skins were used by ladies to place around their shoulders for extra warmth. When not required for this purpose they were carried in the hand (see Figs. 674 and 679). Queen Elizabeth had one presented to her by the Earl of Leicester in 1584. It is described as 'a sable skin, the head and four feet of gold fully garnished with diamonds and rubies of sundry sort.' In Fig. 709 is shown a sable skin lined with silk and edged with a piping of the same.

The Officers of the Household of the Queens-Regnant, Mary and Elizabeth, were the same as in the households of kings, and with two exceptions they performed the same duties.

Maids of Honour, the daughters and granddaughters of the nobility, under the special supervision of the *Mother of the Maids*,[1] took the place of Gentlemen of the Privy Chamber. They formed an aristocratic background for their Sovereign, and were also her personal companions. While Gentlemen of the Privy Chamber were retained, but were exempt from any intimate duties, esquires of the body were replaced by *Ladies-in-waiting* and *Gentlewomen of the Bedchamber*.

Those who superintended the Queen's wardrobe were naturally ladies of influence and the highest importance, and correspondingly autocratic in their methods.

First and foremost comes Mary, whose father Sir John Shelton of Shelton, Norfolk, had been Controller of Elizabeth's household (1538); she was Maid of Honour about 1571, and married in 1576 James (later Sir James) Scudamore. When the Queen heard of this she was furiously angry, but forgave and appointed Mary Scudamore a gentlewoman of the bedchamber. After a time she held the important and difficult post of *Keeper of the Queen's Wardrobe*.

Rauff Hope was 'Yeoman of the Queen's Robes' in 1578.

---

[1] At a much later date the title 'Mistress of the Robes' was given to this official, who was usually a duchess.

Tailors and dressmakers of the Elizabethan era did not have an easy time, and the following quotation from Harrison gives some idea of the fussiness of their clients, gentlemen as well as ladies.

'How long time is asked in decking up' the body with much finery. 'How curious, how nice also, are a number of men and women, and how hardly can the tailor please them in making it fit for their bodies! How many times must it be sent back again to him that made it! What chafing, what fretting, what reproachful language, doth the poor workman bear away! And many times when he doth nothing to it at all, yet when it is brought home again it is very fit and handsome. Then must we put it on, then must the long seams of our hose be set by a plumb-line, then we puff, then we blow, and finally sweat till we drop, that our clothes may stand well upon us.'

It has been mentioned that Queen Elizabeth was enamoured of both French and Italian fashions, and it was not beneath her dignity to make surreptitious inquires about them for her own benefit. Thus at her instigation Lord Burleigh writes to Sir Henry Norris, then Her Majesty's representative in Paris, as follows: 'The Queen's Majesty would fain have a tailor that has skill to make her apparel both after the French and Italian manner, and she thinketh you might use some means to obtain such one as suiteth the Queen without mentioning any manner of request in the Queen's Majesty's name . . . as she does not want to be beholden to her.' The reference is, of course, to Catherine de' Medici, who would have been justifiably annoyed if she had known of such an attempt to entice away not only the creators of Court fashions but also the skilled dressmakers who carried out their designs.

A tire-woman (see Chapter II, p. 209) was the Tudor expression for a lady's maid, but the name was also applied to a dressmaker; likewise a tire-glass was a mirror, chiefly of polished metal as glass mirrors were very rare at this time and were of Italian, especially Venetian, manufacture. These glass mirrors were imported into England during this period and were very expensive. Both varieties, metal and glass, were set in frames of period design, which stood upon the tire-table; and a tire-room or tiring chamber was a dressing-room. A small mirror was sometimes attached to a lady's girdle, but more frequently was fixed into the centre of a feather fan. A small rectangular or circular mirror, with a frame and handle, was sometimes used.

Gentlemen carried very small looking-glasses, often worn in the hat as a brooch or ornament which could be detached when required.

Here are a few items from the Queen's privy purse expenses which may amuse those interested in dressmaking bills and sundry items, bearing in mind the value of money at this time, and the fact that Queen Elizabeth's household expenses were £55,000 per annum.

From 8th July 1566 until 23rd April 1567.

To David Smyth, embroderer	.	.	.	.	.	£203 15	7
William Middleton, embroderer		.	.	.	.	25 11	11
Robert Careles, pynner	.	.	.	.	.	127 8	9

To Raphell Hamonde, capper . . . . . £ 68   1   6

Thomas Ludwell, tailor, for apparell, and other neces-
saries for Robert Grene, the Quene's fool and Nicholas
Knyghte Smyth, his servant 111 13 9

Expenses and chardges of Robert Grene, the Queen's
fool, and to Nicholas Knyghte Smythe, his servant, for
wage and bordewage at sondry times. 1569 . . 17   0   0

[The last items show that the Queen supplied her Court jester with raiment
and also that he kept an attendant with a much more aristocratic name.]

Mrs. Mary Radclyffe, one of the maidens of honoure, for
her stipend of £40 per ann. for two years and a half,
ended at the Annunciation of Oure Lady, 1569. . 100   0   0

This lady was the daughter of a romantic marriage. Her father, Sir
Humphrey Radclyffe, a younger son of the first Earl of Sussex, fell in love
with Isabella, the beautiful daughter
of a rich London merchant named Edmund Harvey.   Mary became a Maid
of Honour to the Queen about 1561,
and served her mistress 'honourably,
virtuously, and faithfully for forty
years.'   Like the Queen, who was much
attached to her, she remained a spinster
all her life: the Queen's 'merry
guardian' the courtiers called her.   At
the end of the reign Mary Radclyffe
held the responsible post of Keeper
of the Queen's Jewels.

Blanche Parry was another very close
attendant on the Queen.   Born at New-
court Bacton, Herefordshire, in 1507,
she had known Elizabeth from the
cradle and served her mistress most
faithfully all her life, at first as Gentlewoman of the Privy Chamber, and
later as Keeper of the Queen's Jewels.
This lady died in 1589, and her effigy
in Bacton Church shows her kneeling
before the Queen.   In it she is habited

Fig. 710. Blanche Parry, 1589

in a simple and comfortable costume, suitable for an old woman of eighty:
in black or some dark-coloured surcote with hanging sleeves, over an ordinary
gown (*see* Fig. 710).   Some of Elizabeth's cast-off dresses became the per-
quisites of her gentlewomen-in-waiting, and the altar cloth presented by
Blanche Parry to Bacton Church, and still shown there, was, in all probability,
made up from one of them.

'For jewels of gold, stones, and pearles bought and provided for
Her Majestie within the time [10 months] of this accompte   £2,294 3 3½'

Seed pearls, which were very much used *en masse* for the decoration of
dresses, cost 1*d.* each.

'Silkes bought of sundry persons to the Queen's Majestie's use £101 14   2

'Gold lace bought by Walter Fisher, the Queen's Taylor, for Her
Majestie's use 32 10

'Mrs. Taylor, the Queen's laundress, for her wages at £4 per ann. . . .
with £6 paid her for her livery gown £10.' 1568.   Fig. 719 shows a laundress,
and who knows but that she is the Queen's own?

'The Italian, Carlo Lanfranchi, a trader who was with the Prince of Parma
at Brussels a few days ago [about 1586], has requested His Highness's permission to purchase some silk wares and take them to the Court of the Queen
in England.   So this merchant has bought nearly 12,000 pounds Flemish
worth of all sorts of silk wares and started for England with them yesterday.'
Lanfranchi was a merchant resident at Antwerp; later with one Andrew de
Looe chief partner in a big Italian firm in London.

'NYGHT STUFFE'

LADIES AND GENTLEMEN

What a wonderful vision young Gilbert Talbot must have beheld at eight
of the clock on the morning of 3rd May 1578—the Virgin Queen in her
nightdress!   He writes to his father:

'I happened to walke in the Tylte-yard, under the Gallery where her Matie
useth to stande to see the ruñinge at tylte; where by chaunce she was, and
lokynge out of the wyndow, my eye was full towards her, and she shewed
to be greatly ashamed thereof, for that she was unreddy, and in her nyght
stuffe.'

Elizabeth was then in her forty-fifth year, an age when modesty grows upon
a woman; so naturally 'much ashamed thereof she was,' as she told her Lord
Chamberlain afterwards.   All Gilbert received was 'a great phyllyp on the
forehead.'   We wish he had remembered more, for then we should have had
first-hand particulars of these interesting garments.   Unfortunately they must
be more or less left to conjecture.   In shape, ladies' as well as gentlemen's
nightdresses or 'night-railes' were, without much doubt, similar to those worn
during the reign of Henry VIII (*see* Chapter II, p. 262), and decorated in various
ways.   A few paintings and some original nightdresses reputed to be of the
Elizabethan era show lace insertion, used in vertical, horizontal, and diagonal
lines in parts or over the whole garment.   A night-raile traditionally said to

have been worn at Rycote by Elizabeth, and once owned by the Earl of Abingdon (a substantial proof of its genuineness!), is now exhibited at the London Museum. Fig. 711 is a half-diagram made from it. It is of fine linen with embroidery, insertion, and lace all white.

Amongst items in the Queen's lists of New Year's gifts and wardrobe accounts are the following:

'A smock of cameryck wrought with tawny sylke and black, with ruffs and collar edged with bone lace of silver' (1577).

'A smock of fine Holland, and the bodies and sleeves wrought all over with black silk' (1588).

These garments may be equivalent to chemises, yet on the other hand would serve equally well as nightdresses.

'A nightraile of camberick wrought all over with black silk' (1588).

'A night gown [i.e. a dressing-gown] of tawny satten, allover embrodered, faced with satten heare collour, for the Queen from Sir Francis Walsingham' (1578).

The shape of night-caps, both for men and women, has altered little from time immemorial (see vol. ii, p. xi, and Chapter II, p. 262). One at least appears in the list of New Year's gifts to the Queen: 'By Mrs. Crokson a night coif of white Cipers florisshed ouer with silver' (1578).

All these night-garments were worn by fashionable women in imitation of the Queen, and even by men.

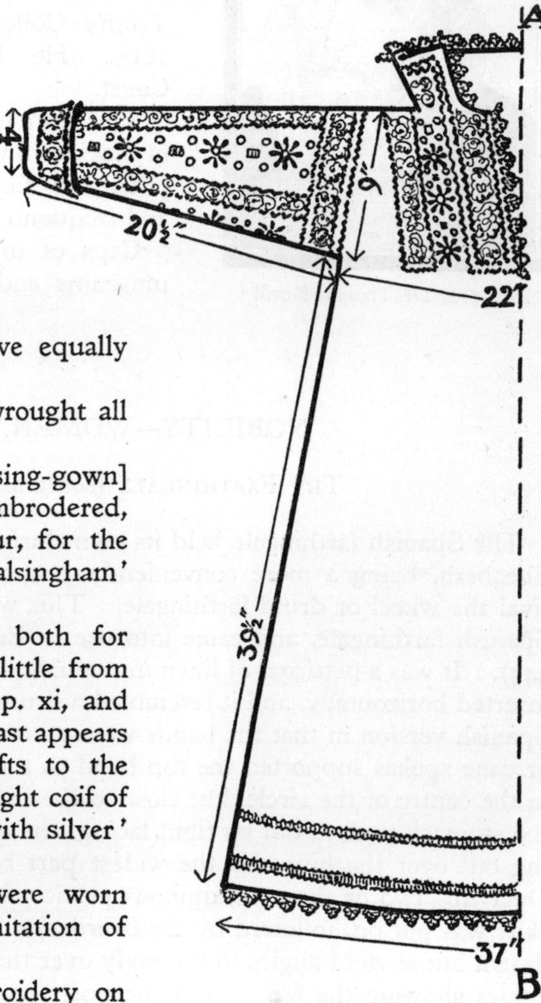

So elaborate did the embroidery on night-caps become, that gentlemen began to wear them in the day-time—

Fig. 711. A Night-raile

especially the elderly who needed protection for their bald pates. Several portraits show them wearing such caps with ordinary day dress, and some in official robes. The full-length painting of Charles, Baron Howard of Effingham (1536–1624), in the Royal Hospital, Greenwich, shows the Lord High Admiral of England (1585–1618) in the full robes

Fig. 712. Dr. Thomas Nevill

of the Order of the Garter and wearing one of these embroidered caps.

In shape they were like a bag round at the top, the end turning up to form a brim and the whole surface usually embroidered. Fig. 712 is drawn from a portrait of Dr. Thomas Nevill, Master of Trinity College, Cambridge, from 1593 to 1615. He built and paid for Nevill's Court.

This cap is made of linen, embroidered in black and white silk and silver gilt thread. Often the embroidery was in coloured silks, and frequently spangles were introduced.

Caps of this type may be seen in many museums and private collections.

NOBILITY—WOMEN, 1580–1603

THE FARTHINGALE (continued from p. 504)

The Spanish farthingale held its own during the remainder of the reign of Elizabeth, being a more conveniently proportioned garment than its close rival the wheel or drum farthingale. This was a development of the earlier Spanish farthingale, and came into use in England only about 1586–8 (Fig. 243). It was a petticoat of linen into which bands of steel or whalebone were inserted horizontally, and it resembled a drum in shape. It differed from the Spanish version in that the bands were all of the same circumference. Steel or cane spokes supported the top band to a waistbelt. This was not placed in the centre of the circle, but close to the frame; in fact, the frame rested on the stomach pushed out by tight lacing, the edges of the circumference bowing out over the hips and the widest part being in the centre of the back. Over this two or three voluminous petticoats were added before the underskirt was put on, followed by the overdress. The skirt of the overdress was drawn out at right angles to the body over the farthingale and then fell to the ankles showing the feet. In some portraits of great ladies of this period a circular top piece is seen on the farthingaled skirt, with box pleats radiating from the waist, resembling the spokes of a wheel; and for this reason it is referred to as the wheel farthingale. This is plainly shown in Fig. 725.

The wheel farthingale, however, had its merits. A dress displayed upon this structure showed the rich and costly material of which it was composed to greater advantage, consequently it became very popular at Court and for ceremonial and full dress.

It required no little skill to wear the cumbersome farthingale with grace and dignity; but use is second nature, and it was not a difficult matter for ladies of quality of the late Elizabethan era to manipulate these hoops with dexterity and effect. The art was born in them, for it must be realized that the farthingale had been worn by their mothers, grandmothers, and great-grandmothers for seventy years or more past.

The correct way to hold the arms when wearing a farthingale was to rest the wrists upon the edge, as shown in Fig. 725, one hand usually carrying a handkerchief, the other perhaps a fan. Two lines from a poem dated 1599 refer to this pose:

> Placing both hands upon her whalebone hips,
> Puffed out with a round circling farthingale.

Amongst the customs for which the wheel farthingale is responsible is that of sitting on piles of cushions on the floor.

The style and shape of chairs in use during the first eighty years of the sixteenth century can be seen from Fig. 215, were, one can understand, quite unsuited for sitting in comfort when the wearer was enveloped in the wheel farthingale. The arms and normal width of the seat were found inconvenient; consequently cushions, always a popular item of furnishing in medieval and Tudor times, were brought into much more general use. As the lady, decked out in all the paraphernalia Court and high society demanded, approached these piles of cushions, in order to avoid disarrangement of the skirt she turned and raised herself high on her toes, and then sank elegantly into their midst and sat upon a soft pedestal, so to speak, encircled by the voluminous skirt and farthingale.

Queen Elizabeth frequently seated herself on the floor on cushions, especially when carrying on a friendly discourse with a lady or gentleman. Taking this into account, it does not appear so incongruous that, during her last illness, this great Queen should prefer to remain upon her cushions instead of going to bed.

It was not until the end of the century that wide chairs, with or without arms, known as farthingale chairs, came into use.

In the Audience or Presence Chambers of the Royal palaces, and houses of the nobility, the number of stools was now greatly increased, amounting to anything from fifty to a hundred and fifty; and in some households cushions of velvet or embroidery were provided for a few of them, being tied by

Fig. 713. Hip Pad

cords and tassels to the legs. Thus, numbers of cushions, or 'quysshens,' are found in household inventories of the sixteenth century, elaborate descriptions being often given. Of oak, these *joint stools* of the mid-Elizabethan period remain with us to-day. Their name does *not* imply that they were used at table for carving; they were so called because made and finished by a joiner. These now took the place of cushions on the floor, and although harder to sit upon were not complained of by the much be-petticoted ladies. Nor was the discomfort of a hard wooden seat noticeable to the gentlemen,

Fig. 714. From an Engraving, 1603

in the days when bombast Venetian breeches were the mode. But in the 1590's fashion decreed a return to the round slops of earlier years *minus* the bombast, as is shown in Figs. 739 and 740. This loss of posterior padding was most likely responsible for more comfortable upholdered seats or 'buffet stools,' so called because they were stuffed with padding or 'buffet' of all kinds. The upholdering was of velvet, damask, brocade, or embroidery—

embroidery of similar design to that shown in Fig. 689. The same privileges connected with the use of stools in the Presence Chambers in the Royal palaces of France, described on p. 664, were adopted in England at this time.

Fig. 715. A Squeamish Townswoman

A faldstool was a similar stool of common make, used by ordinary people in England.

The French farthingale was introduced at the Court of Henry III as late as 1580. It consisted of a single padded hoop, and its modified version was a bolster-like pad (Fig. 713). It fastened round the waist sloping from the back to the point of the stomacher. This was set on top of some petticoats, one or two other petticoats being worn over the hoop or pad. This French type is seen worn by the lady (Fig. 755) in which the very full skirt of rich satin, cut on the circle and gathered into the waist, hangs in many graceful folds well on to the ground. A feature characteristic of the French type is that its widest part is level with the waist-line, the folds of the skirt slightly falling in towards the feet when supple fabrics, such as silk or satin, were used. But when the skirts were of stiff brocades, and some made stiffer by gold metal weaving, the folds took the reverse line and stood out at the hem, having almost the same effect as if the Spanish or wheel farthingale was worn. For example see Fig. 731.

It must have been quite impossible to sit a horse when wearing a Spanish or wheel farthingale, but sometimes the bolster was used.

The French or Italian lady (Fig. 714), taken from a contemporary engraving, is seated upon a special saddle with a very low cantle, and wears a bolster farthingale under the cart-wheel arrangement. Her full skirt drapes over her right leg, which is supported by a pommel, and over the horse's back in quite a pleasing manner. As was the discreet custom with ladies of quality when in public, she is masked, and carries a large feather fan, perhaps as an additional protection.

Fig. 715 is a reproduction of a contemporary engraving, and shows the farthingale as worn by middle-class women. The first impression is that faulty draughtsmanship is responsible for the bottom edge being too much curved and too short, thus showing a very decided and ungraceful ridge when the skirt was let down. Actually this bourgeois lady has hitched up her farthingale with both hands *under* the drapery of her skirt to avoid the canine scavengers; thereby revealing to us the lines of the canes or whalebones which are very clearly defined.

THE CORSET (*continued from p. 504*)

A change in the shape of the corset took place approximately at the time when the wheel farthingale was adopted, in order to accentuate the line of the farthingale.

The Queen was approaching her fiftieth year and her figure, always of slim proportions, became in middle life even more so. All fashionable women wished to emulate the Great Gloriana, consequently a long narrow tapering figure had to be acquired. The construction of steel corsets, without doubt, improved since their first introduction about the year of Elizabeth's birth; and this may account in some measure for the abnormal slenderness of late Elizabethan ladies as seen in their portraits. It is true that the artists who painted them may have exaggerated their narrowness of body, but on the other hand it is extraordinary what impossibilities women of all ages can achieve to be *à la mode*.

The Queen's narrow, flat-chested figure was well adapted to the new style of corset such as is shown in Fig. 716, a drawing made from an original. The front bands of steel extend downwards in a long tapering point as far as the pit of the stomach, and the sides converge as low down as the hip bone will permit. It is the line from this to the lowest point of the corset that deceives the eye and makes the figure look longer and the waist smaller than they really are.

There is no evidence that these corsets hooked, bolted, or padlocked; they were fastened by tight-lacing the back. As previously, the steel work was lined and covered with thin silk or other material, and often decorated with *flat* embroidery which could not add to the bulk. The lady (Fig. 243) is wearing a corset of this kind. The bodice of the dress was cut to fit the corset without a crease, and the front of it was generally covered by the stom-acher, which took the lines of the constructional converging bands of steel.

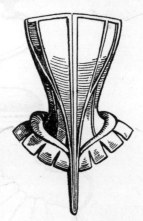

Fig. 716. The Corset

A less expensive contrivance was a broad slightly convex piece of wood which was used by the middle-class women to keep their busts flat, and make their figures straight and erect.

The following lines from *Pleasant Quippes for Upstart Gentlewomen*, by Stephen Gosson, 1596, describe the type of corset worn by both men and women of the middle classes:

> Those privie coats by art made strong,
> With bones, with paste, and such like ware,
> Whereby their backs and sides grow long.

THE RUFF OR BAND (*continued from p. 505*)

During the latter half of this reign the ruff assumed vast dimensions, its width varying from nine to fifteen inches from the neck on either side. When unset and drawn out to its full length the band was sometimes eight yards long. The Queen wore hers higher, wider, and stiffer than any one else in Europe, save the Queen of Navarre, Marguerite de Valois, who had a 'yellow throat,' and desired to conceal it with the addition of 'chin ruffs.' These consisted of one or more frills, themselves small circular ruffs worn close up under the jaw, which also helped to mask the line where the main ruff sur-rounded the back of the neck. These wonderful face frames of lawn were edged with exquisite lace, cutwork, and insertion. They were also decorated with embroidery, and sometimes in complete contrast were quite plain with the edges cut out in points like the head of a small spear.

In 1599 the Countess of Worcester presented the Queen with 'One ruffe

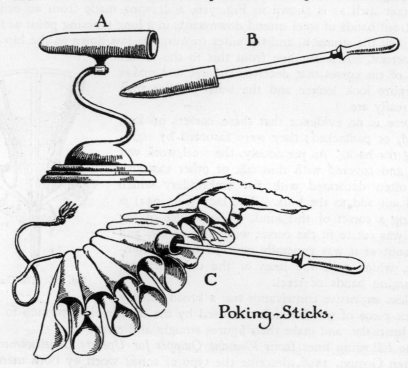

Fig. 717. Poking-sticks

of lawne cut-worke, set with 20 small knottes of gold like mullets [heraldic stars], gar' with small sparkes of rubyes and perle.'

Item 'a sute of ruffes of Lawne, wrought with Spanisshe worke.'

A poking-stick or setting-iron of this period is shown in Fig. 717 drawn from one found at Cowdray. The top of the iron or steel stand, shown at A, was heated in the fire. The stick B was thrust into it, and when sufficiently hot was then placed in that part of the band already damped with starch. This process was repeated all along the flutes of the band until it was complete and well stiffened. This process is seen at C.

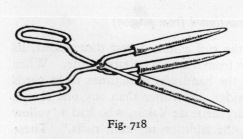

Fig. 718

Fig. 718 shows another kind of poking-stick or setting-tongs made on the principle of modern curling-tongs, except that two sticks were rigid and the third was worked on a pivot, so that three flutes could be goffered at one operation.

Fig. 719 shows a laundress in the act of goffering the set of a ruff. The 'band,' having been dipped in starch, is tied round the ruff-stand and the steel poking-stick is taken from its sheath in the charcoal brazier and thrust into the fold of linen with the aid of the fingers of the left hand. This action is repeated until the ruff is finished; then it is hung up to dry. A complete ruff with one edge attached to a piece of linen, which is fixed inside the collar of the dress, is seen hanging on a rod in the illustration. When the time came for the delivery of the band to its owner, it was placed in a circular box specially made for its reception and known as a 'band-box.' One is shown in the right-hand corner.

Fig. 719.

'There she sat with her poking-stick, stiffening a fall'

Bands and wristbands usually matched, and were made chiefly of lawn. In 1591 Queen Elizabeth paid £10 10s for 'three suits of good lawn cutwork ruffs edged with bone lace'—i.e. three ruffs and three pairs of cuffs.

Three ruffs, one on top of the other, were known as 'three-piled ruffs.'

That arch-craftsman in the art of grousing, Philip Stubbes, has much to say which is worth repeating with regard to the ruff:

'They have great and monsterous ruffs, made either of cambrick, holland, lawn, or else of some other of the finest cloth that can be got for money, whereof some be a quarter of a yard deep, yea, some more, very few less, so that they stand a full quarter of a yard and more from their necks, hanging over their shoulder points, instead of a veil. But . . . if the storms chance to hit upon the crafty bark of their brused ruffs, then they go flip flap in the wind, like rags flying abroad, and lye upon their shoulders like the dish-clouts of a slut. . . . They have them wrought all over with silk work, and peradventure laced with gold and silver, or other costly lace of no small price.'

Gentlemen 'have now newly [1595] found out a more monstrous kind of ruff, of twelve, yea, sixteen lengths apiece, set three or four times double, thence called three steps and a half to the gallows.'

Referring to the stiffening of the ruff he tells us they have 'a certain kind of liquid matter which they call starch, wherein the devil hath willed them to wash and dive their ruffs well, which, when they be dry will then stand stiff and inflexible about their necks.   And this starch they make of divers substances, sometimes of wheatflour, of bran, and other grains; sometimes of roots, and sometimes of other things, of all colours and hues, as white, red, blew, purple, and the like.'   Ben Jonson mentions goose-green starch, but one does not find these coloured ruffs depicted in portraits.

Fig. 720. Supportasse

Despite these stiffening methods it appears that the breezes still played havoc with the ruff. Stubbes describes 'a certain device made of wires, crested for the purpose, whipped over either with gold thread, silver or silk, and this be called a SUPPORTASSE or underprop.   This is to be applied round about their necks under the ruff, upon the outside of the band, to bear up the whole frame and body of the ruff from falling and hanging down.'   Fig. 720 shows one of these supportasses made from a sixteenth-century Flemish engraving.   Rebarto was another name for it.

Late in the period another kind of support was used with large circular ruffs.   This contrivance originated possibly in Spain, and is seen in Fig. 886.   It was a circular gold or silver wire frame fitting the neck, whence wires or spokes radiated to the circumference. To this was sewn a narrow fringe in gold, silver, or silk giving a very pleasing effect.

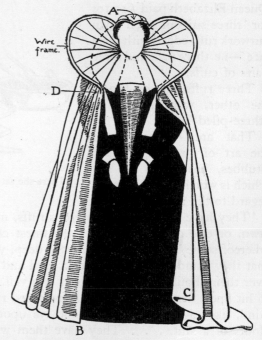

Fig. 721. The Wired-out Veil

THE VEIL (cont. from p. 505)

Now that fashionable costume had undergone various changes both in shape and decoration, elaborate yet grotesque, a new method of arranging the veil was devised.   This was brought about chiefly by the increase in the width of the ruff.   In shape this new veil was a large *square* of filmy transparent gauze or other material edged all round with cutwork, reticella, or gold or silver lace. Its arrangement, shown in diagram (Fig. 721) was as follows:

One corner, A, was attached to the headdress or coiffure; if to the latter, the corner was usually brought well on to the centre of the forehead. In the former case it was slightly gathered and fixed to the headdress, whatever shape it might be. It was again gathered or pleated into the nape of the neck, forming a cap over the back of the head. From the nape the edges of the veil were wired out in two large semicircles or three-quarter-circles on either side of the head behind the ruff, the wire being secured to the bodice just in front of the arm-pit at D. This arrangement kept the veil free from entanglement with the ruff, and did not impede the movement of the head. From the armpit and from over the shoulders two corners of the veil, B and C, fell to the feet. The re-maining fourth corner trailed upon the ground behind: E, Fig. 722. The dotted line indicates the edge of the ruff worn *over* the front of the veil. The earliest example of the veil treated in this manner is seen in the 'Siena' portrait of Queen Elizabeth, 1578, and the more elaborate arrangement is shown in Plate XXXVIII and other illustrations in this section.

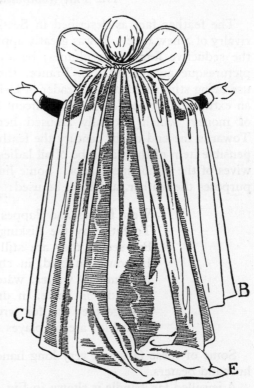

Fig. 722. Back view of Veil

In the National Portrait Gallery portrait, No. 2471 (Plate XXXII B), the gauze veil is decorated with bands of cutwork but not wired; as an alternative, a circular collar worn behind the ruff distends the veil beyond the shoulders.

THE SLEEVES

To balance the width of the wheel farthingale and so enhance the effect of squareness, sleeves were large, of leg-of-mutton shape, and padded out at the shoulders.

In nearly every case there were long loose over-sleeves, cut as an oblong about twenty-five inches wide and forty inches long, though sometimes falling to the hem of the skirt, as seen in Plates XXXVIII, XLI B and C,

XLII, and Figs. 726 and 729. These over-sleeves were gathered or pleated into the armhole, starting from the shoulder and going round the back to the armpit.

THE FAN (continued from p. 507)

The feather fan, as described in Section I, held its own in spite of the rivalry of a new type. It was greatly appreciated for its graceful line, and for the seductive flow of its plumes; besides, no one could possible deny its picturesque advantages. In France, the feather fan was pre-eminent, its use being stimulated by that leader of fashion, Marguerite de Valois, who had an extraordinary passion for magnificent fans. These cost a very great deal of money, which naturally aroused her husband's justifiable displeasure. Towards the end of the century the feather fan had become an almost indispensible item of the wardrobe of all ladies and gentlewomen, and even of the wives of the minor merchants. Some lines dated 1598 show for what other purposes the feather fan might be used:

> Were fannes and flappes of feathers fond
> To flit away the flisking flies . . .
> But seeing they are still in hand,
> In house, in field, in church, in street
> In summer, winter, water, land,
> In colde, in heate, in dry, in weet,
> I judge they are for wives such tooles
> As bables are in playes for fooles.

Some of these fans had very long handles and were found very useful as husband beaters.

A jewelled fan-handle is shown in Fig. 937.

THE SEMICIRCULAR OR FOLDING FAN

It was during the late 1580's or early 1590's that a fan made to open and shut first appeared in England. Such fans were used much earlier in China, and the first European country to adopt them was Italy, where they were represented in paintings earlier in the sixteenth century. In France and Spain they came into vogue at much the same time as in England. One of the first English ladies to possess such a fan had her portrait painted displaying it very prominently: she was evidently very pleased with it, and with reason, since at this time such fans from far-off Cathay were very rare. Many of these fans of European make are seen in portraits of English ladies of the late years of the sixteenth century, but there are unfortunately none

shown fully open. Fig. 723 is a larger-scale drawing
of the fan carried by the Countess of Nottingham
(see Fig. 728). The 'guard' is wider than that of
a modern fan: it is black, inlaid with ivory, with
puff-balls of silk down the outside and along the
top. Fig. 724 is a drawing from a portrait dated
1590, and is given because it is one of the earliest
examples of a fan painted half open. It will be
seen that the same principle of carved sticks and a
decorated 'leaf' that we know to-day was adopted
by fan-makers [1] of the sixteenth century. The sticks
are of carved ivory, the two guards tapering, but the
sticks are of uniform width and are fixed by stitches
of gold thread between the two layers of white gauze
which form the 'leaf': the guards are whipped across
with red silk. The edges of the gauze are bound
together with fine stitches of gold and a row of small
gold knots. The leaf is very finely embroidered in a
design of roses and pansies in their natural colourings.
The pivot is kept in place with a gold filigree ornament set with a ruby.

Fig. 723.
Closed semicircular Fan

This fan has no ring to take
a riband, but many fans had
one as shown in some of the
drawings.

Mica or vellum was often
used for the leaf.

Whether it was a feather
fan on a rigid handle, or one
made to open or close, Brantôme does not say; but he
mentions that Marguerite,
Queen of Navarre, 'on one
occasion . . . gave Queen
Louise of France a fan made
of mother-of-pearl enriched
with precious stones and pearls
of price, so beautiful and rich
that it was called a masterpiece and valued at more
than fifteen thousand crowns.'
This fan certainly appears to
have been of the semi-
circular shape.

Fig. 724. Fan, 1580

[1] The Fan-makers' Company was not incorporated until 1709.

It was customary for ladies, when out of doors, to have a page or servant to carry the fan.

Even men used fans; at least, Pierre de l'Étoile relates that Henry III fanned himself like a woman with a richly ornamented fan of this kind, which opened with a simple flick of the finger, and fell closed.   Some of the courtiers also used fans, chiefly of taffeta decorated with gold and silk embroidery.

STOCKINGS (continued from p. 546)

As late as 1595 stockings of worsted are mentioned as being worn by smart folk.   Silk gradually superseded worsted for best wear, and so great a reputation did English silk stockings attain on the Continent, that Duke Frederick of Württemburg commissioned his secretary, Hans Jacob Breuning von Buchenbach, who was on a visit to this country in 1595, to replenish his stock.   He writes to his master:

'The twelve pairs of stockings I have bought as cheap and as best I could. They are according to Your Grace's wish, in various colours, but no black or green.   They are of excellent quality and picked from a large assortment. Twelve pair fine silk stockings, at 6 French crowns a pair.'

THE STOCKING FRAME

In 1589 William Lee invented the stocking frame, a device which enabled stockings to be mechanically knitted.   He was a clergyman, having matriculated at Christ's College, Cambridge, and was a B.A. of St. John's College. He resigned his living and devoted himself to the manufacture of stockings in worsted at Calverton, the scene of his ministerial labours.   When he came to London his work was brought to the notice of the Queen by Lord Hunsdon, but this fastidious lady who had already worn hand-knitted silk stockings turned up her Royal nose with scorn at hosiery of such coarse make and refused to grant him a patent of monopoly.   The inventor adapted his frame to the use of silk in 1598, but Elizabeth feared that the invention would prejudice the hand-knitters, and therefore discouraged the reverend gentleman.   For the same reason, James I was not interested; but Henry IV invited Lee to settle in France.   At the very moment when he was about to obtain the promised privileges, Henry IV was assassinated (1610), and Concini, the virtual Regent of France, was not willing to assist Lee in his enterprise. The disappointment so distressed the poor man that he gave way to despair, and died of privation and grief the same year.   James Lee, his brother, returned to England with his craft and frames, and eventually obtained the patronage of James I; and with the assistance of a former apprentice of William's he became successful, and his trade increased rapidly. From this time knitted stockings in silk, worsted, and other materials became general throughout Europe.

The foregoing items of costume are seen illustrated in the portraits of the Queen already reproduced, as also in the drawings of Court and Noble ladies which follow. For example, the costume worn by the lady (Fig. 725), which was in vogue during the 1580's, shows large sleeves, long pointed stomacher,

Fig. 725. La Mode, 1580's

Fig. 726. The Lady Elizabeth Howard, 1582

skirt over the wheel farthingale with the cart-wheel effect on top and the huge ruff and high-dressed coiffure surmounted by a coronet like a stephane. The dress is without much decoration, and would be made of satin, silk, velvet or brocade, although the last does not appear to have been much favoured during this decade.

THE LADY ELIZABETH HOWARD, 1580–90

The portrait of Lady Elizabeth Howard (Fig. 726) illustrates further the hanging sleeves, as well as a new method of draping the skirt over the wheel farthingale.   She was daughter of the Earl and Countess of Nottingham, and is shown in one of the many dresses she wore as Maid of Honour to the Queen. It was Elizabeth's wish—nay, command—that all her ladies-in-waiting should dress in white and silver when in attendance, so as to form an ameliorative background for Her Majesty.   Some of them strongly resented being mere backgrounds.   Many made excellent marriages: the Lady Elizabeth wedded Sir Robert Southwell about 1582.   Fig. 726 depicts an interesting costume of hers.   The bodice and skirt are of plain white satin; the very large sleeves and stomacher of this material are decorated with oval ornaments of clusters of pearls.   Behind these sleeves are pleated into the armholes at the back of the *hanging sleeves*, a feature appearing here for the first time. These hang behind the skirt; the outer edge, and probably the inner also, is serrated and stiffened by flexible wire so as to carry projecting ornaments of pearls or tiny buttons in groups of three.   The skirt cut all in one, a large circle, is pleated into a waistband and falls in folds over the wheel farthingale. No cart-wheel effect is here, but instead, the skirt is draped very skilfully at, and over, the edge.   The Lady Southwell's headdress is composed of fern-like leaves in silver, pearls, and diamonds and worn over high hairdressing. There is no lace edging to the ruff: instead, it is cut out in points like *little spear-heads*, while the inner edge is masked where it rests on the neck by puffings of gauze.

CATHERINE CAREY

Countess of Nottingham, died 1603

The Lady Southwell's mother (Fig. 728) is 'Kate' Carey, eldest daughter of Henry, first Baron Hunsdon, and a granddaughter of Mary Boleyn, and so first cousin to Queen Elizabeth.   She was one of the Queen's many Maids of Honour, and in 1563 married Charles, second Baron Howard of Effingham (1573), who was created Earl of Nottingham in 1596.   The Countess's portrait is interesting because it shows distinctly the new arrangement of the veil. One corner is attached to the head in a series of pleats, the lace edging forming a coronet effect.   The lines of the very transparent veil can be traced, first wired out behind the ruff, secondly fixing in front of the armpit, and thirdly descending to the ground behind the skirt.   Her ladyship's dress is of black velvet, made on fashionable lines, the bodice and sleeves embroidered with silver of a different design from the skirt—a new feature.   The skirt draped over the wheel farthingale is also embroidered in silver, and up the front is a puffing of gauze fixed with jewels.   She is holding in her right hand a profusely decorated fan of the newest shape.   Below a dog-collar of jewels, and surrounding the throat, is placed a twist or ruche of gauze—a beneficent fashion for those who have scraggy necks—which also masks the edge of the elaborately worked ruff.   From beneath this, long ropes of pearls fall to the point of the stomacher.   These ropes of pearls and chains of jewels worn round the neck were now given the name of NECKLACES, carcanets being the former appellation for them.   Her hair—or is it a wig?—is closely curled, and adorned with numerous tiny horse-shoes of pearls.

Fig. 727. Noble Lady

Reproduced by kind permission of Archibald G. B. Russell, Esq.

The Countess is celebrated for having withheld the Earl of Essex's ring, confessing to the Queen on her death-bed in 1603 (*see* p. 780).

Quite a different style of dress is worn by the lady of quality (Fig. 727), which shows that the Spanish farthingale was still in favour.   The original drawing was made by Nicholas Hilliard in the 1580's.   The lady portrayed is in full dress wearing large sleeves, but not padded so stiffly as those worn for full State, as shown in some of the preceding and following illustrations. The stomacher is moderately long, but the Spanish farthingale is immoderately voluminous.   This figure is especially interesting as it reproduces all the important features seen in some of Queen Elizabeth's portraits, thereby allocating them within this decade. One of these portraits is shown in Plate XLI A. In Fig. 727 the bodice has tapering rolls converging from the shoulders to the point below the waist. They are studded part of the way with groups of gems, and on the shoulders with bows caught down with jewels. These bows are repeated down the front and hem of the skirt, and down the centre of the under-skirt. This garment displays rich embroidery between bands of gold set with rows of pearls. A circular ruff surrounds the head, and the headdress with attifet front closely resembles the French hood.

There is a portrait, in a private collection, of a young woman wearing a costume very much on the lines of the foregoing. Her dress is composed of green and gold brocade; the headdress is of the same shape as Fig. 727; and round her neck a heavy gold chain is wound four times, descending to the low point of the stomacher—and this portrait is dated 1597.

MARY STUART, 1580–7 (continued from p. 517)

In 1580 Mary Queen of Scots was in captivity at Sheffield Castle, where she spent in all fourteen years until 1584. During the two following years the Queen was retained at four different places until the tragedy at Fotheringay, 1587.

After the death of Bothwell in 1576, Mary appears to have adopted plain black velvet for her gowns, as exemplified by the many well-known portraits of her. The full-length by P. Oudry at Hardwick Hall and the three-quarter, No. 429 in the National Portrait Gallery, which are practically identical, are pronounced the most authentic likenesses of the Queen at this time. A similar portrait, said to have been painted in 1578, originally belonged to the Earl of Darnley and is now in the Scottish National Portrait Gallery. The costume is exactly the same in all three portraits. The dress has a close-fitting bodice, rounded at the neck opening, over a partlet of goffered lawn surmounted by a moderate-sized ruff. The sleeves, fairly large at the shoulders and a little raised, taper towards the wrists. The waist-line is pointed and outlined by a small girdle of jet; from this hangs a Latin cross in gold from which is suspended a rosary of beads, some gold and others of dark metal enamelled with a design in red. From the headdress, reproduced in Fig. 876, hangs a fine white transparent veil edged with lace and wired out as described on p. 748.

Queen Mary's wardrobe was not well stocked, and her dresses were few. Queen Elizabeth took compassion on her 'dear sister,' and sent her as a gift some cast-off garments of her own which Mary haughtily declined.

On the first day of her trial in October 1586 at nine of the clock, Her Majesty of Scotland entered the Great Hall of Fotheringay escorted by a guard of Halberdiers and took her seat.[1] She was dressed, we are told, in a gown with

[1] This fourteenth-century chair in carved oak used to stand by the altar in Fotheringay Church. It was brought into the Castle Hall especially for the Queen's use; and can now be seen in the church at Connington. Mary Queen of Scots at Madame Tussaud's is seated in a replica.

an over-robe like Fig. 602 of black velvet, and over her pointed coif a long gauze veil (see Fig. 875). Her train was borne by her Maid of Honour, Renée Beauregard.

On the fatal morning, 8th February 1587, the Queen of Scotland and Queen-Dowager of France robed herself in a skirt and bodice of black satin over an under-skirt of russet-brown velvet. Above these she wore a long-sleeved mantle (see Fig. 602) of black satin embroidered with gold and edged with sable.

From a contemporary manuscript other details are gathered, but they vary slightly from the foregoing. The original text is as follows:

'Her borrowed hair a BOURNE (see p. 515) having on her head a dressing of lawn edged with bone lace, a pomander chain, an Agnus Dei about her neck, a Crucifix in her hand, and a pair of Beads at her girdle with a golden Cross at the end of them, a veil of lawn fastened to her caul bowed out with wire and edged round about with bone lace, a gown of black satin printed [of formal cut] with a train, and long sleeves to the ground set with acorn buttons of jet garnished with pearl, and short sleeves of black satin cut [cutte] with a pair of sleeves of purple velvet, whole under them a whole kyrtle of figured satin black, her petticote upper body's unlaced in the back of crimson satin, and her petticote skirts of crimson velvet, her shoes of Spanish leather with the rough side outward, a pair of green silk garters, her nether stocks of worsted coloured watchette, clocked with silver, and edged on the tops with silver, and next her legs a pair of Jersey [1] hose white.'

The purple sleeves mentioned above were 'false sleeves.'

One authority mentions that the Queen was 'putting on a paire of sleeves with her owne hands which they [the executioners] had pulled off.'

Another description of the Queen on the scaffold is afforded by the memorial portrait in Blairs College, Aberdeen, which was painted at a little later date under the supervision of Elizabeth Curle, for eight years a personal attendant of the Queen's, and who was, with Jane Kennedy, present at the execution. Her brother, Gilbert Curle, was the Queen's assistant secretary. The picture is an excellent authority for the dress and other details of this mournful event, and the portrait of the Queen, as she appeared at the end of her life, is pronounced an authentic likeness. In it she is robed in a black gown with close-fitting sleeves finishing in plain lawn cuffs; the over-robe, also black, has wider sleeves to the elbow cut up the front and edged with fur, and a stole-like effect of fur edges the fronts of the garment. A plain circular ruff and a black riband carrying a small crucifix surround the neck; and the usual coif (see Fig. 876), and wired-out veil are worn. In her right hand she holds an ebony cross with the Body of Our Lord in carved ivory, and in her left a vellum-bound book of prayers.

After the head had been severed from the body by three strokes of the axe, the executioner 'did lift up her head to the view of all the assembly, and bad God save the Queene. Then her dressing of lawne falling of from her head

---

[1] Jersey was the finest kind of wool, separated from the rest by combing.

it appeared as grey as one of threescore and tenn yeares old polled very shorte.
. . . Then one of the executioners pulling of her garters espied her litle
dogg which was crept under her clothes which could not be gotten forth
but by force, yet afterward wold not departe from the dead corpes but came
and lay betweene her head and her shoulders.'

Brantôme reports that the executioner 'uncoifed her in derision to show her
hair, now white; which, however, she had never shrunk from showing, twisting and curling it as when her hair was beautiful, so fair and golden; for it
was not age had changed it at thirty-five years old (being now but forty);
it was the griefs, the woes, the sadness she had borne in her kingdom and in
her prison.'

The charitable Brantôme is a little out with his calculations when he says
the Queen died at the age of forty.   She was forty-five.

'IN MY END IS MY BEGINNING.'

Fig. 729 is a great lady of the English Court dressed to the full in the very
latest vogue of the 1590's.   During this decade it was most modish to have
the bodice and sleeves of a different material from the skirt.   In this dress
they are of a metallic fabric—a sort of cloud design in gold or silver upon a
ground of coloured silk or satin, perhaps shot with one or the other metal.
The long hanging sleeves, instead of falling at the back of the skirt like those
in Fig. 726, are draped over the top of the farthingale and fall half-way down
the skirt.   The outer edges and the ends are decorated in the same fanciful
manner as is affected by Lady Southwell.   The skirt of plain velvet or silk
suggests the cart-wheel effect, but the spoke-like folds are not so regular;
and an unusual note is the width of brocade let into the front, extending up
to the point of the stomacher.   The wired-out ruff is of cutwork in a simple
design, and edged with tiny white balls at the apexes of stiffened threads or
covered wires, and puffings of lawn or gauze mask where the ruff meets the neck.

'MRS.' MARY FITTON, 1578 *until* 1603

A portrait of Mary Fitton or Phytton is reproduced in Plate XLIV by
courtesy of the owner.   This lady was the younger daughter of Sir Edward
Phytton of Gawsworth, Cheshire.   In her earliest portrait (1592) at Arbury,

wherein she is seen with her elder sister. Anne, she wears a dress veiled like fine gauze ... ruff ... is circular instead of fan-shaped, and that the lace of ...

Made ...

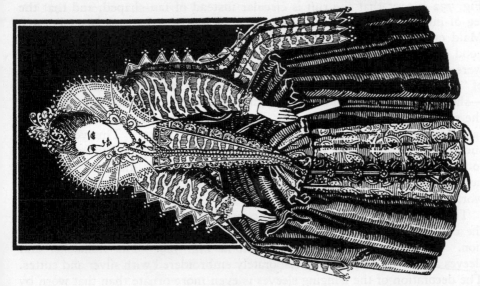

Fig. 729. ENGLISH COURT LADY

sleeve ... apparently embroidered with silver and tinsel.

The decoration of the hanging sleeves is even more elaborate than that worn by the lady before mentioned, for the points edge three three sides of them. The skirt of pale strawberry satin draped over the wheel farthingale is covered with embroidery of close bars of silver to accent it, bodice, over which flowers and leaves are mingled with frog, then, birds, beetles, butterflies, caterpillars, snakes and slues, ... and colourings. A charming aigret of a miniature ... with a gold rim, and suspended at the most ...

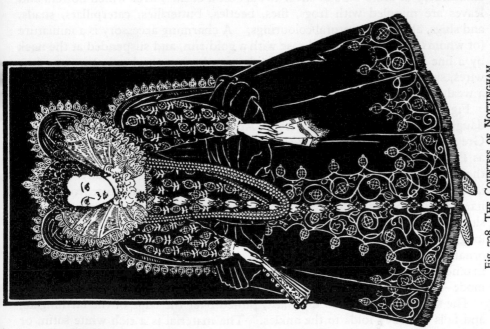

Fig. 728. THE COUNTESS OF NOTTINGHAM

... points to the smaller ... The material is a rich warm white or ...

At the ... of the temple ... robe worn by the Countess ... which lift of damask ...

wherein she is shown with her elder sister Anne, she wears a dress very like Fig. 732 except that the ruff is circular instead of fan-shaped, and that the leg-of-mutton sleeves resemble those of Plate XLIV.   In 1595 Mary became Maid of Honour to the Queen.   She was a clever vivacious girl, and her good looks, and especially her fair complexion, brown hair, and grey eyes, were much admired.   A beautiful dancer—she led a masque [1] in the character of 'Affection,' performed at Lady Anne Russell's wedding festivities in 1600 —she played havoc with many hearts; in fact, she was an arrant flirt, and about the same time carried on a serious intrigue with Lord Herbert (born 1580), 'a proper person, well set, and of graceful deportment.'   This young man succeeded to the Earldom of Pembroke in the following year, but no marriage took place—at least, not with Mistress Fitton!   This indiscretion caused her father to take her from Court, and Mary was packed off home to Gawsworth forthwith.

The portrait (Plate XLIV) was, of course, painted before this disaster, and the costume exemplifies the climax of late-Elizabethan fashion and elaboration.   In style it resembles that shown in Fig. 729.   The stomacher and sleeves are of white satin, very elaborately embroidered with silver and cuttes. The decoration of the hanging sleeves is even more ornate than that worn by the lady before mentioned, for the points edge three sides of them.   The skirt of pale strawberry satin draped over the wheel farthingale is covered with embroidery of cross-bars of silver to suggest a basket, over which flowers and leaves are mingled with frogs, flies, beetles, butterflies, caterpillars, snails, and slugs, all in their natural colourings.   A charming accessory is a miniature (of whom?) in a black enamel case with a gold rim, and suspended at the neck by a fine black cord.   The ruff is fairly simple, but the head attire of silver wires, spangles, and pearls is indeed wonderful.   Sir Edward must have been a wealthy man to supply his daughter with a dress like this!

Fig. 730 is a drawing of the portrait of Anne Fitton's chief friend, Elizabeth, daughter of Edward Nevill, Lord Abergavenny, and wife of Sir John Grey, eldest son of Lord Grey of Groby; this dates about the same time as Plate XLIV; it shows another example of the fashionable mode of having the bodice and sleeves of a different material from the skirt.   In this illustration they are of white satin, worked in half-circles of silver from which hang tiny drop-pearls.   Notice the jewelled pendant hung from the left sleeve, and the gold and enamelled necklace (see also Fig. 912).   The usual long hanging sleeves are of black silk with escalloped edges; a jewelled ornament (see inset) is sewn on each.   These sleeves hang in the correct manner from the shoulders, back, and front, behind the skirt—the very latest mode—almost to the ground.

The skirt is pleated into the waist, puffed over the edge of the farthingale, and falls in heavy folds to the ankles.   The material is a rich white satin, or

[1] At the close of the masque 'Mrs Fitton went to the Queen, and wooed her to daunce.   Her Majesty asked what she was?   "Affection," she said.   "Affection?   Affection," said the Queen, "is false!"   Yet Her Majesty rose and daunced.'   The ingratitude of Essex was no doubt in her mind.

PLATE XLIV. MARY FITTON, AGED 17, 1596: Portrait by an unknown artist
Arbury Park. *By kind permission of Mrs FitzRoy Newdigate*

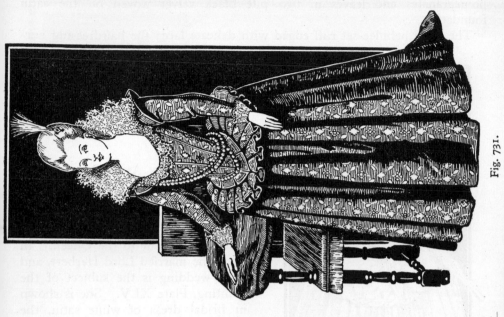
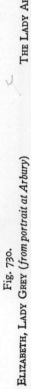

Fig. 731.
THE LADY ARABELLA STUART, 1603 (after Marcus Gheeraerts)

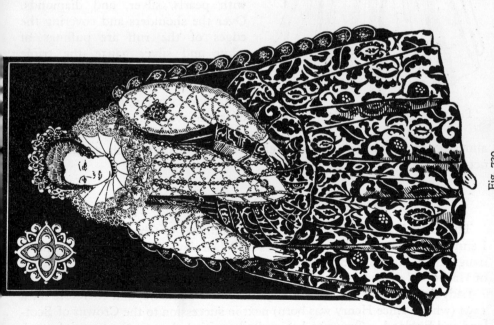

Fig. 730.
ELIZABETH, LADY GREY (from portrait at Arbury)

it could be a pale tone of (say) pink or blue, with a meandering pattern of pomegranates and leaves in two - pile black velvet woven on the satin foundation.

The large nebulée-set ruff edged with delicate lace; the hairdressing surmounted by a wreath of pearls and silver wire—a veritable billement—complete the *tout ensemble* of this fashionably dressed Court and Society lady of the 1590's.

Fig. 732. The Lady Anne Russell, 1600

THE LADY ANNE RUSSELL

Lady Anne Russell (Fig. 732) was daughter of the Earl of Bedford and, like her sister Elizabeth, was Maid of Honour to the Queen. In 1600 she married Lord Herbert, and their wedding is the subject of the painting, Plate XLV. She is shown in bridal dress of white satin, the bodice and sleeves being embroidered with pearls, silver, and diamonds. Over the shoulders and covering the edges of the ruff are puffings of white and silver gauze, the triple ruff itself being plain and edged with tiny points. The skirt is without any decoration, and is puffed out over the wheel farthingale, hanging to the feet in radiating box-pleats—altogether a simple yet rich and effective costume for such an important occasion.

THE LADY ARABELLA STUART, 1575 *until* 1603

The Lady Arabella, born 1575, was the daughter of Charles Stuart, Earl of Lennox (younger brother of Henry, Lord Darnley), and his wife Elizabeth, daughter of Sir William Cavendish and his wife Elizabeth, known as 'Bess of Hardwick' of architectural fame.

Lady Arabella was first cousin to James VI of Scotland, and therefore until 1594 (when Prince Henry was born) next in succession to the Crowns of Scotland and England. Owing to her exalted position she was the cause of much anxiety both to Elizabeth and to James, but the latter treated her with the consideration and affection due to a cousin.

There is a delightful full-length portrait of this lady at Woburn Abbey, painted by Marcus Gheeraerts, when she was about twelve years of age (1587). She wears a dress of what appears to be white brocade made in exactly the same way as that shown in Fig. 726. Her fair hair is flowing over her shoulders, and is surmounted by a wreath of silver and pearls. She evidently had a number of exotic pets, for she is painted with a parrot, a macaw, a monkey, a little dog, and two small parrots which nestle in her right hand. The Lady Arabella was somewhat odd; very vain, extravagant, fond of rich raiment, fantastic costumes (there is a portrait of her in one at Hampton Court), and particularly of jewellery.

Several portraits of this lady exist, and one owned by the Duke of Portland, painted in 1589, shows her wearing a plain white satin dress with long pointed stomacher over the bolster farthingale. Red and gold enamel ornaments decorate the front of the skirt, and smaller ones are set upon the full sleeves. No ruff is worn, which is unusual—she had eccentric tastes!

Fig. 731 is drawn from a very old photograph, dating about the 1880's, of the original by Marcus Gheeraerts in the possession of the Duke of Northumberland at Syon House.[1] It shows the most up-to-date style for February 1602-3, and the Lady Arabella's tall and stately figure carries it off to advantage. The bodice is close-fitting, but the straight lines terminate a little below the waist in striking contrast to the long point of the stomacher previously worn (see Fig. 732). The bodice finishes with tabs at the waist, and has pronounced shoulder pieces or wings and close-fitting sleeves. The skirt hangs in heavy folds over the bolster or wheel farthingale surmounted by the cart-wheel. The whole dress is made of a deep green and gold brocade. The collar of Italian needlepoint lace, 'punto in aria,' is backed by a second collar of starched white lawn; the wrist-cuffs match the two collars; the same lace edges the décolletage; from the right shoulder two strings of magnificent pearls are draped across the figure, and more pearls also encircle the waist. The hairdressing has not changed appreciably since Fig. 732, though an aigrette is fixed by jewels to the left side—the very latest vogue—already worn in Spain.

The artist's mannerism by which a cushion is placed over the arms of the farthingale chair, merely to support the right hand, is a feature of several of the portraits painted by Marcus Gheeraerts the Younger.

MOURNING ROBES

At Sir Christopher Hatton's funeral, 1591, Lord Cobham was Chief Mourner (Fig. 733), whose train was held by a trainbearer. He wears a hood with liripipe of the old fashion, but tasselled; and the sleeves of his doole-robe, which

---

[1] No recent negative of this portrait exists, otherwise His Grace would have allowed the author to use a print from it. The portrait itself is inaccessible at the moment.

bulges over his slops underneath, are padded on the shoulders.   The ladies accompanying him are Countesses, whose only period details are the small ruffs and the curve of the veils over the foreheads.

For widows' weeds, see p. 715; and for the French style, pp. 752, 753.

Fig. 733. Doole-robes, 1591

NOBILITY—MEN: 1580–1603

PERSONAGES OF DISTINCTION ABOUT THE COURT

WILLIAM CECIL (*continued from p. 533*)

Lord Burleigh, 1580–98

Lord Treasurer Burleigh during the remaining years of his life attained the highest honours of the State, including the Garter, but received no greater title than baron, which was intensely galling to him.

The National Portrait Gallery portrait, No. 2184, was painted in the early 1580's when he was about sixty.   In it he is wearing the same dress as in No. 604, but with the addition of the Collar of the Garter.   Another, No. 362, was painted later still when he was a white-haired old man.   He is fully dressed in the Robes of the Garter, still holding his rod of office.   The bulkiness of the crimson velvet surcote or robe around the hips is due to the padded slops worn underneath.

His death, which took place 15th August 1598, was greatly lamented by his Royal mistress, whom he had faithfully served for the greater part of his life without once thwarting her.

Sir Christopher Hatton, 1580–91 (continued from p. 535)

Having incurred the Queen's displeasure over some money matters—he was some £56,000 in her debt—Sir Christopher Hatton withdrew from Court in 1584 and sulked at Holdenby. 'The Queen seldom gave boons, and never forgave due debts. She rigorously demanded the payment of some arrears which Sir Christopher did not hope to have remitted . . . failing herein in his expectations, it went to his heart.' However, Elizabeth desired his return and wrote him two letters to that effect. He obeyed, and was appointed a member of both Commissions which in 1586 tried the conspirators who favoured Mary Stuart. He was also on the Commission which tried this unfortunate Queen. In 1588 he was appointed Lord Chancellor and made a K.G. On Lord Leicester's death the same year he became Lord Chancellor of Oxford. There is a curious portrait of him (National Portrait Gallery, No. 1518), painted at this time, showing him in his robes and holding with great pride the Lesser George which hangs around his neck by a triple chain.

During his last illness the Queen was very attentive, 'bringing cordial broths unto him with her own hands, but all would not do.' He died at Ely, 20th November 1591.

Robert Devereux

Earl of Essex, 1566–1601

Robert Devereux was the son of Walter, Earl of Essex and Eu, Viscount Hereford and Bourchier, and Baron Ferrers of Chartley, Bourchier, and Louvain; and was born 10th November 1566. He succeeded as second Earl of Essex at the age of twelve, and entered Trinity College, Cambridge, taking his M.A. degree in 1581. His first appearance at Court was made in 1584. 'There was in this young lord,' says Sir Robert Naunton, 'a kinde of urbanity or innate courtesy, which both won the Queene, and too much tooke up the people to gaze on the new adopted son of her favour.' For on the death of the Earl of Leicester he succeeded him in the Royal affections.

His complexion was pale with brown eyes and hair, his beard of a golden red, and his moustache lighter and more yellow.

'A body hath he made of iron,' 'of straight and goodly stature,' tall and strong; but he 'did bend a little in the neck, though rather forward than downwards, and he was so far from being a good dancer, that he was no graceful goer.' He is said to have 'exceeded in the incomparable fairness and fine shape of his hands, which . . . he took from his father.'

In 1590 the young earl secretly married Frances, daughter and heiress of Sir Francis Walsingham, and widow of Sir Philip Sidney; and in 1588, at the early age of twenty-two, he was created a Knight of the Garter.

Fig. 734. The Earl of Essex

There are many portraits of the second Earl of Essex, and the costumes he is wearing in nearly all of them are similar. Fig. 734 is adapted from these portraits. He wears a suit entirely of white silk decorated with lines of stitchery, the doublet with wide wings, close sleeves, and a basque which stands out at right angles at the waist. Attention is called to the stitchery round the armholes. The panes of the hip-pad are folded into a series of oblique tucks, but the decoration of this garment varies in the different portraits. The canions and netherstocks are of plain white silk, and the shoes are black. Both waistbelt and swordbelt are gold-embroidered and have a narrow edging of deep red: the sword is elaborate, and the usual dagger is stuck through at the back. The Lesser George is hung by the blue riband, and the Garter is worn. A special feature for notice is the turned-down collar, similar to those shown in Figs. 625 and 627, worn in conjunction with the ruff. In his right hand he holds a baton of command. In one portrait at least the costume is carried out in a pale dove-grey satin, woven with a small silk spot diapered all over its surface. This kind of material was very fashionable at this time.

Fig. 735

Fig. 735 is a detail of the braid with which a suit similar to that described above is decorated. It is from a three-quarter portrait dated 1599 in the Dining Hall, Trinity College, Cambridge, wherein Essex wears a suit of white silk banded with this braid in gold having small pearls set in the middle.   A circular ruff of several layers and the Lesser George on a blue riband are worn.

In 1593, when only twenty-seven, Essex was admitted to the Council, and forsook 'all his former youthful tricks,' carrying himself with 'very honourable gravity.'   Nevertheless, he became recklessly extravagant and improvident, so that even the most generous allowance that the Queen could afford to make him proved quite inadequate to meet the growing expenses of an elaborate household.   The details of his toilet which follow illustrate that of a fashionable and influential courtier of the period.   'The Earl as he grew more and more attentive to business and matter, so less and less curious of clothing, insomuch as I do remember those about him had a conceit, that possibly sometime when he went up to the Queen, he might scant know what he had on: for this was his manner; his chamber being commonly stived with friends or suitors of one kind or other, when he gave his legs, arms, and breast to his ordinary servants to button and dress him with little heed, his head and face to his barber, his eyes to his letters, and ears to petitioners, and many times all at once; then the gentlemen of his robes throwing a cloak over his shoulders, he would make a step into his closet, and after a short prayer he was gone: only in his baths he was somewhat delicate.'

Essex had reached the pinnacle of popularity both with the Queen and her people when, in 1596, he was sent on the Cadiz expedition; and on his return the Queen, 'loving him for his beauty, gallantry, and devotion to her,' entrusted him with the still more difficult task of pacifying the Irish.   'The General of our Gracious Empress' completely mismanaged everything, and was recalled and confined in the Tower, but shortly afterwards released.   He then sought to win back by force the favour which the Queen still withheld from him, and in 1601 madly put himself at the head of a revolt of the Londoners, hoping by their help to drive from power his enemy, Sir Robert Cecil, Keeper of the Privy Seal, and to recover his position.   'His misconduct in Ireland, and his project of displacing his enemies, would have been more easily pardoned by the Queen, than the vulgar and opprobrious words reported by Sir Walter Raleigh to have been spoken by him: "the late Earl says, he told Queen Elizabeth, that her conditions were as crooked as her carcase," but it cost him his head, which his insurrection had not cost him but for that speech.'   He was in consequence sent back captive to the Tower, and after a trial condemned to death.   His execution took place 25th February 1601, and his tragic fall only established Cecil the more firmly in the Queen's favour.

SIR FRANCIS DRAKE, 1540–95

Prominent amongst the 'Sea Lions' was young Francis Drake, who was born at Tavistock about 1540, and educated at the expense of his kinsman, Sir John Hawkyns.   It was not until he was approaching forty that he leapt into fame on account of his voyage round the world.   On his return from this voyage he finally moored his ship, *The Golden Hind*, at Deptford, and on 4th April 1581, 'the Queen made Drake a visit on board, and there, on the deck of the first English ship to have encompassed the Globe, did she Knight the first man of any nation who had commanded through such a voyage.'   Knighthood was conferred upon him ostensibly in recognition of his fame as a navigator, but no doubt also because of the rich spoils, estimated at £200,000, which he was able to lay at Elizabeth's feet.

Fig. 736. Sir Francis Drake

In appearance Drake was 'of small size with a reddish beard, and is one of the greatest sailors that exist.'

Fig. 736 shows Sir Francis about this time.   It is constructed from one or two portraits, all of which show a similar style of dress.   His costume consists of a doublet with sleeves which button into loops up the front seam showing a sleeve of a different colour underneath, and venetians in a small patterned damask of some dark shade, the edges being braided or bound with silk or velvet.   A goffered ruff with plain cuffs of lawn or linen, kersey netherstocks, and leather shoes, sometimes decorated with cuttes or sometimes plain, are worn.   In later life he possessed a small medallion portrait of the Queen which he wore hung by a riband or a chain round his neck.   Notice that he is raising his hat in the approved style.

Drake was Vice-Admiral under Lord Howard of Effingham, and assisted in repelling the Armada in 1588; in fact, men held him in such honour that none had the effrontery to sit in his presence, nor did they presume to keep on their hats without his permission.

The West Indian expedition of 1595 cost the lives of both Drake and Hawkyns.   Admiral Sir John Hawkyns died at sea off Porto Rico, and 'as quiet as a sleeping child the sea-king died' off Porto Bello; but neither his own countrymen nor the Spaniards could believe it, and long expected his return.

Sir Walter Raleigh, 1552–1603

A newcomer to Court, introduced by Lord Leicester in 1582, was Walter Raleigh, aged thirty. This young man was born at Hayes, Budleigh, Devon, and entered Oriel College, Oxford, in 1566, where he remained three years but took no degree. He then took rooms in the Temple, it being fashionable for a young man to take chambers there as a sort of finish to a gentleman's education, and to qualify him as a man of affairs. In 1569 Raleigh was one of a hundred young gentlemen sent by the Queen to France to assist Marguerite de Valois, and there served with the Huguenot Army. He was at sea during 1578, and in Ireland in 1580. Returning to England as Captain Raleigh in 1581, he first came to the notice of Queen Elizabeth. It is said that his cloak was primary instrumental in obtaining the Queen's favour. So popular did he become at Court that even his strong west-country brogue was not only tolerated, but even adopted, by the smart set! He obtained a patent for the settlement of 'Virginia'; and though he never visited it himself, it gave to England potatoes and tobacco. He was

Fig. 737. Sir Walter Raleigh, 1588

knighted by the Queen in 1584, who commissioned him Captain of the Yeomen of the Guard, which post he held from 1587 until her death. Fig. 737 shows Sir Walter at the age of thirty-six, and is taken from a portrait in the National Portrait Gallery, No. 7, dated 1588. There is another in America, but full length, painted in the same year, in which he is wearing a slightly different doublet and slops, but the same cloak.

In Fig. 737 the white silk doublet is pinked in squares, but otherwise unornamented except for the large silver buttons. The square collar has a second of cambric folded over it. The silver embroidery on the black velvet waist and sword-belts is repeated on the black velvet panes of the slops. Over one shoulder is hung the cloak in the modish manner: it is of black velvet lined and turned back with sable, with sun-rays worked in seed pearls or silver and ending with three large pearls.

His attentions to Elizabeth Throckmorton, one of the Queen's Maids of Honour, checked his progress in the Royal favour. Their marriage so enraged

Her Majesty that she sent them both to the Tower for two months.   Their son (Fig. 743) was born there.   With the idea of establishing colonies in the West he set out on voyages of discovery, and also made an expedition against the Spaniards at Cadiz (1596) and the Azores in 1597.

Duke Frederick I (succeeded 1593, died 1608) of Württemburg and Teck had, since 1592, conceived the idea that Queen Elizabeth would confer upon him the much coveted Order of the Garter.   It is not known if she actually made the promise, or, having made it, had any intention of fulfilling it; but the Duke in his impatience sent his envoy, Herr Johann Jacob Breuning von Buchenbach, to London to remind the Queen of her plighted word.   In spite of reams of correspondence, the Garter failed to materialize.   In slighting the Duke the Queen little realized that one of the descendants of this dis-illusioned potentate would one day occupy her throne.   He received better treatment, however, from James Stuart, who conferred it in 1603.

To further his master's suit, Herr Breuning equipped himself with a new Court dress, made by London tailors.   As will be seen from the following account, this cost him £14 4s. in English money, and all to no purpose!

An Account for a Court Dress, 1595

	Gulden	Batzen
For velvet for breeches 6¾ yds., the yard at 3 crowns makes 20 crowns 3½s.	32	6
Four yards fustian or corduroy, 4s.	1	1
½ ell double taffeta, 1 crown	1	9
Cloth for a cloak 3½ yds., the yard 13s., that makes 42s. 3d.	11	4
1 yard of lining, 2s. 9d.		11
Gold braid for cloak 2¼ oz., gold lace for the dress, 1⅛ oz. at 10s. an ounce makes 33s. 9d.	9	
For silk 2½		10
Besides this for lining, 9s. 3d.	2	7
For a pair of silk hose, 6 crowns	9	9
Three dozen buttons for the doublet, 2 crowns . .	3	3
For making the cloak, 6s.	1	9
For making the doublet and breeches . . .	2	2
	75	11

Plate XLV is a reproduction of the painting by Marcus Gheeraerts of the wedding procession at Blackfriars (16th June 1600) of Lord Herbert, eldest son of the Earl of Worcester, and Lady Anne Russell, daughter of the Earl of Bedford.   There are two pictures of this subject, both by the same artist. The original from which Plate XLV is taken is owned by Colonel Wingfield-Digby, who has kindly given permission for its reproduction.

PLATE XLV. QUEEN ELIZABETH AT BLACKFRIARS, 1600: Painting by Marcus Gheeraerts
Sherborne Castle. *By kind permission of Colonel Wingfield Digby*

Fig. 738. KEY TO PLATE XLV

Fig. 738 is a key plan, giving the names of the principal persons and the predominating colourings of their clothes.

1. The Queen . . . White
2. Lord Howard de Walden . Rose colour, grey netherstocks
3. The Earl of Nottingham . White
4. The Earl of Cumberland . Pale scarlet
5. Lord Hunsdon . . . Grey
6. Lord Cobham, with sword . Deep peacock-blue
7. Sir Robert Cecil . . White, dove jerkin, pale green netherstocks
8. The Earl of Worcester . Pale pink
9. The Earl of Bedford . . Dark bottle-green, dove jerkin
10. Lord Herbert . . . White
11. Lady Anne Russell . . White

Fig. 739. Fig. 740.
Noblemen, 1600

Most of the costumes are of silk or satin embroidered with gold and pearls, and all the cloaks are black velvet decorated with gold or silver. Nos. 2, 3, 4, 5, 6, and 8 wear the Collar of the Garter, and Nos. 2, 3, 6, and 8 have each a portrait miniature of the Queen suspended by a riband from his neck.

Yeomen of the Guard and Gentlemen Pensioners line the way.

The young bridegroom (born 1577), Fig. 740, is dressed (as all bridegrooms should be) entirely in white silk brocaded with a fine trellis pattern. The whole costume is extremely simple, yet thoroughly up to date and most elegant.

Fig. 739 is taken from the same painting and represents Henry Brooke, Lord Cobham, K.G., carrying the Sword of State. His suit, in deep peacock-blue satin with a tiny silk spot woven diaperwise in the material, is of the fashionable style as worn at the end of the century. The doublet is without the peascod paunch and has close rather rucked sleeves and a moderate basque. The buttons and waist- and sword-belts are of gold. The slops are quite plain, without any bombast or padding, being gathered or pleated round the waist and thighs. The canions or upperstocks are of the same material. Netherstocks and shoes are of white, the cloak is of black velvet braided with gold, and the Collar with Badge and the Garter are in evidence. Lord Cobham wears a triple ruff; and from a blue riband hanging round his neck is suspended a cameo portrait of the Queen in a jewelled frame with three peardrop pearls attached.

Fig. 741. A Nobleman's Son

The baby boy, Fig. 741, a nobleman's son, comes from a portrait painted about the 1590's. His white silk gown and hanging sleeves are banded with black velvet, and the full sleeves slashed with black. The black hat with a gold rim to the brim, worn over a white biggen, is decorated with a white feather and a rose of red ribbon. A pouch of black velvet and gold is attached to the waist-belt, and the silver and coral teether is slung on a red ribbon round the neck. Both are inset.

At the age of fifty (1602) Sir Walter Raleigh is seen in a portrait by Marcus Gheeraerts, in company with his son. Fig. 742 is made from this portrait. The doublet, slops, and canions are of white silk; oblique tucks edged with silver decorate the panes, and there is a line of silver down the seams of the somewhat rucked sleeves and down the front of the doublet, which is fastened by small silver buttons. Pearl and silver embroidery worked on very fine white cambric is laid on the brown velvet jerkin, and converges down the fronts and down and across the rather deep basques and round the pronounced wings. The waist, sword-belt, and hanger are of buff leather covered with silver embroidery. Pale buff netherstocks, tied with white silk garters having silver fringed ends, are worn with buff leather shoes. The black beaver hat of the newest shape, obviously having its origin in the same source as that worn by the Duke of Infantado (*see* Fig. 853), but slightly modified, has a jewelled feather and is tilted at an angle. Raleigh's pipes and pipe-case are in the Wallace Collection.

Figs. 742–3.
Sir Walter Raleigh and Son, 1602

A coming young man of the seventeenth century, Master Raleigh, unfortunately died in youth. In Fig. 743 he has a complete suit of dark blue silk braided with silver. The waist- and sword-belts and miniature sword are of silver.

'Sir' John Harington is introduced here with apologies. His only interest with regard to this book is that he gives us considerable information on numerous details which have been taken chiefly from his *Nugae Antiquae*. He was born in 1561, the son of Sir John Harington and Isabella Markham, a Maid of Honour to Elizabeth when Princess. 'Boy Jack' was a godson of the Queen—'my saucy godson,' she called him; and as he himself admits, he both loved and feared her greatly. He went to Ireland with the Earl of Essex, from whom he received a knighthood (1598) which was not altogether to the Queen's liking, as she had not conferred the honour herself. Sir John had the reputation at Court of being a wit of more than usual brilliancy.

One item of his wardrobe has become historical: 'The Queen loveth to see me in my last frize jerkin,' he writes, preening himself complacently, 'and faith its well enough cut. I will have another made liken to it.' He proceeds to put on record a most lady-like action of the Great Tudor Queen. 'I do remember,' he writes, 'she spit on Sir Mathew's fringed cloth, and said, "the fool's wit was gone to rags."' No wonder he took the precaution of ordering a second frieze jerkin: 'Heaven spare me from such jibing,' concludes Boy Jack.

He remained the Queen's affectionate if 'saucy godson' throughout her declining years, and helped to cheer her last days. In 1612 Sir John died, at the age of fifty-one.

His own mordant words, descriptive of the fashionable man of his time, **may** fittingly close this account of Sir John, who as a man of the world ought to know what he was talking about.

'We goe brave in apparell that wee may be taken for better men than wee bee; we use much bumbastings and quiltings to seem fitter formed, better shouldered, smaller waisted, fulled thyght than we are; wee barbe and shave often to seeme younger than wee are; we use perfumes both inward and outward to seem sweeter than we bee; we use courteous salutations to seem kinder than we be; and somtymes graver and Godly communications, to seem wyser than wee bee.'

In the sixteenth-century hall of Christ's Hospital, Abingdon, hangs the portrait, dated 1602, of a smart young man—William Bostock. Born in 1572 he was governor of the hospital from 1602 until 1624, when he was removed 'by reason he is departed the Towne.' He died some time before 1642. In Fig. 744 the fashionable doublet is of white cloth pinked, or cutte, the edges being overcast with black silk and outlined with six French knots. It has small overlaying picadils or tabs at the waist-line, and a dagger is stuck through the waist-belt on the right side. The collar of lawn is edged with beautiful

Fig. 744. William Bostock, Esq., 1602

lace and the cuffs match the collar. There is not sufficient indication in the painting to decide whether he is wearing slops or galligaskins; they are of black velvet, decorated with double rows of silver passamayne. The high-crowned white beaver hat, 'well brushed a mornings,' lying on the table has a rich silver hatband and a panache of *uncurled* ostrich feathers standing up high in the approved fashion. In the right hand he carries leather gloves banded with silver lace—altogether an excellent specimen of a well-dressed man of the first few years of the seventeenth century.

With the help of Jeffrey Chorlton and Sir Thomas Overbury, we may here picture an elegant coxcomb of the end of the reign. He has decked himself out in doublet, trunks, hosen, hat, and cloak, all in the height of fashion and of the latest cut. From one ear hangs a pearl, above the other is tucked a rose or other flower in the most fetching manner. In his hat, or mouth,

III ²—T

he carries a pick-tooth; in his pouch a tobacco pipe.   He indulges mincingly in every eccentricity of mannerism: 'the brush upon the beard, the kiss of the hand, the stoop of the head, the lear of the eye.'

'Behold, a most accomplished Cavaleer,
That the World's Ape of Fashion doth appear,
Walking the streets, his humours to disclose
In the French Doublet, and the German hose:
The Muffes [1] Cloake, Spanish Hat, Toledo Blade,
Italian ruff, a shoe right Flemish made.'

FRENCH FASHIONS: 1580–1603

HENRY III

King of France, 1580–9

(continued from p. 560)

The Duc d'Anjou, on ascending the throne of France in 1574 as Henry III, became so spoiled by his favourites that he lost the respect of every one.

Fig. 745. Henry III of France

Like his brother, Charles IX, he was indolent, and left the administration of the kingdom to his mother while he indulged in all kinds of frivolities and debauchery. Very fond of dress, this 'King of fashion and pattern of the exquisite' invented 'novelties' in which he was assisted by his gentlemen friends. These were designated 'Les Mignons,' and copied every detail and gesture of the King. 'Le Roi s'amuse,' we are told by the Duc de Sully, who writes: 'I found him in his closet, a sword by his side, a short cloak on his shoulders, little turban on his head, and about his neck was hung a basket, in which were two or three little dogs, no bigger than my fist.' Teaching parrots to mimic and monkeys to perform tricks were other accomplishments of this puerile monarch, who also played at cup-and-ball,[2] an occupation which was copied not only by the courtiers, but also by the pages and lackeys who were perpetually engaged in it.

[1] A contemptuous term for a German or Swiss.
[2] The ball could also be caught on a peg; see Fig. 751, inset.

So vain had this last Valois become that he cosmeticized his face, stained his eyes, lips, and ears, and dyed his hair and beard. The result was premature baldness, necessitating the wearing of wigs and fantastic turbans, as seen in all his later portraits. Fig. 745 is a drawing from one of these. To keep his hands white and delicate he slept in perfumed and unctuous gloves.

Of the numerous portraits, the one in the Louvre, given in Fig. 746, is chosen as being the most eccentric costume. It is entirely in black—so becoming to a slim tall figure; the doublet of black satin is banded with velvet, but is without the peascod effect. It finishes at the low-cut waist-line, where there is a massive gold girdle with four pendent ornaments in goldsmith's work set with rubies. Similar ornaments are set up the front and on the cloak, and a large diamond in front of the turban. The moderately close sleeves are of plain black velvet, and the hosen extending from waist to toe, and the short cloak faced with sable, are of the same material. Wodges of silk, covered in priceless pearls, which look like corn-cobs, are fixed to the doublet in two places by jewelled ornaments, and extend from the right shoulder to the waist. The Badge of the St. Esprit or Holy Ghost is suspended by a blue riband round the neck, and the star is embroidered on the cloak as being the outer garment. The ruff is circular and small-pleated: a false hair front is tucked into the turban with a made-up white feather, and one peardrop pearl earring is worn. The

Fig. 746. Henry III, King of France, 1585

velvet-covered feet have scarlet heels attached to white kid heel pieces which fasten round the instep. A masculine touch is given by the sword hung high at the waist, and the indispensable laced cambric handkerchief is carried in the left hand, the right resting on the velvet-covered table.

In 1578 Henry III had instituted the Order of the Holy Ghost. The insignia consisted of a Collar of fleurs-de-lys of gold cantoned with flames of the same enamelled red, interspersed with three monograms of gold composed of the letters H, L, and HL, in white enamel.

The Badge (Fig. 747) is a gold cross of eight points enamelled with an edge of white, and gold fleurs-de-lys at each angle; upon a circular centre of green is a white dove, the wings, tail, and head extending downwards over part of the principal quarters of the cross.   The Badge hung from the collar or from a sky-blue riband—'the Cordon Bleu,' as the Order is sometimes designated.

A Star of silver, formed exactly like the Badge with the same details in the centre, was embroidered on the left side of the *outer garment* by all members of the Order.   The surcote was of white cloth of silver; and the mantle of black velvet, lined with orange taffeta and besprinkled with gold flames diaperwise, had a border of gold fleurs-de-lys and lacs d'amour—true lover's knots—of silver arranged alternately.   A short mantle of green cloth of silver was sometimes worn in place of the black velvet mantle; it was embroidered diaperwise with doves in silver, and lined with orange taffeta.

Fig. 747. Badge of Saint-Esprit

After the murder of the Duc de Guise, 1588, for which the King was rightly blamed, he became hateful to his subjects, and shortly after this event a Bull from Rome excommunicated the assassin.   The wrath of the Catholics forced the King to make a reconciliation with Henry, King of Navarre, and together the two monarchs marched on Paris; but the knife of the Dominican, Jacques Clément, ended his life—the last of the thirteen kings of the House of Valois—sovereigns who were for the most part brave, magnificent, and lovers of the fine arts.   With his dying breath Henry III recognized the right of Henry of Navarre to the French throne, and expired 2nd August 1589.

His younger brother, François, Duc d'Anjou, paid a second visit to England, an official one this time, in May 1581 to see the Queen.

During this time there was quite a lot of love-making going on between the mature spinster of forty-eight and her young man of twenty-seven—her 'Frog' or 'Froggy,' as she lovingly called him after her manner, just as she named his Ambassador 'the Monkey.'   This pleasant time induced the Duc d'Anjou to pay a third visit in October 1581, which lasted until February 1582: things seemed to be going most favourably, when fever carried off this unfortunate Prince in June 1584, before he could carry off his prize.

There are two paintings in the Louvre representing balls at the Court of Henry III.   One dated 1581—Ball No. I—was given in honour of the marriage of the Queen's sister, Marguerite of Lorraine, with the Duc de Joyeuse. The other—Ball No. II—is dated 1585, and shows some courtiers engaged in a round dance.   Both of these are valuable as authorities for the costumes of their respective dates.   The painting, Ball No. I, is attributed to François Clouet.   On the left is seen Henry III seated under a crimson velvet canopy; next him is his mother, and on her left his Queen, Louise of Lorraine.   The bride and bridegroom occupy the centre of the scene, advancing hand in hand;

the crowd of courtiers includes Henry, Duc de Guise, who stands on the King's right. On the opposite side is the consort. From this picture are taken Figs. 749, 754, and 748. In Ball No. II the King and Queen, as also the Queen-Mother, stand on the left. This picture has been used for Figs. 750, 755, and 756.

Anne, Duc de Joyeuse, was a great favourite with Henry III; they were very close friends, and Anne was a less covetous and self-seeking courtier

Fig. 748.   Fig. 749.

Duc and Duchesse de Joyeuse, 1581

than the general run of such ambitious noblemen. Honours were heaped upon him. First, he was made a Peer of France, then a Duke, an Admiral, first Gentleman of the Bedchamber, and Governor of Normandy; and lastly became brother-in-law of Queen Louise. In fact, the King could deny him nothing, and could be led by Anne as easily as one of his own lap-dogs, whimpering when the Duke was absent: so that the people used to say that there were three Kings of France: Henry, the *nominal* king; Anne, the *King's* king; and Henry de Guise, the *people's* king. He is shown in Fig. 749 as he appears in the Ball picture No. I, wearing a suit—a doublet, venetians, and hip-roll in deep green satin. The short cloak is of reseda green velvet lined with rose satin, and turns back forming revers with a step-back collar. The hat is black, with a panache of white plumes. The stockings are rose and the shoes green.

The gentleman (Fig. 750) is one of those taking part in the dance, Ball No. II. Some may argue that he is wearing a masquer's costume, but in the same painting Henry III is represented wearing a dress almost identical, except that a short cloak and turban headdress are added.

In Fig. 750 the peascod doublet and hip-roll are of light-coloured silk, velvet, or cloth cutte in perpendicular slits. The bombast sleeves are very

Fig. 750. A French Courtier, 1585   Fig. 751. A Mignon

wide at the shoulders and taper to the wrists; and venetians, gradually decreasing in circumference from hip to knee, match in colour (as do the shoes and stockings), but are banded transversely with coloured braid or gold lace. A circular ruff and a black hat with an upstanding ostrich feather are worn.

The mignon in Fig. 751, or mignonette, dainty, sweet-smelling, and green(?), is playing with his 'bilboquet.' Here, again, the prevailing scheme of black and white is exemplified. The slight peascod doublet with bolonnoise or bouillon sleeves is of white satin, folded or cutte perpendicularly between transverse bands of black velvet. The panes of the hip-roll are of the same material and are edged with black silk braid and worn over white silk hosen and shoes. A black velvet turban with white feather surmounts his own dyed hair, brushed back and upward, and sprayed with violet-scented powder. In bed the made-up face is protected by a face mask, and the delicate white hands by gloves. His eyebrows, and (when old enough) his moustaches, were plucked so as to form thin lines.

Most of these mignons were expert swordsmen, and in later life became men of some worth. Chief among them were Bussy d'Amboise; Anne de Joyeuse (*see* Fig. 749) and his brother, Henri; François d'O, Seigneur d'O, de Maillebois, and de Fresne, Master of the Wardrobe, first Gentleman of the Chamber, Superintendent of Finances, Governor of Paris and the Isle of France; and Jean Louis Nogaret de la Valette (born 1554), also known as Caumont, later created Duc d'Épernon, Lord High Admiral, Colonel-General of the line, and Governor of half the provinces of the kingdom.

It is appropriate that Mr. Punch should make his début upon the stage of history in these days of folly. His name is said to have been crossed in its orthography with the Italian *Pulcinello*, a buffoon of Acerra, and *paunch*. The original puppet Pulcinello had a face like a Greek mask, and a nose like the beak of a bird. Punch's dress is of this period—a large ruff, peascod paunched doublet, and venetians. His cap and bauble are those which appertain to fools. During his travels over the Continent he acquired a humpback, and when he arrived in England he was thus deformed.

In a similar way, the conventional appearance of Mephistopheles illustrates the eccentric fashions prevailing at the French Court. In fact, he may even be a caricature of Henry III as suggested by Fig. 746.

HENRY IV

King of France and Navarre, 1589 until 1603

Henry of Navarre was the first of the Royal House of Bourbon. Born in the Castle of Pau in 1553, he was the son of Antoine, Duc de Vendôme, and Jeanne d'Albret, Queen-Regnant of Navarre and Béarn. As a young man, Henry devoted little attention to dress. He is accused of rough manners, of 'Gascon inelegance,' and of a despicable disregard for clothes, at a Court of such an exquisite coxcomb as Henry III. His slovenly habits caused his mother much uneasiness of mind, although she did all she could to reform him. She procured first-class tailors and expert broderers to supervise his wardrobe, without much success.

A sketch portrait of Henry as a young man is given in Fig. 842.

In 1572 he married Marguerite de Valois, sister of Henry III; his wedded life was not too pleasant, and in consequence he solaced himself with many an intrigue with lovely ladies, chief among them being Gabrielle d'Estrées and Henriette d'Entragues.

In 1589 Henry of Navarre became King of France.

His claim to the French throne was not undisputed (he was eleventh in descent from St. Louis IX of France), largely because he had been brought up in the Protestant faith. The Catholic nobles refused allegiance to him; and the intervening ten years were occupied in warfare against the League. Most of his time was spent in camp and field, experiencing to the full their inevitable hardships, with a few brief intervals of relaxation. These opportunities were seized by the King for flying visits to his lady friends.

We have it on authority that during this period his usual garb was of burgher-like drabness and modesty, and the shabbiness of his *grey* doublet was almost openly ridiculed by the nobles in attendance. It appears that he nearly always wore this neutral hue. When he entered Paris, September 1594, he was dressed in a suit of grey velvet, laced with gold, and wore a grey hat and white plume. Even the horse he rode was mottled grey. His reply to the deputation of clergy, who came to remonstrate against the edict upon the Parliament of Bordeaux (1599), has point: 'My predecessors,' he said, 'gave you words with a great deal of glittering parade. I, in spite of my grey doublet, would give you deeds. I am grey without, but inside all gold.' Hardship and poverty caused him to complain to his friend and minister, the Marquis de Rosny, that 'my shirts are all torn, and I have no doublet which is not out at elbow, and not a suit of armour I can wear.'

Fig. 752. Henry IV, King of France, 1596

Always of simple taste in dress, he endeavoured to encourage his courtiers to curb their lavishness in apparel; he even tried the Spanish method of issuing a pragmatic in 1594. This prohibited the ornamentation of costume with gold and silver, but it proved quite ineffective.

An earlier effort met a similar fate. For, according to de l'Étoile's journal, fifty young women of good family had been imprisoned for 'contravening both in clothes and jewellery the edict of reform promulgated several months before.' These failures did not deter Henry, for in 1601 and 1606 he issued two further ordinances, of which one forbade 'any of the inhabitants of the kingdom to wear either gold or silver on their clothes, except the *filles de joie* and pickpockets, in whom [the King said] we do not take sufficient interest to trouble ourselves about their conduct.'

On the other hand, when absolutely necessary, the King made a very good appearance and was quite in the vogue. For the ceremony of his Act of Abjuration, by which he renounced the Protestant for the Catholic faith, he appeared magnificently attired in *pure* white satin embroidered with gold, a black velvet cloak, and black hat and feather.

The well-known portrait by Pourbus (in the Louvre) of Henry IV, at the age of forty or forty-five, is reproduced in Fig. 752, as it gives the 'line' worn in Europe during the latter years of the sixteenth century. The suit is all black, having the doublet of velvet and the close sleeves and full breeches of black satin. There is nothing elegant about the cut of these garments; the waist is normal and rather short, with no suggestion of a peascod paunch; the gallyhosen or galligaskins —*Chausses larges à l'Antique* —do not enhance the figure

Fig. 753. Collar of Saint-Esprit

of a man, be he tall and slim or short and stout. The hat which lies upon the table is of black blocked felt, with high crown and wide brim, the hatband composed of twisted silk or cords with a rose of black silk on one side. Roses also decorate the shoes—a new mode. The Cordon Bleu suspends the Badge of the Holy Ghost. Henry IV made considerable changes in the Collar of the Order of the Holy Ghost. Only the fleurs-de-lys remained; and for the original monograms were substituted a trophy of arms, and the letter H, surmounted by the Royal Crown, with ducal coronets in gold on each side and cantoned with flames. These emblems were linked to the fleurs-de-lys by golden chains (Fig. 753).

There are portraits of Henry wearing the robes of this Order, and very dignified he looks in them, a great contrast to his earlier slovenly self.

A very beautiful equestrian painting of the King is at Chantilly, in which he wears a doublet with close sleeves, hosen and shoes of white satin with gold roses. The panes of his white slops are black and embroidered with gold in a design not unlike that shown in Fig. 625. The short cloak of black velvet is heavily embroidered in gold and lined with a rich white and gold brocade, with the Star of the Holy Ghost on the left side. The Badge is suspended by a sky-blue watered riband round his neck. His hat, shaped like the one shown in Fig. 752, is black with jewelled ornaments round the brim and short white ostrich feathers on either side; possibly there are two or three round the back as well.

Another portrait shows Henry wearing a suit shaped exactly like that in Fig. 752, but made of a brocade, the groundwork being in black silk with a trellis design in black velvet.

In 1599, Pope Clement VII granted Henry and Marguerite a divorce; and in December of the following year he married Marie de' Medici (born 1573), daughter of Francesco de' Medici, Grand Duke of Tuscany, and of the Archduchess Joanna of Austria.

The children of Henry IV and Marie were:

Louis, born 1601, who succeeded his father.
Elizabeth, born 1603, married Philip IV of Spain.   Died 1644.
Gaston Jean Baptiste, Duc d'Orléans, born 1608.
Christiana, married the Duke of Savoy.
Henrietta Maria, born 1610, married Charles I of England.

Not until Henry had forced his last enemy, the Duke of Savoy, into submission in 1601, was he firmly established on the throne of France.   He made an excellent King, and was most popular, ruling with admirable wisdom and patriotism, and earning for himself the title of 'le Grand.'   His subjects called him 'a father and friend.'   He was affable, indulgent, quick-witted, good-hearted, of a great courage, and skilled in reading the characters of those about him.

Maximilien de Béthune, Marquis de Rosny,[1] the great statesman, was born in 1560 of an impoverished Huguenot family.   At the age of twelve he entered the service of Henry of Navarre, and later did good administrative work for his master with untiring industry and perfect method.

François de Bassompierre was born in 1579 of a noble family in Alsace. After being educated in Germany and Italy, he arrived in Paris in 1598. He captivated the King, who at once took him into his service: in course of time he became Colonel-General of the Swiss, and Maréchal of France.   His *Memoirs* may be dull, but they contain some interesting passages.

NOBLE LADIES: 1580–1603

LOUISE

Queen-Consort of Henry III, 1580 until 1603

(continued from p. 564)

In the picture, Ball No. I, Queen Louise is seated, and Fig. 754 is a standing version showing the dress she wears.   It is in a deep shade of velvet, and the bodice has sleeves à la Bolonnoise slashed with white, and a long tapering stomacher.   The skirt is very full, being cut as a complete circle, with a short train, and worn over the bolster.   The circular ruff is open in front and surrounded with very fine lace standing out from the goffered edge.   This

---

[1] In 1606 he was created Duc de Sully.   His celebrated *Memoirs* were written in his later years.

portrait is of exceptional interest as it shows Queen Louise in a different style of dress from that of most of her portraits.

Louise of Lorraine was of a very religious turn of mind, spending most of her time in good works and prayer. After the King's death in 1589 'she did the same, employing her time in mourning and regretting him, and in praying to God for his soul; so that her widowed life was much the same as her married life.'

Queen Louise had a sister, Marguerite de Lorraine, who became the wife of Henry III's favourite, the Duc de Joyeuse. She is reproduced with her husband in Fig. 748, taken from Ball No. I, and is garbed as a bride should be in white satin. The bodice and skirt are made like those of the Queen (Fig. 754); but the sleeves are not so bolonnoise and are ornamented with horizontal bands of gold embroidery or lace between rows of pearls mounted on red velvet. Over these are worn long, hanging sleeves, but a new fashion note, originating in Spain, is struck here: the edges of these hanging sleeves are caught together by a rich jewel, showing the lining of white and gold-figured silk. The circular ruff and cuffs are edged with reticella. The head-dress is a cap of red velvet edged with gold, like the front of a French hood, having a jewelled ornament with three prongs of black enamel tipped with a pearl in front of a made-up white feather.

Fig. 754.
Louise de Vaudemont, Queen of France, 1581

The Duchesse de Joyeuse was left a widow; 'she was a good and virtuous princess, who deserves honour for the grief she gave to the ashes of her husband for some time, although she remarried in the end with M. de Luxembourg. Being a woman, why should she languish?' as Brantôme aptly asks.

In both the ball paintings the ladies wear costumes similar in most details, although there is a space of four years between the dates. Two of the ladies in Ball No. I are dressed in much the same style as those in Ball No. II, and the noble lady (Fig. 755) is a generalized version of the costumes of these ladies. The dress is entirely of white satin or of a delicate tone of colour, with attenuated stomacher, bolonnoise sleeves, and full circular skirt. The well-stuffed sleeves afforded a good excuse for all kinds of decoration: in this figure one or two rows of gold or silver cord or braids, caught at intervals with jewels set in mounts, form oblique lines. The same arrangement outlines the pointed stomacher. The deep lawn collar is edged with lace, its lower points descending well below the waist-line and revealing a plastron front, over which the pearl and jewelled carcanet or collier falls. A back view of the hairdressing is seen in the following Fig. 756.

The seated lady (Fig. 756) is seen in the foreground to the left of the painting of Ball No. II. The front of her dress is exactly the same as that in Fig. 755, and is of satin in a pale shade. The sleeves are embroidered with a design arranged diaperwise over the whole surface. Other small motifs or fancy ornaments were used to decorate such bolonnoise sleeves. A modish note is the manner in which the collier or riband, or both, worn round the décolletage is fastened with an ornament or bow in the centre of the back. Also the back of the coiffure should be noticed.

Fig. 755.
Lady of the Court of Henry III, 1581

At Penshurst Place is a French painting of a ball scene said to represent Queen Elizabeth dancing with the Earl of Leicester at Kenilworth. It must have been painted at the same time as the two ball pictures in the Louvre; the costumes, especially those of the ladies, are precisely similar, and a lady sitting on a stool in the left foreground is a duplicate of Fig. 756. The figure said to be Leicester does not in the least resemble the Earl. There must be some mistake in the title of this painting, which is much more likely to be a representation of yet another ball at the French Court; or possibly the artist, knowing that Queen Elizabeth had a great passion for dancing, conceived the idea of painting her engaged in this pastime with the two Louvre pictures in his mind.

The seat shown in Fig. 756 is of peculiar interest. Such seats, or rather, stools, superseded at the French Court the use of a cushion or piles of cushions heaped upon the floor: the embroidered border of one such cushion is shown inset. Many of these stools or 'tabourets' stood along the walls of the salons in the various Royal palaces and castles for the convenience of the company. In a short time a custom grew up whereby the wives of the highest personages should have the privilege of occupying tabourets nearest the Royal presence. These were placed, or brought into the chamber by lackeys for those entitled to sit upon them, including the wives of princes, dukes, and some of the high Court dignitaries.   The right to occupy a tabouret depended upon the rank of the husband, and was supposed to be relinquished at his death, unless great exertions and much influence were brought to bear to retain it.   Late in the century this article of furniture was adopted in England for the same purpose, but the rule of precedence was not quite so rigidly enforced.

A note on etiquette at the French Court:

To receive a visitor of great distinction, the King or Queen, if amiably disposed, would advance from the Royal group 'to the middle of the room, not a step beyond, and rather nearer the door than farther

Fig. 756. Lady of the Court of Henry III, 1585

from it.'   A lady on such occasions would, on reaching the sovereign, make a very low curtsy.

MARGUERITE DE VALOIS

Queen of France and Navarre, 1580–1615

(*continued from p. 566*)

For three and a half years Queen Marguerite of Navarre spent her time in Gascony, probably but not necessarily with her husband.   Their undomestic life was definitely unusual according to the sixteenth-century standard of morals: whether they lived together or with someone else, they remained on very friendly terms, and Henry would often appeal to his wife for sympathy and help on important affairs.   In 1581 Marguerite took up her residence at the French Court.   She was then a remarkably intelligent, good-natured, handsome woman of twenty-eight, and a resolute setter of fashion.   As years rolled by, and as a means of holding on to her reputation as a high society beauty, she resorted to all kinds of washes and receipts for the preservation of her skin, so much so that by the time she reached forty-five she had completely ruined her complexion and was a victim to erysipelas and pimples.

By 1585 she had begun to quarrel openly with her husband, Henry of Navarre, and also with her brother Henry III, so that for the time being she was regarded as Queen by courtesy only, much to her annoyance. She therefore sought refuge in the impregnable fortress of Carlet in Auvergne, with her ladies-in-waiting, wardrobe, furniture, coaches, and horses; a lengthy business. By Henry III's orders she was removed to the Castle of Usson in 1587, where she was practically a prisoner in charge of the Marquis de Canillac. Her warder, however, proved too susceptible to the lady's charms,

LA REINE MARGOT.

Fig. 757

so that she gained entire control of the castle, where she remained until the troubles of the League were well over. It is said that 'many common frailties happened there, but less odious than are told by bitter and dishonourable chroniclers, the only authorities for the tales they put forth,' yet during this period she frequently corresponded amicably with her husband.

The King had meanwhile tentatively suggested a divorce: Marguerite was at first very unwilling, being suspicious that her husband, now King of France as well as Navarre, wished to marry Gabrielle d'Estrées. Only after the death of the latter, in 1599, did she consent, and in the same year the Pope granted the decree. If their marriage was commonplace their divorce at any rate was Royal: and before the end of the year the King had married Marie de' Medici.

Fig. 757 is from an engraving by Crispin van de Pass the Elder of 'La Reine Margot.' The portrait is dated 1598, and was therefore made while she was in retirement at Usson. It gives a good example of the large collar made of transparent lawn and edged with lace, insertion, and wire. The part which rested on the shoulders was also of wire, and from this framework uprights of wire supported the collar. A detail of the lace is given in Fig. 694.

Marguerite, still by courtesy Queen of France and Navarre, returned from Usson to Paris in 1605 where she held her Court at the Hôtel de Sens. After her long retirement she found herself on her re-entry into the fashionable world completely out of date, and no longer able to reign as the arbiter of fashion. Her attempt to do so met with much ridicule.

Queen Marguerite made a last magnificent appearance at the coronation of Marie de' Medici at Saint-Denis, 13th May 1610. This ceremony is commemorated by Peter Paul Rubens (1577–1640) in the painting in the Louvre. Marguerite is seen seated on the left, crowned and attired in Royal robes, and at fifty-seven the possessor of a very pronounced double chin. She died in Paris 27th March 1615, aged sixty-two; 'sole remains of the Race of Valois, who did no harm to any but herself,' says a contemporary writer.

MARIE DE' MEDICI

Queen-Consort of Henry IV, 1600 until 1603

Even before her marriage, Marie's interest in dress was well known to her future husband. She herself took pains to see that he was informed of her preferences in this important matter: 'Fontenac [the King's messenger] tells me,' Henry writes, 'that you desired to have some models of the fashion of dress in France. I am sending you some dressed dolls, and will send you with the Duc de Bellegarde [his proxy] a good tailor.'

In her widowhood, Marie still gave much attention to the subject of dress. When she returned from her exile in 1620, she occupied herself with the embellishment of her newly built Luxembourg palace, and commissioned Peter Paul Rubens to paint a series of twenty-one canvases illustrating her history. Rubens did not become famous until after 1603. These pictures were painted between 1621 and 1625 and are now in the Louvre. The allegories were entirely Rubens's own ideas, but the Queen-Mother supervised and directed him in all details concerning the historical matter; therefore, it is safe to rely on the earlier subjects of these pictures as correct representations of the personages, costume, and other details of the years 1600–3. All his preliminary designs and sketches were submitted to the Queen, and we are told that during the time that Rubens was thus occupied, she spent many hours with him in the gallery, eagerly watching the artist at work and delighting in his conversation.

In No. V of the series, 'Her Marriage by Proxy,' Marie de' Medici wears a costume of white and gold brocade made exactly like that shown in Fig. 774, except that the neck of the bodice is cut low and the skirt is heavily braided with gold down the front and hem. Loops and aiglettes decorate the front. The dress the Queen wears in No. VI, 'Her landing at Marseilles,' is illustrated in Fig. 758. It is of plain substantial white satin, the bodice and sleeves being of the same pattern as shown in Fig. 774 and trimmed with gold and jewels. The skirt hangs in rich and heavy folds, most probably over the Spanish farthingale, and has a moderately long train. In both paintings the ruff is of large gofferings and surrounds the back of the neck leaving the throat bare. There is a string of pearls round the neck, and clusters of the same encircle the head behind the high hairdressing. The costume is, in fact, exceptional because of the small quantity of jewels displayed upon it. At the end of the century the costumes of the French Court ladies became not only very costly because of the rich materials

Fig. 758.
Marie de' Medici, Queen of France (*after Rubens*)

used, but also uncomfortably heavy by reason of the excessive quantities of gold and silver bullion and jewels which ornamented them. It is said that the wearers were often scarcely able to move, or even stand, in these gorgeous gowns.

ITALIAN INFLUENCES, 1580–1603

A gentleman of Verona (Fig. 759) is taken from a plan of that city dated 1580. His suit is of the fashion shown in many of the preceding figures, both English and French. The hood of the cloak is of a large size. Hoods were fixed to the cloak, or they were separate garments. The one shown here is probably of a new fashion which later found its way into the wardrobes of western Europe from Italy.

Fig. 759. A Gentleman of Verona, 1580   Fig. 760

The hood shown in diagram (Fig. 760) is all in one with the cloak, cut as a segment of a circle about $3\frac{3}{4}$ yards long and about 30 inches at its widest. The points A and B on the straight edge, $\frac{7}{18}$ of its length from the ends, are caught together; and when the cloak is worn, this junction is placed in the centre of the back of the neck as seen at C. The loop forms a hood 'à la burnoise.'

In Fig. 759 the cloak has a double border of cuttes on the curved edge, and a simple band of gold braid on the straight. The part between A and B is set with a row of tiny silk tassels. The left side of the cloak is draped over the left arm, and the right side hangs from the shoulder. The hairdressing is curious, and the boots are of the fashion in England at the end of the fifteenth century.

III ²—U

Fig. 761.
A Gentleman of Florence, 1590

A representative costume of the next decade is given in Fig. 761, a young gentleman of Florence in the 1590's. His doublet, sleeves, and venetians are well padded, and are of cloth or silk decorated with black or coloured billets set at alternate angles on the doublet and venetians. The sleeves are treated in a slightly different arrangement. The band of embroidery up the seams of the venetians is common to all nationalities of breeches, but the pocket slit incorporated with it is a novelty, as is also the semi-circular decoration at the knee. A cloak with a collar attached to it, velvet hat, jewelled ornament hung by a riband, and sword complete the characteristic costume of an Italian noble.

The lady (Fig. 765) is taken from an engraving (1597) which shows her in the company of a Roman gentleman, shown back view. He wears a small ruff, doublet, trunks, and hosen in the French fashion. His hat has a high crown and a moderate-sized brim; the circular cloak of brocade has a plain velvet border and a hood of the same fastened up the fronts with laces and aiglettes.

ITALIAN LADIES, 1580–1603

The same difficulty is encountered in Part II as with Part I; space allows of only a few drawings of Italian ladies being given, and it is difficult with so much material to find characteristic examples.

The materials used by Italian ladies were exquisite: they always had been, but in the sixteenth century, and especially in its second half, they excelled anything previously created. Italian silks and 'broccate' were of exceptionally fine workmanship and design, and were woven at Bologna, Florence, Genoa, Milan, Modena, and Venice. These factories supplied every country in Europe.

The lady of the 1580's, shown in Fig. 762, is a composite drawing embodying modes borrowed from Rome and Venice. The bodice, the close-fitting sleeves with (probable) puffs on the shoulders, and skirt are both Roman and Venetian, and were the models on which French fashions of the middle of the century were founded. The over-robe or surcote is Venetian, and claims kinship with the surcote of Spain, from which country the high collar is derived. The moderate circular ruff is international; the fan is one of the new models made to open and shut.

Fig. 763 shows a noble lady of Florence; the authority from which it is taken dates 1589. The main features to be noticed are the normal waist-line, the bodice open in a V at the throat and surrounded by a goffered ruff such as is seen in paintings of many Italian ladies, including the well-known portrait of Bianca Cappello by Bronzino. The armholes and waist are

Fig. 763. A Lady of Florence, 1589

Fig. 762 (*left*). An Italian Lady

decorated with a row of small tabs or ruchings, and the sleeves are much like the Spanish, but with under-sleeves of soft silk, lawn, or gauze. The skirt of rich brocade hangs stiffly without folds, and is *not* worn over a farthingale. It opens up the front, and fastens if desired by buttons and loops attached to tulip-like motifs. The neck-chain is of massive rectangular gold links, and the fan, of characteristic Italian design, is framed square and fixed to a long handle very like a flag.

The Grandes Dames of Venice were always very richly attired. The city produced magnificent brocades, lace, and jewellery, and the ladies took the opportunity of displaying these commodities on their persons. The matron of Venice (Fig. 764) wears a gown of simple though definitely Venetian style. Of some stiff brocade in gold and colour, the skirt is ample and forms heavy folds: it is quite plain, and gathered in to the sloping line of the waist.   The portly figure is accentuated by the point of the stomacher being padded, rather like the peascod paunches worn by men.   The sleeves are unattached at the shoulders, but tied to the bodice by laces and aiglettes, which also appear just above the wrists.   Escaping from the space between them is

Fig. 765. Roman Lady, 1597 (*after Boissard*)

Fig. 764 (*left*). A Noble Lady of Venice

a row of beautiful point de Venise lace, which also surrounds the stand-up collar or ruff.   This is all in one with the partlet and stomacher, and made of transparent silk-gauze, sometimes shot with gold or silver.   The fan when not in use hangs at the end of the chain girdle.

Italian ladies are accused of excessive painting, so that this lady of mature age has no doubt attempted to add to her charms by adopting this pernicious habit.

The ladies of Rome were simply, yet very beautifully, dressed, as is shown by Fig. 765.   This is a copy of an engraving by Jean Jacques Boissard, published in 1597, and therefore can well be taken as a fashion

PLATE XLVI. PHILIP II, KING OF SPAIN, c. 1580

of the 1590's. The dress, with close-fitting and puffed sleeves, bodice cut low, and ample trained skirt gathered to the hip-line, is of rich silk or satin. The partlet is edged with a small frill, suggesting a miniature ruff, and the same frill is repeated at the wrists. Attached to the hair is a wide veil, soft and transparent; one corner is caught in the left hand together with the skirt. The corresponding corner is fixed to the ornament at the point of the bodice. This vogue was a very usual one with Roman ladies, and often both corners of the veil were fixed at the same point.

SPANISH STYLES, 1580–1603

PHILIP II, 1580–98

(continued from p. 576)

The eyes of all Europe, especially of Rome, were at this time turned towards one man—Philip of Spain, who was crowned King of Portugal at Lisbon in 1581, thus adding to his many titles —and cares.

As the hostility of Spain became more definite, culminating in the Invincible Armada, anything Spanish naturally fell into disfavour. Nevertheless we see the current influences of Spain influencing English costume via France.

From this time forward His Catholic Majesty is said to have dressed entirely in black. Plate XLVI shows him so garbed in a plain suit of dull black silk. His moderate - sized slops are the only part decorated with cuttes on the piped panes.   Nether stocks are rolled up over the upper stocks, and the cloak and collar of black velvet are lined with a glossy black silk. The hat of blocked felt has a twisted silk band and a rose.

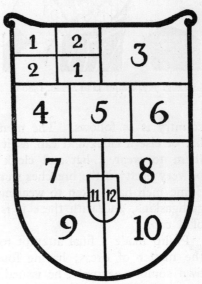

Fig. 766. Key to Armorials

Following his invariable custom he is wearing the Golden Fleece suspended by a small gold chain, well set off by its sombre background.

In striking contrast we see the brilliant tinctures of the Armorial Bearings of the States ruled by Philip before he became King of Portugal in 1581. Fig. 766 gives the names of these quarterings:

(1) Castile, (2) Leon, (3) Aragon, (4) Jerusalem, (5) Hungary (*unseen*), (6) Sicily, (7) Austria, (8) Modern Burgundy, (9) Ancient Burgundy, (10) Brabant, (11) Flanders (*unseen*), and (12) Tyrol (*unseen*). They are surmounted by the Spanish Royal Crown.

Although it is said that Philip usually dressed in unrelieved black, there are one or two portraits which show that the black suit was sometimes ornamented with a minimum amount of fine gold. He also wore a muceta of black silk or velvet, also relieved with gold, and sometimes lined with sable.

Fig. 767. Philip II of Spain, 1586

A head-and-shoulders drawing taken from a portrait of Philip II at the age of fifty-nine and dated 1586 is given in Fig. 767.

The King appears to have been too busy with affairs of State to trouble much about his subjects' apparel, for after 1564 no more pragmatics were issued for some time.

A description of the costume worn in the meantime by men (for women *see* p. 683) is given in the writings of Camillo Borghese, who came to Madrid in 1593 on a mission from Pope Clement VIII. The following is his account: 'The dress of this country is as follows. The men wear long breeches, with a surcote and hat or else a cloak and cap, as it would be a great breach of decorum with them to wear a hat and cloak together. This costume would certainly be very pretty if the breeches were not cut so long as to be disproportionate. Some men have taken to wearing hose in the Seville style, which they call galligaskins, and with these it is proper to wear a cloak and hat instead of a cap.'

Philip made a final attempt to check the extravagance of his subjects in the matter of dress; having found them, perhaps, reluctant to follow his own sombre example, he issued a last pragmatic in 1594:

'No man may wear either at his neck or wrists on any sort of ruff or frill, fixed or loose, any trimming, fringe, ravelling, or netting, starch, rice, gums, rods, wires, gold or silver threads, or any brass wiring or anything else to extend or support them, but only a plain holland or linen ruff with one or two little pleats, on pain of forfeiture of shirt and ruff and a fine of 50 ducats.'

These restrictions aroused so much indignation that the Council of State solemnly gave the subject its attention: and in the matter of ruffs a compromise was reached by which these adornments might be worn so long as they did not exceed three inches in width from band to hem, and were pure white. The penalties were enormous. Similar concessions were made regarding the materials of men's doublets, jerkins, and breeches, which might now be made of gold or fancy silk material (whose manufacture in Spain had of recent years much declined), as also of quilted silk, satin, or taffeta, while for the first time for many years stamped patterns might be used; trunk hose might be slashed and double-stitched at the edge of the slashings, and breeches stiffened

Fig. 768. Don Enrique de Guzman, 1595

by a single thickness of baize. Thus, luxury in dress was allowed to continue unchecked during the last years of the reign.

Philip II, who suffered from a lingering, loathsome disease, died in his palace-monastery on 13th September 1598, and is buried in the Escorial church. His reign marks the climax of Spanish power, and the commencement of its decline by secession of its New World possessions.

On the south side of the high altar is a monument to himself and his family. The effigies, five in number, are in gilt bronze, by Leoni. The King kneels in front at a prie-dieu and wears full armour under a State mantle with ermine cape quartering the armorial bearings of the Hapsburg inheritance. Grouped

Fig. 769. Don Luis de Velasco

around him are three of his wives—Marie of Portugal, Elizabeth of France, and Anne of Austria, and, behind, his son Don Carlos, all wearing armorial mantles in their proper tinctures.

As an example of the great simplicity of the costume worn by Spanish nobles of the highest degree in the 1580's and 1590's, the head-and-shoulders drawing (Fig. 768) of Don Enrique de Guzman, Conde de Olivares, Spanish Ambassador to the Holy See from 1584 onwards, is given.   An unpretentious

Fig. 770.
Philip, Prince of the Asturias, 1596

doublet of black silk, slashed on the breast over black and buttoned up the front, has a high collar, small ruff, and close-fitting sleeves with small shoulder rolls. This doublet must have had a narrow basque, although this is not shown. The rest of the dress consisted of equally plain nether garments—slops and hosen, and in addition an ample black cloth Spanish cloak and a high crowned almost brimless black felt hat.

Don Luis de Velasco, Viceroy of Mexico (Fig. 769), was a knight of the Order of St. James of the Sword in Spain. This Order was instituted in the twelfth century, but the Emperor Charles V made some additions and alterations. The badge (inset) was a red-enamelled cross of gold formed like a sword, the pommel like a heart reversed, and the guards terminating in fleurs-de-lys. Upon the centre was a white escallop shell. This badge was hung from a red riband round the neck, and on ceremonial occasions from a triple gold chain.

The robes of the Order consisted of a tunic of black silk or velvet, and the white mantle had a red cross embroidered on the left shoulder. A black velvet hat adorned with white ostrich feathers had a small red feather in the middle.

Don Luis is not wearing these full robes in his portrait (Fig. 769), but those worn for semi-State. The red badge on the black tunic is without the escallop shell, and is repeated on the shoulder of his *black* mantle. The hat he wears, with three rolls round the brim, is typically Spanish, and his gold-rimmed spectacles are attached to his ears by black leather straps.

Ladies were admitted to this Order; their robes were black, with the badge and cross.

The costume worn by a Spanish nobleman at the end of the century is illustrated in Fig. 770. It is taken from a portrait at Shottesbrooke Park, and is said to be of the Infante Philip, afterwards Philip III: if not, it represents some Spanish grandee. It was painted by Pantoja de la Cruz about 1596. The 'line' or cut of the doublet and trunks is different from that of the previous era, and shows the emergence of the form characteristic of the first part of the seventeenth century. The very angular effect of the trunks or slops should be noticed. The doublet and trunks are composed of vertical bands of dark green velvet embroidered in scarlet, white, and gold. The black velvet cloak is draped in the latest mode over the left upper arm; it is lined with white satin covered with lines of narrow gold cord set about one and a half inches apart and forming double loops. The sleeves are of the same embroidered white satin. A small plain circular ruff, black velvet belts, white silk hosen, and golden satin shoes with gold lace roses complete the attractions of this young Prince.

Philip III

King of Spain, 1598 until 1603

Philip, son of Philip II and Anne of Austria, was born in Madrid, 14th April 1578, and ascended the throne in 1598.

His long face with lack-lustre eyes, black hair, and heavy Hapsburg lip and jaw was anything but pleasing, as is evidenced by the crayon drawing by Daniel Dumoustier from which Fig. 771 is made. He was a sickly young man and subject to scrofula, with the mind of a silly pious child given over entirely to futile pleasures. The exact opposite of his father in everything except his beliefs, he squandered fabulous sums on Court festivals. He lacked his father's industry and intelligence, leaving the administration of the kingdom to Francisco de Sandoval y Rojas (born 1552), the chief minister, who was created Duke of Lerma in 1599. Later (1611) the Duke was superseded by his son, the Duke of Uceda. Philip married Margaret of Austria in the same year.

The sumptuary pragmatics had been ignored for many years, and extravagance in dress had reached such a pitch that it had become a national scandal. Hence in 1600 Philip issued a new pragmatic, quite

Fig. 771.
Philip III of Spain

different from previous ones, which formed the pattern of all similar enactments for the next hundred years. No one except the King and the Royal family might wear any sort of brocade or cloth of gold or silver, or silk in which these metals were woven, nor might ornamentation of any kind, or embroidery or pearls or jewels, be used on garments. Ruffs, however, could now be four and a half inches wide, as long as they had no lace edgings or ravellings and were pure white.

The following dress is alone prescribed: the cape or other over-garment may be of any sort of silk with stripes, on each edge of which may be an ornamental stitching. Surcotes and ropillas (a sort of half-tight over-jacket with double sleeves, the outer ones hanging loose from the shoulders) may be also of silk and trimmed in the same way, and, if desired, a piping of another sort of silk, but not the same, may be put between the stripes. The inside of the capes may have similar stripes of silk, satin, or taffeta, but not velvet. Shoulder-capes may be made of velvet, and the hoods of riding-cloaks or rain-capes may be lined with the same. Silk gimp and frogs may be sewn on to *duffel* cloaks, etc. The trunks may be worn of any kind of silk, and each slashing may be edged with a velvet or silk piping and an *eyelash* border. If the slashing is a wide one, this edging may be worn on both sides of it, but if otherwise only on one side. The slashings may be lined with taffeta. Silk gimp or braid of any sort may be worn on the trunks excepting *lutestrings* or crewels. Galligaskins may also be made of silk, but with no trimming but a row of gimp on each side and at the opening. Dressing-gowns for women and men may be of any material or fashion, so long as gold or silver is not used. Doublets, ropillas, or trunks made of satin may be ornamented by silk stitching of any colour, but on no account may the stuff be pinked, ravelled, or fringed.

The rules generally apply to women as well as men, but the former are allowed to wear *jackets* of light cloth of gold or silver, which may be trimmed with a braid of the same over the seams, and the whole jacket may be covered with 'whirligigs' or scrolls of gold or silver, so long as there is no working in the stuff itself. The frills and flounces of these garments may also be ornamented in the same fashion. Hats, belts, baldricks, etc., were all treated in the same way; gold or silver gimp, braid, and lace were allowed to be sewn on, but not embroidered or woven in, the texture.[1]

It should be explained that *eyelash* was a stitching very like what is known as 'blanket stitch.' Lutestring was a glossy silk cord or ribbon.

Philip's gloomy forebodings as to what would happen when the Crown should pass to his incompetent son were more than realized.

NOBLE LADIES, 1580–1603

The Great Infanta, 1566 *until* 1603

Isabella Clara Eugenia, eldest daughter of Philip II and Elizabeth or Isabel de Valois, was born at Balsain, near Segovia, in 1566. She was named after Queen Isabella the Catholic and her mother; Clara because she was born on that Saint's day, 1st August; and Eugenia out of gratitude to the efficacious body of St. Eugène which had restored her mother to health.

---

[1] The whole of this description is taken from Martin Hume's *The Year after the Armada*.

Fig. 772. THE INFANTA ISABELLA CLARA EUGENIA

Her father, who was devotedly fond of her, describing her on his death-bed as 'le miroir et la lumière de ses yeux,' endeavoured to bring about a marriage between her and Henry, Duc d'Anjou.   This project was extremely unpopular in France, especially with the Huguenots, and was the subject of much satire on account of her age and swarthy complexion.   The negotiations did not mature.   This middle-aged spinster—she was nearly thirty—was still left without a husband or a crown, despite the fact that was she the greatest catch of Europe 'ever since Elizabeth of England had definitely retired from the matrimonial market.'   However, as some compensation, her father bestowed upon her first the Netherlands (21st May 1598) and then her cousin the Cardinal Archduke, Albert of Austria, whom she married in 1599, the Pope releasing him from his religious vows.   As Governess of the Netherlands conjointly with her husband, the Archduchess persecuted her new subjects with zest, as was usual with some members of the Hapsburg family.   The famous siege of Ostend in 1601 was undertaken with this object.

The Great Infanta was frequently painted at different periods of her life by such artists as Pantoja de la Cruz, Coello, Liano, Pourbus the Younger, and—in late life—by Rubens: these portraits may be seen in the Prado, at Versailles, Munich, and Hampton Court.

Fig. 772 is founded on more than one of these portraits.   There are several apparently trifling details about the costume which repay study.   The characteristic surcote of Spain, mentioned as far back as 1550 (see Fig. 516), is still in vogue, and continued to be so well into the seventeenth century, but the shoulders and back are now cut to fit close as evidenced by the way the folds of the skirt part, gored behind at the waist, hang.   The slits on the breast remain; but turning the front back to waist-level instead of fastening it at the throat (see Fig. 592), and raising the hem in front, are new ideas. So also are the lace wrist-frills which form the transition from the turned-back cuffs of the sixteenth century to the flounces of lace worn during the whole of the seventeenth and eighteenth centuries.

The hanging sleeves, farthingale, hairdressing, and headdress are truly Spanish.   In Fig. 772 the whole dress is made of one of those magnificent brocades so much used at this time; it has a raised velvet pattern of more delicate design than hitherto, on a different coloured satin ground.   The surcote and underdress have a fancy gold lace set on all edges, and in some portraits there are two rows and even three placed close together.   In more than one painting the whole surface of the surcote and underdress is covered with bands of gold lace, about an inch in width, set close in horizontal, perpendicular, and oblique lines.   The underdress is shaped like that shown in Fig. 774 and nearly always made of the same material as the surcote.

Portraits of the Archduchess's younger sister, the Infanta Catherine Michela, who was born in 1567, show her as a very good-looking girl with a round face, beautiful dark eyes and hair, and without any Hapsburg characteristics.   The one by Coello, in the Prado, is a specially good example. Fig. 773 is drawn from it.

Fig. 773. THE INFANTA CATHERINE MICHELA.   After Sanchez Coello

The Infanta married before her elder sister, her husband being Emmanuel I, Duke of Savoy; and their wedding festivities were so magnificent as to call from this very haughty young Princess the remark that such ostentatious display was unnecessary for a 'mere duchess.' However, she had nine children, and died at the age of thirty in 1597.

Although the art of weaving brocades, damasks, plain velvets, and silks had reached such a high standard in Spain during the fifteenth century, owing to the excellent craftsmanship of the Moorish weavers who were alone responsible for the textile manufacture (*see* vol. i, p. 218), a certain quantity of silken material was imported from Italy.

Spanish woven fabrics had been entirely of Moorish design; but with the advent of the Renaissance, the pomegranate and the method of spacing out patterns in pointed ovals became incorporated with Morisco features. Towards the end of the sixteenth century the oval motif gave place to a lighter and more flexible ornament, such as are seen in the brocades worn by Spanish ladies of this time in their portraits. When the Moriscos were finally banished from Spain by Philip III in 1609, the country was deprived of the services of these expert silk weavers and designers. Henceforth Spain had to rely on Italy and France for the gorgeous stuffs wherewith to create magnificent clothes, upholder furniture, and decorate apartments.

Fig. 774. Spanish Lady of the Court

The noble ladies of Spain who were in the entourage of the Great Infanta, and later the Archduchess, followed her example in their toilets and sumptuous apparel, and were entirely outside the pale of any pragmatics.

Fig. 774 is a representative costume carried out in a brocade of rich colouring, in which the most important motif is the tulip—a new flower lately introduced from Turkey. The bodice, cut high at the neck, and the farthingale, were regulated for the dress of Royal ladies, the Court, and the aristocracy. Usually the neck was high, having a stiff collar almost reaching the lobe of the ear. The circular ruff was attached to the top of this collar, as shown in Fig. 772; but there are a few instances in portraits of great ladies turning the edges and corners down, showing a little of the bare throat, the circular ruff being supported at the sides and back as seen in Fig. 774. In this, the bodice is cut to fit the corseted figure, descending in a point well below the waist; it has three lines, sometimes more, of gold set with jewels in gold mounts converging from shoulders to waist and point. Tabs surround the armholes and the sloping waist-line.

The hanging sleeves of deep-toned velvet are the most distinctive feature of this typical Spanish costume. Fig. 775 is a diagram of one. It is cut in two sections; AB is pleated or gathered into the armhole; from B to D it is seamed, leaving a reversed T opening at C; DE is the wrist; and from E it is seamed along the curved portion to A.

These sleeves were ornamented in many different ways, but usually with rows of gold braid, as seen in Figs. 774 and 775, showing a decidedly Moorish influence. Loops and aiglettes were often added, and as a matter of course the sleeve could be worn on the arm or hanging behind. The close under-sleeves, of different but plain material, were almost covered with transverse braids, the joins and front and back seams being masked with a single row of braid. The skirt is without folds in front and at the sides, being cut on the circular plan; but sometimes a train was worn (*see* Fig. 772), when the skirt would become an oval. The seams are joined with care so as not to mutilate the pattern more than possible when

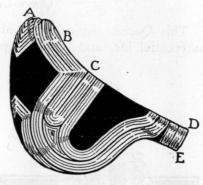

Fig. 775

using brocade or damask. If, of necessity, there must be a seam down the centre of the skirt, which was often left open, it was marked with braids. Velvet, satin, and silk were other materials much used for these costumes.

With regard to the costume of the Spanish ladies in general, we are told by Camillo Borghese in 1593 that it was usually of black relieved only by the large circular white ruff. Ruffs were not so frequently worn as voluminous black veils: 'They have a veil round their faces like nuns, their heads being enveloped by their MANTILLAS in such a way that their faces are hardly visible.' This is a very early reference to that very characteristic item of Spanish costume, as the mantilla of lace did not become important until much later. Velazquez's two portraits of a lady of middle class, one belonging to the Duke of Devonshire, the other, No. 88, in the Wallace Collection, are perhaps the earliest paintings which show the mantilla.

Straight-cut jackets with sleeves reaching to the elbow, or even sleeveless, were frequently worn over ordinary dress. These used to be very elaborately braided with gold or silver round the edges and over the seams, and were of Moorish origin; for this reason such decoration was no longer allowed by the pragmatic of 1594, but this restriction was not enforced by Philip III in 1600 (*see* p. 677).

Spanish ladies were notorious for painting their faces. Being dark-skinned they used many kinds of paint and cosmetics to make themselves appear fair, blonde complexions being greatly admired by all Spaniards. 'Though small of stature they wear pattens to make them look tall,' a method of increasing their height which had been in use from the early part of the century (*see* Fig. 248).

MARGARET OF AUSTRIA

Queen-Consort of Philip III

This Queen, the daughter of the Archduke Charles of Styria, led an uneventful life, and brought up her children to the best of her ability.

They were:

Fig. 776. Marguerite of Austria, Wife of Philip III, 1602

Anne, born 1602, married Louis XIII of France.

Philip, born 1605, succeeded as Philip IV, and married Mary, daughter of the Emperor Ferdinand III.

Mary married Ferdinand III.

Margaret realized from the outset that she was unequal to the task of supporting the important position thrust upon her, though bidden by her relentless parents to sacrifice everything to duty; tending the poor and sick in her native land, where she led an almost nun-like life, was much more suited to her temperament. However, she was much loved and venerated by her Spanish subjects.

The jacket mentioned on p. 678 was a garment often worn, but seldom seen in portraits or illustrations. Fortunately, in a full-length engraving by Crispin van de Pass the Elder, dated 1602, Margaret of Austria is wearing this interesting jacket. Fig. 776 is a drawing of it, in black or some dark-coloured velvet, the surface covered with a beautiful scroll design in gold and, possibly, some silver. The borders and shoulder pieces are edged with gold braid. It should be noticed that the funnel-shaped sleeves give the same effect as the fashionable sleeves worn by the lady (Fig. 774) but lack the lower part. This jacket is worn over a dress, of which the dark front of the bodice set with jewels is the only part visible; the close-fitting sleeves, finishing at the wrists with the new style of wrist-ruffs, are of light-coloured satin or silk. The skirt hanging in stiff folds over the Spanish farthingale is of white and gold

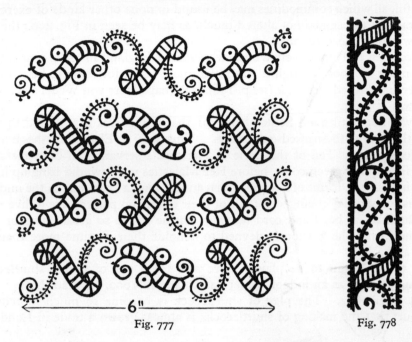

Fig. 777   Fig. 778

brocade, and opens over an embroidered underskirt. The fronts, like those of the jacket, are formally turned back to show the silk lining. A circular ruff edged with picadils, and a high jewelled coronet, are worn.

.A three-quarter portrait by Gonzalez of Queen Margaret with her hand on the head of her dog 'Valliante,' in the Prado, shows her in a dress of white with a black pattern (Fig. 777) fashioned somewhat on the lines as that seen in Fig. 774, but heavily braided with black silk braid, a portion of which is given in Fig. 778. She wears a circular lace edged ruff and a coronet of upstanding pear-shaped pearls at the back of her head.

TENYSE (*continued from p.* 196)

Tennis still remained a popular game, and in 1584 a Fellow of Oriel College, Oxford, wrote with reference to this enjoyable pastime, that it 'exercises all parts of the body alike and greatly delighteth the minde, making it lusty and cheerful, all which commodities may be found in none other kinde of exercise.' The racquet in use had not altered much, as may be seen in Fig. 490; the top is now rather more rounded.

According to Lupold von Wedel, who visited England in 1584, tennis balls were made of wood, though it was much more usual for them to be made of leather and stuffed with hair (*see* p. 196). Perhaps Herr von Wedel's observation was at fault.

It was not until 22nd September 1591 that tennis was first played upon a smooth lawn with marked-out courts. This was at Elvetham, the Earl of Hertford's seat: 'Ten of the Earle of Hertford's servants, all Somersetshire men, in a square green court, before Her Majesties window, did hang up lines, squaring out the forme of a tennis court, and making a cross line in the middle. In this square they (being stript out of their doublets) played, five to five with the handball, at bord and cord (as they tearme it), to so great liking of Her Highness, that she graciously deyned to beholde their pastime more than an hour and a half.'

As tennis began to be played more and more out of doors, shuttlecock became popular as an indoor winter game; and in 1602, we read that:

'24 Dec. 1602. The play of shuttlecock is become so much in request at Court that the making of shuttlecocks is almost grown a trade in London.'

THE YEOMEN OF THE GUARD (*continued from p.* 424)

During the first years of Queen Elizabeth's reign the number of the 'Yeomen in Ordinary' was increased to two hundred, and that of the 'Yeomen Extraordinary' reduced to one hundred and seven. There were thirty 'Yeomen of the Crown' who were usually in attendance near the Queen's person, and four 'Yeomen Ushers,' a number subsequently increased to fifteen and ultimately reduced to eight.

The predominating colours of the State liveries of the Yeomen of the Guard during this reign are shown in contemporary illustrations as red, black, and yellow.

One of the corps in attendance at Queen Elizabeth's coronation is given in Fig. 779, reproduced from the pen-and-ink drawing referred to on p. 485. Comparison of A, Plate XXIII, with the rough drawing, will show that the only difference in their dress is the hat, which in Fig. 779 is a trifle larger. It is noticeable that in the original drawing the yeomen do not wear hats all of the same shape; there are three varieties, as shown inset. Some wear high-crowned hats, others a large bonet with a feather.

The captain of the Yeomen of the Guard, Sir William St. Loo (second husband of the Countess of Shrewsbury, 'Bess of Hardwick'), rides at the head of the corps on a finely caparisoned horse like Fig. 957, and wears rich clothes exactly as shown in Fig. 610, but with a high-crowned hat and feather.

Some time after the accession of Elizabeth the black gards shown on the sleeves and bases of the tunic in Plate XXIII A were edged with a narrow gold braid.

B in Plate XXIII illustrates the livery of the Yeomen of the Guard in use from about 1575 to 1595. The body part of the tunic is decorated in the same manner as the last example, the only differences being that some time before 1580 the black gards were edged with narrow gold and the Royal cipher was added, the letters 'E.R.' in gold being placed on either side of the rose. From this time onwards to the present day, the initials of the sovereign, together with the rose and crown, have been embroidered upon the breast of the State liveries. The gold-embroidered gards, which descend on each side of the tunic front, are repeated round the neck opening. The collar is attached to the doublet and supports the band.

The puffed sleeves finish with a gard of black velvet through which pass the close sleeves of the dark purple doublet. The basque seen in Plate XXIII A has been superseded by a reversion to the earlier bases—hence the opening up the front (seen in the basque) has disappeared

Fig. 779. 1559

—descending to the middle of the thigh and showing a small portion of the lower part of the dark purple slops. The legs are clothed in kersey hose, also of dark purple, and over them are drawn netherstocks of white kersey, tied with dark purple garters below the knee. Black shoes with black roses are worn.

From 1570 onwards Yeomen of the Guard wore a hat of black velvet, in place of the earlier bonet, as seen in the drawing (B Plate XXIII). Round the crown was folded a band of white silk or linen with a rose of the same on the left side, securing a bunch of white ostrich feathers.

A gilt halberd, together with a gilt-handled sword in a black scabbard slung from a black sword-carriage and belt, was carried.

The Yeomen of the Guard were present on all occasions of State and ceremony in numbers graduated according to the importance of the function. Thus Samuel Kiechel writing in 1586 says: 'Before the Queen marched her bodyguard. They are all tall, strong, picked men. There are said to be two hundred of them, but this day they were not all present. They bore gilt halberts and wore red coats trimmed with black velvet. On their coats in front and behind are the Queen's arms in beaten gilt silver.'

In the great Presence Chamber the Yeomen of the Guard, drawn up in lines in various positions, kept order. On occasions when a State banquet was given, or when the Queen dined in public,[1] one detachment was on guard as previously noted (p. 50), while the other served the different courses. The men of this latter detachment performed their duties bareheaded; and while serving, or when addressed by the Queen, they always knelt on one knee. These two customs, it should be remembered, were in use only during the reign of Elizabeth.

Fig. 780

Since the Yeomen wore their hats at all other times when in attendance on the Sovereign, whether indoors or out, it is difficult to understand why they are shown in black *skull-caps* in the picture of Elizabeth at Blackfriars (Plate XLIII); or why the Gentlemen Pensioners in the same picture are bareheaded. Perhaps special consideration for the bald heads of these old men superseded a general order that no *hats* should be worn on this particular occasion.

The French Ambassador, 1598, informs us that 'the Queen for her ordinary Guard has about one hundred and fifty Englishmen clad in red *velvet*, who live in the first chamber of her palace; and besides she has sixty Gentlemen that she calls her Pensioners, who are an ordinary part of her household, scions and gentlemen of good family.'

A slight change occurred in the tunic during the last ten years of Elizabeth's reign. The full puffed sleeves became shorter, little more than shoulder puffs; the horizontal gards disappeared from these reduced puffs, and were transferred to the elongated 'cuffs' on the upper arm. Sometimes one, sometimes two, gards are shown (*see* Fig. 780).

The Yeomen of the Guard numbered one hundred and fifty in the year 1601. Their active service equipment at this time is recorded as follows: 'The cuirass complete with breast and back pieces; taces, and tassets, and arm pieces; gorgets, morions (*see* Fig. 512), targets, muskets and musket rests, bandoliers for carrying ammunition, and long and short pikes.'

On the occasion of the funeral procession of Queen Elizabeth on 28th April 1603, the Yeomen of the Guard carried their halberds reversed and veiled in black.

---

[1] A custom very prevalent among Royalty.

GENTLEMEN PENSIONERS

At the coronation of Queen Elizabeth the Gentlemen Pensioners wore rich suits of crimson damask and carried gilt battle-axes.

'This Princess in imitation of her father, Henry VIII, did admit none about her for Pensioners, Privy Chambermen, Squires of the Body, etc., but persons of station, strength, and birth.' Queen Elizabeth's pensioners and guard were 'always the tallest and goodliest gentlemen and Yeomen in the Kingdom,' though they were by this time evidently ceasing to be men of small fortunes: in fact, the wealth of the Corps must have been as noticeable as the high birth and physical prowess of its members. The Gentlemen Pensioners were held in very high esteem by Elizabeth, who treated them as personal friends and liked to have them in attendance near her on every possible occasion, and seldom, if ever, went on her progresses without a considerable number. When out in the darkness of the night they carried 'torch-staves' as well as their battle-axes.

It is stated that the Gentlemen Pensioners were at some time during this reign dressed all in black with black cloaks and golden chains about their necks; but this must have been when they were attending the Queen at some funeral ceremony. On the other hand, Elizabeth was fond of display and pageantry, and it is beyond all doubt that on other occasions these Gentlemen of Blood made a brave show in the Tudor colours of white and green, or crimson. In the picture of Elizabeth attending a wedding at Blackfriars, 1600, the Gentlemen Pensioners are seen, though not very distinctly; they all wear black cloaks with gold chains over their shoulders, but the other parts of their dress are of different colours, without uniformity.

At the Queen's funeral the corps were dressed entirely in black, if we may rely upon an Illum. MS. depicting this event. They were attired like ordinary gentlemen in doublets, slops, upper and netherstocks and shoes, ample cloaks, and high hats with round crowns and wide brims. They carried their halberds, of gilt garnished with crimson and gold like those in Plate XXIII B, point downwards, and covered with black.

SECTION III: 1558–1603

MIDDLE CLASSES—MEN

The social position of the *professional* classes was assured. Originally of the middle class, the learning of many gained them titles, sometimes, and so raised them to a higher sphere—the nobility. Harrison explains all this most aptly:

'The King doth dubbe knights, and createth the Barons and higher degrees,

Fig. 781. A Bishop

so gentlemen whose ancestors are not known to come in with William, Duke of Normandy (for of the Saxon races yet remaining we now make none account, much less of the British issue) do take their beginning in England, after this manner in our time. Whosoever studieth the laws of the realm, whoso abideth in the university, giving his mind to his book, or professeth Physick and the liberal sciences, or beside his service in the room of a captain in the wars or good council given at home, whereby his commonwealth is benefited, can live without manual labour and thereto is able and will bear the port [style of living], charge, and countenance of a gentleman, he shall for money have a coat of arms bestowed upon him by heralds, who in the charter of the same do of custom pretend antiquity and service, and many gay things, and thereunto, being made so good cheap, be called master.'

The Bishop of Lincoln (Fig. 781), although an ecclesiastic, appears in these pages from the funeral procession of Mary Queen of Scots, 29th July 1587, on account of his biretta, which is now in process of development into the square-shaped cap. It shows one of the earlier examples of the transition of the academic cap—a skull cap with a soft square top to it. After the Reformation 'a square cap without any stiffening which causes such corners to flap' took the place of the biretta amongst the Protestant clergy.

A square cap stiffened is seen in Fig. 854.

The scarlet robes of a judge are shown in Fig. 782, and consist of a long gown with sleeves turned back at the wrists with budge, a hood with deep cape edged with the same fur, a mantle lined with white and edged with budge, and a square black velvet or cloth cap, worn when not on the bench or tucked into the black satin waist sash on State occasions. Underneath is the coif, the 'principal and chief insignment of habit wherewith serjeants-at-law on their creation are decked.' It should be noticed that the mantle is placed *on top* of the cape, the hood being turned back over it. The mantle was worn only at coronations, opening of Parliament, cathedral services, and on the first day of term. A broad black silk scarf was sometimes hung round the neck, stole fashion, when the mantle was dispensed with. These robes remain in use up to the present day.[1]

Fig. 782. A Judge   Fig. 783. A Physician

In portraits of judges of the following centuries a 'modern' detail is always in evidence, and that around the neck. In the Elizabethan and early Stuart period it was the ruff; in the late Stuart the 'rabato'; in the Georgian, the 'cravat'; and in the nineteenth century the collar and tie.

Some judges were privileged to surround their shoulders with a collar consisting of a rose in the centre between two portcullises, SS, and cord knots, like that worn by the Lord Mayor (Figs. 797 and 431).

The earlier austere monastic garb affected by the medical profession is now out of date, and in Fig. 783 we see a physician of the Elizabethan era. His

[1] During the second half of the seventeenth century the periwig was worn over the coif which was completely concealed by it; and in the reign of George II the white curled wig took the place of the periwig, and this, with some modifications, became the judge's wig of the nineteenth and twentieth centuries.

underdress is a suit of the period, and so is his flat black velvet cap.   The wrap-over cloth gown of a dark colour or black, lined throughout or turned back only with fur, has sleeves of the fashionable shape; and to the waist-belt is attached a commodious pouch.   The professional coif of white linen, the only symbol of his calling, is worn under the cap.   At the neck there is sure to be a small ruff.   For a cap worn by an Italian doctor of medicine see Fig. 666.

A case of *cuir boulli* (Italian, of the sixteenth century, containing surgeons' instruments) may be seen in the British Museum.

Fig. 784.   Fig. 785.
A Doctor and Student

Fig. 786.
A Schoolmaster

A don reprimanding an Oxford student (Figs. 784 and 785) clearly shows the caps and gowns worn at the universities during the greater part of Queen Elizabeth's reign.   These garments of black were, of course, worn over the ordinary everyday dress of the period.   According to Anthony Wood 'the Scholars are supposed in their dress to have imitated the Benedictine Monks, who were the chief restorers of literature,' so that the gowns must have been made of a soft woollen material.

Lord Burleigh's orders as Chancellor of the University of Cambridge (1585) were as follows: 'They might walk in cloak and hat to and from the fields.   Also within his College, Hall, Hostel, or Habitation it was lawful for any student to wear a gown, or gaberdine of plain Turkey fashion with a round falling cap without gard, welt, lace, cutte, or silk except one cutte in the sleeves thereof to put out his arms only. . . . Also that every graduate wearing the above gown and gaberdine within the University or town out of his chamber or lodging do wear withal in the daytime a square cap and none other, no hat to be worn except for infirmities sake with a kerchief about his head, or in going to and from the fields, or in the street or open air when it shall happen to rain, hail, or snow; the hat which shall be worn to be black, and the band or lace of the hat to be of the same colour, plain, and not excessive in bigness, without feather brooch or such like uncomely for students.'

The gown of a schoolmaster is illustrated in Fig. 786, from the brass to the memory of Edward Harris, M.A., born 1534. He matriculated at Oxford 1564, and was appointed in 1570 first head master of Lord Williams's Grammar School, Thame. Master Harris was especially instrumental in founding the school, and was, in consequence, nominated for the period of his life, which ended in 1597. His hood, not worn in the brass, would have been of black cloth lined with white fur of superior quality. A bachelor's hood was similar, but lined with less expensive fur, which it retains to this day. Even undergraduates wore hoods at this period, longer in the point which hung behind (liripipe) and without any fur lining (*see* vol. ii, p. 213). Over his ordinary suit of cloth he wears his academic gown of black cloth slit up the sides and falling back down the open fronts. The

Fig. 787.
A Gentleman, 1578

conventional tubular sleeves are edged and frogged with black braid. His ruff is by no means smartly dressed.

GENTRY

The sixteenth-century opinion of what constituted a gentleman was very different from that held in the twelfth and following centuries (*see* vol. ii, p. 68).

According to William Harrison, any one who had the means to live comfortably without doing manual labour could be termed a gentleman. If he could afford to buy a coat of arms and register himself and his family at the College of Arms, he was, without doubt, a gentleman and an armiger, and would be addressed as 'esquire' or 'master.'

The gentleman dressed all in black (Fig. 787) is attending a society interment; nevertheless, his clothes are of the fashionable cut of the 1570's. His slightly padded doublet, with full sleeves and shoulder roll, has remarkably deep and full basques. His venetians are not stuffed, but form folds round the thigh, the lower part of the legs being clothed in netherstocks and ankle-boots.   The hat is of the Italian shape.

The two young gentlemen (Figs. 789 and 791) are escorting their lady friends to Bermondsey.   They come from the picture at Hatfield House painted by Joris Hoefwagel between 1582, when he came to London, and 1590.   Some authorities suggest that the painting dates 1570.   The ladies' costumes, if not the gentlemen's, have characteristics of that year.   The

Fig. 788.   Fig. 789.   Fig. 790.   Fig. 791.
Ladies and Gentlemen at a Marriage Feast

clothes of the gentlemen are on the fashionable lines as worn by the nobility, and would be made of cloth.   The high-crowned hats, whether with wide or narrow brim, are much in vogue at this time.   Fig. 789 wears a buff doublet over dull pink trunks and hosen; his hat and cloak are black.   Fig. 791 is dressed entirely in black.

Two bright young people of the gentlefolk (Figs. 792 and 793) are performing a bow or 'reverence' prior to taking part in a dance.   They have gained their instruction in deportment from Thoinot Arbeau in his *Orchéso-graphie*, published at Langres in 1588.

'At the moment when the musicians begin to play make your reverence, holding the damsel by the hand.   To perform the reverence you will keep the left foot firmly on the ground and, bending the right knee, carry the point of the toe a little to the rear of the left foot, at the same time doffing your bonet or hat and saluting your damsel and the company as you see in this picture. When the reverence has been performed, straighten the body, and replace your bonet: then, advancing your right foot, bring and keep the two feet together. The reverence done, assume a goodly modest attitude.'

Fig. 792.   Fig. 793.
The Reverence of the 1580's

The pleasing young man (Fig. 793) is well dressed in a doublet of simple cut, having sleeves puffed on the shoulders; a fine lawn collar surrounds the high collar of his doublet. His slops are paned, and his hosen cross-gartered.

He is uncovered at the moment, and shows his hair dressed à la Don Juan.

Fig. 794 is a woodcut of Gabriel Harvey as caricatured by Thomas Nash in 1596. He is a fashionable young man, with his high-crowned hat and fierce moustaches, and is wearing rather antiquated paned slops, which is a vogue revived. The attitude of this young gentleman in getting out his purse to stand treat makes it obvious that *trouser pockets* were inserted in the amplifications of the slops. He is a good specimen of a gentleman of this decade.

The exploits of the sword-and-buckler man were somewhat handicapped by Proclamation. Two examples are given below:

'viij May 1562. Proclamation of the Acts of Array and great ruffs and great breeches, and that no man to have but a yard and half of kersey, that no sword be but a yard and a quarter in length of blade, and daggers but xij inches the blade and that bucklers shall not have long pikes, but of a fixed form.'

In 1580 another proclamation ordained further reduction in the length of

Fig. 794. Gabriel Harvey, 1596
Have with you to Saffron Walden

Fig. 795.
Young Gentleman, 1577

the sword blade to three feet. Pikes on bucklers were to be no more than two inches.

Fig. 795 shows a young gentleman of the 1570's and 1580's who is an expert in the art of sword-and-buckler play. He looks very smart in his doublet of cloth garded with black or dark velvet, but it is more in the fashion of the previous reign than of this. His hat with a high crown bulging at the top is more up to date, and his shoes are decorated with cuttes and loops. He is armed with a good long hefty sword and a *small* buckler known as a 'rondel,' 'rondelle à poing,' or 'boce.' This particular art of self-defence or aggression began to decline towards the end of the century owing to the increasing popularity of the rapier, which caused a certain amount of dissatisfaction.

One of the characters in *The Two Angry Women of Abingdon,* 1599, expresses public opinion in the following words:

'Sword and Buckler play begins to grow out of use . . . if it be once gone, this poking fight of rapier and dagger will come up: then a good *tall* Sword and Buckler Man will be spitted like a cat or rabbit.'

The word 'tall' was often used to mean courageous.

This country esquire (Fig. 796), Justice of the Peace and of the Quorum and Custos Rotulorum, 'who writes himself armigero [1] in any bill, warrant, quittance, or obligation,' is soberly and substantially clad in a gown with tubular sleeves of cloth decorated with bands of velvet. It is a comfortable garment worn over a suit of sombre hue, and girded with a leathern belt to which a pouch is attached. A set of small goffered cuffs and ruff, a hat perhaps of velvet, and a medallion or mounted jewel hung round the neck, add to the old gentleman's dignity.

MERCHANTS AND BURGHERS

'Citizens and burgesses have next place to gentlemen, who be those that are free within the cities and are of some likely substance to bear office in the same. . . In this place also are our merchants to be installed as amongst the citizens, although they often change estate with gentlemen, as gentlemen do with them.'

English burghers and yeomen were

Fig. 796. A Country Gentleman

all wealthy, and all, high and low, displayed great ostentation. Merchants still kept to the former gravity befitting burgesses, but their young wives were more frivolous than women of higher estate.

A Lord Mayor's show of the sixteenth century was very much as we see it on 9th November in our time. Several contemporary descriptions of it are extant, and mention that His Worship was accompanied by the sheriffs, aldermen, burghers, and craftsmen of the various city companies all mounted on goodly horses, and richly garbed with heavy gold chains about their necks. The Elizabethans loved pageants, and these played an important part in the procession; but a comic touch was given to the otherwise dignified proceedings by a row or two of servitors, who walked in front carrying squirts,

---

[1] One entitled to armorial bearings by birth, and very superior to those who have merely purchased them.

'such as are used for quenching a fire. With these they squirted water at the crowd, for the street was full of people, so that they were forced to make way.' An excellent idea for dispersing crowds.

The chief actor on the municipal stage was dressed, according to an eye-witness (1585), as shown in Fig. 797. The robe or gown, worn over a very smart yet sober suit, was of scarlet velvet or cloth; some state that it was lined with ermine, others sable. The cut of the gown is familiar, but from effigies of Lord Mayors and aldermen of this time one sees that the material is

Fig. 797. A Lord Mayor   Fig. 798. Lawrence Sheriff

gathered or pleated into a yoke at the back, and also that the tubular sleeve was intricately shaped at the back as shown in the drawing. It is particularly mentioned that over the gown 'hung great golden chains, which before and behind reached to the girdles.' A detail of the Lord Mayor's chain or collar is given in Fig. 431. On the day of his election—28th October—both the retiring Lord Mayor and his successor wore gowns of pimpillo-brown cloth faced with ermine. Over these they wore fig-brown hoods lined with squirrel. The hats on both occasions were of the usual Italian fashion in black velvet.

The mayors of Oxford, according to the brass to the memory of Randolph Flexney, who died in 1578, wore a gown shaped like the preceding but of red cloth; it appears to be quite plain, without any fur. Round the neck is hung a black silk scarf or stole which reaches to the knees.

In Fig. 798 is seen a drawing of Lawrence Sheriff, a native of Rugby, who was apprenticed to a grocer in London and afterwards owned a first-class grocery establishment in Newgate Street. He supplied the household of the Princess Elizabeth with groceries, and after she became Queen she made him an esquire and granted him a coat of arms.[1] In 1561 he presented the Queen with a New Year's gift consisting of 'a sugar loaf; a box of ginger; a box of nutmegs, and a pound of cynomon,' and she returned the compliment by sending him 'oone guilt salt with a cover per oz. 7 oz.' Sheriff was nominated

Fig. 799.
A Merchant of the 1570's

Fig. 800.
A Merchant of the 1590's

Vice-Warden of the Grocers' Company in 1566, and would have been Lord Mayor had he not died in 1567, leaving a wife, Elizabeth, but no children. He was the founder of Rugby School.

The gown in Fig. 798 is of the usual shape, which as a rule had long tubular sleeves with a slit at elbow level; but in this drawing, taken from a contemporary one, the top part forms a small shoulder cape with a long pendent end, somewhat similar to that shown in Fig. 797. Livery gowns were at this time bereft of their gay colourings, being no longer made in the livery colours of the various companies, and as Stow relates (see p. 788) 'of the saddest.'

The best were of black silk, others of a kind of black material having the appearance of modern repp. Lawrence Sheriff carries his chaperon (see

[1] Now the armorial bearings of Rugby School.

description under Fig. 623), parti-coloured crimson and violet, the livery colours of the Grocers' Company, by the tippet over his shoulder. The cap is of the fashion of Henry VIII's time in black velvet. For a description of the headgear of city aldermen refer to Stow on p. 788. Underneath the livery gown is worn the usual costume of the time; the sleeves on the forearm, the band or ruff, and the shoes only are visible.

This opulent burgher (Fig. 799), clutching his money bag, comes from a painting of Abingdon Bridge dated about 1590, and now in the hall at Christ's Hospital. It is supposed to represent Geoffrey Barbour, who took a leading part in the building of the bridge during the reign of Henry V. He is dressed, however, as a rich burgher of the sixteenth century, and affords another blatant example of the custom, arising from sheer ignorance, of painting people of past ages arrayed in costume of the artist's time. Barbour died in 1417; and the little that is seen of his dress, depicted in his brass in St. Helen's Church erected at this date, suggests it is exactly the same as shown in Fig. 582, vol. ii, except that he is wearing in addition a hood thrown back off his head. The costume in Fig. 799 is reminiscent of that worn during the reign of Henry VII: long under-robe with close-fitting sleeves, over-robe with tubular sleeves and lined with fur, and bonet. The only Elizabethan touches are the tiny ruff, and the slight raising of the sleeves on the shoulders.

Fig. 801. A Schoolboy

Fig. 800 shows the unpretentious dress of a well-to-do burgher of the 1580's and 1590's. His suit of cloth is of the ordinary cut, and with it he wears netherstocks over his upperstocks, and an ample cloak reaching down to his knees. This is a good example of the ordinary dress of the people in general.

As has been mentioned before, boys of all periods were dressed like their fathers. This may appear, to their modern counterpart, excessively uncomfortable as restricting their freedom of movement; but, because for many generations these garments had been customary, such complaints would not even occur to William Brome (Fig. 801). He is shown at the age of ten on his brass in Holton Church, Oxon, wearing a slightly padded doublet, full slops, upperstocks and netherstocks, and (for additional comfort or because he is in full dress) an ample cloak.

All readers of this book will agree that a tailor was a very important person despite the fact that Harrison classifies him with 'the last sort.' The Queen and both sexes of the nobility thought differently, and thoroughly appreciated his skill. Besides creating marvellous costumes, tailors manufactured 'pavilions for our Kings, robes of State for our nobles, and tents, etc., for our soldiers.' They also condescended to become 'makers of ordinary garments by stitching jerkins for our prentices, doublets for our shopmen, and trunk-hose for our cooks.' Linen armourers, makers of linen garments to wear under armour, were associated with the tailors.

A Spanish tailor is shown in Fig. 672, and an Italian tailor was honoured by having his portrait painted by Moroni. It can be seen in the National Gallery, London, No. 697.

LONDON APPRENTICES

Here is an apprentice (Fig. 802) of the early years of Elizabeth's reign. Compared with Figs. 337 and 338 the dress has not altered much, the only difference being in the collar of the tunic, which is surmounted by a neatly goffered band.

Luxury in clothing prevailed amongst the London apprentices as it did amongst people of all degrees. The merchants, naturally enough, disapproved of such ostentation on the part of their apprentices: and in consequence the Lord Mayor and Common Council enacted the following *Regulations recommended for the Apparel of London Apprentices* in 1582:

'That from thenceforth no Apprentice whatsoever should presume, (1) To wear any apparel but what he receives from his Master.

(2) 'To wear no hat within the City and Liberty thereof, nor anything instead thereof, but a woollen cap, without any silk in or about the same.

(3) 'To wear no ruffles, cuffs, loose collar, nor other thing than a ruff at the collar, and that only of a yard and a half long.

(4) 'To wear no doublets, but what were made of canvas, fustian, sackcloth, English leather, or woollen cloth, and without being enriched with any manner of gold, silver, or silk.

Fig. 802.
Apprentice of the
1560's–70's

(5) 'To wear no other coloured cloth or kersey, in hose or stockings, than white, blue, or russet.

(6) 'To wear little breeches, of the same stuffs as the doublets, and without being stitched, laced, or bordered.

(7) 'To wear a plain upper coat of cloth or leather, without pinking, stitching, edging, or silk about it.

(8) 'To wear no other surcote than a cloth gown or cloak, lined or faced with cloth, cotton, or bays, with a fixed round collar, without stitching, garding, lace, or silk.

(9) 'To wear no pumps, slippers, nor shoes, but of English leather, without being pinked, edged, or stitched; nor girdles, nor garters, other than of crewel, woollen, thread, or leather, without being garnished.

Fig. 803.   Fig. 804.
Apprentices of the 1580's-90's

(10) 'To wear no sword, dagger, or other weapon but a knife; nor a ring, jewel of gold, nor silver, nor silk in any part of his apparel.

'That no apprentice should frequent, or go to any dancing, fencing, or musical schools, nor keep any chest, press, or other place for the keeping of apparel or goods, but in his Master's house.'

Here are two of these jolly fellows (Figs. 803 and 804), apprentices of the 1580's and onwards. They filled the pit at the theatre, and indulged in all kinds of pranks and escapades, to say nothing of smashing windows and pates with their cudgels. They are dressed as regulations prescribed. The caps should be noticed: Fig. 803 has a knitted woollen cap, like that in Fig. 855, while his companion, wearing his winter 'surcote' or cloak, sports a wool cap of the only type which might bear slight ornamentation in needlework.

YEOMEN

'Yeomen,' says Harrison, 'are those, which by our law (and lawyers) are called "Legales hommes," free men born English, and may dispend of their own free land in yearly revenue to the sum of 40s. sterling—or six pound as mony goeth in our times.'

'Yeoman—a settled or staid man—married and of some years, betaketh himself to stay in the place of his abode for the better maintenance of himself and his family.'

But the yeoman soon ceased to be a stay-at-home.

'This sort of people have a certain pre-eminence and more estimation than labourers, and (the common sort) of artificers, and these commonly live wealthily, keep good houses, and travel to get riches. They are also for the most part farmers to gentlemen, and with grazing, frequenting of markets, and keeping servants (not idle servants as the gentlemen doth, but such as get both their own and part of their masters' living) do come to great wealth, insomuch that many of them are able, and do buy the lands of unthrifty gentlemen, and often setting their sons to the schools, to the universities, and to the Inns of Court; or otherwise leaving them sufficient lands whereupon they may live without labour, do make them (their said sons) by those means to become gentlemen.'

Fig. 805. A Farmer

Yeomen were not addressed 'Master,' but 'Goodman,' as 'Goodman Smith.' 'In matters of law these and the like are called thus Giles Jewd, yeoman, by which addition they are exempt from the vulger and common sorts.'

The wealth of English yeomen always attracted the envious attention of foreigners. 'Many a yeoman here keeps greater state and a more opulent table than the nobles in Germany. He must be an unskilled farmer who does not possess gilt silver salt-cellars, silver cups and spoons.'

A yeoman in his best attire would pass for any well-to-do burgher, and his costume is exemplified in Fig. 800.

An opulent farmer living in the wilds of the country is seen in Fig. 805. His cote or coat is not unlike that worn by Fig. 610, except that it is made of cloth or linen.[1] It is worn over his shirt, to which the small ruff is attached, but he has a doublet at home. Trunk hose, hosen, long boots of soft leather, and a curiously shaped straw hat comprise his outfit when attending a market at the nearest town.

LOWER CLASSES

A young man of the people (Fig. 806) is quite smartly dressed. Over his linen shirt with turned-down collar and cuffs, he might wear a doublet, but our friend here has a jerkin of soft leather with a turned-down collar,

[1] Ancestor of the smock worn by countrymen.

and fastened by pewter buttons. To this, sleeves of cloth are tied at the shoulders by ribands, so that when the fancy takes him he can wear his jerkin without sleeves, exposing those of his shirt which he could roll up at will. His trunk-hose or slops, of moderate proportions, are of cloth braided and stitched with a contrasting colour. The hosen are hand-knitted, or perhaps they are the latest machine-made, and are tied with garters. A cloth cloak

Fig. 806.
A Dashing Young Fellow

Fig. 807. A Master Seaman
(late sixteenth century)

is slung from the back, and the hat of beaver or felt has pheasants' feathers stuck through the band. Altogether a pleasing costume.

No history of costume of the Elizabethan era is complete without a description of the dress worn by seamen. It must be understood that at this time there was no recognized uniform, but a serviceable outfit was provided for men attached to the Navy.

Fig. 807 is taken from a woodcut on a work on *Navigation* by Mariner Martine Curtis, and shows a master seaman of the latter part of the sixteenth century. The jacket, sometimes with sleeves, sometimes without, is cut to fit the shoulders, and hangs in folds to just below the waist-line; this one has close-fitting sleeves, and fastens with one button at the throat, and is not unlike that worn by Chaucer's shipman (Fig. 374, vol. ii). Under this was worn a shirt with small collar of white Hamborough linen or canvas. The galli-gaskins of coarse cloth, cut very wide and pleated into a waist-band buckled in front, taper down and fasten round the knee. These and the jacket were made of woollen cloth or rugge lined with canvas. His stockings are of thick knitted wool or kersey and his shoes of strong leather. The high crown cap of cloth lined with canvas turns up round the head to form a brim. A seaman always carried a dagger or knife slung to the waist-belt,

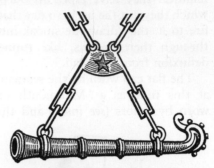

Fig. 808. An Admiral's Whistle

and some more important seamen had a whistle hung round the neck, a master mariner's being of silver and a high officer's of gold.

Fig. 808 shows a mariner's whistle and chain from the painted glass in

Fig. 809. A Seaman, 1580's–90's

Castle Hedingham Church. It was the badge, charged with a mullet, of the thirteenth Earl of Oxford as Lord High Admiral.

The power of the magnet was known as early as the twelfth century, and by the sixteenth century the mariner's compass became the germ of the new science of navigation, and was being used by all the seamen of Europe. The seaman (Fig. 807) holds one in his left hand, and in his right a 'cross-staff' or 'forestaff,' a contrivance for measuring the angles between the fixed stars or the sun and the sea horizon.

The seaman (Fig. 809) comes from an Illum. MS. and belongs to the 1590's. His doublet is just an ordinary one like those worn by people in general, but his leg-coverings called 'trousers' are a distinctive item of nautical dress. These were made of coarse white linen and frequently striped with colour: in the drawing a spiral band of two colours encircles the leg. Socks or stockings of any shade and black shoes were worn ordinarily, but on deck seamen often went bare-footed; and a full-fledged seafaring man was hardly ever without his tobacco and pipe. Fig. 810 shows a sixteenth-century clay pipe four and a half inches long from bowl to mouthpiece. According to

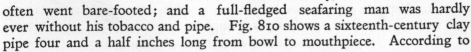

a foreigner the art of smoking has changed very little since Elizabethan days; for he tells us that 'the English are constantly smoaking tobacco and in this manner: they have pipes on purpose made of clay, into the farther end of which they put the herb, so dry that it may be rubbed into powder, and putting fire to it, they draw the smoak into their mouths, which they puff out again through their nostrils, like funnels, along with it plenty of phlegm and defluxion from the head.'

The flat cap worn by the seaman (Fig. 809) was of knitted wool, and known at this time as a 'Monmouth cap' (see p. 734). A 'thrum cap' was also worn by sailors (see inset) and this is described on p. 734.

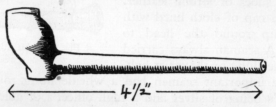

Fig. 810. A Clay Pipe

A person of no importance volunteered his services under Don Juan of Austria for the extermination of the Turks. On the morning of the Battle of Lepanto, this soldier lay sick of the fever in the *Marquesa*, the flagship of Giovanni Andrea Doria,[1] but rose, sought, and obtained the command of twelve soldiers posted in a position of importance exposed to the hottest of the enemy's fire. There he remained until the battle was over at four of the clock, receiving the only distinction ever conferred upon him—the loss of 'the movement of his left hand for the honour of the right.' Don Juan, Doria, and Colonna, world-wide heroes of the sixteenth century, joined their ancestors and were forgotten, for who in the twentieth century has ever heard of them? The warrior sleeps in the Convent of Trinitarian Nuns, Madrid; his work is known to all the world, for every one has read *Don Quixote*.

Fig. 811. Cervantes, 1571

Miguel de Cervantes was baptized at Alcalá de Henares, 9th October 1547, and studied at Salamanca and Madrid. His early career was adventurous; some time after his Lepanto experiences he was captured by Algerian pirates (1575), and made galley-slave for five years until he was ransomed. From 1582

[1] Nephew and heir of the great Andrea Doria (see p. 386).

he was writing copiously for the stage, so that it seems unlikely that he served at sea again.   The immortal *Don Quixote* appeared in Madrid in 1605, and instantly attained such popularity that it was translated into almost every language.

Cervantes died in his house in the Calle de León, Madrid, 23rd April 1616. Fig. 811 is from a portrait pronounced by a great authority on the subject to be a good likeness, and shows the kind of hat sometimes worn by Spanish seamen (*see also* Figs. 342 and 343).

PEASANTS AND THE POOR

'The Last sort of People of England are day labourers, poor husbandmen, and some retailers (which have no free land) copyholders, and all artificers,

Fig. 812. A Peasant or Farm Hand   Fig. 813. A Peasant

as tailors, shoemakers, carpenters, brickmakers, masons, etc.   As for slaves and bondmen we have none'—which is not quite true about bondmen. 'Labourers have neither voice nor authority in the commonwealth, but are to be ruled, and not to rule others.'   'Husbandmen and artificers were never so excellent in their trades as at this present.'

Although we of to-day may think that the lower classes of the sixteenth century were downtrodden, they loved their Queen and were very grateful to her. They were certainly happier during her reign than they had ever been before and long retained an affectionate regard for her memory.

In Fig. 812, a well-to-do farm hand in working kit wears a heuk of coarse linen over an ill-fitting doublet or shirt bound at the waist by a leather belt; his breeches are of cloth, his stockings of thick knitted wool, and his rather clumsy shoes of black leather. Various hats were worn, but most of them had wide brims and were made of cloth, felt, or straw. A leather wallet is slung over his shoulders, and he carries a shepherd's crook with shovel-like end.

As regards the real poor, their style of clothing was much the same as that of the early Tudor period, its chief characteristics being a long-sleeved tunic reaching to the knees, cloth hosen, and a felt or straw hat. They were usually content with the cast-off clothing of their betters.

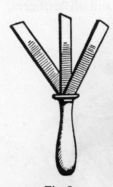

Fig. 814.
Leper's Rattle

There is a trace of the medieval lingering in this (Fig. 813) costume of a peasant. The tunic is loose, made of a coarse material fastened up the front by two straps and bound at the waist with a strap to which a pouch is attached. Sometimes full slops are seen worn under the tunic; the legs are covered with ill-fitting hosen, often tied below the knee, and the feet thrust into cockers. A hood sometimes took the place of a hat, but often both were worn, as of old. If necessary a cloak would be thrown over the shoulders.

A poor man is described at this time as 'having an old ragged doublet, and a torn pair of breeches with his hose out at heels, and a pair of old broken slip shoon on his feete, a rope about his middle instead of a girdle, on his head an old greasie cap, which had so many holes in it that his haire started through it.'

The enclosures for sheep pasture had been going on since the beginning of the century and in consequence many peasants were deprived of their livelihood and turned adrift. The dissolution of the monasteries (1536–9) greatly increased the number of beggars, outcasts, and vagabonds, many of whom had previously lived in the service of the monasteries, and now had to take to the roads and huddle on common or waste land. These, the genuine paupers, known as the 'upright,' swelled the lawless throng considerably, joining dispossessed monks and 'rufflers'—men disbanded from the army, with their families. 'Counterfeit cranks' simulated all kinds of ailments and diseases, including leprosy if they cared to ostracize themselves from the public (though not from their fellows) by carrying a leper's rattle (Fig. 814). Of wood, the centre was rigid, the two flaps being attached to it by a piece of leather.

'Clapperdudgeons' ingeniously disfigured their persons with artificial sores and wounds, besides being ever ready with a dagger. Most of them were addicted to strong liquors whenever they got a chance of purloining any; in fact, the word 'booze' first came into use among them.

Fig. 815 is a vagabond of the most dilapidated sort, whose threadbare and ragged garments beggar description. The hat (probably stolen) is the only respectable part of his attire: cloak, 'patched and unseemly' cote, hosen in process of separation into fashionable upper- and netherstocks, and single shoe, all combine to produce a picturesque ensemble. His wallet is interest-

Fig. 815. A Vagabond

Fig. 816. A Gaoler with Keys

ing because it shows the primitive method of rolling up his few belongings in a piece of material and tying it to a strap over the shoulder, as first mentioned under Fig. 91.

From such a plausible vagabond to a gaoler is but a step. One can hardly place a gaoler (Fig. 816) socially, but his position *after* a vagabond is suitable. His clothes are very ordinary: a leather tunic over the doublet as a safeguard against molesting, slops, hosen, and shoon. The block felt hat has a twisted hatband. A bunch of keys (*one inset*) is attached to his waistbelt by a chain, and he carries a rod. This drawing is made from an engraving of Alexander Andrew, the brutal gaoler of Newgate.

MIDDLE - CLASS WOMEN

Foreign visitors were naturally interested in Englishwomen, and commented favourably upon their good looks and smart appearance; the amount of liberty they enjoyed caused no little surprise. Thus: 'The women are charming and by nature so mighty pretty. They do not falsify, paint, or bedaub themselves [?] as in Italy or other places; but they are somewhat awkward in their style of dress: they dress in splendid stuffs, and many a one wears three cloth gowns or petticotes, one over the other.' Again: 'The women are beautiful, fair, well-dressed, and modest—they go about the streets without any covering either of huke or mantle, hood, veil, or the like. Married women only wear a hat both in the street and in the house; those unmarried go without a hat. Ladies of distinction cover their faces with silken masks or vizards.'

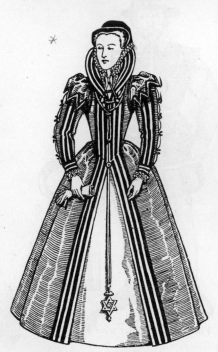

'The women have much more liberty than perhaps in any other place; they also know well how to make use of it, for they go dressed out in exceedingly fine clothes, and give all their attention to their ruffs and stuffs. All English women are accustomed to wear hats and gowns cut after the old German fashion.'

In fact, 'the womenfolk in England wish to be in at everything.'

Fig. 817. A Gentlewoman, 1567

GENTLEWOMEN

The disdainful lady (Fig. 817) steps from her portrait dating 1567. Her high collar and ruff have been alluded to under Fig. 607, but the shoulder pieces are rather unusual. The dress is of black silk banded with black velvet, and is of the style worn by gentlewomen in both town and country during the first half of the reign, indoors as well as for walking. An Elizabethan lady when out walking had one man servitor before, and another behind.

The drawing (Fig. 818) is of Catherine, the second wife of Randolph Flexney, Mayor of Oxford, and is taken from the mural enamelled brass in St. Michael's Church. She died in 1567 and her husband in 1578, so the costume shown is that worn as a 'best gown' during the 60's and 70's. There is an old-fashioned touch about the black velvet partlet and the turned-back sleeves of the red cloth dress; as also about the false sleeves of cloth of gold

and the white waist scarf. The skirt with a short train edged with passamayne opens over a black velvet underskirt. The headdress is shown in

Fig. 818. Mistress Flexney, 1567

Fig. 819. fflorence Wyndham, 1572

more detail in Fig. 887. This costume was worn by the lady when she joined
her husband at municipal ceremonies.

This lady (Fig. 819) possesses the unusual name
of fflorence.[1] She is the wife of John Wyndham, Esq., of St. Decumin's, Watchet, who died
in 1572, to whose memory this dutiful spouse
erected the brass which includes herself, although
she did not pass out until twenty-four years
later. The style of dress is that worn during
the period 1565–75, and the material would be
cloth or perhaps velvet, braided with silk or gold.
The mahoitered sleeves are very up to date
with their slashings and braidings. Fig. 820
gives this sleeve on a larger scale. The cross-
barred braided sleeves on the forearms are in
the fashion of the moment. Fig. 949 is a rubbing
of the pattern on the under-skirt (not shown in
Fig. 819) which doubtless was a brocade. The

Fig. 820. Mahoitered Sleeve

[1] It has usually been understood that Florence Nightingale was the first to bear this name, having
been born at Florence in 1823.

reader should notice the French hood and the ornament at the end of the girdle. Her shoe is described under Fig. 902.

One of Mary Stuart's many faithful attendants is represented in Fig. 821, which is taken partly from a portrait and partly from a contemporary engraving, dating 1572, of Mary Ann Waltham, who was with the Scottish Queen during her imprisonment at Fotheringay Castle. Her dress is of black silk garded with black velvet. The bodice is cut low off the shoulders; the sleeves fit closely below the elbow, and are mahoitered above; surrounding the waist-line are small loops of the same materials. The chemisette is

Fig. 822. A Lady of 1571
(Crest of the Goldsmiths)

Fig. 821 (*left*). Mistress Waltham, 1572

embroidered with fine black silk over the folds of the white cambric round the throat, low-cut shoulders, and bust. There is a necklace of jet beads; and a girdle of black leather, decorated throughout with cut steel, holds the black velvet pouch with mirror. The headdress is given in Fig. 868.

The original grant of crest and supporters to the arms of the Goldsmiths' Company, dated 1571, shows the crest of a demi-lady rising from clouds above the crest-wreath. This was 'tricked' and tinctured at the time, and the lady is dressed in the fashion of that year. She is drawn to a larger scale in Fig. 822. The dress is violet velvet trimmed with gold passamayne, and notice should be taken of the lines on the bodice. Mahoitered sleeves are of velvet, with close ones of turquoise blue silk banded with gold, and white puffings; the under-skirt is of cloth of gold. A small ruff surrounds the face above a stand-up collar of black velvet, to which the white lawn partlet is attached; over this is placed a carcanet of jewels. The headdress of blue silk and gold has an attifet front which surrounds the puffed-out hair. Scales of the period are just like modern ones, only these have a loop with a tassel hanging from the top (*see also* p. 763).

The two ladies (Figs. 788 and 790), although visiting Bermondsey some time in the 1580's, are not so up to date in their costumes as the gentlemen accompanying them. The all-in-one garment worn by the lady (Fig. 790), of maize colour braided with black over an under-skirt of turquoise blue, is very similar to the over-robe shown in Fig. 607, but the fawn hat and feather,

Fig. 823. Mistress Southcote, 1585   Fig. 824. Mistress D'Arcy, 1593

as also the black hat worn by the other lady (Fig. 788), are definitely of a later period. The latter wears a fawn dress with a gold-coloured under-skirt. Each lady carries a small wrap draped over the right forearm, and both are obviously unmarried—their partlets being open at the throat.

Fig. 823 represents the dress with over-robe worn by many women of gentle birth and position during the latter part of the reign, and frequently met with in effigies and brasses. This is from the effigy of Elizabeth, wife of Sir John Southcote at Witham, who died in 1585. The plain underdress is of black silk, the front of the pointed bodice being buttoned up to the high collar supporting the small ruff. The overdress is of black velvet, with two rolled shoulder pieces and full sleeves. It is turned back with sable. The whole, which resembles that of Mary Stuart (Fig. 602), is of dignified richness and simplicity. It must be borne in mind that such ladies were shown wearing their best gowns, which often dated twenty years earlier.

The gentle damosel (Fig. 792) wears a simplified edition of fashionable attire of the 1580's, although the sleeves are not very up to date and at the neck is a wide frill instead of a goffered ruff. The hairdressing, of course, is quite stylish.

Margaret Syllyarde, the wife of Thomas D'Arcy of Tolleshunt D'Arcy (Fig. 824), well represents the costume of her class, and dates 1593. The dress is in the same style as Lady Southcote's underdress, but with the

Fig. 825. Dame Steward, 1596   Fig. 826. A Widow   Fig. 827

skirt open up the front. The full sleeves are decorated with embroidery after the French fashion.

There is quite a French flavour, too, about the dress worn by Dame Steward (Fig. 825) and yet it is not unlike Fig. 824. The only differences are that the former wears a larger ruff and the sleeves are spirally puffed or padded, a mode quite usual at this time. The French hairdressing is uncovered, whereas Mistress D'Arcy and Lady Southcote wear French hoods. The front of the bodice in both figures shows the same lines and absence of decoration; though Mistress D'Arcy's is formed of folds of silk, the other being of braids. The effigy of Dame Steward at Teversham, Cambs, dates 1596.

The kneeling figure (Fig. 826) of Dame Constantia, 'widdow' of Sir Thomas Lucy, Kt., of Charlecote, Warwickshire, who died in 1603, shows widow's garb at the end of the century.   The plain black silk or cloth dress is of fashionable cut, worn over the wheel farthingale, and has a wide fold of the same material hanging from the shoulders down the back and well on to the ground.   Over this is worn a hood lined with white, wired out to frame the face and ruff. A side view is given in Fig. 827.

'Mistress Minx, a *Merchant's* wife, that will eat no cherries forsooth, but when they are at twenty shillings a pound, that looks as simperingly as if she were besmeared, and jets it as gingerly as if she were dancing the canaries:

Fig. 828. A Merchant's Wife

Fig. 829.   Fig. 830.

Town Gossips

she is so finical in her speech, as though she spake nothing but what she had first sewed over before in her samplers, and the puling accent of her voice is like a feigned treble, or one's voice that interprets to the puppets.   What should I tell how squeamish she is in her diet, what toil she puts her poor servants unto, to make her looking glasses in the pavement?   How she will not go into the fields, to cower on the green grass, but she must have a coach for her convoy; and spends half a day in pranking herself if she be invited to any strange place?'   The merchant's wife in Fig. 828 well illustrates Thomas Nash's description of 1592; she might be one of the Merry Wives of Windsor.

The details of the doublet are taken from the original in the London Museum, made of a dull red woollen stuff spotted with white.   The black braidings down the front and forearms are frayed at the ends, and fixed down with a button in the centre. The welts, wings, and cuttes are edged with the same braid. A bolster sets her skirt well out at the back. 'The women also hath doublets and jerkins, as men hath here, buttoned up the breast, and made with wings, welts, and pinions on the shoulder points, as man's apparel is in all respects.'

'Good morrow, Mistress Gossip; how by my truly I am glad to see you in health.' No doubt the conversation soon turns to the subject of clothes,

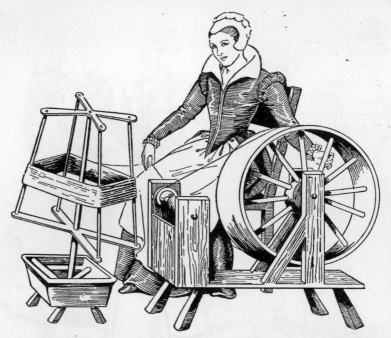

Fig. 831. An Elizabethan Spinster

in which Fig. 830 would have a decided advantage by reason of her smarter costume—in fact, her companion seems to be meditating a reply when given the opportunity. Both are typical women of the bourgeois class. They step from an Illum. MS. dated about 1568. Fig. 829 is the simpler of the two, and in the original her dress is of grey woollen material with a collar and garding of black velvet. The under-sleeves are treated somewhat in the same manner as shown in Fig. 819, but appear to be tucked and banded with braid. The under-skirt is a dull pink, and she wears a posy on her bosom.

The other (Fig. 830) is in a rich brown garded with black velvet; her under-skirt is pink ornamented with appliqué work. A white sash is tied round the waist, and both carry gloves.

LOWER CLASSES

The spinster (Fig. 831) of the latter part of the century, is a cheerful little person and sits all alone, so the contemporary saying 'Women's tongues are like lambs' tails which seldom stand still' cannot apply to her. She is using the old-fashioned wheel to wind bobbins, revolving the wheel with her left hand and with the other guiding the flax or wool from off the winder to the bobbin which is set in the spindle.

Spinning-wheels with a treadle attached were invented by a German in 1533, but they were not in general use in England until about this time.[1]

This woman (Fig. 831) is plainly dressed in a dark gown, with just a touch of smartness in the rolled shoulder pieces and well-fitting pointed bodice. The starched collar denotes that she belongs to the latter part of the century.

The dress of the laundress (Fig. 718) is homely, but a certain modishness is given to it by the turn-over collar, puffs on the shoulders, and smart little ruff. The sleeves which extend to the wrists are rolled up, as she is so much engaged with her goffering.

This sober matron (Fig. 832) going to market is not above doing a bit of charing now and again. 'Chare-women' were pretty general in the second

Fig. 832. A Market Woman

half of the century, and some of these ladies had a liking for the bottle. 'Brains waxt as mellow as a pippin at Michaelmas' was said of an old woman who drank too much. This good woman (Fig. 832) appears in her best gown of substantial woollen cloth, in dull greens, browns, or blues and banded with black velvet. Under the bodice and over the shift or chemisette was often worn a corset-like bodice, usually without sleeves, but occasionally with close-fitting ones. The apron is almost indispensable with this class of person, and so is the pouch. It must be a fine day for her marketing, otherwise she would have a cloak.

The country woman (Fig. 833) is clothed in brown homespun, a white linen apron, ungathered and pinned round the waist like a towel, a folded kerchief round her shoulders, and a muffler over her mouth as a protection against cold.

Fig. 833. A Farmer's Wife

[1] No spinning-wheel of the late sixteenth century seems to have survived in England.

III ²—Z

It should be noticed that some of these women of middle and lower class are wearing goffered ruffs and turnover collars to their bodices, and carry gloves, thus adding greatly to their respectability.

A young country girl of the early and middle part of the reign is shown in Fig. 834. The plain stuff dress has a full skirt gathered to a bodice which is tied up the front with bows of riband: the full sleeves are also tied on in the same way, and could be dispensed with at will. This dress is lined with cotton, perhaps of ochre colour, which is seen on the turned-down collar and where the skirt is turned up to show a striped petticote. The stand-up ruff is attached to the chemisette, and the sleeves of the latter are rolled up because this young person is very business-like.

A.

B.

Fig. 834. A Country Girl

Another treatment of a bodice is shown in A. This would be worn over a similar chemisette, with a skirt of the same or of a different material. A third bodice is shown in B, which was attached to the skirt. It buttons up the front, and has a roll collar, loops on the shoulders, and sewn-on sleeves.

Since a wedding interests only the womenfolk the following description of

A Tudor Country Wedding Procession

is inserted in the section devoted to them, although it also includes the costume of the men. The details are taken from an account of an actual wedding at which it was hoped the Queen, who was staying in the neighbourhood, would be present. Those taking part were marshalled thus:

'First, all the lusty lads and bold bachelors of the parish, suitably every one with his blue buckram bridelace upon a branch of green broom (cos rosemary is skant there) tied on his left arm (for at that side lies the heart), and his alder pole for a spear in his right hand, in martial order ranged on afore, two and two in rank: some with a hat, some in a cap, some a cote, some a jerkin, some for lightness in his doublet and his hose, clean trussed with a point [of the doublet] afore: some boots and no spurs, he spurs and no boots, and he neither nother: one a saddle, another a pad or a pannell fastened with a cord, for girts [girths] were scarce; and these to the number of sixteen active riding men and well beseen: but the bridegroom formost, in his father's tawny worsted jacket (for his friends were fain that he should be a bridegroom before the Queen), a fair straw hat with a capital crown steeple-wise on his head: a pair of harvest gloves on his hands, as a sign of good husbandry: a pen and ink-horn at his back; for he would be known to be bookish: lame of a leg that in his youth was broken at football: well beloved yet of his mother that lent him a new muffler for a napkin that was tied to his girdle for loosing. After these horsemen, a lively Morris dance, according to the ancient manner, six dancers, Maid Marian, and the fool. Then, three pretty pusels, as bright as a breast of bacon, of a thirty year old apiece, that carried three special spice-cakes of a bushel of wheat (they had it by measure out of my Lord's bakehouse) before the Bride: coyly with set countenance, and lips as demurely simpering, as it had been a mare cropping of a thistle. After these a lonely lubber walked, freckle-faced, red-headed, clean trussed in his doublet and his hosen taken up now in deed by commission, for that he was so loth to come forward, for reverence belike of his new cut canvas doublet; and would by his good will have been but an onlooker, but found to be a meet actor for his office: that was to bear the bridecup, formed of a sweet sucket barrel, a fair turned foot set to it, all seemly be-silvered and parcel gilt, adorned with a beautiful branch of broom, gaily begilded for rosemary: from which, two broad bridelaces of red and yellow buckram begilded, and gallantly streaming by such wind as there was (for he carried it aloft). This gentle cupbearer, yet had his freckled physiognomy somewhat unhappily infested as he went, by the busy flies, that flocked about the bridecup for the sweetness of the sucket that it savoured on: but he like a tall fellow, withstood their malice stoutly (see what manhood may do) beat them away, killed them by scores, stood his charge and marched on in good order.

'Then followed the worshipful Bride, led (after the country manner) between two ancient parishioners, honest townsmen. God wot, and an ill-smelling was she; a thirty year old, of colour brown bay, not very beautiful indeed, but ugly, foul ill favoured; yet marvellous fain of the office, because she heard say she should dance before the Queen, in which feat she thought she would foot it as finely as the best. Well, after this bride came there by two and two, a dozen damsels for bridesmaids: that for favour, attire, for fashion and cleanliness; were as meet for such a bride as a wooden ladle for a porridge pot.'

A few notes are necessary to explain some of the details in the above.

The 'lusty lads' escorting the bridegroom would be wearing clothes of all styles, the genuine country louts in garments like Figs. 812 and 813. The more polished, if such there were, might appear garbed as Fig. 805, or even 806. Each lad carried an accessory to show that he was a good horseman, and also to suggest that he formed one of a mounted escort. The 'pannell' carried was a saddle, a treeless pad without cantle, such as was generally used when riding a donkey. The awkward 'lonely lubber,' like so many of his type, looked most unsuitably dressed in his smart new-cut doublet. Had he the good sense to appear in his everyday peasant togs, clean and tidy, he would have cut a much more presentable figure. 'Sucket' was a confection of fruits preserved in sugar, either candied or in syrup. The bridegroom himself would certainly endeavour to rig himself out smartly, either as shown in Fig. 806, or even 800. It is particularly stated that he wore a jacket or jerkin, which was probably at least twenty years old, having been worn by his father. The crown of his hat was high—quite in the fashion of the time. The costume worn by Fig. 806 would suit this young man admirably.

The three 'pretty pusels' or maidens of not too tender years would be in the style shown in Fig. 834, but, of course, with the skirt let down. The bridesmaids were clothed much the same, and probably had made themselves new dresses for the occasion.

For a description of the wedding dress of a Tudor bride of middle class, we use the *Delectable Historie of Ihon Winchcombe*, as this work was not published until 1596. The descriptions nevertheless apply to the costume of the reign of Henry VIII as well as to that of Elizabeth.

Winchecombe's first wife was a widow much older than himself, and possessed a considerable fortune. In fact, it was her money which financed the business of the wealthy clothier 'Jack of Newbury,' as he was familiarly known.

The second Mistress Winchecombe was a young woman, and we have a description of her as she appeared on her wedding day. She wore 'a gown of sheep's russet and a kyrtle of fine worsted: her head attired with a billiment of gold and her hair as yellow as gold hanging down behind her curiously combed and plaited after the manner of those days. Shee was led to Church between two sweete boyes, with Bridelaces and rosemary tied about their silken sleeves.'

Her head attire consisted of a network caul on either side of the head, but no veil is mentioned because such an accessory was not included in a Tudor bride's wedding dress. The special adornments of a bride of the sixteenth century were rosemary and bridelaces; little posies of the former were set in the headdress or worn on the left side of the bodice, and attached to these were long narrow streamers of silk in green and blue known as 'bridelaces.'

SECTION IV: 1558–1603

HAIRDRESSING—MEN

Men's hair during the reign of Elizabeth was generally short, and several variations were introduced from abroad during the period. There was the French mode, which was short and sometimes included a wisp of hair on the cheek; the Italian, short and curled with tongs; and the Spanish, short, but long at the ears. The English nobility and gentry as a rule preferred the French (*see* p. 725) and Spanish (*see* p. 726) styles to the Italian.

While the above national characteristics will be found to be generally correct the differences between them are actually small, so that a fashionable man of any country might adopt any style which pleased or suited him.

Perhaps the simplest and most convenient style is that shown in the drawing (Fig. 835) of Philip II about 1565. The hair is quite short and straight, and smartly brushed from the forehead and temples.

The style of hairdressing worn by fashionable men in the early years of the reign is seen in Figs. 609, 611, 618, and 619. The hair was brushed forward from the crown of the head, forming curves of hair on the forehead and temples; sometimes it was long at the ears and curled. This is the early Spanish mode, and a side view of it is seen in Fig. 537.

Fig. 835. Philip II of Spain, 1565

The portrait of Sir Philip Sidney, 1577, No. 2096 in the National Portrait Gallery, shows slightly wavy hair brushed up off the face—an intermediate stage between Figs. 835 and 843.

Soon after 1571 (Lepanto) a new Spanish mode, set by Don Juan of Austria and shown in Fig. 843, was adopted by self-respecting men of all ages. The hero's hair was naturally beautifully waved, worn fairly long all over the head, and moderately brushed back: his admirers, less blessed by nature, imitated this style artificially. It is worn by the courtier (Fig. 621); the gentleman (Fig. 630) has adopted this Spanish method of brushing his hair back, but the embryo lovelock is French.

Hair curled by nature or artifice in the Italian style was becoming more favoured, and we see it in the portrait of Sir Henry Lee dated 1568, No. 2095 in the National Portrait Gallery.   Fig. 836 is a drawing of it.

For a typical style of hairdressing for men of middle class during the greater part of the reign, the portrait of the tailor by Moroni, No. 697 in the National Gallery, is a good example.

Harrison writing about the middle of the reign, and commenting upon the variety of styles, 'will say nothing of our heads, which sometimes are polled, sometimes curled, or suffered to grow at length like women's locks, many times cut off, above or under the ears, round as by a wooden dish.'

The fashions in hairdressing for the period covered by Part II are well illustrated in the various drawings commencing with Fig. 734.

The young gentleman (Fig. 837) has his hair smartly brushed off the forehead and sides in the true Don Juan style, but he has included a wisp of hair

Fig. 836. Sir Henry Lee, 1568

Fig. 837. Aetat. xxiij

or lovelock in front of his ears.   His moustaches are dressed with a sticky preparation and neatly twisted into small points; his beard of fluff is as much as he can grow at the early age of twenty-three.

Toward the end of the century it was the mode for gentlemen to 'cut their hair close on the middle of the head, letting it grow on either side.   The noblemen (Figs. 739 and 740) wear their hair decidedly long over the ears, but it is anything but close cut on the middle of the head.

It was at this period that gentlemen with scanty locks, who yearned to be in the mode, had resource to 'perriwigges' (1595); Shakespeare refers to this when he describes one of the actors in *Hamlet* (Act III, Sc. ii) as a 'periwig-pated fellow,' a ruffian whose length of hair hung about the ears and 'curled like the two ends of an old cast periwig.'

Regarding these fashions we learn from Stubbes that the barbers 'have invented such strange fashions and monstrous manners of cuttings, trimmings, shavings, and washings, that you would wonder to see.   They have one manner of cut called the French cut, another the Spanish cut; one the Dutch cut, another the Italian; one the new cut, another the old; one of the bravado-fashion, another of the mean fashion; one a gentleman's cut, another the common cut; one cut of the court, another of the country, with infinite the like varieties, which I overpass. They have also other kinds of cuts innumerable; and therefore when you come to be trimmed, they will ask you whether you will be cut to look terrible to your enemy, or amiable to your friend, grim and stern in countenance, or pleasant and demure (for they have divers kinds of cuts for all these purposes, or else they lie).'

Beards and moustaches were very general among men of all classes, and the fashions in dressing the beard are too numerous to describe. Many kinds may be seen by referring to the various drawings; Figs. 712, 851, and 854 give three varieties. Harrison writes: 'Neither will I meddle with our variety of beards, of which some are shaven from the chin like those of Turks, not a few cut short like to the beard of Marquess Otto, some made round like a rubbing-brush, others with a *pique de vant* (O! fine fashion), or now and then

Fig. 838. The Pique de Vant

suffered to grow long, the barbers being grown to be so cunning in this behalf as the tailors. And therefore if a man have a lean and straight face, a Marquess Otto's cut will make it broad and large; if it be platter-like, a long, slender beard will make it seem the narrower; if he be weasel-beaked, then much

hair left on the cheeks will make the owner look big like a bowdled hen, and so grim as a goose, if Cornelis of Chelmeresford [1] say true: many old men do wear no beards at all.' The dressing of the beard known as pique de vant, (Fig. 838) is seen worn by Henry III of France (Fig. 745), Henry of Navarre (Fig. 842), and Dr. Nevill (Fig. 712).

Besides these numerous styles and cuts of beards there were the following: the swallow-tail cut mentioned in 1596; this was also called a fork-beard, and is seen in Fig. 839; it is worn by Prince Philip (Fig. 670) and by the gentlemen (Figs. 845 and 854). 'The broad

Fig. 839. The Swallow-tail

or cathedral beard, so called because bishops and grave men of the Church anciently did wear such beards.'

---

[1] Nothing seems to be known of this worthy, but from the context he would seem to have been the author of a book on hairdressing. How interesting such a book would be if only a copy could be discovered.

'The British beard has long mochedoes [mustachios] on the higher lip, hanging down either side the chin, all the rest of the face being bare; the mouse-eaten beard is when the beard groweth scatteringly, here a tuft and there a tuft.' A 'bodkin beard' was pointed; a spade beard is shown in Fig. 840,

and a 'great round beard like a glover's paring-knife' in Fig. 841. This tool, now obsolete, is shown inset. A Cain-coloured beard was small and yellowish red, so called because in old tapestries Cain (and Judas) were represented with such beards.

'Then when the barbers had wasted a lot of time and concluded all these feats . . . it is a world to consider, how their mustachios must be preserved and laid out, from one cheek to another, yea, almost from one ear to another, and turned up like two horns towards the forehead.'

Fig. 840. The Spade

The barber asks in 1591: 'Will you have . . . a pent-house on your upper lip [a straight tooth-brush moustache] or an ally on your chin? A low curl on your head like a Bull, or dangling locke like a spaniell? Your Mustachoes sharpe at the ends like shoemakers' aules, or hanging downe to your mouth like goates' flakes? Your love-lockes wreathed with a silken twist, or shaggie to fall on your shoulders?'

Small brushes, carried in the panes and cuttes of the slops, were made expressly for the use of the beard and moustache: these, together with ornamental beard combs and 'an instrument for dividing the hair'—a comb —known as a 'gallon,' were much used, even in public.

Although the Earl of Essex is shown in Fig. 734 as a comparatively young man, he wears a full beard. It should be borne in mind that during the Elizabethan period the beard was a very much coveted appendage, and all young men of fashion anxiously cultivated its growth. Remembering this, Rosalind's

Fig. 841. The Round

kind offer, made in the epilogue of As You Like It, has considerable point:

'I would kiss as many of you as had beards that pleased me.'

This is particularly so if the part was played by a boy!

FRENCH HAIRDRESSING

The French style of hairdressing during the middle of the sixteenth century was similar to that worn at the present time, the hair being cut short.

After 1571 the hair was allowed to grow a little longer, and was brushed off the forehead in the Spanish fashion. This is shown in Figs. 654 and 655; in the nobleman (Fig. 658) it is even more pronounced.

A 'lac d'amour,' nœud, or wisp of hair, known in England as a 'love-lock,' and worn on the cheeks in front of the ears, originated amongst the coxcombs of France, and was adopted by some gentlemen of England (*see* Fig. 630). The style adopted by young Henry of Navarre about 1580 (Fig. 842) is decidedly distinctive. His hair was naturally wavy and wiry, and stood up from the head, while that of his brother-in-law, the Duc d'Anjou (Fig. 656), fast falling off from too much application of dye, is probably a periwig. 'Per-ruque' was the French for a lock of hair, and the words 'peruke' and 'periwig' are derived from it. In his later portraits as King Henry III a peruke is obvious (*see* Figs. 745 and 746). He evidently retained a certain amount of hair on his forehead which enabled him to brush it up over the peruke, thus masking the hard line.

Fig. 842. Henry of Navarre

The youth (Fig. 751) has his hair rolled back to perfection, equal to any of the ladies. By the time Henry of Navarre came to the throne, his hair must have become more amenable, or the Royal barber, in his 'checkerd-apron,' must have been specially at work for the 'sitting' of this (Fig. 752) portrait. It is certainly not so wild, and more in the mode of the day.

The type of beard worn at the French Court during the reigns of Francis II and Charles IX is illustrated in Fig. 845. Later, under Henry III, they became very pointed—the pique de vant—with little if any hair growing on the sides of the face; and moustaches were narrow with the ends turned up and sometimes down (*see* Figs. 745, 746, and 749). In Henry IV's time moustaches became more normal.

ITALIAN HAIRDRESSING

The styles of hairdressing worn by the Italian aristocracy are illustrated in Figs. 662 and 663. The young noble (Fig. 761) has adopted the earlier Spanish style, while the later Spanish mode is to be recognized in Fig. 664. Hair crimped with curling tongs was fairly general among Italians, but the coiffure worn by the gentleman in Fig. 759 suggests the East End of London in the twentieth century.

Beards dressed in the style most usual all over Europe are worn by the noble in Fig. 848 and by the doctor (Fig. 666) as well as in Fig. 759.

SPANISH HAIRDRESSING

Only the length of hair over the ears distinguished the hairdressing characteristic of Spaniards from their contemporaries in other countries. Most of the hair was cut close to the head like that worn by the upper classes in England and on the Continent.

Fig. 843 is made from the colossal statue of the Hero of Lepanto, 1571, Don Juan of Austria in full armour. It was erected at Messina in 1572, and

Fig. 843.
Don Juan of Austria,
1571

is one of the masterpieces of Andrea Calamech. It shows the method with which he dressed his golden hair—the envy of all the young bloods of Europe. Admiring him, most likely, more for this than for all his feats of military or naval glory, they made haste to cultivate the same style. The hair is waved and left moderately long, and is brushed and combed up and back off the forehead and puffed slightly above the ears, the ends mingling in waves with the hair on the back of the head. The more sober of the Spanish grandees displayed nothing out of the ordinary in their hairdressing; Fig. 768, typically Spanish of the earlier period, is an example. The hair is allowed to grow rather long over the ears and to curl slightly at the ends. That worn by the Spanish Infante (Fig. 770) has the ends rolled back over the ears.

With regard to beards, reference to Fig. 671, the usual style, and to Fig. 670, the forked or swallow-tail type, will show those generally worn during the period 1556 to 1580, when mustachios were quite normal.

During the latter part of the period—to 1603—those shown in Figs. 767 and 768 illustrate the style usually worn. The beard and mustachios seen in Fig. 769, were not unusual and certainly have distinct character. In Fig. 853 very little beard appears, and the ends of the mustachios turn up slightly.

HEADGEAR, 1558–1603

In this section the division hitherto adopted, into two periods and separate countries, cannot be followed, as it is practically impossible to distinguish the various national styles. During the first twelve years of Elizabeth's reign, the flat velvet cap, described in Chapter III, was the usual headgear of the nobility, gentry, and (in other materials) of the lower classes.

Afterwards, the crown of the cap became slightly fuller. Those shown in Figs. 653 and 611 are definitely of the flat or plate variety of older fashion, the former worn by a French, the latter by a Scottish, nobleman. The cap worn by the gentleman (Fig. 610) is in this later mode; and to prove how

Fig. 844. Charles IX, 1566

Fig. 845. Duc de Guise

universal the wearing of this type of headgear was at this period, Fig. 844 gives a French cap. It is from a portrait drawing of Charles IX made by Clouet in 1566; the same shaped cap is worn by this King in Fig. 650 (1569). In Fig. 845, a similar shaped cap, the decoration of portions of passamayne set at angles on the crown and brim, is shown; the braiding and aiglettes on the doublet of this French nobleman should be observed. Fig. 670 shows the same kind of cap worn by Philip II, and Fig. 666 by an Italian doctor.

HATS

It was about 1570 that a new shaped hat, imported from Italy, came into general fashion among well-dressed men everywhere, and became a serious rival to the flat cap. For the first appearance in this book, refer to Figs. 662 and 663—two Italian gentlemen of the late 1560's and onwards. The crown of the hat is much fuller, and the material—velvet or silk—is lined with something moderately stiff, such as a coarse muslin or fine buckram, to give richness to the folds and to prevent them from flopping too much. The crown is pleated into the brim of moderate width in Fig. 662, with a hatband to conceal the join. Fig. 663 has the same kind of crown, but the brim is very narrow and almost covered by a rouleau of twisted velvet which forms the hatband.

Possibly the introduction of this new kind of hat from Italy into England was due to the young Earl of Oxford in 1573. It is seen in Fig. 846, a drawing from his portrait; and has a much more exaggerated crown of folded velvet, a narrow brim, and a band of two rouleaux fixed by pairs of gold buttons at intervals. The hat is most rakishly worn on one side, this being a feature of young coxcombs at this period. The dignified Knights of the Garter (Fig. 623) wear similar hats, but of much more reasonable proportions and poise.

Fig. 847—this is Mr. Edward Hoby (born 1560, knighted 1582, died 1617), a smart young gentleman in his eighteenth year, who as a nephew of Lord

Fig. 846.
The Earl of Oxford, 1573

Fig. 847.
Edward Hoby, Esq., 1577

Burleigh had the entry into High Society. His youth must be the excuse for his outrageous headgear. It is made on the same principle as that worn by Lord Oxford, but is tilted at a more moderate angle; it has some beautiful gold ornaments set round the hatband, and a straight plume of deep crimson. The two gold buttons and acorn placed towards the top strike one as odd; but such fancies often took modish men. The same eccentric arrangement of the crown is apparent in the hat worn by the Duc d'Anjou in 1573 (see Fig. 656); the hatband is of gold cords caught by jewels in gold settings.

Lord Burleigh (Fig. 624), Lord Leicester (Fig. 625), and Sir Christopher Hatton (Fig. 627), all wear this type of hat, but with moderate-sized crowns, much more like the original Italian hats, shown in Figs. 662 and 663.

An Italian hat of 1589, worn by an Italian nobleman, is shown in Fig. 848. Made of velvet, usually black, the crown is cut and pleated, as mentioned earlier, into a stiff and slightly rolled brim. The join between this and the crown is masked by a fold of silk or a band of velvet, a rose or bow being placed at the side. The appearance of the crown clearly indicates that it is mounted on a stiff lining or foundation. The skull-cap worn underneath probably suggested to the ladies of Europe the use of cauls beneath their chapeaux à l'Italienne. The patterned or embroidered material used for the doublet of this gentlemen (Fig. 848) should be noticed; it is of a bold and effective design in keeping with the Italian mode.

The hat worn by Philip III of Spain (Fig. 771) although of later date (1598) is of the same shape.

Hats with stiff or hard foundations appeared in fashionable England about 1575. An actual hat of this period is in the London Museum, and Fig. 849 is a drawing of it. The crown is hard and shaped like an inverted flower-pot, and covered with a small patterned black silk and velvet brocade. The brim is bound with a small fancy braid; and the hatband is of folded satin twisted

Fig. 848. The Italian Hat

round with a braid three-eighths of an inch wide, with loops of braid one-eighth wide forming bows along its length (*inset*). The dimensions of the hat are: brim of plain black velvet $1\frac{1}{2}$ inches wide and $30\frac{1}{2}$ in circumference; the crown is $5\frac{3}{4}$ inches high and 23 round the base. The hat worn by Sir Henry Unton, 1586 (born 1557, died 1596) (Fig. 850), is shaped very much like Fig. 849, except that the top of the crown is rounded. The black silk is moulded to the foundation by silk thread

Fig. 849

worked into a pattern. The hatband of twisted silk is very wide, and almost covers the moderately wide brim. The ornament at the side is of a new design in gold and black enamel, and from it spring the fronds of an ostrich feather and an aigrette.

Sir John Hawkyns (Fig. 851) wears a hat of similar fashion which has a brim very much curled up at the sides.   The stiff crown is covered with black velvet pleated down to the hatband, the latter being ornamented with pearl and diamond buttons.   The button with the silver pin stuck through it is, indeed, a pretty conceit.   This Italian hat, worn at a jauntish angle by the admiral, shows that this famous sea-dog did not disdain the latest fashion even at the age of fifty-eight.

In Spain this type of hat was the vogue, and it is seen in Fig. 767.

Fig. 850.
Sir Henry Unton, 1586

Fig. 851.
Sir John Hawkyns

Simultaneously with the hats last described was worn another of a slightly different kind (Fig. 852) from the original in the London Museum.   It is of soft light-biscuit-coloured leather, blocked stiff and decorated with cuttes and brown silk stitchery.   The lining is rose-coloured satin which is pulled through the cuttes.   Descending from the top of the crown across the brim are strips of leather with brown silk braid down the centres and brown silk stitches set diagonally (*see at* A): the hatband is trimmed in the same way. A button fixes the top.   The flat brim, which is of double thickness, has the under-part of brown leather, cutte as shown in the portion B.   The dimensions are: brim, $1\frac{1}{2}$ inches wide and 34 in circumference; crown, 8 inches high and $28\frac{1}{2}$ in circumference at base.   In the centre front is embroidered a coat of arms of seven gold fleurs-de-lys on a blue shield.   In the drawing, the centre back is shown where there is a holder of leather and brown braid fixed to take the quill of a feather. Most feathers were attached to the hat in this manner. Hats of soft or blocked felt having high crowns and small brims were worn in England and on the Continent from about 1570 onwards. Figs. 616 and 617 show two of this kind.

In France, headgear, as lately described, was popular at the Court of Henry III, although this monarch adopted the turban (Figs. 745 and 746) which was copied by a very select few (*see* Fig. 751).

The blocked felt worn by the courtier (Fig. 750) is high-crowned with parallel sides and a moderately wide flat brim, and is decorated in front with an upstanding plume. The Duc de Joyeuse (Fig. 749) wears a similar one, but with a narrower stand-up brim edged with gold and a panache of ostrich feathers in front. Henry IV has placed his hat on the table beside him (*see* Fig. 752). Its brim is rather wider than usual. In Spain these blocked black felt hats were very general; the crowns varied in height (*see* Plate XLVI

Fig. 852

and Fig. 769) and their brims were usually narrow, a Spanish characteristic (*see also* Fig. 767). Brims also went to the other extreme, and were very wide; but these were worn by the Spanish people of all classes as a protection from sun or rain, the name 'sombrero' being applied to them.

The life-size equestrian portrait by Rubens, painted in 1602, of the Duke of Infantado, chief of the family of Mendoza and first Grandee of Spain, furnishes us with a very smart and *becoming* hat at the beginning of the seventeenth century (Fig. 853). It is probably made of black felt, but its shape could also be carried out in black velvet, silk, or satin. Its wide brim is caught on one side to the fez-shaped crown by a large ornament of jewels, in which is set a brush of black feather-fronds.

This style of hat soon found its way into England, for we find Sir Walter Raleigh painted in the same year wearing one (*see* Fig. 742). It is true it is not so large as the Spanish original, and the brim is just caught by the pointed bejewelled feather with peardrop pearl.

The date of the appearance of this stylish hat in England may be earlier if the satirist, John Marston, in his lines of 1598 is referring to this style: 'His hat, himself, small crown and huge great brim, and all the band with feathers he doth fill, which is a sign of a fantastick still.'

It is interesting to reflect that this particular befeathered shaped hat became a very handsome piece of headgear in the seventeenth century.

However, hats with high crowns were in very general use at the end of the reign, as evidenced by many contemporary illustrations.

The 'copatain' hat, i.e. coppid-peaked, of high conical or sugar-loaf shape, is represented in several drawings (Figs. 789, 791, and 798). It is usually made of blocked felt with a brim of varying width.

Fig. 853. The Duke of Infantado

Two hats of curious shape are shown in Figs. 795 and 805. The former is of blocked felt; that of the farmer is in plaited straw: both have twisted hatbands, one of silk, the other of cloth with a cord round it.

A hard blocked hat of cloth with a twisted hatband is worn by the gaoler, Fig. 816. This type of headgear was in very general use during the latter part of the reign.

A soft felt hat of conical shape, such as was used in the fifteenth century, was still worn by the commonalty, a thong of leather or cloth being tied round it to make it fit the head. The shape of one is well seen in Fig. 806, where it is decorated by a band of colour and three pheasant's feathers, but the peasant (Fig. 813) has only a plain band of cloth or leather. (Refer also to Figs. 90 and 105.)

Stubbes, as usual, unburdens himself of many caustic gibes at the expense of the headgear worn by his better-dressed fellows:

'Sometimes they wear them sharp on the crowns, pearking up like a sphere, or shaft of a steeple, standing a quarter of a yard above the crown of their heads; some more, some less, as please the phantasies of their minds. Othersome be flat and broad on the crown, like the battlements of a house. An other sort have round crowns, sometimes with one kind of band, sometimes with an other; now black, now white, now russet, now red, now green, now yellow, now this, now that, never content with one colour or fashion two days to an end . . . their Hattes be made diverse also; for some are of silk, some of velvet, some of taffetie, some of sarcenet, some of wool: and which is more curious, some of a certain kind of fine hair. These they call Bever hattes of xx, xxx, or xl shillings price fetched from beyond the seas, from whence a great sort of other varieties do come. And so common a thing it is, that every servingman, countryman, and other, even all indifferently, do wear of these hattes. For he is of no account or estimation amongst men, if he have not a velvet or a taffatie hatte, and that must be pincked and cunningly carved of the best fashion; and good profitable hattes be they, for the longer you wear them the fewer holes they have. They have also taffeta hatts of all colours quilted, and imbroydered with gold, silver, and silks of sundry sorts, with monsters, antiques, beasts, foules, and all manner of pictures and images upon them, wonderful to behold. Besides this, of late there is a new fashion of wearing their hatts sprung up amongst them, which they father upon the Frenchman, namely to wear them without bands; but how unseemely (I will not say how assy) a fashion that is, let the wise judge. . . . An other sort (as phantastical as the rest) are content with no kind of hatt without a great bunch of feathers of diverse and sundry colours, peaking on top of their heads, not unlike (I dare not say) cockscombes.'

Unfortunately, few of these curiosities have been handed down to us in portraits.

CAPS

A 'mortar-board' of the latter part of this reign is worn by Gabriel Good-man, Dean of Westminster 1561–1601, in his portrait bust in Ruthin Church, Fig. 854. The square top is thick, about an inch, and is attached to a cap pointed on the forehead and covering the back of the head to the level of the lobes of the ears. For the headgear of another Doctor of Divinity, see Fig. 781; of the Law, see Figs. 782, 783, and 666. Caps worn by members of the universities are shown in Figs. 784 and 785.

A cap, a development of the French bonet, is worn by the liveryman (Fig. 798), and hats modelled on the Italian fashion are seen in Figs. 797 and 796.

Knitted wool caps were much worn by apprentices and young men of the lower orders. School-boys were supposed to wear caps, and the Colloquies contain directions

Fig. 854. The Dean of Westminster

as to what was to be done with them: but boys went bareheaded when they could and despised the cap as effeminate.

III²—2 A

The construction of these caps is explained under Fig. 377; and Fig. 855 shows an Elizabethan boy wearing one of these wool caps.

Another kind of wool cap, chiefly worn by apprentices, is seen in Fig. 804; this is flower-pot shape, and round it some kind girl friend (or his mother) has worked three rows of coloured wool.

Sailors also wore a knitted woollen cap, something like Fig. 855, but more of the nineteenth-century tam-o'-shanter shape. This kind was known as a 'Monmouth cap,' and is well shown in Fig. 809. During the first part of the sixteenth century the best were made at Monmouth. In 1590 the manufacture removed to Worcestershire, but the name of Monmouth caps [1] was still retained.

Fig. 855. Woollen Cap

For extra warmth seamen often wore a cap that fitted tight, and could not be blown off. It was composed of coarse canvas shaped like a shallow flower-pot; the ends of the wool, cut off from woven lengths of cloth, were knotted through the canvas like wool mats to-day. Such caps, known as 'thrummed caps' (see inset, Fig. 809), had a shaggy appearance, and were dyed a brown or blue.

The master seaman (Fig. 807) wears a superior cap of cloth made like an elongated flower-pot and fairly stiff to stand up high: the base of it is turned up to form a brim and show the lining. The hat worn by the Spanish marine (Fig. 811) is exactly like the felt hat with a brim which one often sees to-day.

For the description of *night-caps* see p. 617.

ETIQUETTE CONNECTED WITH HEADGEAR

Raising the hat was a fashion in vogue at the Court of Burgundy towards the end of the fifteenth century, and became universal on the Continent during the sixteenth century and in England during Elizabeth's reign (*see* Fig. 736). Towards the end of the century it became the general custom for gentlemen to remove their hats indoors, and in the presence of the Queen out of doors. Certain people had the privilege granted them by the sovereign to wear their hats in the Presence. This hereditary privilege was recognized in France from this time almost to the beginning of the nineteenth century. In the two celebrated paintings of a Court ball given at the Louvre in the 1580's, several of the gentlemen have their hats on, and, of course, the bridegroom (Fig. 749), who was a special friend of Henry III.

The custom of remaining uncovered in the presence of the Queen, which had grown up (perhaps more in compliment to her womanhood than to her

[1] Fluellen in *Henry V* says that Welshmen wore leeks in their Monmouth caps (Act IV, Sc. vii). It must be remembered that this play was first acted in 1599, and Monmouth caps were well established before this date. But in the days of Henry V they were unknown. Another snag!

sovereignty) during the early years of her reign (if not during Mary's) became firmly established before the end of the century. Thus: on one occasion in 1597 when the French Ambassador was summoned to an audience with the Queen, who was awaiting him in the Privy Chamber, De Maisse writes that he was led 'across a chamber of moderate size wherein were the Guards of the Queen and thence into the Presence Chamber, as they call it, in which all present, even though the Queen be absent, remain uncovered.' The same observer relates that when in the Queen's presence 'because I was uncovered, from time to time she signed to me with her hand to be covered, which I did. Soon after she caused a stool (*see* p. 619) to be brought, whereon I sat and began to talk to her.'

Visitors from abroad noticed that all the gentlemen in attendance on the Queen were bareheaded. 'Whoever speaks to her, it is kneeling; now and then she raises some with her hand.'

It was considered bad form to appear in a hat on public or ceremonial occasions without a cloak or gown over the doublet. The privilege of remaining covered, not only at Court, was fairly common during the sixteenth century in cases of *baldness, ringworm,* or *other scalp diseases.*

It may be surprising to learn that the male portion of the congregation kept their hats on in church, and more astonishing still that they were covered during the celebration of Mass.

HAIRDRESSING—WOMEN: 1558–1603

At the commencement of the Elizabethan period the hair was dressed simply, as in the two previous reigns. The portrait of the Queen (Fig. 571) shows it so arranged, with the side hair brought slightly forward in a small puff. This method is also seen in Fig. 575. Fig. 540 exemplifies the usual style adopted by most ladies when wearing the French hood, as described in Chapter III.

A side view, showing the hair somewhat raised on the top of the head, is seen in Fig. 549. This also shows a small caul of gold network and pearls used to encase the hair at the back of the head. In several figures the caul may be seen worn in this manner. It was the usual way of decorating the knob of hair when the headdress worn exposed the back of the head (*see* Fig. 592).

During the period that the French hood was of narrower proportions (*see* Fig. 867), the hair was very little puffed, to make it conform with the line then in vogue.

For some years after Elizabeth had ascended the throne, hair of all natural colourings was the mode. As the popularity of the Queen increased, the ladies of the Court and aristocracy craved for hair of the same colour as the Queen's. This was easily achieved, of course, by the aid of dye, and before the end of the period covered by Part I every woman of fashion wore hair of auburn, gold, or bright yellow.   These colours predominated during the remaining years of Elizabeth's reign, few ladies having the courage to differ from the rest.

The machinations of fashionable women are thus described by a contemporary:

'They are not simply content with their own hair but buy other hair, dyeing it of what colour they list themselves.   And if there be any poor woman that hath fair hair these nice dames will not rest, till they have bought it.'

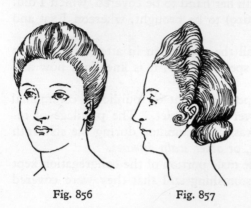

Fig. 856   Fig. 857

The fashion for using the crescent-shaped pads worn in France (*see* p. 738) was not popular amongst English ladies.   Sometimes one sees in portraits the style described under Fig. 860, but in a much modified and less rigid form, which suggests that the hair was arranged without the use of pads.

To magnify their height, these winged and farthingaled Court ladies of the latter part of the reign built up their heads with quantities of curls and puffings mounted on false hair pads known as 'attires of false hair,' or—a simpler way of achieving the same ends—wore immense wigs called 'bourns.'   At the opening of Part II the fashionable hairdressing is seen in Fig. 725, where the hair is drawn up high over pads placed on *top* of the head.   A tiara (1555) is set above this.

The mysteries of the coiffeur's salon are thus revealed to us by a mere man, and he a Puritan: 'Then followeth the trimming and tricking of their heads in laying out their hair to the show, which of force must be curled, frisled, and crisped, laid out on *wreaths* and *borders* from one ear to an other. And least it should fall down, it is under-propped with forks, wires, and I can not tell what, rather like grim stern monsters, that chase Christian matrons.' 'Wreaths' and 'borders' here mean plaits or braids of hair encircling the head.

Lady Southwell (1582) (Fig. 726) has her hair dressed in the same manner as Fig. 725, and surmounted by a wreath of silver work and jewels (*see* p. 750).

The development of this high hairdressing can be traced through Figs. 728, 729, and Plate XLIV, all of which have accentuated the height by adding wreaths or garlands, cunningly and curiously wrought.   The hairdressing of Fig. 732 is completed by a high jewelled ornament, almost like a crown, which gives increased height.   Queen Elizabeth obviously much liked this style of hairdressing, it being easily adopted by means of built-up wigs. Many of the Queen's later portraits show her high 'hair frizzled, crimped and curled beyond the limits of nature. This added height was sometimes bought at the price of Royal dignity. 'Coming once to visit Lord Burleigh [1591], being sick of the gout at Burleigh House in the Strand, and being much heightened with her head attire (as the fashion then was), the Lord's servant who conducted her through the door said, "May your Highness be pleased to stoop," the Queen returned "For your Master's sake I will stoop, but not for the King of Spain's."'

At other times Elizabeth wore wigs of circular shape, not so lofty, and a mass of curls.

Ladies of the provincial aristocracy and gentle-folk in the early 1590's began to adopt the earlier French fashion of using crescent-shaped pads as a foundation for their hair. This style is frequently met with in the effigies of noble families to be found in country churches. It is seen in Figs. 856 and 857. In front the hair is taken up over one pad, moderately high in the middle and tapering down to the ears. The side view shows that the hair forms a decided ridge at the back. In front it is slightly puffed in the centre, and

Fig. 858. 1590's

the hair at the back is smoothly taken down into a small roll in the nape. Sometimes a row of small curls surrounds the forehead and temples as shown in Fig. 858, which shows the coiffure of a young girl. It is doubtful if a pad is used in this case; but the hair is pushed up high on top to give the same effect by the gold band set with jewels, whence the hair flows freely on to the shoulders.

The lady (Fig. 872) wears the same style of hair-dressing as shown in Figs. 856 and 857, but with a row of curls on the forehead like Fig. 858.

FANCY HAIRDRESSING

The hairdressing worn by Venus, referred to under Plate XXVIII, is shown in Fig. 859. It is simple compared with that seen in Fig. 413, and much more attractive.

Fig. 859. 'Venus'

The very wavy golden hair, bespangled with gold, is parted in the centre and drawn upward and back from the temples: the ends are plaited, and entwined with a very narrow silver riband and a string of black pearls. The extremities of the plaits are formed into a loop or 8, and bound by one of the encircling plaits to the centre over the parting. At this point a red enamelled star, in a narrow gold setting, is fixed, and from it hangs a pendent sapphire.

Another example of fanciful French hairdressing combined with a head-dress is to be seen on the arm of the French chair in the portrait of Queen Elizabeth (Plate XLII).

FRENCH HAIRDRESSING

By the time Charles IX ascended the throne in 1560 a new way of dressing the hair came into fashion. Straight or waved hair was combed off the fore-head and temples over two pads shaped like crescents, called ARCELETS (Fig. 860), forming two bandeaux and producing the effect of a top-of-a-heart or Cupid's bow: the point where the ends of the two pads met coming in the centre of the forehead. The remainder of the hair was dressed in a flat coil in the nape of the neck, or sometimes a little higher. This arrangement of hair is much more pronounced and formal than that shown in Fig. 540, which is the earlier style both in France and England. In some instances a little curl of hair is worn in front of the ears, and this may be seen in Fig. 882 and later in Fig. 757. Queen Elizabeth of France is shown in several of her portraits wearing her hair dressed in this manner, chiefly with a headdress. In Fig. 659 she wears a jewelled escoffion shaped like that of Mary Stuart (Fig. 599).

Fig. 860. 'Arcelets'

Queen Louise (Fig. 660) is coiffured in this type of hairdressing without any headdress or ornament. Later, during the 1580's, this Queen of France is seen in Fig. 754 with an ornament of small black feathers, made up into a triangle with a few pearls. This is fixed rather forward on the head just behind the arcelets. The ladies of the Court of Henry III dressed their hair as shown in Fig. 755: the pads lost their crescent shape and became a single, semicircular pad, quite flat at the top, or a series of such pads one behind the other, framing the forehead. A back view of the same style is given in Fig. 756, which shows that small plaits of hair, arranged horizontally, are attached to the head by bows or other ornaments. Low in the nape of the neck the ends of hair were done into a coil. An aigrette fixed with a jewel was often set at the side.

The coiffure of Marguerite, Queen of Navarre, and after 1589 Queen of France, is arrived at by the same methods, but (as can be seen in Fig. 757) it is much larger and altogether more massive. It has a small, hardly notice-able puff in front, springing from a peak high up on the forehead, a new touch. This hairdressing is framed at the back with pearls arranged in points.

Marguerite de Valois had very beautiful black lustrous hair, of which she was very proud; but as time went on much of its beauty and substance dis-appeared. 'She did not like the fashion in vogue much and seldom used it, but preferred perukes most daintily fashioned.' Towards the end of her life, when she returned from Usson to hold her Court in Paris, she became antiquated, with no black hair of her own to dress; but ever resourceful, she made great display of blonde perukes. For these she kept a brigade of golden-haired footmen, who were shorn of their locks from time to time to supply Her Majesty's wigmakers. Unconventional as ever 'she never hid behind a mask like other ladies of our Court, for nearly all the time she went uncovered,' it being the custom with most ladies in high circles to wear masks in public.

As would be expected, Marie de' Medici, on her arrival in France on 6th December 1600, was wearing her hair in the Italian mode—that of Rome, if we are to rely on Rubens's portrait (see Fig. 758).

Fig. 861.
Gabrielle d'Estrées, 1560

Fig. 861 is a portrait drawing of Gabrielle, daughter of Antoine d'Estrées, who was born in 1573. She was first seen by Henry IV when she was seventeen, and immediately made a lasting impression by reason of her beauty and grace. On the authority of two contemporaries, we know that she possessed 'a beautifully shaped head, covered with an abundance of fair hair; blue eyes of a peculiar brilliancy; a lily-white complexion, only faintly tinged with rose, . . . the nose well formed, the lively, humorous curves of the mouth set off with fine teeth.' The poet, Guillaume du Sable, praised 'her coral lips, her ivory teeth, and her lovely double chin.' The last, a blemish in these days; but so great was her charm that she was able to carry it off as an attraction.

Sainte-Beuve tells us: 'She was white-skinned and fair, with blonde hair of the finest gold heaped up in a mass on her head and crisping on the sides in little curls.' But La Belle Gabrielle sometimes removed her attractive 'little curls' as Fig. 861 proves. The simplicity of her coiffure is seen in this: she has brushed her hair off the forehead and temples in a perfectly natural manner, perhaps a little high, but that was to conform to the mode of the day. At the back, it is woven into a coil or knob, very like the Roman lady's (see Fig. 765).

To throw a flimsy veil over the intrigue, she was married to one Nicolas d'Amerval de Liancourt, a gentleman of fortune if not otherwise attractive. This was in accordance with the usual practice under such circumstances, the match being arranged by the King, or (as some say) by her father: but she lived at Court as a Princess of the Blood, though actually the King's mistress. Gabrielle was created in 1595 Marquise de Monceaux, and later, in 1597, Duchesse de Beaufort.

She was remarkable, not only for her beauty, but for her great luxury and extravagance, which shocked not only the populace but even the courtiers!

The schedule of toilet articles left by her and drawn up at her death mentions nineteen mantles of the utmost sumptuousness, cotillons (under-petticoats) of Turkish cloth of gold, robes of satin of the colour of *brown bread*, doublées (camisoles, chemises) of incarnadine taffeta, etc.

She also had the distinction of being painted, with her sister, by Frans Pourbus the Younger in her bath, attired in fashionable hairdressing and a pearl earring, with an obvious allusion to the birth of her son, César, created Duc de Vendôme, in 1594. Her second son, Alexandre de Bourbon, was born in 1598.

This celebrated courtesan, and all but Queen of Henry IV, died 'from eating a large citron' in 1599.

ITALIAN HAIRDRESSING

The hairdressing of Italian ladies, like their headdresses, was very varied. Sometimes it was extremely simple, but more often very elaborate, not to say extraordinary.

The coiffure of Fig. 667 is simple, the line over the forehead being *the* mode for every self-respecting well-dressed woman of Europe. The hair is braided at the back, rolled round in the classic manner, and fixed with bows of riband.

The ladies of Rome dressed their hair somewhat on French lines, as shown in Fig. 762. The hair is slightly waved and taken up off the forehead, in this case over two pads, and is worn in conjunction with a black velvet cap fitting close at the back and having a deep rounded point on the forehead, as seen inset.

Sometimes one sees illustrations of Roman ladies at this time with their hair dressed close to the head in a series of very formal curls.

Later, in the 1590's, we find the front hair combed off the forehead over a small pad, and the back hair taken upwards to form with it a coil or knob on the angle of the cranium: this in Fig. 765 is partly hidden by the veil (*see also* Figs. 758 and 861). The effect is less rigid and much more natural than the original stiff and formal French style (*see* Fig. 860) and altogether more pleasing.

The Florentine lady (Fig. 763) wears an extraordinary coiffure. The hair is taken high up over a pad in front like Fig. 856, with the back hair dressed close to the head and ending in a twist, from which a long gauze veil floats. An ornament of pearls on wires is fixed to this twist, and a string of large pearls rests upon the rolled-up hair on the forehead and the puffs of hair at the sides.

The ladies of Venice dressed their hair in a most eccentric manner, with frisettes or curls, or both, mounted on wire frames or pads resembling horns. Fig. 764 is a typical example of the style: compared with some seen in illustrations this is quite inoffensive. The hair on the head itself is dressed in the ordinary manner, being smoothly brushed back and braided into a coil. In front, however, it is curiously wound round horns of material or wire, from which tiny curls escape: in the centre the hair is drawn back off the forehead. A wire support for the hair was called a PALISADO.

SPANISH HAIRDRESSING

Judging by her portraits, Elizabeth de Valois continued to wear the French style of hairdressing after she became Queen-Consort of Spain, and most of the ladies of her Court followed her example. Many of these were French, who had accompanied her to the land of her adoption.

The hairdressing and headdress worn by the lady (Fig. 679) is definitely French, although her dress retains the Spanish characteristics. Similarly, Philip's fourth wife, although Austrian, adopted the French manner of dressing the hair with arcelets and over it the French escoffion, like Fig. 882.

During the first part of the period covered by Section II there was no Queen-Consort of Spain, and the first lady in the land was the Great Infanta. In Fig. 772 she has adopted the style popular in England and France, of dressing her hair high over one or more pads, with small curls on the forehead and temples. The same style is worn by the lady (Fig. 774), but she has arranged some additional curls in front of her ears.

At a little later period, the Infanta changed her style of hairdressing, and Fig. 886 shows her new ideas. The hair is brushed right off the forehead, and arranged in two reversed pronounced high-standing waves. At the sides, waves of hair lie close to the head: the remainder is made into a flat coil at the back.

The coiffure worn by the Infanta Catherine (Fig. 773) is composed of a mass of curls very like the wigs used by Elizabeth of England.

HEADDRESSES: 1558–1603

THE FRENCH HOOD

Without doubt the ladies of the aristocracy and upper classes emulated the young Queen by wearing the same kind of French hood as Her Majesty did. That worn by the Queen at the time of her accession is seen in Fig. 571. It is the same as that worn by Lady Jane Grey (Fig. 516) and described on p. 451, and, like it, is entirely without jewels or other ornamentation. On occasions when the Queen appeared in public, her French hood was more elaborate, having a *wide* coronet or PARURE of jewels like that shown in Fig. 575.

A later type of French hood worn during the 1560's is seen in Fig. 589: a three-quarter view of the same is given in Fig. 862, and a profile in Fig. 863. The front piece of black velvet followed the contour of the head and de-

Fig. 862. The French Hood   Fig. 863. The French Hood

scended well on to the ears. It was shaped like a bow, lay flat on top of the head, curving outward at the sides, the angle level with the eyes, and then

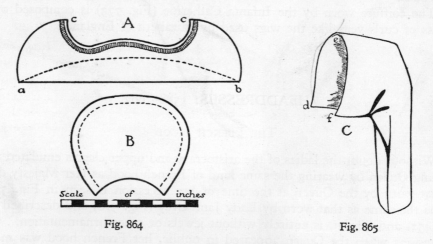

Fig. 864   Fig. 865

descending in a graceful curve to the back of the neck, almost covering the ears. This curve was achieved by the use of wire as described on p. 452. The front top edge was outlined, for a certain distance only, with gold cord or pearls. Behind this was generally a band of gold passamayne or gimp. Joined to the back was the 'coronet,' which, in this example, is headed by a row of ornamental and enamel beads, the parure. In front of it, and resting on the back portion of the headpiece, is a small, shaped band or slip of coloured or white silk tapering to ear level. Attached to the back of the upstanding 'coronet' was a rectangular piece of black velvet—the tube, so arranged as to form two or more pleats on each side of the back of the head, which fell down the back in definite folds. This was, of course, lined with silk.

Fig. 864 gives diagrams, A and B, of the main sections in the construction of the general type of French hood worn in Queen Mary's reign and in Queen Elizabeth's. It is exemplified in Figs. 862, 863, and 866. A shows the front portion which rests on the top of the head, the straight edge, a B, being fixed to the back, B, round the broken line. CC in the front piece A are the corners which come level with the eyes. A band of passamayne ornaments the front. The coloured silk slip covers the portion below the

Fig. 866

broken line. B is the back with the 'coronet'—often surmounted by a parure of jewels—shown between the solid and broken lines. C, Fig. 865, is the hood or tube, the front edge, D E F, being attached to the back of B at the broken line.

An important detail to be remembered is that the French hood was mostly made of black velvet, only *occasionally* was silk or even satin used and then always black.

Lady Denton (Fig. 595) wears a French hood of 1566. Fig. 866 shows the top of her head, as seen by looking at her recumbent effigy from behind. It shows all details which decorated the head portion, and the side pleats of the tube.

The Queen is shown wearing this latest type of French hood in Plate XXIX.

By the middle of the 1560's the French hood became narrower and higher, as shown in the drawing of Lady Walsing-

Fig. 867. Lady Walsingham, 1572

ham (Fig. 867), the original being painted by Hans Eworth in 1572. This type was worn by all the fashionable ladies of the Court, as is seen by their portraits. The Countess of Sussex wears the narrow French hood in Fig. 607.

There is a very pleasing three-quarter-length portrait group dated 1568, in which the noble father wears a jerkin like Fig. 492 and a hat like that worn by Fig. 505. Four small sons, all dressed alike, form a row in front of their parents; but the group is introduced here because of the ladies. The wife is very smart in her fashionable dress, with the latest narrow and high French hood, and small ruff reaching half-way up the ears; but the gaunt grandmother, aged sixty-one, still adheres to the gable headdress which was all the rage in her youth.

Fig. 868
Mistress Waltham, 1572

The quaint headdress worn by Fig. 821 and shown in Fig. 868 is definitely a French hood, but the front is so shaped as almost to suggest the brim of a hat and in one piece with the curved sidepiece, the corner overlapping it. A gold ornamental band secures it to the head.

The French hood, as such, went out of fashion among the well-dressed aristocracy at the end of the 1580's, the finish of the period covered by Part I. Many knights' wives, gentlewomen, and old ladies, however, still wore it during the early years of the seventeenth century. Lady Southcote, 1585 (Fig. 823), wears a simple French hood entirely of folded velvet and without any ornament. Another gentlewoman of about the same date (Fig. 819) wears one with a slightly different arrangement and ornamented.

Fig. 869. Dame Clopton, 1596

A French hood of a late date is shown in Fig. 869, worn by Anne Clopton on her effigy in Trinity Church, Stratford-on-Avon. She died in 1596. In A, we see the hood side view, coming down in a point well on to the forehead, and curving behind the formal arrangement of hair over pads to a point on a level with the mouth. The ridge or 'coronet' is of goldsmith's work

set with floral motifs.[1] In B, one sees the hood from behind, showing
clearly the three sections which form the headpiece. From behind the
ridge hangs the tube pleated into
several folds.

Two elderly and unfashionable ladies
of the aristocracy are shown in Figs.
870 and 871. The former is Lady
Williams from her alabaster effigy in
Thame Church dated 1559. The front
portion of her headdress is reminiscent of the gable, but the back part is
the French hood arranged in folds like
that in Fig. 823. The hair is entirely
concealed by a lawn cap worn underneath and gathered into a very narrow
band which encircles the head.

The other lady (Fig. 871) is Dame
Agnes Sanders, from her painted effigy
in Hatfield Church. This is dated 1588,
a period of twenty-nine years having

Fig. 870. Lady Williams, 1560

elapsed since Fig. 870, yet the headdress is practically the same. One sees
grey hair slightly waved on the temples, with a small frill of the under-cap of

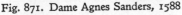

Fig. 871. Dame Agnes Sanders, 1588

Fig. 872. In Shadow

lawn showing over it, and above this is placed the French hood of black
velvet. A band of tubular and spherical beads was often attached round

[1] The shape of these motifs is very undefined in the effigy.

the slightly padded fold A, and hitherto referred to as the coronet. This lady's dress is all in black, and is modelled on the same lines as Lady Southcote's (Fig. 823).

From time to time to the end of her life, Queen Elizabeth continued to wear a type of French hood. In some cameo portraits (a drawing of one is seen in Fig. 698) one sees the front fitting close to the head, but without the flat tube. This is very like the escoffion of an earlier date (*see* Fig. 547). The Queen wore a French hood when opening Parliament in 1600 (*see* Plate XLIII).

Fig. 873. Queen Elizabeth, 1575

Other headdresses, of great variety, worn by the Queen at different periods, are described under the sections dealing with her wardrobe and portraits, Parts I and II.

When the French hood was worn with a ruff of increased circumference, it was found that the *fall* of the tube part was deprived of its perpendicular line. In some instances it was removed from the hood. On the other hand a custom arose of turning it up and arranging the tube attractively over the top of the hood, so that the end projected over the front and shaded the face as is shown in Fig. 872. It was then said to be *à l'ombre*.

It was the ambition of a woman of the people to don a French hood whenever an excuse occurred. 'Every merchant's wife and mean gentlewoman wore her French hood, and every cottager's daughter her taffeta hat.'

To make a perfect 'lady' a husband had only to supply his spouse with a French hood and a silken gown.

HATS

The hats worn during the first part of Elizabeth's reign were of various shapes and sizes. The one referred to under Fig. 597 was that fashionable during the 1560's: one like it is worn by the Countess of Lennox (Fig. 596). These are of the flat variety, with narrow brims. Both are decorated in the same manner, with a row of pearls round the brim and three strands crossing each other over the crown; a tuft of ostrich tips is set at the side. Under the hat the hair is puffed out moderately at the sides of the head and over the ears (*see* Fig. 540), the knob at the back being encased in a network caul of gold or pearls, or both (*see* Fig. 549).

It is said that Mary Stuart wore a 'chapeau à l'Italienne'; without doubt this refers to that shown in Fig. 597. (*Refer also to* Italian headdresses, p. 753.)

The curious high-crowned hat worn by Queen Elizabeth, mentioned under Fig. 578, is one that is seldom met with worn by ladies. It is obviously borrowed from men's headgear, and has the same curled brim as that worn by Sir John Hawkyns (Fig. 851).

Fig. 873 shows the hat the Queen sometimes wore while hunting or riding. It is the same style as is described under Fig. 849. A row of pearls surrounds the bottom of the crown, and a panache of ostrich feathers is set at the back, the hat itself being tipped slightly forward over a network caul at the back.

Amongst other hats known to have belonged to Elizabeth in the 1590's were two sent as a present by Lady Russell, who herself dilates upon their beauty and expensiveness: 'Two hats with two jewels, though I say it, fine hats; the one of white beaver, the jewel of the one above a hundred pounds' price,

Fig. 874. Bourgeois

besides the pendent pearl, which cost me the £30 more.' For their shape we may rely on Figs. 849 and 852.

A hat such as was worn by the wives of the middle classes and merchants is seen in Fig. 874. Of felt, it is ornamented with a feather fastened by a piece of jewellery to the hatband. Another such hat has been chosen by the good lady in Fig. 828. Hats of a little later date, perhaps more *outré*, are worn by the two gentlewomen (Figs. 788 and 790).

Towards the end of the reign hats of this shape and higher in the crown, covered with velvet or silk, were worn by the wives of London merchants.

OTHER HEADDRESSES OF MARY STUART

Headdresses worn by the Scottish Queen already illustrated and described are: Fig. 548, 1559; Figs. 597 and 599, 1560; and Fig. 601, 1561. Another headdress worn by her in 1561 is shown in Fig. 602. A headdress, which was more or less her usual coiffure during the seven years she lived in Scotland,

Fig. 875. Mary Stuart, 1567

Fig. 876. Mary Stuart, 1578

is given in Fig. 875. Here again the cap is of white lawn, with an attifet front edged with lace, the motif of which is seen in the four corners of the drawing; it is covered at the back by a long hanging veil of the same material. In the later years of her life and imprisonment, she changed her style of headdress to that shown in Fig 876. This is founded on the various portraits of her, chief among them being that by P. Oudry in the National Portrait Gallery, London. The usual cap, not quite so bowed or pointed as before, is of white lawn, the front part slightly gathered into the wire frame and edged with narrow lace; the back part is plain. Over this, the veil, edged with the same lace, follows the curve of the head round to the ear, thence curving out and down to the armpit, the bulk of the veil falling in many folds over the trained skirt. This style of headdress was worn by the ill-fated Queen, with very slight variations, during the last tragic months of her life.

Figs. 597, 875, and 876 show, as do many of her portraits, the usual way the ruff or band is arranged at the throat, in the same manner as in Fig. 862.[1] In Fig. 876 one also sees the jet ornaments, or black pearls, Queen Mary wore round her neck at this time: they consist of two larger ornaments, and on either side the letter M.

---

[1] Special notice should be taken of the arrangement of the ruff, and reference should be made to Fig. 862 and the description on p. 504. Mary Stuart was in the habit of wearing her ruff with the collar turned down on the right-hand side. This has misled a nineteenth-century authority into thinking that the ruff on this side was of a different formation from that on the left! Evidently he did not know how the Elizabethan ruff was constructed.

CAULS AND CAPS

It has been mentioned that cauls worn on the knob of hair at the back of the head were used in England. In 1583, Stubbes describes the escoffion (*see* p. 453) as 'made netwise, to the end, as I think, that the cloth of gold, cloth of silver, or else tinsel (for that is the worst) werewith their heads are covered and attired withal underneath their cauls may appear, and show itself in the bravest manner, so that a man that seeth them (their heads glitter and shine in such sort) would think them to have golden heads . . . and some wear lattice caps with three horns, three corners I should say, like the forked caps of Popish priests, with their perriwincles, chitterlings, and the like apish toys of infinite variety.'

Fig. 877. 1584

One seldom, if ever, meets these later monstrosities of head attire, 'these glittering caules of golden plate wherewith their heads were richly dect' in illustrations of English women. Stubbes, exaggerating his countrywomen's head attire for his own purposes, has unconsciously arrived at the Italian coiffures, as may be seen on reference to Figs. 763, 764, and 885.

A caul of quite a new shape is shown in Fig. 877, worn by a gentlewoman of the 1580's. The part which covers the head is bag-shape, secured to the head by three bands or one bound three times round. The front, edged with a

Fig. 878.   Fig. 879.
Anne Fiennes, Lady Dacre, 1594

fancy trimming, is bowed out by wire—the attifet—over the puffed hair at the sides, and this descends in a point on the forehead. A headdress of a similar type but definitely a cap, dated 1594, is shown in Figs. 878 and 879. It is made entirely of white lawn. The cap is a square trellis of puffings, with the horseshoe-shaped back joined to it with two rows of cording. On the front is a shaped piece of double lawn edged with a narrow pleated ruching, and being wired à l'attifet it bows out over the hair dressed in a mass of tiny curls. Underneath this cap is worn a kerchief folded cornerwise, the points coming well on to the forehead, and the sides curving out over the hair in front of the ruching.

Caps of this sort were much worn at the end of the century, and well into the seventeenth.

HEAD ORNAMENTS, WREATHS, AND GARLANDS

The delightful fashion of wearing wreaths and garlands of wirework in gold or silver for the vain purpose of adding the desired cubit to the stature came in late in the 1580's. It is described by our friend Stubbes: 'Then, on

GLORIANA.

Fig. 880

the edges of their bolstred hair (for it standeth crested round about their frontiers, and hanging over their faces like pendices or veils with glass windows on every side) there is laid great wreaths of gold and silver, curiously wrought and cunningly applied to the temples of their heads.'

The first such wreath to be shown is in Fig. 726. This takes the form of fronds of fern and ospreys carried out in silver wire, and backed by a fan-shaped motif of the same mounted with diamonds and pearls. A rich jewel of rubies and diamonds in front sets off the whole headdress—a beautiful effect.

These head ornaments became more elaborate as time went on: an example may be seen in Fig. 729, obviously set in a comb inserted into the back of the hair or wig, and from it springs a spray of silver wires each carrying several hanging diamonds or bugles, giving the effect of lilies of the valley. The wreath which hangs on the hair in front is treated in the same manner.

The wonderful head attire worn by Mistress Mary Fitton in her portrait (Plate XLIV) is a very beautiful example of the mode of the 1590's. The foundation of this is of silver wire; and to its outside edge, as well as to the centre portion, are set sprays of silver wires on which are quantities of pearls interspersed with spangles and bugles. These would quiver and scintillate at the slightest movement of the head. Mounted on Mary's brown hair, dressed high, this would have a magnificent appearance, rather like a shimmering cluster of white and silver elderberries.

De Maisse was very much struck by the garland the Queen was wearing at an audience in 1597, though, unfortunately for our purpose, he omits to describe it. A portrait in St. James's Palace of Queen Elizabeth, shows her wearing a very lovely garland of the 1590's on top of her high hairdressing. It is reproduced in Fig. 880, and has a delicate framework of fine silver wire embodying scrolls, flowers, and leaves of silver gauze, beads, and diamonds, and further embellished with pearls set on upstanding wires forming a complementary design. Large peardrop pearls form a kind of fringe resting on the much-becurled wig. The whole structure tapers up very high in the centre, with wings descending the sides of the hair, the effect suggesting a Russian tiara but more delicate in design. Elizabeth was fully aware of the advantage gained by placing dazzling diamonds close to a face and neck much wrinkled and scraggy through advancing years.

FRENCH HEADDRESSES

In the land of its birth the French hood, after reigning for many years, disappeared as a fashionable headdress by the time Henry III was on the throne.

A French example of it is shown in Fig. 881, which presents a French noble lady of the 1560's. It is worn over the hairdressing described under Fig. 860, and in consequence is placed rather far back on the head. Jewels in gold mounts alternating with double rows of four pearls form the parure, and also edge the front of the hood where it rests on a pleating of gold gauze. On the forehead is an ornament from which three peardrop pearls hang.

The escoffion was still fashionable in France, and in Fig. 599 we see it worn by Mary Stuart, drawn from a medal struck in 1560. The foundation is of silk or gold tissue cross-barred with gold: at the intersections pearls are set, and there are jewels in gold mounts (*see* inset) in the spaces.   A peardrop pearl is suspended from it and hangs well on to the forehead.

An escoffion worn by a French Noble lady is shown in Fig. 882.   It is composed of a dark-coloured silk covered by an intricate network of gold and pearls.   The edge fitting the head is of gold, set with jewels and shaped to

Fig. 881. French Lady in French Hood

Fig. 882. Catherine of Lorraine

come to a point in the centre of the head just behind the hair dressed as described under Fig. 860.   The escoffion disappeared as a headdress among fashionable women after 1560.   A smaller version of it remained in use to cover the knob of hair worn at the back of the head.

WIDOW'S WEEDS

The Deuil Blanc, referred to on p. 514, and reproduced in Fig. 601, shows the characteristic weeds regulated by the Controller of French Court ceremonial for young widows.   To start with, the barbe, described under Fig. 191, vol. ii, and Fig. 149, vol. iii, is tied under the chin and over the head.   On the hair is placed a little coif of very fine lawn, a small portion only being visible on the forehead; and over it is the cap with the bowed attifet front.   Around the back of the cap is pinned the voluminous white lawn veil.

Widow's weeds, as worn by Catherine de' Medici, are referred to under Fig. 661 and Plate XXXV.   Fig. 883 shows another arrangement of the veil, and is taken from a portrait medallion of Catherine dating about 1574. This shows the arrangement clearly.   One corner of the black crêpe veil is pulled forward on to the forehead over the black cap with the attifet front, and tied with itself behind, the remainder falling to the ground. If, however, the edges were set out in curves on both sides of the head, the wire would be inserted at the line A. No barbe is worn. Catherine was apparently the first Royal widow to omit this, as henceforth it does not appear as an item of mourning amongst Royal and noble ladies. Possibly it was an Italian fashion introduced by this Queen of France.

The widow's weeds worn by Queen Elizabeth of Austria, are shown in

Fig. 883.
Catherine de' Medici

Fig. 884. Elizabeth of Austria,
Queen-Dowager of France

Fig. 884, taken from a portrait by François Quesnel dating shortly after 1574. A close-fitting black cap is first put on: then the black crêpe veil, wired into an attifet front, is placed over it. The wire at the sides continues below ear level, producing on a smaller scale the effect described under Fig. 721. This same type of widow's weeds was worn by Queen Jeanne of Navarre (*see* p. 453). For widow's weeds as worn in England at the end of the century, refer to Figs. 826 and 872.

ITALIAN HEADDRESSES

The lady of Pisa (Fig. 669) wears a close-fitting coif composed of folds of soft material with semicircular ornaments of gold round the front. A series of loops gives a coronet effect at the back, from which falls a long gauze veil. No hair is visible.

The head-and-shoulders drawing of the Italian lady (Fig. 885) shows sufficient of her dress to give it a date—about 1550. She has mahoitered sleeves to her surcote, and the rest of the costume may be understood by referring to Fig. 521, remembering that Italy was in advance of England in fashions. The hat is of particular interest; it is typically Italian, and, together

Fig. 885. Bonet à l'Italienne

with the hats worn by Italian men, captivated fashionable women of England and France. It is of black velvet 'moulded on a porringer; a velvet dish—'tis a cockle, or a walnut shell.' Gold buttons set with jewels are placed round it, and on the right side an elaborate ornament of gold, jewels, and pearls stands erect. The hat is poised at an angle over a caul or escoffion, showing the hair through the network. Bunches of curls cluster in front of the ears.

SPANISH HEADDRESSES

The same applies to headdresses as to hairdressing—Spanish ladies of *noble* rank wore much the same styles as English and French. In Figs. 676, 679, and 680, both Queens and the noble lady wear escoffions. The chapeau à l'Italienne is worn over a pearl and jewelled caul by Elizabeth de Valois in Fig. 674.

With the new style of hairdressing worn by the Great Infanta (Fig. 772), the headdress so popular in England was, curiously enough, adopted in Spain. Possibly the attention aroused in Spaniards to the nation of heretics may be the cause of this fantastic head decoration finding its way to Spain. In Fig. 772, the headdress takes the form of a coronet composed of pearls and jewels, and backed by a made-up plume of small feathers.

In Fig. 774 it has become

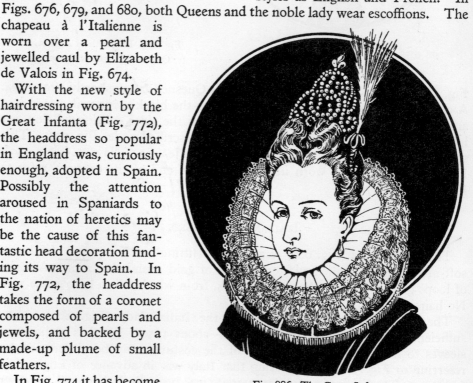

Fig. 886. The Great Infanta

more elaborate, and consists of a wire foundation of steeple shape, and in a scroll design, covered with pearls. An aigrette is fixed to the hair on the left side.

The head attire, shown in Fig. 886, is taken from a portrait of the Infanta Isabella by Pantoja de la Cruz. It is a wonderful erection of pearl scroll-work. From an ornamental holder on the left side of her hairdressing springs an aigrette.

The headdress worn by the Infanta Catherine (Fig. 773) is a Spanish version of the chapeau à l'Italienne, seen in Fig. 885. It is pill-box shape, covered with black velvet and encompassed by folds of the same set with oblique groups of three pearls and jewels in gold mounts. A short curled ostrich tip is fixed by a jewel on the upper side of the tilt. Whether a caul is worn or not it is impossible to see. The same style is seen in one or two other Spanish portraits.

MIDDLE CLASSES

Besides those hats described on p. 747, there were other headdresses worn by the middle-class women and varying in shape.

Fig. 887 shows one of the blocked felt variety. It is in white, formed with

Fig. 887. Mistress Flexney, 1567   Fig. 888. Mistress Dorcas Martin, 1562

a point on the forehead and projecting at the sides; down the back hangs a flat tube. The townswoman (Fig. 830) wears a similar headdress.

Fig. 888 is a felt cap of another shape, or it could be made of cloth and seamed at the sides, worn over a plain linen under-cap. It is taken from a portrait medallion of Dorcas, wife of Richard Martin, Queen Elizabeth's goldsmith. He was Warden and later Master of the Mint, and Lord Mayor for part of the year 1588.

White linen caps worn by the lower orders and country people were very simple in construction. The back part was horseshoe-shape, and to the curved edge was sewn plain or gathered a rectangular front piece (Fig. 889). This

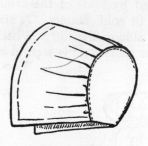

Fig. 889

Fig. 890

was always turned back off the face, as worn by the young girl (Fig. 834). Sometimes the front corners were rounded off.

Another kind of cap much worn is first seen in Fig. 352, and later in Figs. 718 and 831. It has a shaped front piece like that of the French hood, but in linen; and most likely wired at the edge so as to lie close on the forehead, bow round over the hair at the sides, and come close to the cheek. To this is gathered the bag-shaped back, as shown in Fig. 890.

These caps were always made of white or natural-tinted linen, and were worn indoors and out. When it was required to be more dressy, a felt or straw hat was worn on top, as in Figs. 832 and 833.

FOOTGEAR, 1558–1603

The Guild of Cordwainers was granted its third charter by Queen Elizabeth in 1562, which was followed by a grant of arms in 1579. The armorial bearings (Fig. 891) are: azure, a chevron or between three goats' heads rased argent horned and bearded of the chevron. Crest, a goats' head rased argent, the rasures (edges of the hair) gules, the horns wreathed or and azure, mantling gules lined or 'dobled' argent.

For some years after the accession of Queen Elizabeth, footgear was simple and more or less followed the shape of the foot. The material used was chiefly leather: velvet, satin, silk, and cloth were employed by the shoemaker for special shoes.

Fig. 891. Arms of the Cordwainers

A man's shoe, such as was in general use, is shown in Fig. 893. This type was worn by all classes—by the nobility in the best Spanish leather. Most of the examples seen in portraits have no fastenings; they were close-fitting,

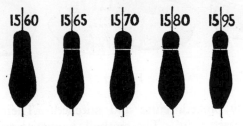

Fig. 892

but it was possible to pass the foot into the shoe with ease despite the rather high instep. Sometimes the shoe was open down the outer side (*see* dotted line at A) and laced; or a strap was cut in the vamp and fastened by a button. In Fig. 895 straps, fixed at the sides, tie in a bow on the instep. A buckle would serve the same purpose.

The soles of ordinary shoes were of uniform thickness, and as yet there were no heels. Shoes worn by the French nobility during the 1550's and 1560's were much decorated with cuttes, a fashion already noticed in Chapter III. Fig. 896 shows a shoe, dated 1561, and made of silk or satin; it has a row of loops over the instep, cuttes piped at the edges, and three ornamental buttons. Comparison with the earlier examples will show that these shoes do not differ

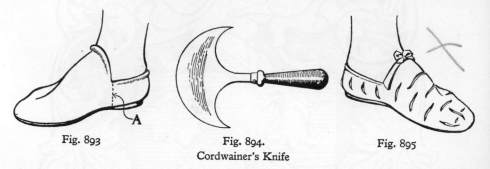

Fig. 893   Fig. 894.   Fig. 895
                    Cordwainer's Knife

appreciably from them; in fact, this style remained in fashion during the greater part of the reign for dress purposes. As late as 1596 one meets it in a portrait of the Infante Philip at Vienna, painted by Pantoja de la Cruz.

Figs. 897 and 898 are drawn from shoes in the Archaeological Museum, Cambridge, which were found in Corpus Christi College. They are still in excellent condition. The soles are thin, and the shoes made of brown

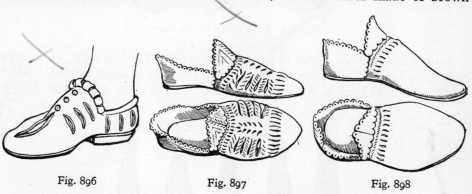

Fig. 896   Fig. 897   Fig. 898

leather, elaborately pinked, cutte and stitched. Their owner must have been a smartly dressed man. The method, known to the Greeks, of raising the foot at the back to give additional height, was not adopted in England until after the middle of the sixteenth century. As seen in Fig. 899, which is taken from an original, the sole of cork gradually increased in thickness from the toe to the heel. Another shoe, a lady's, with a corked sole is shown in Fig. 902.

Comment was, of course, made on this innovation. One such is quoted

on p. 543, and we may be sure Stubbes would seize the opportunity of airing
his disdainful, yet enlightening, remarks on footgear in general:

'They have corked shoes, pinsnets, and fine pantofles, which bear them up
a finger or two from the ground: whereof some be of white leather, some of
black, red, black velvet, white, red, green, raced, carved, cutte, and stitched

Fig. 899

Fig. 900

all over with silk and laid on with gold, silver, and such like: yet not withstanding to what good uses serve these pantofles.'

Fig. 899 is of leather, decorated with cuttes on the toe joints, and with
stitchery above them and on the heelpiece. Shoes were often 'stitched with
silk, and embroidered with gold and silver all over the foot, with other gew-
gawes innumerable.' Heels to shoes began to make their appearance in
France as early as the 1560's, for a low heel is seen in Fig. 896; this, however,
is somewhat exceptional at this date.

In the portrait of Henry III of France, referred to under Fig. 740, there is

Fig. 901

Fig. 902

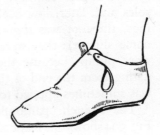

Fig. 903

shown a novel arrangement for attaching the heel (see Fig. 900). The sole
is part of the black velvet hosen; the red heel is separate, attached to a heelpiece of white kid. No fastening appears, so the foot must have passed through
the opening, which strikes one as not being very secure.

Fancy shoes were worn by courtiers during the latter part of the reign,
and Fig. 901 shows one of a pair in white silk, satin, or leather, worn by Lord
Leicester. An ornamental tongue stands up high over the instep, and the
front part of the shoe is stitched with silver thread in a diamond pattern.

In the 1570's a new method of fastening the shoe came into vogue.   The brass to the memory of Mistress Wyndham (*see* Fig. 819) furnishes us with an early example (Fig. 902).   The side pieces are cut down rather low, the fronts curving up over the instep, and the backs curving forward to form a short strap with eyelet holes through which ribands were passed.   These, being tied together in a bow, kept the top of the shoe secure round the ankle. Sir Walter Raleigh (Fig. 742) wears the same type of shoe at a later date and Fig. 903 is a detail drawing of it.   This method in its primitive stage is seen in Fig. 630, but at that time shoemakers had not discovered the advantage of the larger open space at the sides which assisted the bend of the foot in a more comfortable manner.   It should be noticed that the toe is cut rather square.

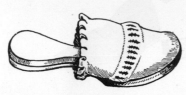

Fig. 904

'With two Provincial roses on my razed shoes.'   This quotation from *Hamlet* (Act III, sc. ii) might perplex some, but the rose referred to was an ornament introduced to the shoe in the 1590's.   'Shoe roses' they were called, and were at first made up of loops of ribands resembling that flower.   Henry IV is wearing them in his portrait (*see* Fig. 752).   A little later they were made of gold or silver lace, as shown in the drawing (Fig. 770). In the following century these roses became the usual decoration for ladies' and gentlemen's smart footwear.

On the tennis court woollen slippers were worn lest ordinary shoes should distract the players by creaking.

The origin of the word 'pumps' is unknown, but it came into use in the middle of the century.   They were shoes with thin soles and, later, low heels.   As there were no fastenings, the foot was *slipped* into them (hence, also, the name slipper); they were used only indoors.   Lackeys wore pumps because they were soft and quiet; and dating from the end of the century, the name 'pumps' was sometimes applied to a lackey.

The French 'pantoufle' means a slipper or mule. Fig. 904 shows one made of leather, having a row of cuttes, pinked at the edges, over the front, and a row of loops at the top of the instep.   The heel rests on padded leather attached to the sole.   The shape of the sole is given

A   B

Fig. 905

in Fig. 905 A.   Pantoufles are worn by Sir Christopher Hatton (Fig. 627).

One often finds these curiously shaped soles when examining the feet of ladies in their effigies recumbent upon altar tombs (Fig. 905 B).

Little of ladies' shoes can be seen when the skirts touch the ground: it may be assumed that their shoes resembled those of the men.   In the 1580's and 1590's, when skirts became a little shorter, more of the shoes can be seen.

Two examples of shoes worn by ladies are given in Figs. 906 and 907, both dating about 1588–95. Those in Fig. 906 are taken from the portrait of Queen Elizabeth (Plate XLII), and are of white satin with numerous small cuttes. They are rather short from toe to heel, and broad across the toe joints, in contrast to Fig. 907, in which the shoes are tapering and flat. These

Fig. 906   Fig. 907

are of white satin, with the addition of three ornamental buttons, and the cuttes are differently arranged.

Long boots, generally worn for riding, but sometimes used for walking, were of the same shape as shown in Fig. 505. The French jack-boot (Fig. 559) is seldom met with in illustrations of English sixteenth-century gentlemen.

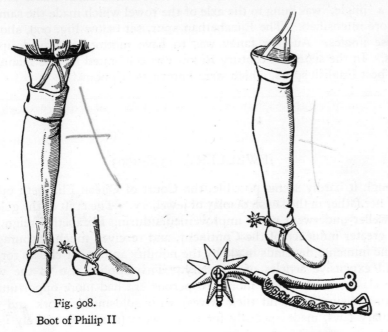

Fig. 908.
Boot of Philip II

Fig. 909. Boot and Spur

The long boot of soft fawn leather, and fitting the leg closely, shown in Fig. 908, is from a portrait of Philip II. The foot is sewn to the leg part underneath the spur strap, and also up the front in the form of a tongue, like that shown in Fig. 901. Above the knee the boot is turned down and up, and two straps sewn inside are attached to the waist-belt underneath the slops. The boot in Fig. 909 is similar, but more rounded in the toe, and without the stitching up the front of the ankle. The top does not turn down, and two straps support the boot as described above.

'They have also boot hose—they be of the finest cloth that may be got, yea, fine enough to make any band, ruff or shirt needful to be worn: yet this is bad enough to wear next their gresie boots . . . they must be wrought all over, from the gartering place upward, with needlework, clogged with silk of all colours, with birds, fowls, beasts, and antiques purtrayed all over in comly sort, so that I have known the very needlework of some one pair of these boothose to stand, some in iiij pound, vi pound and some in x pound a piece. Besides this, they are made so wide to draw over all, and so long to reach up to the waist.'

Boot-hose, known as TRIQUEHOUSE, besides being a leg-bag to draw over the hose under a boot, was also a thick hose to wear instead of a boot.

Spurs worn for either riding or walking often had large loose rowels which caused a jingling sound. Hence this excerpt: '. . . he walked the chamber with such a pestilent gingle'—an effect much sought after by cavaliers towards the end of the century. At this time also a small metal ornament, called a 'jingle,' was hung to the axle of the rowel which made the same noise but more intensified. The Elizabethan spur, set below Fig. 909, shows one of these jingles. Another fancy was to have mottoes engraved upon the shanks. In the sixteenth century Ripon was celebrated for the manufacture of the best English spurs, which were known as 'rippons.'

JEWELLERY, 1558–1603

Though it hardly seems possible, the Court of Queen Elizabeth outshone that of her father in the lavish display of jewellery. The craft of the goldsmith and jeweller underwent many improvements during Elizabeth's reign, owing to the greater influence of the Continent, and received much encouragement from the immense demands made by the nobility and upper classes for splendid and expensive articles of jewellery. This applies also to the wealthy middle classes, who in this more prosperous era had more opportunities of bedecking themselves (and their wives) with goldsmith's work and jewels. Sumptuary laws, made specially for them, were (it seems) entirely ignored, as usual.

This prosperity, no doubt, prompted the Wardens of the Goldsmiths' Company to ask for an augmentation to their existing shield of arms (see p. 117), for in the Memorials of the company we find under date 14 Elizabeth—1571—the following entry:

'Agreed that the Arms of the Company shall be renewed against the Mayor's feast—with helmet, crest and supporters.' They are shown in Fig. 910.

The crest above mentioned is blazoned as a demi-lady rising from clouds above the crest wreath, holding in her dexter hand a pair of scales and in the sinister a touchstone. The dress is described under Fig. 822. The supporters are 'Two Unicorns or, armed, crined, and hoofed argent'; the motto: 'Justitia Virtutum Regina.'

The colours of the livery remained violet and scarlet, but these were confined to the hood, the gowns being of the lately introduced style—all of black and furred with foins. For an alderman in livery see Fig. 798.

Fig. 910. Arms of Goldsmiths' Company

English goldsmiths had serious rivals in Germany, where the craft had reached a very high standard and had acquired universal fame. Many German goldsmiths of an earlier generation had studied in Italy, and by this time they were outrivalling their masters by their delicacy of treatment and richness of invention. 'Never was the working of metals better understood, to bring out the highest brilliancy and mirror effects, to enliven plain flat surfaces with artistic engraving and, above all, how to combine the hard brilliance of precious stones with soft colours in enamels.'

Pure Classic lines gave way to a more mixed style in which strap and ribbon-work, architectural members, and the cartouche framing are prominent features. The German craftsmen thus supplied a large proportion of the jewellery in use in Europe.

The reformed religion, which was occupying the minds of higher and lower classes, is responsible in a great measure for figures of saints and objects of religious significance going out of favour in the decoration of articles of jewellery. They were not excluded altogether, but were replaced by mythological or allegorical figures and animals. These were usually of white enamel with a mauvish hue, and modelled or raised in the round. The design surrounding figures, especially for pendants and brooches, was of scroll and strap-work in enamels, and in the revived champlevé on gold.

Jewels of every sort were used, and diamonds became the most popular, since the method of cutting them was much improved, and the use of foil set underneath greatly enhanced their brilliance.

A great impetus to the popularity of rich jewellery was given by the capture of Spanish trading galleons by the Sea Dogs of the 1580's.

The Handbook of Elizabethan Jewellery, published by the London Museum, is particularly useful for the study of this extensive subject.

CROWNS

The Crown Imperial worn by Queen Elizabeth is shown in Plate XXVII, and has the circlet set with rubies, sapphires, pearls, and diamonds. There are eight crosses patées, from which rise four arches supporting a large cross. The orb, which makes its first appearance in this work in vol. i, Fig. 82, is of iron surrounded and arched with sapphires, rubies, and diamonds. The reason for using iron is obscure: possibly to bring good fortune?

The Imperial Crown is shown also in Figs. 574, 575, and Plate XLIII. It is probable that the crown shown in the coronation portrait, Plate XXVII, is the more authentic, as the artist no doubt painted it from the original. Fig. 575 is from a contemporary engraving.

The crown of France surmounts the drawing of Charles IX (Plate XXXVI); it will be noticed that the design has not altered since the time of Louis XII (Fig. 38).

Plate XLVI shows the Spanish Royal Crown, which consists of eight leaf-motifs rising from the circlet and supporting four arches.

The coronet of the Grand Dukes of Tuscany is seen in the drawing of Marie de' Medici (Fig. 758), surmounting the arms of the Medici family.

COLLARS

The Collar of the Garter is seen in numerous portraits of the time, and the most satisfactory drawing of it in this book is that shown in Fig. 624. But there is always Fig. 339, vol. ii, for convenient reference.

It does not appear that Queen Elizabeth was painted wearing the Collar of the Garter, but she must, of course, have done so on certain occasions, particularly when attending a Chapter of the Order. Nor has the garter worn upon her arm ever been discovered in any painting. Unlike her sister Mary, Elizabeth had no kingly husband to take her place as Sovereign of the Order, and the drawing referred to on p. 495 is perhaps the only representation of her in the insignia and robes.

The following description of a George is found in an inventory of the Queen's jewels dated 1574:

'Item oone George, on horsebacke, the foreparte of the George of Diamoundes the maile of the Curettes and Renettes of the same silver haulfguilt, wᵗ a sworde in his hand of golde, a Lozanged Diamonde like a shilde and a Dragone of gold, posz together iij oz iij qᵃrrt.'

The Lesser George, set in a jewelled frame and suspended on a black riband, is worn by Queen Elizabeth in her portrait (Plate XXXI C).

Below are the costs of some jewels of the insignia of the Order of the Garter:

A Garter of gold with diamonds and rubies, £48.
A George of diamonds, £60.
A wire chain to the same, £10 2s.
A Collar of gold, £210 5s.
Another George, £25.

And one must remember that these sums represent ten or twelve times as much to-day.

Elizabeth conferred the Order of the Garter upon the King of France, March 1586. 'The Garter is valued at fifty thousand crowns. In return the King is said to have prepared a magnificent coach with all fittings to still greater value for presentation to the Queen of England.'

CHAINS

Chains worn by gentlemen during the Elizabethan era gradually lost their 'massy' proportions: their links were decidedly smaller, as for example, Fig. 621, and chiefly oval or round, but sometimes rectangular. In some portraits chains appear to be made of plaited gold wire, as are those described in vol. ii, under Figs. 503 and 513.

Not only were these chains worn once round the neck, but often two or three times, and they were frequently long enough to extend to waist level.

The French were more given to wearing chains than the English, and these were of more ornamental character, as already shown in the last chapter. The portrait, of which Fig. 650 is a drawing, shows a chain of gold beads of a more delicate nature; a cross of gold set with jewels is suspended from it.

That noble Frenchmen did wear the heavier gold chain to which a pendant

III²—2 C

is attached, is shown in Fig. 653; and a Spaniard wearing a longer one wound three times round the neck is seen in Fig. 671. Admiral Sir John Hawkyns (Fig. 851) has a very long chain of small links worn in like manner.

Attached to the neck-chain, or hung round the neck by a riband or chain, were *pick-tooths* and *ear-picks*, very generally used by both ladies and gentlemen and often richly gemmed and enamelled.   These necessities were sometimes contained in an ornament in the shape of a whistle like Fig. 471.   An excerpt from Queen Elizabeth's list of New Year gifts, 1576–7, gives an example of the decoration bestowed upon such articles.

Fig. 911.   Fig. 912.   Fig. 913.
Necklaces

'Item, a tothe and eare-picke of gold, being a dolphin enamuled with a perle pendaunte, 16 small rubyes being but sparcks, and 5 sparcks of dyamonds—geven by the Lady Cheake.'

CARCANETS

The carcanet, which in the reign of Henry VIII was usually worn by gentlemen only, was now a very favoured decoration for the throat and shoulders of ladies also.   The feminine carcanet was equally rich, and was composed of jewels in gold mounts and groups of pearls set between.

A very handsome carcanet is worn on the shoulders by the Countess of Sussex (Fig. 607); and Queen Elizabeth of Spain (Fig. 676) wears another close up round the throat.

See also the carcanets worn by Queen Elizabeth, p. 770.

NECKLACES

In the 1580's the word 'necklace' came into general use with ladies in place of 'carcanet,' which gradually became obsolete.   There was a great difference between the massive carcanet and the lighter necklace, the latter being a small linked chain in which ornaments and jewels were inserted. Figs. 911 and 912 are good examples.

The former, taken from a portrait dated 1589, has three differently shaped ornaments, in gold, black enamel, and pearls, strung together by three links.

Fig. 912 is a detail of the necklace worn by the lady in Fig. 730, and is also in gold, black enamel, and pearls. Fig. 913 shows a necklace taken from a portrait dated 1600; it is composed of three links, with ornaments in gold and two different coloured enamels with a pearl set in the centre of each. All these necklaces are very long, and are worn twice round the neck, extending to below the waist.

Ropes or strings of pearls were also referred to as necklaces. They were worn close up round the throat, and often consisted of two or three strands, sometimes with pearls in loops hung from the lower strand, as seen in Plate XLIV.

Many great ladies in full dress wore a number of long strands of pearls round the neck hanging well below the point of the stomacher; and it will be seen in some of the illustrations that these necklaces were sometimes knotted on the bosom. A graceful mode was to drape the necklace from the neck or shoulder and under one arm, as in Fig. 731.

PENDANTS, JEWELS, MINIATURES

Pendants were most elaborate in design, quite different from the oval shapes in fashion previously. They were composed of all kinds of objects, from monkeys to ships in full sail, carried out in enamels and jewels, and hung from chains of jewels. Frequent subjects composing the designs were enamelled flowers, leaves, jewelled motifs perfect in themselves, and varied ornaments. Strap-work and scrolls also formed an important feature of the settings, especially of the frame.

Characteristics appear to be a cartouche-shaped frame with a comparatively unbroken outline, enriched with scroll ornament, and occasionally with human figures and grotesques, a slight use of open work, and the general employment of a central ornament.

Although of Spanish workmanship, Fig. 914 is a good specimen of the pendant with quaint animals introduced. A spotted dog in white enamel, and set with two diamonds, stands upon gold and enamel scrolls rising from a crescent of rubies. This is hung by two chains of gold and white enamel with four motifs set with rubies, from a red and gold ornament having an emerald in the centre. Five pearls form pendants. The total length is three inches.

A pendant worn by a gentlewoman, 1586, is given in Fig. 916. It measures two and a half inches without the three grey pearl pendants, and is cross-shaped, having an emerald in the centre surrounded by four rubies. The chain by which the ornament is hung is somewhat massive considering the small size of the pendant.

Fig. 918 is a pendant of rather unusual design in which enamel, rubies, sapphires, and pearls are arranged symmetrically. That shown in Fig. 915 is worn upon a lady's sleeve of 1590. The eagle of gold and enamel, bearing

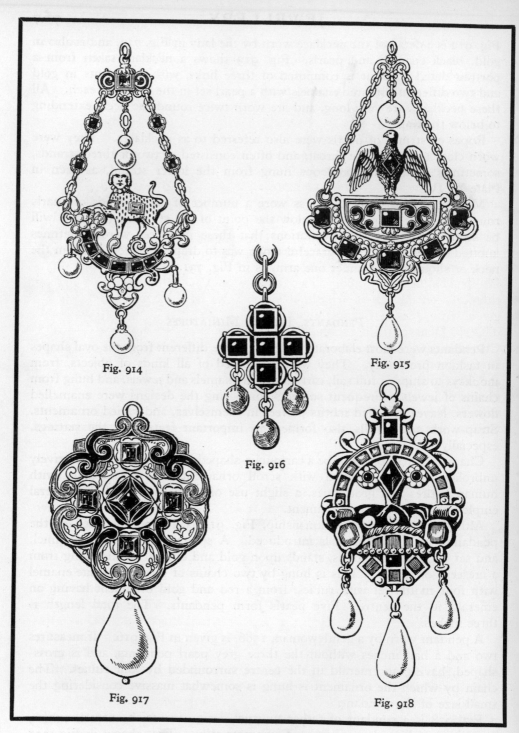

Fig. 914

Fig. 915

Fig. 916

Fig. 917

Fig. 918

PENDANTS

a lozenge-shaped ruby on its breast, stands upon a gold ornament decorated with coloured enamels and a square emerald. Around the base are rubies, emeralds, and small pearls set in gold open-work scrolls with a pear pearl suspended from it. The pendant is hung by chains from a small ornament with a pearl hanging in the centre.

A pendant of the usual shape is given in Fig. 917, and is composed of two coloured enamels, four small sapphires, and a large one in the centre. The large pear pearl is hung close up to the base, which rather detracts from its beauty.

Fig. 919 is the celebrated Armada jewel, produced after the defeat of Philip II's fleet in 1588. Two and three-quarter inches in length, it was given by Queen Elizabeth to Sir Thomas Heneage (died 1595), her Vice-Chamberlain. On the front, which is here reproduced, is a profile bust of the Queen in gold upon an enamelled ground of aventurine blue, inscribed with the Royal title. On the reverse, and covered by a lid enamelled outside with the Ark and inside with a Tudor rose, is a miniature of Elizabeth painted

Fig. 919. The Armada Jewel

by Hilliard and dated 1580. The jewel has a border in blue, red, and white enamel set with diamonds and rubies. The original may now be seen in the Victoria and Albert Museum (M. 81-1935).

Cameos and intaglios became very fashionable, especially towards the end of Elizabeth's reign, partly owing to the fact that the Queen was very fond of such gems set in jewelled frames. *Miniatures* and cameos thus ornamented, usually portraits of herself, were presented by Her Majesty

Fig. 920.   Fig. 921.

Cameos

as marks of esteem to such courtiers and other subjects as she favoured. Several of the noblemen in Plate XLV wear these gifts at waist level, suspended on long ribands beneath the Collars of the Garter. Two examples of portrait cameos are given in Figs. 920 and 921. The former is set in an elaborate frame of enamel and pearls, and the latter has a moulded gold frame with four square rubies 'garnished with their gold'—a period term for jewels in gold mounts.

Miniature cases, known at the time as 'picture boxes,' were among the most important of pendent jewels (*see* Plate XLIV). Such boxes were elaborately enamelled on the back and front, the latter being set with jewels as well.

Fig. E, Plate XVIII, shows the back of a miniature case, dated about 1580, three inches over all, enamelled with a lovely design of dolphins and arabesque scrolls in several colours on a black ground. The front is pierced in gold scroll work set with rubies and diamonds, through which the miniature portrait underneath can be seen. Such miniature cases were worn attached to the bodice, and often caught up round the neck by a cord as well (*see* Plate XLIV).

Many museums, notably the Victoria and Albert, possess original examples of Elizabethan pendants.

JEWELS OF QUEEN ELIZABETH

Carcanets and Pendants

We must here interrupt the description of jewellery in general to describe that worn by the Queen, as seen in her portraits.

Her great love of jewellery and the manner in which she loaded herself with jewels and pearls, already well known, is commented upon by the French Ambassador, de Maisse, in 1597:

'She wore innumerable jewels on her person, not only on her head, but also within her collar, about her arms, and on her hands, with a very great quantity of pearls, round her neck and in her bracelets. She had two bands, one on each arm, which were worth a great price.'

Attention is called to one of these bands in D, Plate XXXI.

The Queen was in the habit of frequently losing her jewels, as these were sewn on or even pinned to various parts of her dresses. Notices were issued to the effect that such and such a jewel was missing, and if found please return.

Carcanets

A very beautiful carcanet is worn over the ermine cape of the Queen's coronation robes in Plate XXVII. It is composed of table-cut rubies each set square and surrounded by six pearls, alternating with oval sapphires set in small diamonds; to each of these a pear pearl is attached. In the middle of the carcanet is a larger ruby set lozengewise and surrounded by six groups of diamonds; a pear-shaped pearl hangs from this. The carcanet encircling the throat is of the same design but on a smaller scale. The waist girdle is of the same jewels, but contains fewer pearls and no drop pearls.

In Fig. 575, the Spanish surcote being closed, the carcanet with pendant is worn over it. In Plate XXIX the carcanet with pendant of rubies and pearls is worn on the bodice and *under* the open Spanish surcote.

The carcanets seen in B, C, and D Plate XXXI, vary slightly in design, consisting of groups of pearls alternating with jewels set in gold mounts. They are worn close up round the throat.

The carcanet seen in D, Plate XXXI, has rubies in settings of enamel and gold alternating with groups of five pearls. The bracelets are bands, and match, being of the same jewels. To the carcanet is added a centre ornament of a large diamond or sapphire, and to this and to the rubies are attached peardrop pearls. An ornament in the form of a bracelet worn on the upper right arm is of rubies, sapphires, diamonds, and pearls. Quantities of pearls, sapphires, and diamonds are scattered with regularity over the whole dress and headdress.

In the Portland portrait, C, Plate XXXII, the jewellery worn by the Queen consists of a carcanet of jewels in gold mounts joined by groups of eight pearls, and from it hangs an oval pendant; another pendant of similar design with a pearl hanging therefrom is suspended by a riband from the girdle. This is quite a new

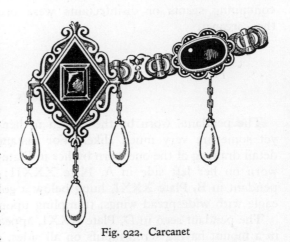

Fig. 922. Carcanet

fancy, and can be seen in the portraits A, Plate XXXI, C, Plate XLI, and Plate XLII. The jewels on the shoulder rolls, waist-girdle, and frogging down the front all match.

Plate XXXVIII D, the Ermine portrait, shows one of the wider carcanets, and the arrangements of the eight pearls which come between the jewels is of quite a different design from any hitherto met with.

On close investigation it will be seen that the Queen in A, Plate XLI, is wearing the same carcanet as shown in Plate XLII. Fig. 922 gives a small part of it which is attached to the central jewel. This is a lozenge-shaped ornament in black enamel, framed in gold scroll work, and having a ruby set in the centre. The ornamental links, or rather hinges, connect oval rubies set in gold and black enamel mounts; and from each of these—and there must be at least a dozen to complete the carcanet—hangs a pear pearl on a gold chain. Three more pearls are suspended from the central ornament.

A few items referring to carcanets, and taken from various lists of New Year's gifts to Her Majesty, are set forth below:

'Item, one riche carkenet or collar of golde, having in it two emeraldes,

4 rubyes, and fully garnished with small rubyes and dyamondes.   Geven by the Erle of Lecetor [Leicester].

'A collar of golde contayning 13 peecies, wherein are 13 great emeraldes and 13 pieces of golde, with 13 troches [clusters] of perles, 5 perles in every troche, and in every peece 4 small rubyes, geven by therle Lecetor.'

'Item, a carkenet, upper and nether habilliment of christalles, and small pomaunders slightly garnished with golde. Geven by the Countyes of Lyncolne.'

The 'upper' refers to a carcanet worn close round the throat, and the 'nether' to a larger one of the same design worn over the shoulders. 'Pomaunders' must mean that little filigree gold buttons or balls containing scents or disinfectants were used as additional ornaments to the carcanet.

Pendants

The pendants worn by the Queen in her portraits are of varied design, yet some are very much alike. For instance, that shown in Fig. 923, a detail drawing of the one worn by her in Plate XXIX, is very like the pendant worn on her left side in A, Plate XXXII; possibly it is the same. The pendant in B, Plate XXXI, hung below a golden rose set with a ruby, is an eagle with widespread wings, trampling upon scorpions.

The pendant seen in D, Plate XXXI, appears to be a large square sapphire in a mount having scroll motifs on all sides, each set with a diamond; from this hangs a pelican in enamel perched on a rectangular ruby in a corresponding gold mount, and to this is attached a lace of pearls festooned round the bodice.

In the Siena portrait, A, Plate XXXII, Elizabeth has hung a beautiful pendant on the left side of her bodice. It consists of an immense jewel in a gold setting, with two female figures supporting it; a round pearl is attached. The pendant shown in B, Plate XLI, is of square shape, with the frame of gold and red enamel.

Fig. 927 is a detail of the pendant worn in B, Plate XXXII. It is an amber heart in a mount of black enamel and gold, surrounded by two rows of black enamel and headed by two rubies. A third and smaller ruby holds the pendent pearl.

The Ermine portrait, D, Plate XXXII, at Hatfield, which the Marquess of Salisbury has kindly allowed to be reproduced together with the 'Rainbow' portrait, is particularly interesting. Apart from the carcanet already referred to it has lately been discovered by the author that the Queen is wearing, suspended by a chain from this carcanet, the historic jewel known as the 'Three Brothers.' Fig. 427, which is made from the Ermine portrait, is probably

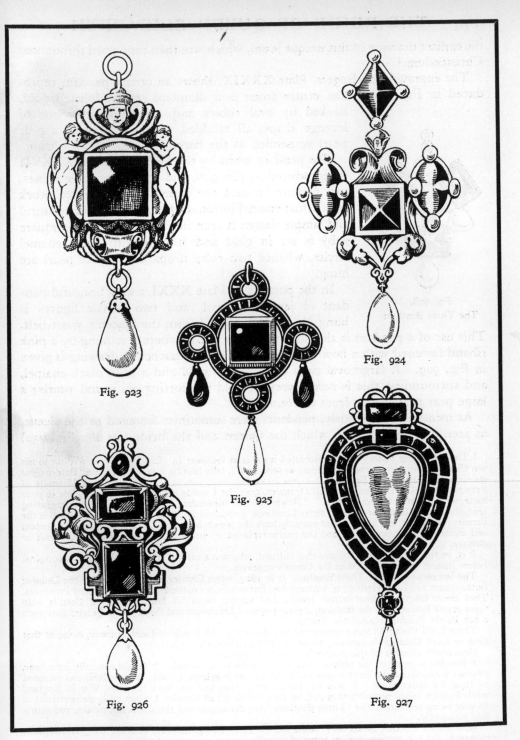

Fig. 923

Fig. 924

Fig. 925

Fig. 926

Fig. 927

PENDANTS WORN BY QUEEN ELIZABETH

the earliest drawing of this unique jewel, which was then renowned throughout Christendom.[1]

The engraving by Rogers, Plate XXXIX, shows an ornate pendant reproduced in Fig. 924. The centre stone is a diamond set on foliated gold, flanked by oval rubies and surmounted by one of lozenge shape, all studded with pearls, with a pear pearl suspended at the base.

Fig. 928.
The Three Brothers

The pendant worn by the Queen in Plate XXXVII is reproduced in Fig. 926, and comprises three rubies, two rectangular and one round, in open scroll work with a little enamel introduced. A pendant of beautiful and simple design is seen in Fig. 925. A large square ruby is set in gold and framed with black enamel circles, whence two ruby drops and a pear pearl are hung.

In the portrait A, Plate XXXI, a very beautiful pendant of jewels, enamel, and two female figures is hung by a black riband from the Queen's waist-belt. This use of a pendant is also shown in Plate XLII where it is hung by a pink riband fastened with a bow to the point of her stomacher; a drawing is given in Fig. 929. A large oval ruby is framed in gold and a little black enamel, and surrounding this is scroll work in gold supporting six round pearls; a large pear pearl hangs from the centre.

As mentioned previously, pendants were sometimes fastened to the sleeve, as seen in Plate XLV, in which the Queen and the bride (*see also* Fig. 732)

[1] The remaining history of the celebrated jewel is as follows: In 1623 James I, in writing to his son Charles, about to journey into Spain to seek a wife, tells him he is sending for his 'Babies owin wearing . . . the Three Brothers that you know full well, but newlie sette, and the Mirroure of Frawnce, the fellowe of the Portugall Dyamont, quhiche I wolde wishe you to weare alone in your hatte with a little blakke feather.' 'Newly set' is misleading. In comparing the engraving (Fig. 928) taken from the work of Peter Lambeck, published in 1669, with the jewel shown in the Ermine portrait, it will be seen that not only have the jewels been reset, but apparently both rubies and diamonds have been recut and the pearls replaced by smaller ones—perhaps through loss or damage.

It is, on the whole, more probable that Hilliard, who was a careful artist and who had the original before him, is more correct than the Count's engraver.

The last record of the 'Three Brothers' is in 1625, when Charles, now King, sends the Duke of Buckingham and Lord Holland as Ambassadors Extraordinary to the States of the United Provinces. They are to take with them certain jewels, and among them 'A faire Flower of Goulde with three greate Ballasses in the middest, a great poynted Dyamond and three greate Pearles fixte with a fair Pearle Pendant, called the Brethren.'

These Lord Compton was commanded to deliver into the hands of Lord Conway, being at that time in Lord Compton's custody, to be pawned in Holland.

Henceforth all trace of this interesting jewel disappears.

A possible solution of the ultimate fate of this jewel is suggested. It would naturally have been pawned with one of the most important financiers or jewellers in, say, Amsterdam, and retained by them for redemption. It may be that at some date, but not until the Civil War in England when English credit probably slumped, or after the death of Charles I when no hope remained of its ever being reclaimed, the 'Three Brothers' was dissected, and the diamond, rubies, and pearls sold separately.

Who knows whether Louis XIV, noted for his love of magnificence, or some other ostentatious monarch, did not acquire one, or some of them?

It would be an interesting mystery for someone with the necessary time, industry, and means to follow up.

are both wearing such a decoration. Another example is given in Fig. 730.

The following descriptions apply to other pendants belonging to the Queen:

'A juell of golde, being a catt, and myce playing with her.'

'One green frog, the back of emeralds, smale and greate, and a pendaunte emeralde, and a smale chegne of gold to hang by.'

'A juell of golde, being an anker.'

'Two snakes wounde together.'

Some excerpts from lists of New Year's gifts which show the varied subjects introduced into pendants are given below:

'Item, a juell of golde, being a shippe, set with a table dyamonde of fyve sparcks of dyamondes, and a smale perle pendaunte. Geven by the Lorde Howarde.

'Item, one juell of golde, wherein is a pelly-cane garnished with small rubyes and dia-mondes, hanging by a small chegne, and one perle pendaunt. Geven by the Lady Mary Sidney. Geven by her Majestie to the young Countyes of Huntingdon.' 1572.

The above may refer to the pelican pen-dant worn by the Queen in the portrait, D, Plate XXXI.

Fig. 929. Pendant

'Item a Falcone or parret, the body chris-tall, the hedd, tayle, leggs, and crest of golde; fully garnished with sparcks of rubyes and eme014uldes, hanging by a very short and small chegne of golde.' 1574.

'Item, a riche juell, being a clocke of golde, garnished with dyamondes, rubyes, emeraldes, and perles, with one very fayre rubye in the bottome, and a fayre emeralde pendante sett in golde, and two mene perles pendaunte, all 9 oz 3 ge. Geven by Mr. Hatton, Capitayne of the Garde.' 1575.

The following story illustrates the lengths to which Elizabeth would go to secure a coveted jewel—a greed which she shared with Catherine de' Medici. Soon after Portugal became a province of Spain under Philip II in 1581, the claimant to the throne, Dom Antonio, was driven out of the country and fled first to France and then to England. Arriving at the English Court penniless but with the bulk of the Portuguese crown jewels, Dom Antonio was made much of by Queen Elizabeth and Leicester, and treated with Royal honours solely on account of his great wealth in jewels. 'The greedy crew that sur-rounded the Queen soon scented plunder, and money for warlike preparations, the purchase of ships and the like [for the recovery of Dom Antonio's lost crown] was speedily forthcoming.' Elizabeth and Leicester managed to grab some of the best, advancing £5,000 for a magnificent diamond of the purest water, weighing eight carats and called 'The Portuguese.' After a good deal of haggling with merchants about loans, etc., the Queen annexed the diamond for £8,000 (it was valued at about £30,000) and in England it remained for forty-two years.[1] 'In dudgeon with the greedy English,' poor though he still had a considerable quantity of jewels left, Dom Antonio went back to France, only to be treated in like manner by that other coveter of rich jewels, Catherine de' Medici.

This finishes the list of a few of the Queen's jewels.

HAT AND HEAD ORNAMENTS

There seems to be no rule as to the kind of jewellery worn by gentlemen in their headgear. Although there might be a particular vogue at a given time, men of fashion decorated their hats with whatever took their fancy at the moment.

The gold ornaments and the jewelled pin worn by Mr. Edward Hoby in 1577 (Fig. 847) are imitated by Sir John Hawkyns (Fig. 851). The decoration of young Oxford's hat, 1575 (Fig. 846), of fastening the hatband with jewelled buttons, is one that was frequently used on smart headgear for some time. Later we find Sir Henry Unton in 1586 (Fig. 850) wearing an elaborate jewel, such as at a later date (1602) is set upon a Spanish hat; and at a much later period (beyond the limit of this volume) similar elaborate jewels in hats were very much in vogue.

Fig. 930. Parure of French Hood

The women copied the men, as with headgear, and their outdoor hats glistened with ornaments. The Spanish ladies of the aristocracy were profuse in the adornment of their hats, as seen in Fig. 674 (the Queen of Spain) and Fig. 773.

The band of jewels or parure which ornamented the arch of the French hood, referred to in this volume as a 'coronet,' varied very considerably, as will be seen by the many illustrations of French hoods. Fig. 930 shows part of a parure of unusual design in which jewels do not appear; instead, it is decorated with coloured enamels on a band of gold and set with large pearls. The portrait from which this drawing is taken dates about the 1570's.

Headdresses in the form of coronets or cauls, especially those worn by Queen Elizabeth, were masses of jewels; and the wreaths, or billiments as they were called (see especially Fig. 880), and tiaras such as were in fashion during the 1590's, are so elaborate as to be almost indescribable. Some illustrations are given in Figs. 729, 730, 732, 772, 774, and Plate XLIV.

[1] This diamond was ultimately given by Charles, Prince of Wales, to the Duke of Olivares in 1623.

Another head ornament much used during the second half of the reign was the bodkin. This was a kind of skewer, but for practical purposes it must have been shaped like a hairpin. At the top of this bodkin was usually set some jewel, often a diamond, or a round or pear pearl; sometimes a diamond suspended by pearls. A number of these ornaments were stuck over the whole coiffure. Queen Elizabeth was very fond of piercing her padded wigs with jewelled bodkins, as seen in her portraits, Plates XXXII A and XLI, A, C, and D, Plates XLII and XLV.

These ornaments might be termed buttons, as they could, without the pin, be used as such; and excerpts from an inventory of the Queen's are:

'Item, 3 dozen of buttones of golde, havinge 3 pearles and a sparcke of an emeralde or rubyes in every button. 3 ounces and a half.

'Item, 84 buttons of golde enamuled, and every of them sett with a small sparcke of emeralds, rubyes, and perles. Geven by therle of Warwicke.

'Item, twoe bodkins of golde, thone a flye, thother a spyder, the spider's body being a perle and a sparke of a rubye, the fly garnished with sparks of dyamondes. Geven by Sir Henry Lee, Master of the Armorye.' 1586–7.

'Item, a bodkinne of silver, with a little ostridg of gold, pendant, enamuled, and two waspes of golde lose enamuled. Geven by Mr. Carmanden.

'Item, a bodkin of golde, with a pendant emrald with a smale perle therat. Geven by Mrs. Sakeford.' 1584–5.

GIRDLES

The ornamentation of girdles with long ends reached its climax in the reigns of Henry VIII and Mary. No new features are noticeable, and girdles worn were of the same styles as described in Chapters II and III.

By the 1580's the girdle with a long pendent end was definitely out of fashion.

BRACELETS

Bracelets were not much used, as they could be worn only with sleeves of a certain kind; for instance, the one of embroidered linen shown in the portrait of Queen Elizabeth, Plate XXXI D. Also bracelets were not consistent with the elaborate lace cuffs which were so general. In some portraits one sees a single row of pearls between the edge of the cuff and wrist and falling well on to the hand (see Plate XXXII D, and Plate XLI D).

A wide band of jewels is worn round the upper arm by the Queen in D, Plate XXXI, and the Spanish Infanta (Fig. 772) also wears one in the same position.

That bracelets could be used as carcanets is verified by the following gift to the Queen:

'Item, a payre of braceletts, which may serve for a carkenett, fully garnished with ophales and rubyes very fayre, enamuleted with an ophall pendaunt. Geven by Mr. Hatton, Capitaine of the Garde.'

Fig. 931.
Cuff Ornament

Fig. 932.
Sleeve Ornament

A jewel fixed on to the lace cuff was quite usual, as shown in C, Plate XLI. This is given in larger scale in Fig. 931.

Fig. 932 shows another ornament which could be used for the same purpose, but this one is taken from a portrait of a lady dated 1599. In this she is wearing several of these ornaments sewn at the top of her full-puffed sleeves.

EARRINGS

Earrings—when they were worn, which was not very often it appears—were, as a rule, circular or peardrop pearls. Other kinds were occasionally used, and Fig. 933 gives one of a pair worn by the Queen in D, Plate XLI; the main element in the design, thrice repeated, is a peardrop pearl and an almond-shaped ruby set in gold, both hanging from the same link.

Elizabeth preferred pearl earrings, and a peardrop hanging from a cluster of pearls is seen in Plate XL; in B, Plate XLI, the pear pearl is hung from an ornamental disc in gold and red enamel.

Mary Fitton, Plate XLIV, has chosen earrings each consisting of a hoop of pearls or diamonds, probably both, from which a peardrop pearl is suspended.

It has already been mentioned that gentlemen wore *one* earring, and that a pearl.

Fig. 933.
Earring

RUFF ORNAMENTS

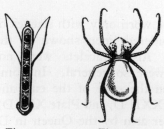

Fig. 934.   Fig. 935.
Ruff Ornaments

The use of jewelled ornaments pinned on to the ruff was a charming idea in vogue during the 1590's. These are particularly conspicuous in Plate XL, where they take the form of arrows in gold and red enamel set with rubies or diamonds, with the feathers in pearl (Fig. 934). It was noticed on one occasion that a large black spider was sitting on the ruff of Queen Elizabeth; this was a realistic piece of jewellery in jet with diamond eyes. Another spider is shown in Fig. 935, with the head and legs in gold and enamel, diamond or emerald eyes, and a pear-pearl body.

Some portraits of the Queen and noble ladies show a rose of the new variety fastened on the left side of the ruff, and there are several others where a rose or other flower is fixed to the bodice.

AIGLETTES

Throughout the latter half of the sixteenth century the attractive decoration of aiglettes and loops plastered on sleeves and down the fronts of skirts was very much the mode. This fashion originated in Spain, where it was very generously used upon the elaborate dresses of the no-bility (*see* Figs. 674, 676, 680). These loops with ends are first seen worn by an English lady (Fig. 589), dating 1560, where the reason for their introduction is explained; but, as so often happens in the history of costume, utility soon gave way to decoration. Henceforth we find these aiglettes and loops much in evidence, but used only as ornaments mainly by ladies of the land of their origin, and of France, and in England from about 1600. Fig. 936 shows a pair of jewelled aiglettes of coloured enamel and gold, with spirals

Fig. 936.	Fig. 937.
A Pair of Aiglettes	Handle of Fan

of pearls. Each is attached to one end of a piece of silk or riband, which is knotted, forming an erect loop.

Fig. 937 is the jewelled handle of a feather fan carried by Queen Elizabeth in the portrait Plate XLII.

FINGER RINGS

In the Bodleian is a book of original designs for finger rings by Pierre VVoerior of Lorraine, 1561; from this source Figs. 938, 939, and 940 have been reproduced.

Fig. 939 shows the side and end views of two of these rings. The ring (Fig. 938) with grotesque men's heads which terminate the shanks supporting the flange and bezel, is set with a pointed diamond. In Fig. 940 the shanks develop into rams' heads and forelegs, and are mounted by a circular watch. It is very ornate, and so minute that one wonders if it is practicable.

Another ring of the same kind, but dating the end of the century, is given in Fig. 941. Scrolls set with diamonds decorate the shanks, bezel, and lid, the latter covering a very small dial.   This ring is drawn from an actual example, which shows that a watch-ring such as is described above *could* be made.

Fig. 942 is a ring of romance — the Essex ring which the Countess of Nottingham failed to bring to Queen Elizabeth, with such fatal results.   The

Fig. 938.

Fig. 939.
Four Finger Rings, 1561

Fig. 940.

delicate shank, somewhat worn by age, supports a heavy flange engraved in lines with tiny globules surrounding the bezel.   This contains a cameo portrait of the Queen cut from a three-strata sardonyx.   A blue enamelled cinquefoil ornaments the top and base.   After the execution of the Earl of Essex, the ring was returned to his daughter, the Lady Frances Devereux, and thereafter it passed from mother to daughter for several generations.[1]

It was still not uncommon to wear a ring on the middle joint and one on the thumb as well as on the fingers.   Two rings worn on the right hand are shown attached for safety by a fine gold chain to the bracelet in the Arbury portrait of Katherine Nevill, wife of Francis Fitton, Esq., who was married in 1588.

Fig. 941. Dial Ring

Fig. 942.
The Essex Ring

It was stated recently that the wedding ring of Mary Stuart and Lord Darnley was a rather clumsy, rough one of tawny gold, bearing the initials M. H. entwined with true lovers' knots.   In her list of bequests (made in

---

[1] Later this ring came successively into the possession of six noble ladies, three peers, and four old bachelors, and was sold to Lord Michelham in 1910 for £3,412.   From him it was purchased in 1927 by an historical enthusiast, Mr. Ernest Makower, for £546 to present to Westminster Abbey, where it can now be seen upon the tomb of Queen Elizabeth.

1566) a wedding ring is mentioned of red and gold enamel set with a large diamond, and in her handwriting in the margin beside it are these words: 'Cest celui de quoy ie fus espousee. Au Roy qui la me donne.'

The English Envoy at Edinburgh, in his contemporary account of the Queen's marriage, writes: 'The words were spoken; the rings, which were three, the middle a rich diamond, were put upon her finger, they kneel together, and many prayers said over them.' The other two rings were plain guards.

French Jewellery

The amount of jewellery produced in France during the reigns of Charles IX and Henry III was greater than at any previous period, and many French masters of the jeweller's art became famous. In design their work very closely resembled the Italian, being greatly influenced by the school of Cellini of the previous generation.

Some very delightful jewellery of about 1550–60 is to be seen in the portrait, French School, of the Duchesse d'Angoulême, No. 2617 in the National Gallery. She wears a pale mauve-grey dress; the carcanet, waist-girdle, bracelets, and the ornaments on her French hood all match. They are of gold with black enamel, and set with rubies and pearls.

A few of the presents, sent from the French Royal family to the Archduchess Elizabeth of Austria before her marriage to Charles IX in 1572, are quoted:

'List of the presents with which the Royal Princess of France has been honoured by His Majesty, his Lady Mother, and his brethren. The King of France caused to be given: To his Bride, the said Princess Elizabeth, the daughter of His Imperial Majesty: A necklace, that is valued in all at 50,000 scudi,[1] consisting of three diamonds in clusters, the least of which is valued at 10,000 scudi, four large rubies, sixteen large pearls, each one of which is valued at 100 scudi.

'A ring with a diamond hanging, set in four golden bands, so that it can be seen on all sides. It is valued at 12,000 scudi.

'To the Archduke Ferdinand: To lave the hands, a pitcher or can for water made of agate, set with pearls and a handle with an emerald to lift the lid thereof. . . .

'The Old Queen, Mother of the King of France, has presented: A chain all of rubies, diamonds and emeralds from which is suspended a large diamond. At the top there is a large ruby, and thereunder hangs a large pearl like a pear. This all is valued at 20,000 scudi. . . .

'Besides these presents, four white harriers have been sent to Vienna as a gift to the Emperor. Each of these has a red velvet and gold collar. The value of all this is 500 scudi.'

Elizabeth of Austria possessed the largest oriental ruby in the world. It was the size of a hen's egg, and at her death became the property of her brother, the Emperor Rudolph II.

[1] An Italian coin worth about four shillings.

JEWELS OF MARY STUART

Mary Stuart possessed many beautiful jewels of her own, chiefly of French workmanship. Amongst them were some remarkably fine pearls, including seven of exceptional size (*see* p. 277), the wedding gift of Catherine de' Medici. When Queen-Consort of France she had use of the French as well as the Scottish crown jewels in addition to her own, but the former she relinquished when she returned to Scotland in 1561.

In her will, drawn up in June 1566 by Mary Livingston, Keeper of Her Majesty's jewels, and Margaret Carwood, bedchamber woman in charge of the Queen's cabinet, Mary Stuart left certain jewels of her own to the Crown of Scotland in remembrance of herself and the Scottish alliance with the House of Lorraine. The items include seven jewels containing her largest diamonds for ornaments to the succeeding Queens-Consort of Scotland. To the Crown itself she devised a diamond cross, a chain enriched with rubies and diamonds, a carcanet of diamonds, rubies, and pearls, and the 'Great Harry.' This jewel contained a large diamond 'taillé à faces' set in gold, a cabochon ruby, and the cipher ♄ set in diamonds, hanging by a chain of gold 'with a ruby pendant thereat.' This was a gift to Queen Mary from her father-in-law, Henry II, whose cipher it bore.[1]

In 1570 the 'Great Harry' was bestowed by the Regent Moray upon his wife, and later much pressure was brought to bear upon the widowed Countess to give it up—apparently without success, as it was not until 1574 that she, now Countess of Argyll, was compelled by Parliament to restore it to James VI.

After 1567 Mary's own jewels and those of the Scottish Crown began an adventurous career. She left them behind, with most of her wardrobe, on her hurried escape from Edinburgh Castle in May 1567, some of them hidden, it is said, in a crevice in the castle rock. Others, chiefly those belonging to the Crown, including the Regalia, were discovered in the castle 'hidden in a wooden chest in a cave.' Her own personal jewels fared worse. At Carberry Hill (June 1567) Mary gave 20,000 crowns' worth (£6,000) to Bothwell, and these fell into the hands of the Confederate Lords, along with most of her belongings.

Shortly afterwards the Queen entrusted her own diamonds and pearls to the Earl of Moray, who was visiting her at Loch Leven. The trust was ill-kept; they passed, to the value of 20,000 or 30,000 crowns, into the hands of the Earl of Morton, and many of them were subsequently pawned or sold. Numbers of diamonds and pearls were pawned to many different persons, from whom the Regent Morton recovered them by powers granted by Parliament in 1574. Some came to London for sale, and among them were 'six cordons of large pearls, strung as paternosters; but there are five and twenty separate from the rest, much finer and larger than those which are strung; these are for the most part like black muscates'—the famous black

---

[1] In James I's reign the large diamond of the 'Great Harry' was incorporated in the more magnificent 'Mirror of Great Britain.'

pearls, the most magnificent in Europe. Many offers were made for them, but Queen Elizabeth, who had always kept a keen eye on her dear sister's jewels, bought the pearls [1] for 12,000 crowns, not a third of their value, in April 1568. This was done under the covetous eyes of Catherine de' Medici and, indeed, of most of Europe.

The little jewel casket, which afterwards became so celebrated, is described thrice—by the Regent Moray in 1568 as 'a silver box'; by the Privy Council in 1568 and 1571 as 'a silver box owergilt with gold'; and by Buchanan as 'a small gilt coffer not fully a foot long, being garnished in sundry places with the Roman letter F under a king's crown.'

Gabrielle d'Estrées was noted for the marvellous jewels she possessed, and at a Court function in 1594 her dress of black satin was so loaded with diamonds, rubies, emeralds, and pearls, that she was only able to stand for a few minutes at a time. By special permission this overweighted lady was allowed to sit in the Royal presence.

Another bejewelled lady, this time a Royal one, was Marie de' Medici, over whose gown were strewn 32,000 pearls and 3,000 diamonds. It was so heavy that she sat all through some State ceremony, but this was her privilege as Queen-Consort.

A beautiful Indian diamond of almond shape and faceted on both sides ultimately became one of the English Crown jewels, but not without a history of some interest.

Henry III's Ambassador at the Turkish Court was Nicolas Harlai, Seigneur de Sancy, who, while at Constantinople in 1570, bought this Indian diamond for a very large sum. On his return to France, Harlai sold it to the King, who prized it so much that he often wore it in front of his turban (see Figs. 745 and 746). At Henry's death in 1589 the diamond was returned to the Lord of Sancy, and henceforth this precious stone was named after him.

In order to raise money for the strengthening of his army, Henry IV borrowed the 'Sancy' from its owner, who had now become superintendent of the King's finances, and in course of time returned it. Later, when fulfilling his term of office as Henry's Ambassador to England, Harlai sold it to Queen Elizabeth.[2]

[1] The seven pearls, the gift of Catherine de' Medici, still form part of the crown jewels of Great Britain.
[2] After Queen Elizabeth's death this large diamond was taken, together with the diamond from the 'Great Harry,' to adorn a still more splendid jewel known as the 'Mirror of Great Britain,' and in an inventory dated 1605 it is described as follows:
'A greate and rich jewell of golde called the Myrror of Greate Brytayne conteyninge one verie fayre table dyamonde, one verie fayre table rubye, twoe other lardge dyamondes, cut lozengewyse, the one of them called the Stone of the letter H of Scotlande garnyshed with smalle dyamondes, two rounde perles, fixed, and one fayre dyamonde, cutt in fawcettis bought of Sauncey.'
So set, the Sancy remained among the British crown jewels until 1689, when it passed (detached) to the crown jewels of France, appearing again in an inventory of 1791. In the nineteenth century it came into the possession of the Princess Paula Demidoff, from whose family it was purchased in 1856 for the sum of £20,000 by the wealthy Parsee merchant, Sir Jamsetjee Jeejeebhoy. At his decease it returned to France and was shown at the Paris Exhibition of 1867, where it was priced at a million francs. Thence it passed to the Maharajah of Patiala, after whose death William Waldorf Astor purchased it as a wedding present to his daughter-in-law in 1906. This diamond is still in the possession of the Viscountess Astor.

The most confusing stories are told about famous jewels, but it is hoped that the accounts of those which have been given in this volume are reasonably correct.

CLOCKS

Perpendicular standing clocks, anything from twelve to twenty-four or more inches in height, were very elaborate during the reign of Elizabeth, following the designs popularized by Holbein.   A description of one is given on p. 501.

Another, mentioned in a list of jewels delivered into the custody of M^{ris} Mary Radeclyffe, one of the gentlewomen of 'the Quenes Majesties privie chambre' by Mistress Blanche Parry, is described as follows:

'Item one clocke of golde curiouslye wrought with flowers and beastes with a Quene in the toppe on thone side, and on the other side a beare and a ragged staffe of sparkes of diamondes fullie furnished with diamondes and rubies of sundrye sortes and bignes one Emerode under it a faier table dia-monde with a ragged staffe in the foyle thereof and a faier Rubie under it squared, and a pearle pendaunt on eyther side of the clocke.'

A clock in the form of a ship, dated 1580, can be examined in the Franks Room of the British Museum; and another, dated 1589, and resembling a three-storied tower, can also be seen there.

WATCHES

In the second half of the century the clockmakers of southern Germany and France supplied an increasing demand for standing clocks, table clocks, and pectoral or pendent clocks—i.e. watches.   By their ingenuity they were able to reduce the size of the works so as to take up as little space as possible, reducing the clock to a very small compass.

Watches were of different shapes, their dials being circular, square, octagonal, or oval; and in thickness flat, semi-spherical, pumpkin, or egg-shaped, the last being known as 'Nuremberg eggs.'   'Memento mori' watches were set in gold, silver, or ivory carved in the form of a skull, and were as much as three by two and a half inches; they were usually attached by a chain to the waist-girdle.

Circular watches were worn as pendants at the neck, on the hip, and at the waist or end of the girdle.

Mary Stuart possessed at least two octagonal watches or dials as they were often called.   One of them, the work of D. du Chemin of Rouen, 1570, measures one and five-eighth inches in diameter, and has an engraved gold dial; the lid is of rock crystal set in a narrow gold frame.   The other watch is almost identical in design, except that the dial is not engraved.   Both these watches are similar to that shown in Fig. 945.

The Queen of Scots left to Darnley, by her will dated 1566: 'One watch garnished with ten diamonds, two rubies, and a cord of gold,' and 'one little dial curiously wrought and set with eight diamonds, two rubies, one pearl pendant, one little chain of gold to which is attached a pomander garnished with little turquoises and garnets.'

Fig. 943 is a German-made watch dating about 1560. Its case is flat, curiously shaped, and decorated with enamel. As a rule, German watches were circular boxes and struck the hours; they had the same appearance as a reliquary, being hung round the neck like a pendant. Augsburg was an important place for the manufacture of watches, and several of those now existing bear this name upon them. In 1558 it is stated that fashionable young men wore these circular watches suspended by a chain upon their breasts.

It is more than likely that the circular pendant worn by Queen Elizabeth on her right hip in the portrait (Plate XXXII C) is a jewelled watch. The Earl of Leicester presented her with a watch, sometimes called a dial or even clock, as a New Year's gift, 1578-9. It was 'a verey feyer juell of golde, being a clocke fully furnished with small diamonds pointed and a pendaunte of golde, diamonds, and rubies, very smale, and upon each side a lozenge diamond, and an apple of golde enamuled grene and russet.'

Fig. 943. German Watch, 1560

According to the design by VVoerior (Fig. 940) watches were sometimes set as finger rings, and perhaps the first wrist watch recorded in history was the Earl of Leicester's New Year's gift to Elizabeth, 1571-2. It is described as 'one armlet or shakell [shackle] of golde, all over fairely garnishedd with rubyes and dyamondes, having in the closing thereof a clocke, and in the fore parte of the same a fayre lozengie dyamonde without a foyle, hanging thereat a rounde juell fully garnished with dyamondes, and perle pendant; weying 11 oz. qu^a dim. and farthing golde weight. In a case of purple vellate all over embranderid with Venice golde, and lyned with greene vellat.'

The portrait, dated 1586, of Joyce Frankland at Brasenose College, Oxford, shows the lady holding a circular watch in her hands (Fig. 944). She was the daughter of Robert Trappes, a goldsmith, and married first Henry Saxey and secondly William Frankland, both goldsmiths of London. It is said that she was the first citizeness to possess a gold watch. Being thrice associated with the goldsmith's craft, this is not surprising. Certainly the watch, which measures two and a half inches across, is an excellent specimen. The dial, A, of gold is plain with the exception of very delicate engraving in the centre. The hours are engraved, and round the edge is a cord moulding.

The lid, B, has an openwork design reproduced on a larger scale in E. The back part, C, which shows in perspective in the original painting, has rectangular incisions forming a decorative border. D is a section through the back. To the watch is attached a black silk riband, and at the end is strung the golden key.

The pendant (Fig. 916) is worn by Mistress Frankland in this portrait.

Fig. 945 is a watch dating the 1590's, hexagonal and flat in shape, the dial

Fig. 944. Mistress Frankland's Watch, 1586   Fig. 945

and sides being decorated with enamel. The front and back are covered with rock crystal lids set in narrow moulded gold frames, and to it is attached a plaited gold chain bearing the key.

An instance of the diplomatic use of jewels—a very frequent occurrence —is cited below:

'Venice, 3 March 1600.

'We are advised from Constantinople that the Sultan has sent magnificent gifts of rubies, pearls, and diamonds to the Queen of England with a request that she should effect a peace between him and His Imperial Majesty.'

Should students of historical jewellery wish to pursue the subject more comprehensively, they will find H. Clifford Smith's book, *Jewellery*, 1908, most useful.

GUILDS AND TRADE (*continued from p. 464*)

In the early days of Elizabeth's reign, trade in the Mediterranean was made dangerous, even impossible, owing to the rise of the Turkish sea power dating about the middle of the century. Consequently, England was still dependent on the merchant galleys of Venice for her supplies of luxuries and gorgeous fabrics. In 1571 the Ottoman Empire received a tremendous blow at Lepanto, which completely crushed its naval ambitions. The first English representative was installed at Constantinople in 1578, and in 1580 the Charter of Liberties to English merchants, which opened trade relations with Turkey, was formally issued.

Russia had already, in 1553, made commercial overtures to the English nation, and again in 1582 a special envoy was sent by Ivan the Terrible to undertake matrimonial negotiations with one of Queen Elizabeth's relatives, but without success. A year later Sir Jerome Bowes was sent, as first Ambassador to Moscow, in order to obtain exemption from the duties on English exports to Russia.

Apparently Japan had trade relations with Spain in 1595, and China with England. The latter could not have been very extensive, for, according to a report dated 1599, 'a vessel richly laden with gold and silk is said to have reached England from China after a three years' voyage.'

Ever since it was established at the Styleyard, the Hanseatic League had enjoyed many and great privileges by special treaty; but owing to its arbitrary bearing, these were abolished by order of Queen Elizabeth in 1578. However, the merchants still remained at their headquarters, and continued to cling blindly to their old prerogatives; in consequence of which the exasperated Queen expelled them from London in 1598. A nasty blow was dealt them by Sir Francis Drake, who captured sixty-one of their ships. Piracy was a popular amusement carried on even against countries with which England was normally at peace; and the Queen herself thought no shame in protecting the pirates and in accepting a large share of the loot.

So remarkable was the development of the Merchant Adventurers in the Netherlands during this reign, that at the height of their prosperity they employed fifty thousand persons in Holland, and the annual value of the trade reached twelve million ducats. In 1578 the foreign headquarters were moved to Hamburg, whence the merchants were for a time expelled under pressure from the Hanseatic League, but after the Queen closed the Styleyard the Adventurers soon recovered their position in Hamburg, and there the Company continued to function until 1808.

In 1600 Queen Elizabeth granted a charter to the East India Company, whereupon the various Dutch societies trading in the Indies were consolidated in 1602 into the Dutch East India Company.

Alas! all the picturesqueness of the London Livery Companies disappeared with the Middle Ages, owing to the commercial instincts of Sir William Bayly, Draper, described on p. 367.

It is quite certain that the Queen did not approve of this change. She would have much preferred homage and ovations from a colourful crowd of City worthies rather than from a collection of black-robed Dominicans, as they might have appeared but for the coloured hoods they carried.

There is a note of regret in the following excerpt from Stow:

'But yet in London among the graver sort (I mean the Liveries of Companies) remaineth a memory of the hoods of old time worn by their predecessors: these hoods were worn, the roundlets [the roll part] upon their heads, the skirts [the shoulder part] to hang behind in their necks to keep them warm, the tippet [liripipe] to lie on their shoulder or to wind about their necks; these hoods were of old time made in colours according to their gowns, which were of two colours, as red and blue, or red and purple, murrey, or as it pleased their masters and wardens to appoint to the companies. But now of late time they have used their gowns to be all of one colour, and those of the saddest, but their hoods being made the one half of the same cloth their gowns be of, the other half remaineth red as of old time.'

For the dress of a member of one of the City Companies see Fig. 798 and the description given under it.

One of the most popular of the Livery Companies of London was 'the Fraternity of the Art and Mistery of the Haberdashers . . . indifferently called Hurrers and Milliners, the Latter from the Merchandizes they chiefly dealt in, which came from the City of Milan.' Their wares comprised all kinds of articles necessary for dress, adornment, and utility: such as aiglettes, buttons of silk, metal or bone, brooches and ouches, French and Spanish gloves, head ornaments of every kind, caps, hats, French hoods, cauls, escoffions, spurs, ink-horns and penners, earpicks and toothpicks, trinkets and gewgaws, needles and pins.

WEAVING AND MATERIALS

During the course of the last two reigns there had been a repetition of many fraudulent practices in the making of cloth. Again in 1597 the same practices were denounced when 'flocks, sollace, flour, chalk, and other deceitful things' were mentioned as ingredients injurious to cloth, 'the use of which made them rewey, pursey, squally, cockling, light, and notably faulty . . . the same cloth having only for the most part an outward show, wanting that substance and strength which oftentimes it appears to have.' Fraudulent imitations of gold threads were made from copper-gilt wire, from gold leaf hammered upon vellum and afterwards cut into strips, and by covering fabrics with gold leaf.

The weaving industry received a tremendous impetus during this reign by the immigration of Flemings. Amongst them were a great number of weavers, dyers, and other skilled craftsmen, who fled to England to escape the persecutions of the Duke of Alba in 1568. A similar influx occurred in 1585, when the Duke of Parma captured Antwerp.

The prices of various materials will be found in Philip Henslowe's *Diary*.

LIST OF MATERIALS

Bays, bayze, introduced into England in 1561 by the Walloons; so called from its colour, a reddish brown. In 1568 the Flemish refugees were granted permission to settle at Norwich, Colchester, Maidstone, Sandwich, and Southampton.

Bewpers, beaupers, some kind of cloth, but its character is unknown. Probably a light woollen stuff.

Boulters, boulting cloth, a thin woollen material of coarse mesh, like a sieve or bolter.

Burra, borra, diminutive *burrell,* a kind of stuffing or padding.

Callimancoes, material made of camel hair or wool in stripes, checks, patterns, or plain colours, and glazed in finishing.

Cambric. See *Lawn.*

Carrells, a material like bays and fustians, only mixed with silk, worsted, or linen yarn.

Cobweb lawn, an especially fine transparent linen, as the name implies.

Crape, crêpe, thin transparent cotton or silk material with a small crinkled surface, usually black, and used for mourning. Also in white, but smooth.

Cyprus, a very fine transparent curled linen. Both black and white were made, but the former was much more common. This was chiefly used for mourning. Originally introduced from Cyprus, hence its name.

Damask, first made in England by the Netherlands weavers, who sought refuge in this country in 1568 and again in 1585. Its price was from about nine to ten shillings per yard.

Dornicks, dornock, checked table linen.

Estamel, same as stammell.

Harden, a common linen made from the coarsest quality of hemp or flax, and sometimes even of tow.

Galloon, braid of gold, silver, or silk thread.

Lawn. Stow is not correct in stating that lawn and cambric 'began to be known,' and were first imported to England in 1562. Both materials had been known for more than a century (*see* vol. ii, p. 463).

Luzarnes, fur from the Russian lynx, the shade of which depends upon the climate, as described on p. 130.

Mockadoes, an imitation velvet; a fabric either of wool or silk on which a pattern was formed with loops, which being afterwards cut, in the same way that velvet was sheared, left the pattern in pile.

Nettle cloth, a material said to have been woven from the fibres of nettles.

New draperies, a term used to denote light woollen fabrics introduced into England from the Netherlands by Protestant refugees, hence a name given to any novelty in cloth weaving.

Paillettes, pailles. See *Spangles.*

Fig. 946. Border, 1590

Pampilion also referred to a livery coat worn by servants, not necessarily furred.

Passamayne, gold or silver braid. Also applied, after 1578, to coloured braids.

Perpetuana, a term used to denote substantial fabrics. Also a strong *everlasting* glossy cloth, like parchment.

Fig. 947. Border, 1600

Plush, material made as shag having a long nap either in silk or of hair. Its use came in at the latter part of the sixteenth century.

Sammeron, a linen cloth 'between flaxen and hempen, finer than one and coarser than the other.'

Satin became so general and so inexpensive — about eight shillings, the

Fig. 948. Border, 1600

very best twelve shillings, per yard—that almost every one of any importance wore it.

Say, saye, sayes. The craft of weaving this coarse woollen cloth was brought to England by some Flemings in 1567. They settled at Braintree, Norwich, and Sudbury.

Shag, a rough hairy cloth woven with a single thread woof and a double warp; the one wool of two threads twisted, the other of goat or camel hair.

Spangles, musers, pailles, paillettes. Spangles were now much more scintillating. They were stamped in facets, and some were engraved.

Stammell, a coarse red cloth used by the commonalty as a substitute for the expensive scarlet cloth worn by the nobility. Estamel is another name for it.

Swansdown, the dressed down and skin of the swan fashionable for trimmings in the late sixteenth century. It was often dyed in colour.

Taffeta, a cheap substitute for the rich thin silk so popular amongst the nobility and upper classes, made in linen.

Thrum, the ends of the threads of the warp cut off from the extremities of the weaver's web.

Tiffany, a very transparent fine linen or gauze, sometimes classified under *Cobweb lawn.* Made in silk late in the sixteenth century as a silky transparent gauze.

Velure, a material something like velvet but made of cotton and sometimes wool.

Velvet. In the days of Queen Elizabeth velvet cost twenty shillings and thirty shillings per yard.

PATTERNS

The patterns of materials used during the first half of Queen Elizabeth's reign were much the same as those used during the reign of Henry VIII.

During the late 1570's, when skirts became fuller and the surface was broken up into many folds, large patterns became distorted. The Italian designers and weavers realized this change, and were the first to adopt much smaller and more compact designs, chiefly floral and often of a diaper or semée nature. France produced brocades of similar design, which is accounted for by the fact that many Italian weavers had emigrated to that country and brought the newest ideas with them. The first appearance of this type of smaller pattern in this volume is to be seen in the Darnley portrait of the Queen, A, Plate XXXI: a semi-floral scroll design, in delicate curves and broken sprays of gold, is woven upon a white satin or silk foundation.

Later, in 1580, we find the Queen, Plate XXXII C, gowned in a very beautiful brocade in the very latest style; conventional flowers and leaves in colours alternate diaperwise with motifs in gold having a jewelled button sewn in the centre; the design is woven into the white satin ground.

A pleasing design is given in Fig. 949, taken from the brass of the lady (Fig. 819), and dated 1572, where the under-skirt is of a brocade of this pattern.

Fig. 950 is an Italian brocade showing one element of a floral design enclosed in ogival bands, which is repeated over the whole fabric. The

Fig. 949. English

Fig. 950. Italian

Fig. 951. Franco-Italian

Fig. 952. Italian

pomegranate is still prominent; and there are definite Japanese features introduced, e.g. the motifs on the ogival bands, which may have come direct from Japan or via China to Spain or Italy.

A very characteristic pattern of smaller and more compact design, used by the Italian and French weavers of the latter part of the sixteenth century, is shown in Fig. 951. The introduction of flowers and foliage springing from vases, coronets, and birds shows how very persistent these types of motifs were. The fabric would be woven in silk of two colours.

Fig. 953. Spanish

A good example of the single motif placed diaperwise or semée over the surface of a silken material of Italian weave is shown in Fig. 952. Each motif could be of the same design, but in this example two slightly different designs are employed, each occupying different rows—diaperwise, and two colours are used upon a light ground.

Fig. 953 is a motif, from four to six inches in width, showing Moorish influences. It is repeated diaperwise over the surface of the silken material. This brocade is of Spanish manufacture: it is taken from a portrait of the Great Infanta, and in this case the ground is cloth of gold with the central design woven in close globules of gold; the four scroll-motifs which enclose it are of silver.

A prevalent type of design used at the end of the century is illustrated in

Fig. 954. Spanish

Fig. 954, showing one lozenge-shaped floral motif. This might be woven in a coloured or black velvet upon a cloth of gold, silk, or satin ground.

The pattern (Fig. 955) is one section from a late sixteenth-century wall painting in which the squares set diaperwise contain a design suggestive of acanthus leaves and a vase with flowers; it is also a pattern that could be used for a material. In the original the ground is pale yellow and the pattern black.

The brocade worn by the Queen of Spain, referred to on p. 685, is of white satin with a pattern of the latest mode in black silk woven upon it. It is shown in Fig. 777, and consists of two motifs arranged diaperwise, one suggesting the letter N and the other a caterpillar.

A very serious rival to patterned fabrics and brocades at this time was embroidery: the former retired somewhat from the fashionable wardrobe for a time. All the same, patterned fabrics were worn, as is evidenced by the fashionable lady (Fig. 730) who wears quite a large pattern in velvet upon a satin ground.

Fig. 955. English

LIST OF COLOURS

Ash-colour = grey: also *Cendré* (see vol. ii, p. 124)

Beasar = brownish like the bezoar-stone

Bice = a pale blue

Blecche = orange

Carnaĉon = carnation

Claie-colour = a deep cream

Clodie-colour = an off-white or light grey

Dead Spaniard: perhaps the colour of a corpse-like sallow complexion

Devil in the Hedge

Dove = a grey

Drakes-colour: possibly the flaming red of the Tudor 'dragon' or of the resin known as 'dragon's blood.'

Fig-brown = a brownish heliotrope

Flax-seed-colour. See *Isabella*

Goose-turd-green = a green darker and slightly more yellow than grass

Gozelinge = a pale yellowish-green

Hearecolour = brown, the colour of a hare

Horsefleshe-colour = a brown-pink

Isabella-colour. For the origin of this, see Chap. I, p. 133.

Ladie Blushe = pale pink or deep flesh colour

Lion-tawny = an ochre-orange colour

Lust Gallant

Marigold = an orange-yellow

Peache = yellow flushed with pink

Pease-porridge-tawny = a brownish-green

Pimpillo is a sixteenth-century name for a pin pillow. It is also applied to the prickly pear, from its appearance of a pin-cushion stuck full of pins.

A dye was prepared from the pulp of the prickly pear, of a colour between a raw umber, which is too red, and a raw sienna, which is too yellow

Pincke = pink

Popingay-blue = a blue-green

Pounde-Gythrone

Virli = a vivid green

Watchet = a light blue

The Dutch developed an extensive dyeing industry during the second half of the sixteenth century, and quantities of materials, chiefly cloth, were sent to Holland yearly to be dyed. According to Sir Walter Raleigh, as much as £400,000 per annum was spent out of England on this business.

The art of the dyer made much progress in France during the same period, and the following list gives the names of a few fancy French colours:

Amarante = amethyst-purple.

Céladon = sea-green.

Nacarade = pale orange-red.

Zinzolin = a red-violet.

Astrée. Astraea, the star-maiden, was a goddess who became the constellation Virgo, but what colour is intended, let another decide!

Espagnol malade = a variant of *Dead Spaniard*, above.

Fleur mourante ⎫
Triste amie   ⎬ sad colour or neutral tint.

Ventre de biche = a reddish-white.

VEHICLES (*continued from p. 466*)

The Litter

The litter continued to be a State vehicle, and according to custom Queen Elizabeth went to her coronation in an elaborately decorated horse-borne litter (Fig. 956), reproduced from the contemporary drawing in the College of Arms.

The body of the litter has ornate spiral ends, and the sides are decorated with lions' heads, scrolls, and a pelmet-like edging. The litter is borne by two richly caparisoned palfreys with nodding plumes on their heads, the first one led by Lord Giles Paulet and the second by Lord Ambrose Dudley. The Queen sits on a large chair, and over her a canopy of cloth of gold is carried by four noblemen. Her Majesty is preceded by an Earl carrying the Sword of State, and the Earl of Oxford as Lord Great Chamberlain of England. Behind the litter, Lord Robert Dudley leads the palfrey of honour (Fig. 957). On both sides walk 'Esquires and footmen near about Her Highnesses litter,' all dressed in crimson velvet; and outside them came 'The Gentlemen Pensioners on foot with polleaxes in their hands.' Both sets of gentlemen are garbed as shown in Figs. 609 and 610; the latter dressed in crimson damask and carrying gilded battleaxes. Altogether there were a thousand nobles and gentry, richly clad and mounted on gorgeously caparisoned horses. It is particularly stated that *all* were bareheaded.

An innovation in a French Royal litter, the use of *glass*, is described in the following:

Marguerite de Valois's journey to Flanders, in 1577, was undertaken ostensibly to partake of the waters of Spa, but in reality to gain partisans for her brother, the Duc d'Alençon, in his project of wresting the Low Countries from Spain.

'I went,' she says, in her *Memoirs*, 'in a litter with columns covered with rose-coloured Spanish velvet, embroidered in gold and shaded silks with a device; this litter was enclosed in glass, and each glass also bore a device, there being, whether on the velvet or on the glass, forty different devices about the Sun and its effects, with the words in Spanish and Italian.'

When Queen Elizabeth convened her fifth Parliament, 29th October 1586, she was not in the best of health. She therefore was conveyed 'in a semi-covered litter that looked like a half-canopied bed. The litter was entirely of wood upholdered all over with cloth of gold and silver. The cushions, too, on which the Queen reclined were of gold and silver material. . . . The litter was borne by two white steeds with yellow manes and tails; on the horses' heads and tails were plumes of yellow and white, their saddles and cloths being of gold material.'

Preceding the litter was 'a riderless horse, led by a Gentleman. The saddlecloth, the saddle, and the bridle were of pure cloth of gold, studded all

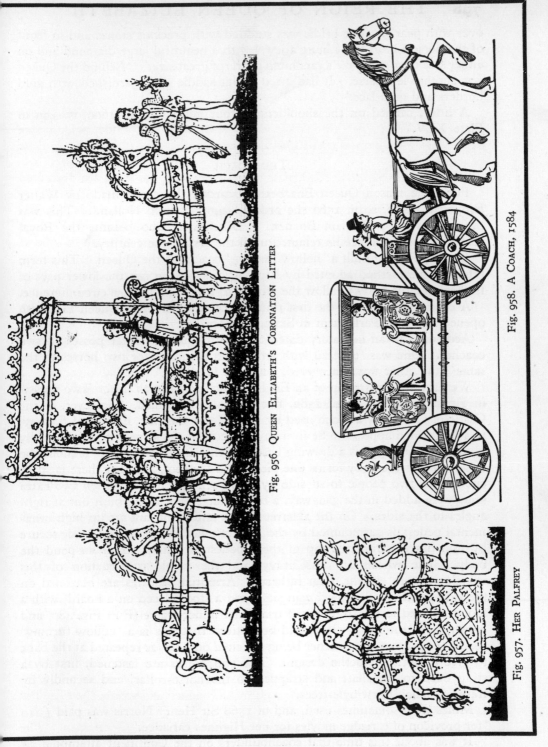

Fig. 956. Queen Elizabeth's Coronation Litter

Fig. 957. Her Palfrey

Fig. 958. A Coach, 1584

over with pearls.   The bridle was studded with precious stones and in front of the horse's head there hung a jewel with a beautiful large diamond and on either side near the horse's ears hung pearls of great size.'   'Behind the Queen was another led horse.   It had a red velvet saddle cloth garnished with gold borders and gold lace.'

A litter, carried on the shoulders of four gentlemen in 1600, is seen in Plate XLV.

THE COACH

For some reason Queen Elizabeth discarded the coach made by Walter Rippon in 1556, so in 1560 she ordered another from Holland.   This was brought over by William Boonen, a Dutchman, who became the Royal coachman, which office he retained until the end of the century.

In 1564 Rippon built a 'hollow turning' coach for the Queen.   This term refers to the method adopted by Rippon, of scooping out the lower part of the front of the body to allow the wheels to turn on a greater circumference.

A coach was used for the first time for ceremonial when Queen Elizabeth opened her third Parliament in State, 2nd April 1571.

According to an inventory dated 1577, Archbishop Parker possessed two coaches.   One was 'covered with lether and furniture for two horses to the same'; the other was 'uncovered, with like furniture.'

We have no illustration of an English coach so early as this.   Two appear in Hofnagel's print dated 1582, but this is rather small.   However, at the Castle of Coburg is a coach used by Duke John Casimir, Elector of Saxony, in 1584, which appears to be in many respects of the same type as shown by Hofnagel.   Fig. 958 is a drawing based on the Elector's coach.   It should be observed that the body forms one piece with the roof, and that there is space enough for two people to sit side by side back and front.   Often two extra seats were added in the gangway, a box arrangement being built out at right angles to the sides.   On the axletrees, back and front, are set up high ornamental pedestals surmounted by the Elector's heraldic lions and made secure by iron braces; from the top of these pedestals leather straps suspend the body.   The wheels are less heavy, and the whole construction of this vehicle is more elegant, than hitherto.   Armorial bearings are blazoned on the side panels.   The coachman sits upon a stool placed on a board, with a foot-rest fixed to the front of the triangular under-frame (F in Fig. 480, and known as a 'futchel').   It should be noticed that this is a 'hollow turning' coach, the bottom front corner being *hollowed* out: this is repeated at the back to give uniformity to the design.   The two horses are fastened, first by a strap fixed to the shaft and strapped to the horse-collar, and secondly by traces attached to swingle-trees.

Mules were sometimes used, and in 1568 Sir Henry Norris was paid £210 'for provicõn of cariadge moyles for her Highnes cariadge.'

It was about this time that coachbuilders on the Continent attempted an improvement on the leather strap suspension by introducing metal springs. Evidently springs of this kind were not in use in England at so early a date: otherwise Queen Elizabeth would not have made her confession (*see* p. 484) in 1568.

An early use of a coach with springs occurred in the marriage procession of the Archduke Ferdinand of Austria in 1582 when 'the betrothed Princess [of Mantua] appeared with her mother, and a stately retinue of ladies-in-waiting in elegant gilt litters, and *carriages on springs*.'

The decorations of Royal coaches were often very elaborate. The one belonging to Marguerite de Valois, discovered outside the lodging of Charles de Balzac d'Entragues by her suspicious brother, Henry III, was 'all gilded, and lined with yellow and silvered velvet.' 'I would wager she is there,' declared the King: but no evidence of any indiscretion was forthcoming, for examination showed that 'the birds have been there, but they have flown.'

In 1585 Queen Elizabeth owned at least three coaches and eighty-one horses. 'One of the coaches was so small that only two persons can sit in it; but it is so contrived that both the fore and hind wheels are attached far from the body of the coach. The second coach was of red leather and studded all over with gilt silver nails. On the third coach the wheels were placed under the axle in a way that I cannot describe. This coach had twelve wheels.' Another coach belonging to the Queen was of gold 'open all round, but having above it a canopy embroidered with gold and pearls. On the front and on the back of the coach were three plumes of various colours. The coach was drawn by four bays in Royal trappings. The coachman was clad in red velvet, and on his coat both before and behind was the Queen's coat of arms and a rose of chaste silver gilt.'

For her progress to St. Paul's to give thanks for the defeat of the Armada, Elizabeth rode in 'a chariette-throne made with four pillars behind to have a canopy, on the toppe whereof was made a crown imperiall, and two lower pillars before whereon stood a lyon and a dragon, supporters of the arms of England, drawne by two white horses . . . her footemen and pensioners about her.'

Whether the following stanza describes Elizabeth's coach accurately is doubtful. It was written by a poet who saw her on this memorable occasion.

> 'He happy was that could but see her coach,
> The sides whereof beset with emeralds
> And diamonds, with sparkling rubies red
> In checkerwise, by strange invention,
> With curious knots embroidered with gold.'

The use of coaches and carriages became more general among the nobility during the latter part of Elizabeth's reign. 'After a while, divers great ladies (with so great jealoussie of the Queen's displeasure) made them coaches, and rid in them up and down the country, to the great admiration of all the beholders.' Towards the end of the century it was scornfully remarked that 'our wantons now in coaches dash.'

The celebrity of English-built coaches is shown by the following extracts. A German who came to England in 1595 on purpose to buy a coach, writes home and says that he had 'walked all over London, I did not overlook a single coachbuilder, and also saw a large number of coaches and carriages.' He eventually bought an English coach, with harness for the horses, for £34.

In 1599 'the presents sent by the Queen of England to the Sultan are said to be a very handsome timepiece and a coach with silver mountings.' In September of the same year Elizabeth made Henry IV a present of 'a coach of great value and some fine horses.'

A mail-coach, 1592, is referred to on p. 563.

Towards the end of the sixteenth century long, immense-wheeled wagons —later known as 'stages'—for the conveyance of passengers and goods began to ply between the chief towns of England and on the Continent.

THE CHAIR

In 1581 a seat enclosed in a box and carried on poles by two men made its first appearance in England. Many years before, similar contrivances were used on the Continent to carry invalids. The Emperor Charles V had one;

Fig. 959. An Italian Chair, 1590

and Henry VIII, when he became very gouty, was moved from room to room in such a seat or chair (see p. 257). In the latter part of the century this chair became popular with the upper and middle classes. It was found very convenient for getting about, especially along narrow streets, for visiting when 'dressed up,' and in inclement weather.

An Italian chair of the late sixteenth century is given in Fig. 959 from a contemporary engraving. The box is of wood covered with some kind of material inside and out, with waxed cloth between to make it waterproof; the window and door are at the side, and the roof is semicircular. Poles pass through the front and back of the box, and these are hung by straps over the left shoulders of the bearers.

The lady appears somewhat cramped but no doubt she is moderately comfortable.

THE END

The following excerpts from contemporary writers give interesting details of the last days of the great Queen.

Sir Robert Carey, a relative of Elizabeth on her mother's side, writes in his *Narrative*: 'I found her in one of her withdrawing chambers, sitting low upon her cushions.' 'She took me by the hand and wrung it hard, and said: "No, Robin, I am not well," and then discoursed to me of her indisposition, and that her heart had been sad and heavy for ten or twelve days; and in her discourse she fetched not so few as forty or fifty great sighs. I was grieved at the first to see her in this plight; for in all my lifetime before I never knew her fetch a sigh, but when the Queen of Scottes was beheaded. Then, in 1587, upon my knowledge, she shedd many tears and sighs, manifesting her innocence that she never gave consent to the death of that Queen.'

'She remained upon her cushions four days and nights at least. All about her could not persuade her either to take any sustenance or to go to bed.'

Beaumont, the French Ambassador, relates that 'the Queen hastens to her end, and is given up by all her physicians. They have put her to bed, almost by force, after she had sat upon cushions for ten days.'

'The Queen kept her bed fifteen days,' reports her lady-in-waiting, Lady Southwell (Elizabeth Howard).

Archbishop Whitgift ministered to the dying Elizabeth at Richmond Palace. She died in her sleep, soon after he had left her, at 3 a.m. on 24th March 1603; and in sign that her soul had passed, Sir Robert Carey conveyed her sapphire ring to James VI of Scotland.

THE QUEEN IS DEAD—LONG LIVE THE KING.

Fig. 960.
Badge of James I

GENERAL INDEX

Note: For names of Individuals and Places, see Index of Names, p. 819

INDEX OF NAMES

This Index does not contain references to the Historical Data

MADE AT THE TEMPLE PRESS LETCHWORTH IN GREAT BRITAIN